Things to Keep in Mind When Interpreting a Dream

- Interpreting dreams doesn't have to be difficult, intellectual, or dry.
- Use your intuition to sense which dreams have that extra "psychic weight" and allow yourself to work with those first.
- Does the dream trigger an experience of love or fear?
- Is the dream about your physical body, the way you use your energy, your hidden emotions, your ideas and belief system, your inspirations, your life purpose, or is it transpersonal and visionary?
- If the dream is helping you become more authentic, what is it trying to tell you?
- If the dream were depicting a literal movement of your awareness, rather than something symbolic, what might you be doing?
- What are the key elements of the dream and how is each an aspect of your life right now?
- What choices did you make and what feelings did you experience in the dream? What does this tell you about yourself?
- Are there any puns, double meanings, or cliches in the dream? What might the secondary meanings denote?
- Was the dream in color, or sepia-toned or black and white? Was it lit brightly or was it dark?
- Did you have any "sidebar" impressions or outside commentary about parts of the dream?

Common Dream Themes

Here are dreams everyone has at one time to another:

- My teeth are falling out!
- I'm naked in public!
- I'm in a play and I forgot my lines!
- Someone is chasing me and I'm paralyzed!
- I'm revisiting an old house I once lived in and it has new rooms!
- I'm making love with a movie star!
- I lost my wallet and can't find my keys!
- I have to take a test and: can't find the examination room/didn't study/forgot to go!
- I'm flying without an airplane!
- I'm in an elevator and it's falling; we're going to crash and die!
- My car: has flat tires/won't start/has brakes that don't work!
- I found: money on the street/buried treasure/jewels in the attic!
- I have to catch a plane/train and am late/can't find my luggage!
- I'm having surgery on my eyes/knees/heart/feet/throat.

Dreams For Dummies®

Ten Tips for Better Dreaming

To help you develop a rich dream life, try any of the following:

- ✔ Start talking about dreams to your friends and family. Dreams increase when you pay attention to them.
- ✔ Get clear about why you want to dream. Know what's possible — dreams have many positive benefits and these can motivate you to dream more.
- ✔ Take a warm bath before bed, and steer clear of alcohol, stimulants, mood altering medications, and too much extraverted social activity in the evening.
- ✔ Sniff a dream pillow scented with mugwort, rosemary, lavender, or sage.
- ✔ Try eating foods rich in tryptophan like turkey, milk, bananas, and cheese, or engage in a period of quiet study in the evening.
- ✔ Learn to wake up without an alarm clock; many dreams are lost when your body is shocked awake suddenly.
- ✔ Start a dream diary and keep it next to your bed. Write your dreams in it every morning.
- ✔ If you can't remember a dream in the morning, make one up and write it in your dream diary! Soon you'll remember the real thing.
- ✔ Learn dream incubation techniques so you can program yourself to dream what you want and remember what you dreamed.
- ✔ Write a poem from your dream or make a drawing or painting inspired by dream imagery.

Ten Questions to Ask Yourself in Order to Trigger Dream Responses

- ✔ What do I need to know about the functioning of my body to improve my health?
- ✔ What beliefs are interfering with my ability to see my life situation clearly?
- ✔ What is the next phase of my life work?
- ✔ How can I connect with my grandparents who died?
- ✔ How can I improve my relationship with my spouse?
- ✔ Which of the possible solutions to this problem would best serve my growth?
- ✔ What is causing my child's anxiety and irritability, and what can I do?
- ✔ How can I move through my writer's block and jumpstart my creativity?
- ✔ What hidden factors are limiting the forward movement of my career?
- ✔ What do I need to know to become more spiritually aware?

For Dummies™: Bestselling Book Series for Beginners

Praise for Dreams For Dummies

"Penney's simple dream strategies taught me how to access a powerhouse of information I never knew existed! I make use of Penney's dream interpretations for clarity, creativity, and decision-making regarding my business, relationships, and health. Anyone who is interested in intuitive development will be enriched by this book."

— Cat Gibson, CEO, Bobcat Advertising

"Penney Peirce is a unique and unusual thinker whose work with dreams bridges the gap between the conscious and unconscious in immediate and practical ways. She has the rare gift of being able to keep the energy of the dream alive and is able to use it to guide and support you through even the most challenging times in life. Perhaps even more importantly, as a teacher, she is able to explain complex ideas in simple and practical ways. . . . Her book will help you discover that you are already much more than you ever thought you could be."

— Larry Leigon, president, Leigon Corporate Training
and Consulting; founder and former CEO,
Ariel Vineyards

"Every dream has a meaning if only you can find it. *Dreams For Dummies* helps you understand your dreams and use this knowledge in your everyday life and on your psychic and spiritual journeys. It's innovative and a valuable traveler's guide for the tangible and intangible worlds."

— Dr. William Roll, State University of West Georgia

"*Dreams For Dummies* is a real standout among dream guides. Penney Peirce provides a thorough and easy-to-follow program that will take you to the heart of your dreams. Under her expert guidance, you will not only understand the messages in your dreams, but also be able to use them as tools for self-improvement and self-empowerment."

— Rosemary Ellen Guiley, author, *Dreamwork for the Soul*

TM

References for the Rest of Us!™

Dreams

FOR

DUMMIES®

by Penney Peirce

Foreword by Carol Adrienne, Ph.D.,
author of *The Purpose of Your Life*

IDG BOOKS WORLDWIDE

IDG Books Worldwide, Inc.
An International Data Group Company

Foster City, CA ◆ Chicago, IL ◆ Indianapolis, IN ◆ New York, NY

Dreams For Dummies®

Published by
IDG Books Worldwide, Inc.
An International Data Group Company
919 E. Hillsdale Blvd.
Suite 300
Foster City, CA 94404
www.idgbooks.com (IDG Books Worldwide Web site)
www.dummies.com (Dummies Press Web site)

Library of Congress Control Number: 00-108209

ISBN: 0-7645-5297-X

Printed in the United States of America

10 9 8 7 6 5 4 3 2 1

1B/RV/RS/QQ/IN

Distributed in the United States by IDG Books Worldwide, Inc.

Distributed by CDG Books Canada Inc. for Canada; by Transworld Publishers Limited in the United Kingdom; by IDG Norge Books for Norway; by IDG Sweden Books for Sweden; by IDG Books Australia Publishing Corporation Pty. Ltd. for Australia and New Zealand; by TransQuest Publishers Pte Ltd. for Singapore, Malaysia, Thailand, Indonesia, and Hong Kong; by Gotop Information Inc. for Taiwan; by ICG Muse, Inc. for Japan; by Intersoft for South Africa; by Eyrolles for France; by International Thomson Publishing for Germany, Austria and Switzerland; by Distribuidora Cuspide for Argentina; by LR International for Brazil; by Galileo Libros for Chile; by Ediciones ZETA S.C.R. Ltda. for Peru; by WS Computer Publishing Corporation, Inc., for the Philippines; by Contemporanea de Ediciones for Venezuela; by Express Computer Distributors for the Caribbean and West Indies; by Micronesia Media Distributor, Inc. for Micronesia; by Chips Computadoras S.A. de C.V. for Mexico; by Editorial Norma de Panama S.A. for Panama; by American Bookshops for Finland.

For general information on IDG Books Worldwide's books in the U.S., please call our Consumer Customer Service department at 800-762-2974. For reseller information, including discounts and premium sales, please call our Reseller Customer Service department at 800-434-3422.

For information on where to purchase IDG Books Worldwide's books outside the U.S., please contact our International Sales department at 317-572-3993 or fax 317-572-4002.

For consumer information on foreign language translations, please contact our Customer Service department at 1-800-434-3422, fax 317-572-4002, or e-mail rights@idgbooks.com.

For information on licensing foreign or domestic rights, please phone +1-650-653-7098.

For sales inquiries and special prices for bulk quantities, please contact our Order Services department at 800-434-4322 or write to the address above.

For information on using IDG Books Worldwide's books in the classroom or for ordering examination copies, please contact our Educational Sales department at 800-434-2086 or fax 317-572-4005.

For press review copies, author interviews, or other publicity information, please contact our Public Relations department at 650-653-7000 or fax 650-653-7500.

For authorization to photocopy items for corporate, personal, or educational use, please contact Copyright Clearance Center, 222 Rosewood Drive, Danvers, MA 01923, or fax 978-750-4470.

is a registered trademark under exclusive license to IDG Books Worldwide, Inc. from International Data Group, Inc.

About the Author

Penney Peirce has been interested in the inner dynamics of perception and the mysteries of consciousness for as long as she can remember. As a child she talked to her animals (dogs, cats, lizards, horses, mice, sheep, and goats) telepathically, drew endless drawings from her imagination, and had inexplicable urges to write poems. She has kept a journal since she was seven. Penney began remembering her dreams and talking about them quite early, a habit that continues to this day.

In college, Penney became part of an experimental program at California Institute of the Arts called Social Design, where she concentrated on projects like "redesign the elevator so people will talk to each other inside, or redesign the funeral, or the doctor-patient relationship." She credits her training in two- and three-dimensional design, as well as the abstract thinking skills she learned in "social design," with helping her eventually discern the hidden patterns in people's lives. "There was no official training for professional intuitives then, but something in me found the skills I needed anyway!" she says.

In California, Penney soaked up courses in Tai Chi, meditation, nutrition, and clairvoyance development. Surprisingly, she found she was quite talented as a clairvoyant, and discovered her dreams were unusual and often precognitive. Within a few years, Penney was focused entirely on developing her skill as a professional intuitive, doing life readings and teaching intuition development trainings. She became affiliated with The Center for Applied Intuition in San Francisco, founded by Dr. William Kautz, a scientist from SRI International, who developed a technique to use intuitives for scientific research.

Today, Penney is a gifted intuitive and a popular lecturer, counselor, and trainer specializing in the art of "skillful perception." She works throughout the United States, Japan, and Europe as a coach to business executives, psychologists, scientists, other trainers, and those on a spiritual path — and is known for her ability to present complex ideas in a common sense, easy-to-understand way. She is the author of *The Present Moment: A Daybook of Clarity and Intuition* (Contemporary Books, 2000), *The Intuitive Way: A Guide to Living from Inner Wisdom* (Beyond Words Publishing, 1997) and is featured in five books: *The Purpose of Your Life* by Carol Adrienne, *The Celestine Prophecy Experiential Guide* and *Tenth Insight Experiential Guide,* both by Adrienne and Redfield, and *Intuiting the Future* and *Channeling: The Intuitive Connection* by Dr. William Kautz of the Center for Applied Intuition. Penney makes her home in Marin County, near San Francisco. You can reach her via her Web site (www.intuitnow.com).

ABOUT IDG BOOKS WORLDWIDE

Welcome to the world of IDG Books Worldwide.

IDG Books Worldwide, Inc., is a subsidiary of International Data Group, the world's largest publisher of computer-related information and the leading global provider of information services on information technology. IDG was founded more than 30 years ago by Patrick J. McGovern and now employs more than 9,000 people worldwide. IDG publishes more than 290 computer publications in over 75 countries. More than 90 million people read one or more IDG publications each month.

Launched in 1990, IDG Books Worldwide is today the #1 publisher of best-selling computer books in the United States. We are proud to have received eight awards from the Computer Press Association in recognition of editorial excellence and three from Computer Currents' First Annual Readers' Choice Awards. Our best-selling ...For Dummies® series has more than 50 million copies in print with translations in 31 languages. IDG Books Worldwide, through a joint venture with IDG's Hi-Tech Beijing, became the first U.S. publisher to publish a computer book in the People's Republic of China. In record time, IDG Books Worldwide has become the first choice for millions of readers around the world who want to learn how to better manage their businesses.

Our mission is simple: Every one of our books is designed to bring extra value and skill-building instructions to the reader. Our books are written by experts who understand and care about our readers. The knowledge base of our editorial staff comes from years of experience in publishing, education, and journalism — experience we use to produce books to carry us into the new millennium. In short, we care about books, so we attract the best people. We devote special attention to details such as audience, interior design, use of icons, and illustrations. And because we use an efficient process of authoring, editing, and desktop publishing our books electronically, we can spend more time ensuring superior content and less time on the technicalities of making books.

You can count on our commitment to deliver high-quality books at competitive prices on topics you want to read about. At IDG Books Worldwide, we continue in the IDG tradition of delivering quality for more than 30 years. You'll find no better book on a subject than one from IDG Books Worldwide.

IDG BOOKS WORLDWIDE

John J. Kilcullen
John Kilcullen
Chairman and CEO
IDG Books Worldwide, Inc.

Eighth Annual Computer Press Awards ≥1992

Ninth Annual Computer Press Awards ≥1993

Tenth Annual Computer Press Awards ≥1994

Eleventh Annual Computer Press Awards ≥1995

IDG is the world's leading IT media, research and exposition company. Founded in 1964, IDG had 1997 revenues of $2.05 billion and has more than 9,000 employees worldwide. IDG offers the widest range of media options that reach IT buyers in 75 countries representing 95% of worldwide IT spending. IDG's diverse product and services portfolio spans six key areas including print publishing, online publishing, expositions and conferences, market research, education and training, and global marketing services. More than 90 million people read one or more of IDG's 290 magazines and newspapers, including IDG's leading global brands — Computerworld, PC World, Network World, Macworld and the Channel World family of publications. IDG Books Worldwide is one of the fastest-growing computer book publishers in the world, with more than 700 titles in 36 languages. The "...For Dummies®" series alone has more than 50 million copies in print. IDG offers online users the largest network of technology-specific Web sites around the world through IDG.net (http://www.idg.net), which comprises more than 225 targeted Web sites in 55 countries worldwide. International Data Corporation (IDC) is the world's largest provider of information technology data, analysis and consulting, with research centers in over 41 countries and more than 400 research analysts worldwide. IDG World Expo is a leading producer of more than 168 globally branded conferences and expositions in 35 countries including E3 (Electronic Entertainment Expo), Macworld Expo, ComNet, Windows World Expo, ICE (Internet Commerce Expo), Agenda, DEMO, and Spotlight. IDG's training subsidiary, ExecuTrain, is the world's largest computer training company, with more than 230 locations worldwide and 785 training courses. IDG Marketing Services helps industry-leading IT companies build international brand recognition by developing global integrated marketing programs via IDG's print, online and exposition products worldwide. Further information about the company can be found at www.idg.com.   1/26/00

Dedication

This book is dedicated to my sister, Paula, who has been my friend and sounding board all my life. Though she doesn't remember her dreams as much as I do, she has always generously made time to listen to me rattle on about mine, and has even seemed interested most of the time! If I hadn't had someone to talk to about my inner life, who knows if I'd have been encouraged enough to pursue the intuitive way of life as much as I have. . . .

Author's Acknowledgments

Gratitude truly is a powerful force. It is the act that opens us to be able to integrate what we've already received, and be ready to receive more of whatever we need. The first thing that occurs to me to be grateful for is the very fact that I've been given the opportunity to write a book about one of my absolute favorite subjects. I never get tired of dreaming, of hearing other people's dreams, or of the amazing work (play?) of weaving together daytime and nighttime reality.

It's been a real pleasure working with the staff at IDG Books — from beginning to end, I experienced clear communication, responsiveness, bright minds, and a compassionate attitude. They have this down to a fine art, and writing in the Dummies format has been downright fun. I am especially grateful to my editor, Kathy Cox, in Indianapolis, with her amazing wisdom and common sense. Good editors are really like healers. Also, thanks to Karen Young in Chicago, who nursed the project along and coordinated the pieces. Dream expert Jeremy Taylor has been exceedingly generous and kind in giving of his time to help make this material come to life, and my dear friend and author, Carol Adrienne, contributed enthusiastically by writing the foreword. Susan St. Thomas and Leslie Schwing were gracious in contributing their fabulous artwork. My agent, Sheryl Fullerton, has once again been solidly present and ever-helpful. Thank you!

My father died unexpectedly three thousand miles away as I was halfway through writing this book, and it threw me for a loop, sending me into the other dimensions to try to communicate with him, while simultaneously shifting into gear as executor of his estate. It was hard to think about dreams and annuities at the same time, and I found it impossible to write. And yet, that two-month period where I stopped creating was an incredibly powerful teaching, a time when my dreams supported me in ways I hadn't expected. They helped me navigate through the grieving process, make sense of what was really happening under the surface, and on the other side as my father acclimated to his new reality. I'm grateful for the experience because it made the other world of dreams and after-death far more real than I'd ever suspected was possible. When I was able to write again, it was with a deep new understanding.

Thank you to my circle of friends who loyally called me with dreams they'd had, and to so many of my clients and colleagues, who contributed dreams for the book. Heartfelt thanks to Larry Leigon, Marcus True, Karen Harvey, Cameron Hogan, Kay Woodside, Donna Hale, Lorraine Anderson, Jon Curtis, Allen Hicks, Pam and Steve Steinberg, and Cynthia Schmidt. Finally, a special kind of gratitude goes to Dr. Koen Kallop, who is a dream come true.

Publisher's Acknowledgments

We're proud of this book; please register your comments through our IDG Books Worldwide Online Registration Form located at http://my2cents.dummies.com.

Some of the people who helped bring this book to market include the following:

Acquisitions, Editorial, and Media Development

Project Editor: Kathleen M. Cox

Senior Acquisitions Editor: Stacy Collins

Associate Acquisitions Editor: Karen S. Young

Copy Editor: Kathleen M. Cox

Technical Editor: Jeremy Taylor

Associate Media Development Specialist: Megan Decraene

Editorial Manager: Jennifer Ehrlich

Editorial Assistant: Jennifer Young

Production

Project Coordinator: Dale White

Layout and Graphics: Amy Adrian, Karl Brandt, Kendra Span, Brian Torwelle, Erin Zeltner

Special Art: Susan St. Thomas, Leslie Schwing

Proofreaders: John Bitter, Marianne Santy, York Production Services, Inc.

Indexer: York Production Services, Inc.

Special Help: Michelle Hacker, Janet Seib, Steve Arany

General and Administrative

IDG Books Worldwide, Inc.: John Kilcullen, CEO; Bill Barry, President and COO

IDG Books Consumer Reference Group

  Business: Kathleen A. Welton, Vice President and Publisher; Kevin Thornton, Acquisitions Manager

  Cooking/Gardening: Jennifer Feldman, Associate Vice President and Publisher

  Education/Reference: Diane Graves Steele, Vice President and Publisher; Greg Tubach, Publishing Director

  Lifestyles: Kathleen Nebenhaus, Vice President and Publisher; Tracy Boggier, Managing Editor

  Pets: Dominique De Vito, Associate Vice President and Publisher; Tracy Boggier, Managing Editor

  Travel: Michael Spring, Vice President and Publisher; Suzanne Jannetta, Editorial Director; Brice Gosnell, Managing Editor

IDG Books Consumer Editorial Services: Kathleen Nebenhaus, Vice President and Publisher; Kristin A. Cocks, Editorial Director; Cindy Kitchel, Editorial Director

IDG Books Consumer Production: Debbie Stailey, Production Director

IDG Books Packaging: Marc J. Mikulich, Vice President, Brand Strategy and Research

◆

The publisher would like to give special thanks to Patrick J. McGovern, without whom this book would not have been possible.

◆

Contents at a Glance

Cartoons at a Glance

By Rich Tennant

page 7

page 93

page 45

page 155

page 217

page 315

Fax: 978-546-7747
E-mail: richtennant@the5thwave.com
World Wide Web: www.the5thwave.com

Table of Contents

Foreword

*W*hen Penney Peirce, whom I've known for many years, invited me to write a foreword for this wonderful book on dreams, I was excited to see how my unconscious would respond. Two nights later, I had a dream which I had great fun interpreting upon awakening. The symbols in dreams are always specific and relevant, though it may take time to find out the real reason they show up when they do. They always present information designed to show you where you need to pay attention in waking life. In my experience, dreams often speak to us on both a personal level and a more collective level. Since I'd been thinking about writing this foreword, I had to consider that my dream might be a clue about what wanted to be said, as well as a personal message to me. In the dream, I've returned to a house I lived in years ago. The entryway needs work — it's empty and the walls are crumbling. To reach the top floor where my bedroom is, I have to walk up many steep stairs and I'm not sure I want to. I'm looking for an easier way to be in the house. I can't find the kitchen, so I go outside to look for another entrance, and sure enough, my house is divided into two structures! Just then my boyfriend drives up in a small truck, upon which he has roped cushions, perhaps for a sofa. He says to me, "We should have brought the baby." I nod in agreement.

On the personal side, my dream shows me in a happy relationship (or a happy integration of my male and female energies) and we seem to be getting even closer since he's moving stuff into my house, which I am also trying to move into. Carl Jung said houses are symbols of the self and I see that the new space/self we are to occupy needs some work. To me, returning to an old house means my subconscious is still operating from old concepts. The dilapidated entryway signals me that I need to put more attention on welcoming the new. That the house is divided means I need to focus on integrating myself internally. That I can't find the kitchen means I need to make sure I'm being nurtured. That I am trying to figure out how to live comfortably in the house without undue effort means I'm getting my priorities straight, and not just putting up with what doesn't work! The baby? Maybe we need to bring into our relationship an awareness of what our inner children need — and maybe we're going to create something new together. . . .

What is this dream saying about dreams in general? Might not this dream's advice to me be pertinent to everyone in some way? Don't we all need to make sure we're open to the new, that we feel comfortable and authentic within ourselves, that we are unified within, and able to feel nurtured? Don't we all need to share our "space," or ourselves, with others in an intimate way? Don't we all need to "remember the baby" — to make space in our lives for creativity and rejuvenation? As an artist myself, I know the power of dreams to inspire. As I have learned more about living on purpose, I see the great power of following your Dream. As a human being, I see the power of dreams to bring me guidance when I'm temporarily confused or distracted by life. Penney Peirce's book provides a thorough, practical, and uplifting understanding of this important, and mysterious, component of life.

Dreams are wonderful and colorful magazines of our inner lives, presenting us with the table of contents, photographs, feature stories, news reports, advertisements (wants and needs), and editorial comments from our unconscious. You have a lifetime subscription to dreams, and I hope you take the time to let them speak to you. Their guidance can make a big difference in how you see the truth behind all your relationships and your very connection to the world.

Carol Adrienne, Ph.D.,
author of *The Purpose of Your Life*

Introduction

· ·

Then let us all deliver ourselves to the interpretation of dreams, men and women, young and old, rich and poor, private citizens and magistrates, inhabitants of the town and of the country, artisans and orators. There is not any privileged, neither by sex, neither by age, nor by fortune or profession. Sleep offers itself to all.

—Synesius of Cyrene, 5th Century Bishop

*W*elcome to what promises to be a fascinating journey! Whether you're already a prolific dreamer or someone who's just peeking over the edge into the unknown, you're sure to get results from the insights, techniques, and tips provided for you in *Dreams For Dummies*. Not only does this book outline all the important dream skills, it goes further, providing an integrative framework for understanding how dreams mesh with everyday life.

You may be interested in dreams casually, but not quite understand the real power they hold. In *Dreams For Dummies* you'll learn to harness your dreams to increase your creativity, solve problems, find purpose in life, and obtain useful, accurate personal guidance. As a result of becoming familiar with the principles of dreaming you will discover that the options in your life are truly limitless.

Your dreams may be elaborate productions reminiscent of *Gone with the Wind*, *Star Wars*, or a Stephen King novel, or perhaps you dream in numbers or simple geometric symbols. If you are a regular, active dreamer, you might like some help interpreting your dreams and finding the hidden meanings. Maybe you'd like to discover more dream options and hone your skills further. Even if you're an expert, when you view things you already know from a subtly different perspective, which this book offers, powerful new insights can often click into place.

On the other hand, you may wake up with a "to do" list in your head, all business from the moment you open your eyes, dreams instantly vaporized. If you don't remember your dreams — even if you think you don't dream at all — *Dreams For Dummies* can help jumpstart your dream life. If you're a novice dreamer, this book will guide you step by step through the process of learning to remember your dreams, making sense of them, and consciously attracting new ones.

I remember seeing George Lucas interviewed on television. He was talking about imagination as he pointed to highly detailed sketches of underwater cities and strange kinds of submarine vehicles that had appeared effortlessly in his mind. He said it was years before he realized that everybody didn't have the same kind of imagination he had, that not everyone saw the intricate details of these complex sci-fi worlds. Dreaming is a realm where imagination rules, and it's important that you honor your own particular type of imagination. Don't compare yourself to anyone else; your own inner world is full to brimming with wonderful, magical content. As you work more concertedly with your dream world, please be sure to honor your own way through the new territory.

Why I Wrote This Book

My background in dream work comes from more than 20 years as a professional intuitive counselor and trainer, and before that as an artist and graphic designer. Dreams have always captured my imagination and heart. But in the years when I was developing my intuitive abilities and working intensely on my own spiritual path, dreams became my touchstones, my teachers, and my main method of receiving guidance for myself. So, I come to dreams because I am fascinated with the art of perception, with using all of our awareness. What's in that unused 90 percent of our brain? My sense now is that it is intuition, imagination, and multidimensional awareness that occupy most of our consciousness. Logic is a very small part. Dreaming is the bulk of what we do, whether we are awake or asleep.

I hold a philosophy about dreams that is very similar to that of many ancient cultures and tribal cultures. The dream world is not separate from the waking world; they are simply extensions of one another. Everything we do in the dream world is real; it's just happening at other dimensions of our awareness. It's absolutely normal for our awareness to move in and out through all the dimensions; we're changing focus continually, day and night, though we may be unaware of what we're doing. What we do in our dreams, we also do in our waking world; the two realms are mutually supportive and co-creative. When I speak of soul in this book, I mean your individual experience of the divine, or the function of consciousness that translates the divine into the personal experience and vice versa — not necessarily association with any particular religious belief.

In this book I want to share my intuitive insight, synthesized from diverse disciplines and my own inner experience over many years, about a broader, more holistic way to view our realms of consciousness, and what dreaming may really mean. This view can help you understand your own multilevel identity and have more freedom and choices in life.

What This Book Can Do for You

You are greater and wiser than you think! My intention in writing this book is to help you gain access to your own higher knowledge and make the "supernatural" world more natural. By helping eliminate needless fear of the unknown, I hope you will be able to expand your idea of how big you are, how much is possible in life, and how much knowledge you have to draw from. You can become a wiser, more creative, more intuitive you.

What so many people assume are far-out, even dangerous psychic phenomena, I believe are innate human gifts. We just haven't known ourselves well enough yet to develop these skills in a reliable way so they become accepted and normal. *Dreams For Dummies* will help you learn to use your intuition as a new perceptual skill, and both your waking dreams and sleep dreams as important tools for emotional, psychological, and spiritual growth.

How to Use This Book

You can use this book in a variety of ways, depending on your time constraints and how much you want to get involved.

Jump in anywhere, or dig in deep

If you're rushed, you may want to jump right in and go immediately to a section that helps you recall or interpret your dreams. If you're patient and willing to do a little more work, you'll benefit from following the chapters in sequence, doing the exercises, and tracking your dreams daily. By working with the book as a step-by-step roadmap, your dreams will become accessible and meaningful. This book is designed to help you develop alignment between your mind, body, and soul so you will actually experience a process of opening and personal growth facilitated by focusing on your inner life of dreams.

Keep a dream diary

The key to improving your intuitive ability and success with dreams is to make your normally intangible, unconscious inner world more conscious and real. This means physicalize your dreams somehow and bring them intentionally into your waking mind. Describing your dreams out loud is one way, but writing them down is even better.

Dreams For Dummies is designed to be used with a journal. You will encounter writing exercises and meditations to help develop your imagination sprinkled throughout the chapters. The meditations become more meaningful if you write about your experience of doing them and the results you achieve afterward. At the end of every chapter, you'll also find seven suggested writing exercises that can prompt you to receive insights from your inner self and help seed your dreams.

I strongly encourage you to record your dreams every morning. In the evening before you go to sleep, write about your dream intentions. You might also want to use your diary to work with the "nightly review" and "daily list" mentioned in Chapter 4. Your dream diary will be a record of your inner process. Why not buy a special notebook just for this purpose, along with colored pens, pencils, and highlighters? Go for it!

Use the book with a support group

Why not gather a few friends together for a dream group and lend each other moral support? An interesting intensification occurs as people commit to hear and validate each other in a group. As you see the special quality and beauty of each person's way of being and dreaming, you'll start to respect their particular path in life and the many wonderful ways we make sense of the world. This, then, helps you respect your own way even more. As the group synthesis evolves, you'll experience how each person becomes an aspect of you, and their dreams an aspect of your dreams. Many dream groups actually start having group dreams.

How This Book Is Organized

Dreams For Dummies is divided into six parts and nineteen chapters. There is a logical progression to the material. It flows like this:

- ✔ **Part I: Open Your Dream Door.** Part I gets you started. Chapter 1 introduces you to the mechanics of sleep and the benefits of an active, creative dream life. Chapter 2 teaches you how to build a reliable dream habit by increasing your intent and learning dream recall techniques. Chapter 3 helps you begin your dream diary and use it to track your personal dream process.

- ✔ **Part II: Explore Your Dreamscape.** Part II sketches an overview of the dream world, one that empowers you to increase your sense of self, gives you more dream possibilities, and helps you discern exactly what you're doing when you're dreaming. Chapter 4 introduces the idea of dreaming twenty-four hours a day and shows you how to increase the connection between day and night for maximum dream proficiency.

Chapter 5 teaches you about your superconscious and subconscious minds — the realms of love and fear — for they are the two sources of your dream content. It also helps you understand how your conscious mind functions as the dream viewpoint. Chapter 6 describes the dream zones, or the kinds of dream experience it's possible to encounter. If you know the characteristics of each zone, you'll be able to interpret your dreams more accurately.

✔ **Part III: See What Dreams May Come.** As preparation for knowing the meaning of your dreams, Part III helps you understand what kinds of dreams are possible. Chapter 7 describes the categories of sleep dreams and which dream zones they involve, while Chapter 8 delineates types of waking dreams and daydreams and their dream zones. Chapter 9 broadens out the territory, describing life dreams, which include the birth vision and originate directly from your soul's purpose.

✔ **Part IV: Decode Your Dreams.** Part IV helps you dig in and make sense of every type of dream experience. Chapter 10 leads you through the basic steps to interpreting a dream. Chapter 11 helps you understand and work constructively with symbolism. Chapter 12 actually interprets a variety of dreams, helps you work with scary/subconscious dreams to find the "gift in the garbage," and shows you what to do when you get stuck.

✔ **Part V: Make Your Dreams Come True.** Once you can interpret dreams, Part V shows you how to use dreams intentionally to improve the quality of your life. Chapter 13 helps you apply dreams to your life work and career, while Chapter 14 helps you use dreams to improve communication and relationships. Chapter 15 gives techniques for using dreams for healing and stress reduction. Chapter 16 focuses specifically on enhancing your imagination and authentic creativity. Chapter 17 discusses ways to use dreams to expand your spiritual growth, receive superconscious guidance, and develop intuition.

✔ **Part VI: The Part of Tens.** Finally, Part VI provides a few more fascinating tidbits — a little "dream dessert." Chapter 18 suggests ten ways to work with kids and their dreams. Chapter 19 presents guidelines for starting your own dream group.

✔ **Appendix A: Dream Resources.** Look here for leads to popular Web sites, magazines, organizations, and other resources to advance your dream life.

✔ **Appendix B: Dream Dictionary.** Look here for the meanings of more than 200 common dream symbols.

Icons Used in This Book

 Dreaming has its own vocabulary. Watch for this symbol to alert you to new terms.

 There are certain nuances and details that it's important to pay attention to in dreamwork, that can increase your efficiency and results. This icon alerts you to these time and trouble-saving ideas.

 The history of dreams is replete with fascinating tidbits of information. Watch for this icon to find some really fun stuff.

 You'll get the best results from working with your dreams when you keep a dream diary. Watch for this symbol — it points out a writing exercise you can do in your diary.

 Becoming an expert dreamer isn't just a matter of remembering your dreams — it's also important to develop your intuition, imagination, ability to focus and concentrate, and your body-mind integration. Look for this icon to find meditations you can do to loosen your imagination and practice clear perception.

 Tie a string around your finger to help you remember these important insights into dreams and dreaming.

Where to Go from Here

Where do you go from here? You enter the fascinating world of the superconscious, from which your higher self strives to help you live a fuller, richer, more authentic life, and the subconscious, which keeps you grounded to the fears and frustrations of the earth. Recognizing these elements of your self and training yourself to hear their voices will help you make decisions about who you are and whom you want to be. So pick a place to start, and dream on.

Any condition is first dreamed before it becomes reality.

—Edgar Cayce

Part I
Open Your Dream Door

In this part . . .

*W*hether you're a beginning dreamer, a lapsed dreamer, or an expert, Part I is designed to give you both an overview of dreams and some valuable grounding in the basic techniques of dream work. You'll become familiar with the mechanics of sleep and the benefits of an active, creative dream life. Next, you'll build a reliable dream habit by increasing your intent and practicing dream recall techniques. Finally, you'll begin your dream diary and use it to track your personal dream process.

Chapter 1

A Few Facts about Dreams

• •

• •

I shut my eyes, in order to see.

—Paul Gaugin

*W*hat is the first dream you can remember? Do you remember special dreams you dreamed as a child? Did they fuel your early crayon drawings, or fill your head with fantastic stories? Perhaps they even laid a foundation for what was to come later in your life. In my family, from as early as I can remember, we shared our dreams. Perhaps that's why over the years dreams have been my best friends, bringing me adventure, romance, learning, nurturing, guidance about everyday problems, and prophetic visions about my future and the future of the world.

In this chapter, I introduce you to a new world of dreams: what science knows about dreaming, what great dreamers have surmised, and how you can start to use that information to enrich not only your dream life but also your personal and professional lives as well.

Dreams Can Make You Happy and Healthy

The Senoi tribe in Malaysia have one of the most sophisticated and sensible systems in the world for working with their dreams. They begin by discussing their dreams each morning at breakfast, the parents gradually teaching the young children to catch and describe their dreams, and then to control them.

Children learn several important dream principles, like developing dream helpers, calling for help in dreams, turning on a dream attacker and killing it (then absorbing its vitality back into oneself), advancing toward pleasure in dreams, asking for gifts from dream characters, and always making sure dreams end with a positive outcome. By honoring their dreams as real activities occurring at a higher level of their awareness, and by developing the habit of confidently influencing their dream experience through positive imagination, Senoi children learn faith in themselves and life. They learn that for each event in their dream world, there is a parallel event in their waking world. If you can positively affect one, you will reap benefits in the other.

The Senoi don't stop with an individual focus on personal, psychological work with dreams. They extend dream guidance to the community level. Once the family's dreams have been shared and compared in the morning, the parents then take their family dreams to the tribal council, where all the family dreams are interpreted and synthesized, and the tribe's projects and actions are then determined from the dream indicators. The Senoi people have virtually no neurosis or mental illness in their society — they are phenomenally well-adjusted, harmonious, productive, and emotionally mature. Could working constructively with dreams be part of the answer?

Use your dream diary to help you focus on the dreams of childhood.

The Dreams of Childhood

1. In your dream diary, write about the earliest dreams you can remember from your childhood. What images come to mind? Did you have scary dreams? Flying dreams? Dreams about animals?

2. What were your favorite images to draw as a child? Write about how it felt to draw these pictures.

3. Did you share your dreams with your family as a child? If so, write about how that felt, what kind of feedback you received, and how your love of dreaming was either nourished or discouraged.

4. If you have children, or are close to other children, ask them to describe their first dream in as much detail as they can recall. Write about it and the child's attitude in your diary.

The dreams of children are shorter than those of adults and often contain animals and monsters. Nearly 40 percent of children's dreams are nightmares, which may be part of the normal developmental process of learning to cope.

Everyone Dreams

Whether you dream every night in glorious technicolor detail, or whether you're one of the many people who claim they don't dream at all, one thing's for certain — science says that everyone dreams, and for as much as one third of their time asleep, which equates to two or three hours per night. Even animals and birds dream. Robbed of vital dreaming activity through sleep deprivation, disturbances, and stress, both people and animals become irritable and disoriented — and will catch up and balance themselves by dreaming excessively the first chance they get.

When do you dream?

Every night you rotate through four basic phases of sleep (see Figure 1-1). In the first phase, your brainwaves slow from their waking frequency, called *beta,* to the more relaxed *alpha* state, where you may experience a feeling of floating. Imaginative pictures or scenes from the day may drift haphazardly through your mind. Your muscles relax, and your pulse, blood pressure, and temperature drop slightly at this point.

In phase two, your brainwaves slow some more until they reach the level known as theta. You are now in a light sleep state characterized by many bursts of brain activity. Most of our dreams occur at level two, during which the eyes move back and forth rapidly beneath the eyelids. This is known as *Rapid Eye Movement,* or *REM sleep,* and it lasts for several minutes the first time it occurs. During REM sleep, your fingers and toes may twitch but the rest of your body is paralyzed, as if in a "fight or flight" mode. Your heart may beat erratically and breathing can become irregular and shallow. If you are awakened during this period, you'll easily remember your dreams.

About 20 to 45 minutes after you fall asleep, your brainwaves slow even more, finally achieving the ultra-slow frequency known as *delta.* These long, regular, delta waves produce a deep, dreamless sleep. The third phase of sleep is characterized by about 20 to 50 percent delta waves. At phase four, an EEG would measure 50 percent or more delta waves. This is the state many refer to as a "dead sleep." If you are awakened at this point, you'll feel fuzzy and lost, resist waking fully, and drop back to sleep almost immediately. Delta waves can last up to an hour.

The four phases of sleep repeat four or five times during the night, approximately every 90 minutes, with the REM state lasting longer the longer you sleep. The longest uninterrupted period of dreaming occurs in the early morning and may last an hour. Figure 1-1 shows how your brain waves look during the different phases of sleep.

The amount of time we spend in REM sleep changes with age. A fetus spends up to 80 percent of its time in REM sleep, and a newborn infant may experience eight to ten hours of REM sleep each day. By the time a child is five years old, the sleep pattern is similar to that of an adult; dreams comprise 20 to 30 percent of sleep time. As we age, especially in our older years, we often sleep more lightly and the disturbed quality of sleep can prevent us from dreaming as deeply.

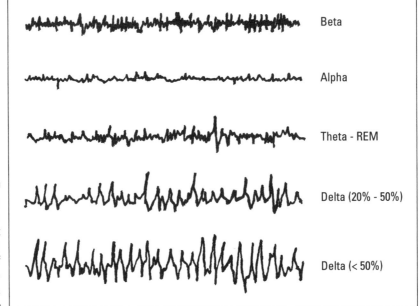

Beta

Alpha

Theta - REM

Delta (20% - 50%)

Delta (< 50%)

Figure 1-1:
The brain waves that indicate the phases of your sleep cycles.

Dream inhibitors

Many substances have been shown to have a negative effect on your REM sleep. Drugs such as marijuana, cocaine, barbiturates, sleeping pills, tranquilizers, muscle relaxants, many mood-stabilizing drugs, as well as alcohol, tobacco, and stimulants like caffeine and amphetamines — can delay sleep and disturb or reduce your amount of REM sleep and your ability for dream recall. Dream activity also often decreases when we are too distracted or overwhelmed by a surplus of social activity. Too much aerobic exercise close to bedtime tends to release adrenaline in the body, which can prevent sleep. It also raises your body temperature, which needs to drop for you to feel drowsy and fall asleep.

Dream enhancers

Dream activity, or REM sleep, occurs more frequently when a person has been engaged in quiet, private activities like reading or studying, and often increases after a period of new learning. Eating foods that contain the amino acid tryptophan (turkey, milk, bananas, or cheese) before going to bed can have a sedating effect and help promote sleep. Similarly, Vitamin B complex, especially B6, has been shown to produce more vivid dreams, as has the herb St. John's Wort. The hormone *melatonin* is secreted by the pituitary gland and seems to help regulate our body clock. More melatonin is released into the bloodstream after dark, and less as the sun comes up in the morning. Melatonin supplements are available at drugstores and even a small amount has been shown to help induce drowsiness.

Ask your physician before you take any kind of supplements, however, and be sure not to exceed the recommended dosage on the label. A warm bath before bed can also lead to a restful, dream-filled night, since as you cool down afterward you tend to get sleepy.

Why Know about Dreams?

Here are seven reasons why knowing your dreams can be important to you:

- ✔ You'll have many more interesting, fun things to talk about with your spouse, friends, and family!

- ✔ You'll have firsthand contact with the fascinating mystery: Who am I? What's happening under your surface? Dreams teach you about your psychological process and the subconscious beliefs and fears that can interfere with happiness.

- ✔ You'll learn to recognize your inner wisdom. Dreams often provide accurate advice from your higher mind, the part of you that always knows the truth.

- ✔ Because dreams can expand your sense of personal identity, you'll start thinking of yourself as more than a physical body; you'll access many realms of experience.

- ✔ You'll realize how naturally intuitive and creative you are.

- ✔ You'll find that dreams can help you in real ways: with problem solving, decision making, improving communication, healing yourself and others, even manifesting the help and resources you need.

- ✔ You'll develop the capacity to know things that are in the past, the future, and in other locations — even to know how it feels to be in someone else's shoes.

Entertaining yourself and others

You may want to develop your dreams for their entertainment value. I speak with many people in my intuition trainings and dream seminars who enthusiastically tell of the joys of learning to fly in dreams, or their dream romances with famous celebrities, or their journeys to faraway lands and other planets. Little Johnny Winters, in my second grade class, stood up for show-and-tell every day to relate his latest epic dream in minute and gory detail. Dreams can definitely be more entertaining than theater, videos, or even the Internet!

If you did nothing more than perform loop-de-loops and take exotic vacations in your dreams, you'd be far richer than if you functioned by logic alone. Dreams keep people childlike and open, helping us to maintain a free, adventurous, joyful spirit, as well as a zest for ordinary life. Because anything goes in dreams, extending that same principle to your waking reality is not much of a stretch.

Discovering what's what in your psyche

Perhaps you've had those long, movie-like dreams, loaded with Freudian symbology (Sigmund Freud, considered the father of modern psychology, used dreams extensively in his practice), where the scene shifts twenty times, you're tossed about in swollen streams, ride in elevators, fall over cliffs, eat as much chocolate as you can stuff in your mouth, and give birth to babies — even if you're a man! These image-laden dreams can give us great insight about the inner workings of our psychological process. What beliefs influence your behavior? What fears might underlie those fixed ideas? Is your energy blocked, or being drained, or over-ampled in certain areas? Your dreams can show you how you might become more free, flexible, tolerant, and loving.

Tapping your inner wisdom

Dreams can act as a direct pipeline to inspirational guidance and a mystical revelation of the divine. They demonstrate how effortless and vast your soul's creativity really is, how wise you are, and how interconnected you are with all other living things. Dreams can reveal your life purpose and notify you when you're off center.

Being all that you can be

When you work consistently with dreams, you'll realize that life isn't limited to the physical world. You are composed of energy, emotions, thoughts, and even higher patterns of awareness. When you learn to recognize and honor the various levels of yourself, you'll develop a broader identity that permits a greater range of knowledge and talent — and is truly empowering for everyone.

Developing intuition and innovation

Recalling dreams, interpreting them, and intending them are all acts that require intuition and imagination. By understanding that intuition and imagination are your allies, not frivolous distractions, you will learn to trust yourself implicitly, and to access and use new parts of your brain to extend your capacities.

Increasing real-life success

You've probably had the experience of bringing a problem home from work and continuing to chew on it until bedtime. Then miraculously, you wake in the morning with the perfect solution. You can extend the use of dreams for practical purposes by intentionally using them to generate problem-solving insights, and new creative angles and possibilities. The dream state is a fertile field awaiting the seeds you sow.

Melting barriers of time and space

Dreams cut through our normal limiting ideas about time and space and show us we are omnipresent. Worried about whether you'll get the job you just interviewed for, you dream you're working at the new company, six months of experience already under your belt. You can see out the window by your desk, know all the people, and are comfortable. When you wake, you sense you'll get the job — and you do!

Perhaps you have a dream premonition that your grandmother has died. She comes to you, smiling, saying she is fine and happy on the other side, yet in real life she's still in good health. Suddenly, two weeks later, she dies in her sleep. Remembering your dream gives you a deep sense of peace. Dreams that come true, or give you information that you couldn't have by normal means, can open you to your ability to encompass more time, space, dimensions, and knowledge — you discover that it's all included in you, right here and now.

Dreams Require You to Pay Attention

Dreams can help you see life's great possibilities and achieve them. They can improve the functioning of your daily life and contribute to your spiritual growth. To know more about all these areas, you need to develop the habit of paying closer attention to what goes on right under your nose, on the inside of your experience.

Dreams that contributed to chemistry

Friedrich August von Kekule, professor of chemistry in Ghent, had for years been searching for the molecular structure of benzene. In 1865, while dozing before his fire, he dreamed of a snake seizing its own tail. He woke suddenly with the then revolutionary idea that certain organic compounds are not open structures, but form closed chains or "rings." And Melvin Calvin, honored as a Nobel Laureate in Chemistry (1961) for his work with photosynthesis, while daydreaming as he waited in his parked car, had the recognition of the structure of phosphoglyceric acid — in a matter of seconds.

Becoming mindful

Using your attention to penetrate more deeply into each experience to find the inner meaning is called *mindfulness,* a term that means being fully alert to whatever's happening in the present moment. By being mindful, you develop neutrality and observation skills, combined with a sense of connectedness with what you're observing. Mindfulness is great practice for developing accurate intuition and penetrating into the heart of your dreams.

Pay attention to your waking world because it's easier to track your results when you're awake. As it becomes second nature to know what's underneath an ordinary event, it will be much simpler to see into your dream world. To become more aware of what your inner self is doing during the night, you need to discover how to traverse a whole new territory, be comfortable with new rhythms of movement, a new sense of time and space, new rules of interaction with others, and amazing new possibilities. One thing is certain — the journey into deeper awareness always begins in the center of the here and now.

Try this meditation to help you pay closer attention to the here and now.

Centering Yourself

Whenever you remember to be mindful, imagine an **X** drawn on the ground under your feet. Say to yourself, "I am standing on the crosshairs of the here and now." Next, imagine a spot in the exact geometric center of your head. In that spot, imagine a pinprick opening, through which pours glossy, clear, diamond light. It radiates out spherically in all directions, giving you a fresh, calm, clear feeling, erasing all doubt and fogginess. Visualize the transparent light burning away any opacity or darkness in your mind and body, establishing neutrality and readiness to know. Draw your attention inside the opening and let the light wash out through you. When you need insight and truth, always come into your center first.

A dream that prompted invention

William Blake, the English artist and poet, related that while searching for a less expensive method of engraving his illustrated songs, he dreamed that his dead younger brother, Robert, appeared to him and revealed a process of copper engraving, which he immediate tested, verified, and began using.

Only you have the right to occupy your own center. If you sense other people in there, ask them mentally to leave.

Centering is especially helpful

- ✔ Before making important decisions
- ✔ Before uttering important communications
- ✔ When you've lost a thought or your car keys
- ✔ When you're looking for insight about what's happening
- ✔ Just before sleep, when you're quieting yourself and intending to dream
- ✔ First thing in the morning, when you're recalling your dreams
- ✔ When you want to interpret your dreams

To get yourself ready to start, do the Dream Diary exercises and meditations listed in this chapter; then talk with your friends and family about your desire to dream, your most recent dreams, and what your friends and family have dreamed lately. Talking about dreams keeps them foremost in your mind and helps prime the pump for an increased flow of dreams in your life.

The outward work will never be puny if the inward work is great.

—Meister Eckhart

Your Dream Diary

1. Start with the following phrases and write several paragraphs on each item until you feel finished. You might want to repeat the phrase several times and see what responses you get.

   - If I could remember what I do in my dreams, I'd _____.

   - If I knew my dream activities were real, it would change my experience of myself because _____.

   - If I knew I could try anything in my dreams and not get hurt, it would encourage me to _____.

2. Write from your body's point of view, in first person, about why you're not remembering your dreams as well as you might. What are your body's recommendations for increasing your dream life?

3. If I could know anything in my dreams, I'd like to know _____. (repeat ten times)

4. If I could go anywhere in my dreams, I'd like to visit _____. (repeat ten times)

5. If I could meet anyone in my dreams, I'd like to get to know _____. (repeat ten times)

6. If I could create or invent anything in my dreams I'd like to create _____. (repeat ten times)

7. If I could avoid dreaming about a particular subject, it would be _____. (repeat ten times)

Chapter 2

Building the Dream Habit

> *When action grows unprofitable, gather information.*
> *When information grows unprofitable, sleep.*
>
> —Ursula K. LeGuin

*I*n ancient Greece, dreams were highly respected as a means of receiving guidance from the gods, foretelling the future, and finding cures for illnesses. Prophetic, or precognitive, dreams often led to key turning points in Greek military and political history. The Greeks even believed dreams enabled them to speak with the dead and witness events happening at great distances. They raised the act of seeking, remembering, and interpreting dreams to a high art.

Greek doctors commonly sought healing remedies and surgical instruction in dreams, and Aesculapius, the famous physician who is believed to have lived in the 11th century B.C., and who was later deified, listened to the words uttered by his dreaming patients to help determine the cures he needed to use. The practice of seeking healing dreams became so popular that hundreds of sleep temples were built, 420 to Aesculapius alone, where the sick and infirm could go to concentrate exclusively on their inner world.

To prepare to receive a healing dream in those days, you first made a pilgrimage to the shrine, on foot, thinking about your hopes for contact with the healing gods and a healing dream with every step. When you arrived, you entered buildings of great beauty occupied by priests and a variety of snakes, the symbol of Aesculapius, living peacefully throughout the temple grounds. Before finding your special sleeping spot in the temple, you would be required to bathe, fast, and perform purification rituals and sacrifices to prepare your mind and body to receive a vision. As you cleansed and dedicated yourself, you were surrounded by other seekers, and by a priesthood specially trained in the art of dream interpretation. Every detail was aligned to open your mind, body, and soul to the dream world.

In this chapter, I show you how to prepare to dream today, and how to begin to develop a dream habit that will serve you well throughout your life.

Creating a Dream Temple Attitude Today

Seeking dreams in ancient Greece was serious business, not just a frivolous desire to have fun at night. Although you no longer have the luxury of checking into the downtown Asklepieon, many elements from the ancient Greek dreaming tradition can help you build a strong, positive attitude and dream habit today. To build a strong, positive dream habit, you must

- Believe in the power and reality of dreams
- Get jazzed and talk often about dreams
- Remove your doubts
- Determine your need
- Set your intention to dream
- Expect results
- Dedicate your bedroom to dreaming

In the following sections, I explain how these practices can promote a successful dream habit.

Believe in the power and reality of dreams

Dreams are more than just a curiosity. They offer useful insight and help in living a more successful life, as well as providing a means for you to increase your spiritual growth. To convince yourself of this — in case you have any doubts — do more research. Read books and articles, visit Web sites, join a dream group, take a dream seminar. Surround yourself with active dreamers. Listen to their testimonials. Be affected by their sense of conviction.

Get jazzed about dreams

Nothing convinces your subconscious mind to do something like enthusiasm. When you want to begin remembering your dreams after a long dry spell, for example, try talking to your friends and family about their dreams, about dreaming in general, about the dream books you're reading. Listen for the word "dream" on the radio and on television. What are other people saying? Keep the topic active and in the front of your mind.

Dream recall decreases when you're stressed and anxious (creating fear-based high energy), yet increases with enthusiasm (creating love-based high energy). Similarly, dream recall decreases with depression (creating fear-based stillness) and increases when you're calm and centered (creating love-based stillness). Use your intuition to stay positive and achieve an equal balance between stillness and high energy.

Remove doubts

You may think you want to dream, but your subconscious mind may be holding onto a few "yes, buts."

> ✔ *"Yes, I want to remember my dreams, but if I do I'll have to face my suppressed anger about my father."*
>
> ✔ *"Yes, I want to dream, but if I remember everything, maybe I'll find out how preoccupied I am with sex and I won't be able to think of myself as being a 'good girl' anymore."*
>
> ✔ *"Yes, dreaming will be fun, but what if I dream my sister is going to die? I don't want to know 'bad' things."*

It stands to reason that you won't let yourself remember your dreams if doing so makes you scared or unhappy. True, it's uncomfortable at first to face your "dark side," but uncovering and clearing subconscious fears will give you permission to get more out of life and it produces an immediate increase in dream range and recall.

Get out your dream diary (see Chapter 3) and use the following exercise to discover your own dream "Yes, buts."

Discovering Your Dream "Yes, But's"

1. Quiet your mind and get centered (see Chapter 1 for more about centering).

2. Make a list of responses to the following statements:

    - I do not want my dreams to bring me information about. . . .

    - I do not want my dreams to make me have to feel. . . .

    - I do not want my dreams to change my waking reality by. . . .

    - I do not want my dreams to cause me to lose control by. . . .

3. Look through the lists you made and for each response, ask yourself "Why not?" Why not have information about monsters? Why not feel what it's like to fall? Why not change my waking world by quitting the job that bores me? Why not let go of controlling the formal way I speak to colleagues?

See if you can find the real reason for your resistances. If you allowed each thing you're afraid of, what might you discover?

Determine your need

Why do you want to dream? How might you apply your dreams to round out your experience in life and feel more successful? Be specific in your answers. It's okay to start with a single dream goal. You may simply want the thrill of increasing your dreams about flying. Maybe you need to decide whether to move across country. Perhaps you want to understand why you keep attracting prospective marriage partners who are bad with money. That understanding may enable you to turn around a debilitating 20-year pattern that's kept you single. Talk to yourself convincingly about your need to dream.

Set your intention to dream

Get serious, but not "heavy" or too parental with yourself. You don't need an internal authority figure standing over you with a whip to force you to remember your dreams. A simple, sincere, enthusiastic desire will do.

One of the most common sabotages to a healthy dream habit is the internal conflict that results when one part of you resists another part of you. The inner authority figure says, "You WILL dream tonight, and you WILL do an excellent job, and you WILL like it!" The dreaming part says, "Oh, YEAH? I don't have to do what you say. I'll dream — but I won't remember it. Ha! So there."

To get yourself together for dreaming, try the following meditation.

Aligning Your Body and Mind for Dreaming

1. During the day before the night you want to start dreaming, think enthusiastic thoughts: "Dreams are SO wonderful! It's really going to be fun to dream freely and imaginatively tonight."

2. Get your anticipation juices going: "Falling asleep tonight is going to be a fantastic adventure! I'm going to pay special attention to flying in my dreams tonight."

3. As you prepare for sleep, sit up for a moment on the side of your bed and close your eyes. Talk to yourself about your intentions for dreaming: "I'm so happy that I'm about to enter my dream world. I feel relaxed and ready. My body (pat or hug your body like it's a puppy dog) knows exactly how to enter the dream state and come back with my dreams in tow. My intuition is functioning perfectly to help deliver my dreams accurately to my mind. My conscious mind knows exactly how to recognize my most important dreams, remember them, and describe them in detail. My soul knows what I really need to know in my dreams and guides my dream movements. I trust all my parts. 'We' are all cooperating to enjoy and benefit from the dream world."

When you feel at ease, happy, and confident, lie down and go to sleep, smiling.

Expect results

Let yourself fall asleep expectantly. Dreaming is a normal human ability, and you're entitled to have dreams and remember them easily. You're good at this. It comes naturally. Of course you'll wake up with a dream! Expectancy, without a shred of doubt, is a powerful force. Think of your dog or cat, who expects to be petted often, or of the beaming toddler, who expects to be loved and played with. Their innocent expectations actually elicit the outcome they expect.

Dreaming in other cultures

EGYPT: The Beatty papyrus, written around 1350 BC and discovered at Thebes, is the oldest dream dictionary existing today. It lists the interpretations of many dream images, as well as incantations and rituals to prevent nightmares. Special dream-interpreting priests were called "Masters of the Secret Things" or "Learned Ones of the Magic Library."

BABYLONIAN TALMUD: Fasting was highly valued as a dream incubation method, especially for obtaining precognitive dreams. The Talmud pays special attention to the individualized aspect of dream symbols, taking into consideration the dreamer's personality and life situation in interpretation.

CHINA: Ancient Chinese visited temples, slept on graves, and performed dream incubation rituals, especially to obtain political guidance. They believed the soul could become cut off from the physical body if the dreamer were awakened suddenly, so even today some Chinese do not trust alarm clocks.

NORTH AMERICA: Native American tribes believe dreams bring healing, especially when a bird or animal appears. Among the Sioux, guidance dreams obtained on a visionquest were considered a rite of passage for young men. The vision, interpreted by a shaman, determined the seeker's future path in life.

AUSTRALIA: The Aborigines believe the dream world is a real place, called the "Dreamtime," and that the soul must travel to meet with wise ancestors who live there. Dreams from the ancestors are considered gifts and often inspire art, songs, and dance.

TIBET: The Dzogchen practice of "Dream Yoga" is focused on spiritual dreamwork, on being and experiencing dreams rather than interpreting them. The practice differentiates between "karmic" dreams and "clarity" dreams.

Dedicate your bedroom to dreaming

Do you read in bed? Entertain friends in your bedroom? Watch television in bed? Work on your laptop *while* you're watching TV *and* reading *and* talking on the bedside telephone?

Instead of using your bed as an office, think of your bedroom as your personal sleep sanctuary and use your bed as a kind of altar on which you place your requests for dream assistance. To quiet your bedroom, remove noise-makers like television, radio, and telephone. Move your bookcases to another room. Meditate in bed, sitting upright so you don't go unconscious, before you fall asleep.

As you develop the habit of working with your dream diary, use the time before bed as a good time to do some quiet writing.

Focusing on Dream Recall Meditations

After you mentally prepare to begin remembering your dreams, what else can you do to help grease the wheels of the dream machine? Try any of the following meditations before bed to help stimulate your imagination and focus your awareness.

Visualize your personal dream temple

Just as you've been using the principles from the ancient temples to prepare your dream attitude, you can actually create an imaginary dream temple in your mind and enter it as you fall asleep.

Try the following meditation to create your own dream temple.

See Your Dream Temple

1. Just before sleep, sit up in bed or in a chair, quiet your mind, and get centered. If you're not familiar with centering, see Chapter 1.

2. Imagine that an exquisite building made of glowing light appears in the clear space out ahead of you. It may be white, or crystalline; perhaps it looks like a pyramid or a mosque.

3. Watch the temple grow in complexity. What kind of entrance does it have? What kinds of trees and landscape surround it? What quality of light falls upon your dream temple?

4. Walk to the front door of the temple and meet the guardian. Tell the guardian what you would like to dream about tonight, what you'd like to experience. If you're sincere, the guardian will let you in.

5. Look around inside your temple. What do you see? A fountain, a sacred pool, or baths?

6. Go to the area where you are to cleanse yourself and allow the priests or priestesses who work in that section to assist you. What does the water feel like? Do your helpers use scented oils to help you relax? Do they have you drink a calming potion?

7. Go next to the area of the temple where you will sleep for the night and find your specially prepared bed. What does it look like? Do you sleep on furs, or silk, or on a mattress of leaves, flower petals, and pine needles? What does it smell like? What kind of light permeates the space? Do you have a dream helper — an animal or a priest? Let yourself receive a blessing from your helper.

8. Quietly lie down in bed and imagine you are lying on your sacred dream bed.

Let yourself fall asleep, remembering the purpose of your visit to the dream temple tonight.

Put an energy ball in the back of your neck!

The art of setting yourself up to intentionally remember your dreams and to dream for specific purposes is called *dream incubation.*

One effective technique for planting the seeds of prolific dreaming directs your attention to a sensitive area at the back of the neck, which is close to and stimulates your primitive reptile brain. This deep part of the brain may well receive and implement suggestions planted in the subconscious mind while the rational mind is resting.

Try the following meditation to plant a dream seed.

Plant a Dream Seed

1. Before sleep, sit up on the side of your bed, close your eyes, quiet your mind, and get centered.

2. Imagine the spot at the back of your neck where your head and neck join. Nod your head up and down so you can feel the spot exactly.

3. Imagine a small ball of golden light about the size of a golfball floating in front of you.

4. Think about what you want to achieve in your dreams tonight and formulate a concise sentence describing your goal. Begin with something like a simple request to remember your dreams. Make it simple and specific. *"In the morning when I wake up I will remember my most important dreams."* As you get good at remembering your dreams you might experiment with other statements like, *"I will fly in my dreams tonight and remember my flying dreams."* Or, *"I will wake in the morning with an insight about how I can understand and heal my back pain."*

5. Repeat the sentence several times to yourself, then visualize it and put it inside the ball of golden light. Let the light illuminate and activate the sentence.

6. Place the ball of golden light, with its dream seed, inside the back of your neck at that magic spot. Let the soft, warm light gently penetrate and dissolve into your reptile brain and carry your message to the place where it can be acted upon. Relax and trust that this will occur during the night as you sleep.

7. Lightly hold the idea that the ball and its message will dissolve entirely and in the morning you will wake refreshed with the response you've requested.

When incubating a dream or planting a dream seed, remember that your subconscious mind takes everything you say literally. It's important, therefore, to say exactly what you mean. If you say, "I want to remember my dreams," you may wake up in the middle of the night when you're having any old run-of-the-mill dream. It's more precise to say, *"In the morning when I wake up* I will remember *my most important* dreams." This way you won't disturb yourself needlessly by waking up all night.

Imagine a dolphin pool

Sometimes thinking about a large, peaceful body of water and friendly dream animals, especially dolphins, creates a sleep and dream-inducing mood.

You might try this meditation to call on your dream dolphins to help you recall your dreams.

Call on the Dream Dolphins

1. Lie down in bed and begin to relax. In your mind, imagine your bed is a large raft, floating on the surface of a peaceful ocean, or a huge lake. The moon and stars are shining above you, it's pleasantly warm, and the air is fresh. Imagine your bed-raft rocking gently on the waters.

2. Send out a call in your mind to the dream dolphins. Imagine the dolphins swimming up underneath your bed-raft, poking their noses up around the sides, and nodding their heads up and down as they squeak their

greetings to you. Let them hook their noses into the tow ropes that exist at the corners of your bed-raft and imagine the dolphins are now pulling you far out into the center of the water, where all the other dolphins live.

3. As you fall asleep, tell yourself that the dolphins will talk to you during the night. They will bring you messages from the deep, and you will be able to understand them perfectly.

In the morning, the dolphins will tow your bed-raft back to your bedroom and you will wake with a "dolphin dream message."

Doing Dream Recall Rituals

How many times have you said, "I wish I could figure out what's causing these headaches of mine"? Or, "I'm going to stop eating so much!" But then you let your mind wander to the next thought, and the next one, and in a few minutes you've forgotten your intention.

The problem is that your body and its close ally, the subconscious mind, have not forgotten. Your body treats seriously each request from your conscious mind. As soon as you ask to find out what's causing your headaches, whether you really mean it or not, your body starts to bring you the information you asked for. But now your mind has moved on and isn't there to receive the answer. Your body gets frustrated. It's like your mind is crying "Wolf!" Soon your body starts sabotaging your requests.

"I want to remember my dreams tonight!" you say with conviction. Your body, now used to the superficial nature of your requests, just says, "Sure, sure. I've heard that one before. I'll believe you when you give me some consistent attention — the kind I *know* is real." Your mind may think something is real just by conceptualizing or saying it, but your body needs sensory, kinesthetic, tactile input to recognize something and be able to act on it. Preferably, your body would like the physical input repeated at least three times, as well.

Because your subconscious mind, which is closely allied with your body, helps bring your dream requests to consciousness, doing a dream ritual as described in the sections that follow can help convince your body that what you ask for is not just a mental whim. After you've experimented with these rituals you may get ideas for rituals of your own that satisfy your particular imagination and physical body.

A *ritual* is the symbolic acting out of an idea in specific physical stages to establish a kind of energetic and thought "blueprint" that will guide the manifestation of an intended result. A dream ritual can help you recall your dreams.

Place a note under your pillow

Many dream researchers have developed techniques for incubating dreams and prompting literal responses from the subconscious mind. Some involve lengthy analysis of why you want to solve the problem at hand, a discussion with yourself about the various aspects of the issue, the benefits of solving or not solving the problem, and what you will do when you achieve the desired outcome. I think, however, that you can achieve good quite simply.

Remember how you used to leave your baby teeth under your pillow, sometimes with a nice note to the tooth fairy, and in the morning she'd have magically replaced your tooth with a gold coin? Well, okay, maybe a dime or a quarter? Even so, wasn't it great? You can do something similar with your dream self, or "dream fairy" — that magical part of you that knows how to facilitate your potentially colorful and prolific dream life. I believe a part of our childlike imaginations still has absolute faith in Tinkerbell and Thumbelina. When seeking dreams, it's always a good idea to use as much child-friendly imagery as possible.

Try the following meditation when you need to reach the dream fairy.

Send an Invitation to the Dream Fairy

1. Quiet your mind and get centered. What do you want to do in your dreams tonight? Think of a specific dream goal that captures your fancy, about which you feel true motivation. *"I want to visit my brother, who's traveling in Europe this week, and dream about what he's doing."* Talk to yourself a moment about it. Why is that particular goal interesting? *"I want to know that he's safe, I'm curious about his discoveries, and I'm a little jealous of his freedom."* Okay. You've got it.

2. Write your dream request, concisely and specifically, on a slip of paper. *"Tonight I want to dream about what my brother is doing on his vacation."* Fold up your note and on the outside write: "To my Dream Fairy."

3. Put the note under your pillow and, as you fall asleep, repeat your request three times to yourself.

4. In the morning, open the note and let it trigger any dream recall. If you don't remember a dream, notice the first impressions or thoughts that come to mind and write them in your dream diary.

Try the water technique

You can use a glass of water to help increase dream recall. Here's how:

1. Before bed, fill a special glass with good water and set it by your bedside.

2. Sit up on the side of your bed and decide what you'd like to do in your dreams. What seed will you plant in your subconscious mind tonight? State your request specifically to yourself; even write it out on paper.

3. Take the glass of water. Say to yourself, "As I drink half this glass of water, my body recognizes and receives my dream request. When I drink the other half in the morning, my body will complete the cycle and convey my dreams to me." Drink half the water, let go and relax, and sleep happily. In the morning first thing, sit up on the side of your bed, remember what you asked for, and drink the remaining water. Notice what comes into your mind.

If you don't get results the first night, try again. Rituals often must be repeated three to seven times before your body gets accustomed to the new behavior and follows through consistently.

Use a dream crystal

Shamans often use natural quartz crystals, especially double-terminated (points on both ends) quartz "wands," to aid in dreaming. If you have a natural crystal, hold it in your hand before bedtime, close your eyes, and let your hand relax so the energy from the crystal can flow into you. You may notice your hand starts to vibrate or tingle. That's just your body starting to raise its level of vibration.

Close your eyes and picture the crystal floating freely in front of you. Imagine it increasing in size, growing so large that soon it encompasses you, your bed, and bedroom. When you feel you are inside the crystal, let your whole body adjust to the higher vibration. The principle here is that as you raise the level of your awareness, the caliber of your dreams will correspondingly rise. Lie down and fall asleep, visualizing yourself protected in this new "room" or aura of high frequency awareness. You may even want to hold the crystal as you fall asleep or put it under your pillow.

Hang up a dream catcher

Dream catchers are Native American devices that look like stylized spider webs stretched in a hoop, decorated with little fetishes and amulets, and a feather, which helps send your intentions to the higher dimensions and attract guidance dreams from the same place. Dream catchers are popular decorative items, available through spiritual bookstores, gift catalogues, and Western gift shops. You might even want to try fashioning your own (see Figure 2-1).

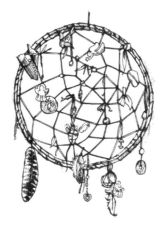

Figure 2-1:
Make your
own dream
catcher.

Native Americans use dream catchers, hung near their beds or in their bed-room window, to help filter out unwanted nightmares or negative dream char-acters. You can use one to help catch your most important dreams, just by intending that it be so, and remembering your intention whenever you look at your dream catcher.

Sniff an herbal dream pillow

Certain aromatic herbs have a reputation as having a positive effect on dream clarity and recall. You can buy small herbal "sleep pillows" at gift shops or make your own using mugwort, which is a universally-known dream activator, as well as rosemary, lavender, sage, rose petals, and other flower scents, such as lilac and jasmine. Keep the small fragrant sachet near your head while you sleep.

Dream during a cat nap

If you have trouble remembering your dreams at night, try taking a nap in the afternoon when possible. Many people find that the concentrated sleep time in a nap promotes dream recall. You'll need to sleep about an hour, though, to reach the REM sleep state (see Chapter 1).

Assume the dreaming position!

Have you ever noticed that sometimes, when you lie down to sleep, dream images from the previous night flit through your mind briefly? My theory about this is that your dreams continue to exist at the level where your mind was focused when you had the dream. By the time you wake up, your mind has narrowed down — or slowed down — to its ordinary worldview; your mind has actually fallen below the threshold where you can recognize the higher dimensions of awareness. Therefore, you are no longer aware of your dreams, which are still at those levels.

When you relax and your consciousness expands again as you fall asleep the next night, you once again match the frequencies of awareness in which your dreams abide. That's why, as you reach the alpha state I discuss in Chapter 1, you may get brief glimpses of what your mind was doing the last time you were consciously in the alpha state. Interestingly, when your body copies the same posture you held when you last slept and dreamed, you may recall previous dreams. Do you wake up on your back, or on your left side with your right leg kicked up and over the left one? Try recreating that position and see if you can tune in to last night's dreams.

Meditate later in the day

Meditation can relax you and expand your awareness into alpha and theta levels (see Chapter 1). You might try an after-work meditation, dream diary at the ready, to see if dream imagery floats back into your mind while you're quiet. The more practice you have at quieting and focusing your mind and body into meditative states, the easier it will be to retrieve dreams at will.

Dream with other people

People who lead dream groups (see Chapter 19 for more information about dream groups) testify that participants who begin a group swearing they never remember their dreams soon remember one every week if the group is of a particular size that allows each person to share one dream per gathering. They remember two dreams if the groups are smaller, allowing time to share two dreams per gathering. Is it peer pressure? Or is the group mind smoothing the way for all? Couples who sleep together and tell each other their dreams as a part of their morning ritual seem to dream more consistently, often of the same things. My teenage niece, Valerie, tells me that when she has her girlfriends over for a slumber party, they don't fall asleep at a set time, and they wake rather organically the next morning. On these occasions, they all seem to dream more actively than usual, remember their dreams, and enjoy sharing them with the group.

The first mystery is simply that there is a mystery. A mystery that can never be explained or understood. Only encountered from time to time. Nothing is obvious. Everything conceals something else.

—Rabbi Lawrence Kushner

Your Dream Diary

1. On a scale of 1-10, with ten the highest or best, rate:

- Your ability to be consistently enthusiastic

- Your ability to be calm and centered

- Your stress and anxiety level

- Your level of depression

- Your energy level in the early morning? the late morning? the early afternoon? the late afternoon? the early evening? the late evening?

Write about how these factors affect your attitude about dreams and your ability to dream.

2. Write about your specific dream goals for the week. As you write, notice which one or two attract you the most.

3. Write about your "innocent expectations" in life. What do you assume will come to you effortlessly? Conversely, what do you expect you will never attain, and what do you expect to be difficult? How might these expectations relate to your dream life?

4. Describe your ideal bedroom in detail. What would you do in your ideal bedroom? How would it feel to dream there?

5. Write about the animals you consider to be your allies, especially those you could imagine helping you move back and forth through the dream world, and helping you remember your dream activities. What is each animal's specialty?

6. Describe in detail a dream recall ritual that comes to you from your inner self, one that will work specifically for you.

7. Meditate and write about the process you experience. How did it feel to your body? What happened to your emotions? What images did you notice? How long could you maintain it? How did you feel afterward? Could you recall any fleeting dream images?

Chapter 3

Keeping a Dream Diary

. . . .

In This Chapter

▶ Harness the power of a daily writing practice
▶ Understand the specifics of creating a dream diary
▶ Determine what goes into your dream diary
▶ Discover how to work with your diary over time

. . . .

The future belongs to those who believe in the beauty of their dreams.

—Eleanor Roosevelt

*W*hen attempting to open and improve the quality of your creativity, or develop your intuition, recording your daily insights and creative urges helps tremendously as you track your progress and watch your growth process unfold. Creativity teacher Julia Cameron, author of *The Artist's Way* (published by Tarcher/Putnam, 1992), recommends writing three pages of stream-of-consciousness observations, which she calls "morning pages," first thing every day. She says that when you just drain your brain onto three pages every day, no matter what, you soon break through the limiting notions that you aren't creative, that your mood affects your output.

The same thing is true with dream work. To help remember your dreams, and even more importantly, to expand the overall scope of your dream life, a dream diary is the single most powerful tool you have. Over time, the diary will reveal the unique pattern of dreaming that is yours alone. At first, writing daily may seem like a stiff discipline, but eventually it becomes a rewarding art form.

Keeping a journal, or dream diary, is a powerful technique for attracting dreams from the higher realms of consciousness into waking reality. You may go from a trickle of memory to a flood. But dreams should never feel burden-some. They're the gravy on our mashed potatoes, the pesto on our pasta! Life would be boring and dry without them.

The Art of Keeping a Dream Diary

Successful dreaming is a process of the mind cooperating with the body so the soul's knowledge can flow through your dreams. So your body plays a key role as the delivery system.

Your body is sweet and animal-like, and loves simple, sensual, repetitive acts. It enjoys bright colors, the swirls, squiggles, and bold strokes of the pen, strong smells, audible sound and music, wild or graceful movement, and complex imagery. If you want your body to help you, you must give it attention, sensory stimulation, and something to do that's physical. To remember your dreams you need to drop them into three-dimensional time and space where your body can interact with them. Keeping a dream diary does this. Writing is a wonderful bridge between the conceptual and the physical. So, ask for dreams and you will receive them — if you create a consistent method for receiving. Give your body a notebook and a fat pen, interesting things to do with that pen, and see what ideas come.

You may prefer to record your dreams first thing in the morning on a cassette recorder you keep by your bedside. This method, because it is physical, also sends a positive reinforcing signal to your body. You can go back later and transcribe the tape into your dream diary so you can work with the dreams in a deeper way.

Fit your diary to your personality

The type of diary you buy should reflect your personality and style of self-expression. What frees your creativity? What helps you focus? What motivates you to write?

- ✔ Are you neat and tidy? Is your handwriting small and precise? Do details matter to you? If so, perhaps you'd do best with a small, bound journal with a beautiful design on the cover and smooth paper with narrow lines inside. Or one with exquisite handmade paper pages. When you touch your diary, you want to feel satisfied because it fits perfectly with your need for focus, good design, precision, and organization. You may have a favorite pen that works perfectly for your style of handwriting. Use this pen for recording your dreams.

- ✔ Maybe your style is more colorful, impulsive, and grand. Is your handwriting large, somewhat messy, and did you always have trouble staying inside the lines when you colored as a child? Do you write fast? Perhaps your perfect dream diary is a large sketchbook, with wide pages that fall open easily, and no lines to restrict you. Or maybe you'd do well with cheap spiral-bound notebooks from the drugstore. You may like pens in a wide variety of colors and nibs to keep you stimulated. Make sure your writing instruments match your mood!

> ✔ Maybe you're someone who, upon waking in the middle of the night or early morning, bleary-eyed with a dream, *would* write your dream down if you could scribble illegibly and get right back to sleep. If you had to be too neat, if it took too much time, you might just pass on the opportunity. If so, you may need two diaries — one that feels comfortable to be messily journalistic in, and one where you recopy the salient points and make sense of it all later.

Some people I know transcribe their dreams into a computer file — a cyber dream diary – and do all their dream analysis at the keyboard. This has the advantage of being speedier, with unlimited space, and you can go back to edit and add on. It has the disadvantage, however, of being overly mental and not particularly visual or tactile.

You have a definite advantage when you can keep your body involved and stimulated by the dream recall process. In a physical diary, you can draw pictures, smell the paper, press hard or softly with your pen, see the subtle changes in your handwriting. Your body interprets all these sensory signals as pleasurable, which reinforces its desire to bring back more dreams. When sitting at your computer monitor, your body may actually feel bored and out of the loop. See what works best for you.

Organize and personalize your diary

You may want to buy a relatively large diary so you have enough space to do some dream analysis, free association of related images and meanings, or sketching right alongside your dream descriptions. Following are some possible dream diary layouts.

Divide each page in half vertically, and use half to record your dreams, half to divine the meaning. Or use two-thirds of the page for writing your dreams and one-third as a margin in which to make notes, as shown in Figure 3-1.

Or use the left-hand page to write your dreams and the right-hand page to analyze and illustrate them, as you see in Figure 3-2.

Just let your process run on in a stream of consciousness fashion, one dream leading to the next day's insight, one day's omen seeding the next night's dream, an analysis about the meaning of it all following next. Try using different colored highlighters, or colored sticky tabs, to mark dreams that seem especially meaningful. Yellow might indicate a teaching dream, green a healing dream, pink a creativity dream, blue a precognitive dream, lavender a spiritual guidance dream, and orange a psychological process dream (I explain these in Part V). Or, underline important words or passages. Create your own system.

I need some help, and some magic, in my life!	March 3 I am running down a dirt road and a man in a pickup truck stops to give me a ride. He has a white rabbit on the seat.	March 5 My brother called me on the phone and I actually heard his voice! He seemed like he wanted help.	I called my brother today and he was depressed. He thinks he might lose his job.
I am wise! I look happy.	March 4 I see my face in the mirror. I look like I'm 100 years old.		

Figure 3-1: Record on two-thirds of a page; interpret on the other third.

Dream/March 3 I am running down a dirt road and a man in a pickup truck stops to give me a ride. He has a white rabbit on the seat.	*I need some help, and some magic in my life! I saw a movie about farmers and thought about the simple life.*
Dream/March 4 I see my face in the mirror. I look like I'm 100 years old.	*I am wise! I look happy in the dream and maybe that person is in me now.*

Figure 3-2: Record on the left page, interpret and sketch on the right page.

You may prefer the kind of spiral notebook that has storage pockets so you can slip in notes, articles, pictures from magazines, or dreams you've remembered and written on the backs of napkins. Some people find that making their diary into a kind of scrapbook adds a new dimension to their dream work. Have you been dreaming about Egypt lately? Why not paste that great photo of the pyramids you found in a travel magazine right next to the dream? Do you want more dreams containing higher guidance? Make a collage of images of angels, innocent children, eagles, and wise elders and write your dream request next to it. See what comes.

Using Your Diary to Prompt Dreams

Think of your dream diary as a record of what's going on in the other, more hidden dimensions of your life. You're a private eye on a stakeout, conducting surveillance on a mysterious subject — the elusive You who lives in the underworld and travels surreptitiously through foreign lands. Your diary is your surveillance report. Some days you jot down notes, some days you take pictures with a long telephoto lens, some days you record snippets of conversations picked up by the "bugs" you've planted. Here are some tips for eliciting dreams:

- ✔ **Discuss your dream goals:** Write out your juicy ideas about what you want to do in your dream world. What do you want to accomplish with your dreams? What are your reasons for wanting to dream more?

- ✔ **Write about your sabotaging ideas:** Explore the ideas that might block your ability to dream and remember your dreams. Dig down to find the insights that will help you resolve the incomplete issues.

- ✔ **Do the Dream Diary writing exercises:** As you work through this book and come across the Dream Diary icon, do the writing exercise in your notebook. Each day, you may also want to pick one of the suggested writing exercises in the "Your Dream Diary" section at the end of the chapter you're reading.

- ✔ **Do the Meditation exercises:** As you encounter the Imagination Meditation icon in this book, do the meditation then write about what you experienced in your dream diary.

- ✔ **Evaluate your dream recall meditations and rituals** (see Chapter 2): Write about the methods you experiment with for improving your dream recall. Which ones work best for you? Which ones are difficult, and why? Did your results improve as you repeated the technique consistently?

- ✔ **Examine your sleep pattern and cycles:** Make notes about how and when you sleep. When do you fall asleep and wake up? Do you sleep through the night or wake up habitually at a certain hour? What stages do you go through as you fall asleep and wake up? What positions do you take as you go to sleep and wake up? Do you always wake up facing the window? Fall asleep on your back? What effect do the moon's cycles have on your sleep pattern? What about the seasons? Do you sleep differently in winter than in spring, summer, or fall?

- ✔ **Detail your "Nightly Review" and "Daily List":** These summary lists can help smooth the transitions between the waking and sleep states. See Chapter 4 for details.

- ✔ **Collect images that trigger dreams:** Paste pictures and mementos into your diary — images of dreamy people, dreamy places, dreamy symbols. Draw little pictures — a cartoon of yourself remembering dreams, sleeping soundly, waking happily.

✔ **Stimulate your mind with quotes, poetry, and prayers:** Copy the inspirational words of others into your diary, and write poems, prayers, or gratitude lists from your heart.

✔ **Pay attention to your waking dreams:** Write about experiences from real life that have a dreamlike quality, are marked by synchronous timing, or seem like omens. I talk more about these in Chapter 8.

✔ **Document your dream incubation statements:** Write out your dream requests in specific, concise terms.

Waking Up and Becoming Conscious

Some people are so sensitive to sound they can be awakened by a dog whistle or the television volume being turned down a notch. Others can sleep through a smoke alarm going off. The way you wake up affects your ability to retrieve your dreams. The following sections help you wake up with a dream whether you wake when a pin drops or sleep through a hurricane.

The hair-trigger waker: Noisy dogs and DJs

If you're a sensitive type, the irritation of a dog barking nearby at 5:30 a.m. could be enough to chase your dreams away and leave you disturbed for the rest of the morning. You certainly wouldn't do well waking to a blaring alarm clock or an AM radio DJ hawking the latest dot-com company. If you have a hair-trigger waking mechanism, consider having a clock radio go off in another room, or using a timer to turn on a small light in your bedroom, or waking to a clock that plays babbling brook or ocean surf sounds. If sound jars you awake painfully, your subconscious will quickly find a way to avoid the shock, and you'll probably have no difficulty programming yourself to wake up ten minutes before your beeper so you can turn off the source of the offending noise pollution. Remembering your dreams is fairly easy when you wake without trauma.

It's time to get up now. Wake UP!

You may sleep like the proverbial log, preferring to wake up naturally about ten or eleven in the morning. When work forces you to rise at 7:30 a.m., even a loud alarm clock right next to your ear may sound like the faintest whisper. Do you hit the snooze bar on your clock radio again and again without realizing it? Then wonder how you overslept, why you're late, and how you lost your dreams so quickly? If this is you, let yourself sleep to your natural waking time, at least once a week, and the rest of the time try a sequence of waking mechanisms combined. Have music start playing across the room half an hour before you get up, a light turn on 15 minutes before, and place a beeping alarm, with no snooze button, next to your bed, set to go off 5 minutes before you want to rise. Before sleep, suggest to yourself that you will hear each of the three signals and wake up gradually and progressively with each.

The dreamer's motto: "Be prepared!"

Keep your dream diary, or your tape recorder, where you can reach it easily, no matter how groggy you might be. The common reasons most people give for failing to remember their dreams and eventually giving up on dream work are:

✔ I forgot to put my dream diary by my bed.

✔ I forgot to put a pen next to my diary.

✔ My diary is too neat for me to write in; I can't control my handwriting before I've washed my face and scrubbed my teeth.

✔ I don't have enough time to write down a dream. I'm late!

✔ I had a dream in the middle of the night and . . .

. . . it's too much trouble to take the top off the pen when I'm sleepy.

. . . it's too dark to see where I put my pen and diary.

. . . it's too dark to see what I'm writing. If I turn on a light I'll wake up too much.

 Be good to yourself. Prepare for writing in your dream diary before you go to sleep. Talk to yourself about doing it. Put your diary next to your bed, open to the right page, easy-writing pen in the gutter of the notebook. Have a small penlight there, too, in case you wake in the dark with a dream. You might even go through the motions of what your body will do in the middle of the night or the morning: "I'll wake up, lie still until I crystallize what I want to write, and then I'll reach over, take my pen, sit up, and write. . . ."

Lie still and float between worlds

Leaving a little extra time for dream work in the morning pays off. Just floating a moment or two before the daily grind imposes itself upon you is an important key to dream recall. Transferring your higher consciousness back to your physical reality smoothly is a bit like landing a jumbo jet at a metropolitan airport. You've got to give your inner pilot a chance to keep the wings level, the nose on the right course, and the angle of decline perfect. That way, you meet the tarmac seamlessly, with all crew and passengers intact. Come back too fast, and you actually feel like you're crashing back into your body, all memory of your journey through the higher atmosphere gone.

There is a stage between sleep and wakefulness where your awareness is relaxed yet engaged, receptive yet creative. This *hypnagogic state* is a fertile kind of awareness where many c images may flow freely through your mind. It is this soft pliable awareness you want to maintain for a little while upon waking, so your dreams have the best chance of seeping through into ordinary reality.

Work backward through the images; no words yet!

Stay in touch with the subtle state you are immersed in as you awaken. You don't need to label it immediately and get verbal. Let it be. Let it inform you. Let it suggest an image. Let that image talk to you. Let that image lead you to a previous image, and that to an even earlier one.

By working backward, and by staying in a tactile and visual mode of perception without any urgency, your dream may be gradually illuminated. As you feel points of recognition, new earlier segments of the dream may suddenly open to you. You cast your awareness toward your dream world and remember a feeling of concern, which leads to an image: Your friend Sara was showing you a growth on her side that she was worried was infected. You give her advice. Suddenly you remember another whole part that preceded this one — the real reason you were visiting Sara was to take a photograph of a piece of unusual Native American art she had. As you focus on the statue, you enter a state of peacefulness, seemingly conveyed by the arrangement of feathers and turquoise adorning the figure. Go as far as you can with your nonverbal re-experiencing. Then let the sequence of scenes, important details, and feeling states come together in your mind, finally putting words around the sensations. NOW, sit up, reach for your pen and diary, and write down the core of your dream experience with as many details as possible.

If no dreams come, write anyway!

So what do you do if you lie there all soft and ready, and no dream presents itself? Not to worry! Sit up, take your diary, and write about the mood or feeling state you woke up in. What does your body feel like? Write about the questions that were in your mind first thing. Write about the first thought you had this morning or the first person you thought about today. Why did she come to mind?

If no dreams come, especially after you specifically requested one the night before, it's important that you follow through anyway and give your body the message that you mean what you say. "I am going to remember a dream in the morning," you said. So, make one up! Fantasies, creativity, and dreams all come from the same place, so your body won't know the difference.

What's critical here is that you write SOMETHING in that diary of yours to complete the process and validate the impression in your subconscious mind. "I fall in a muddy pond and when I stand up I feel a school of minnows tickling me as they nibble at my legs." Later, work with this fantasy image the same way you would a real dream. In short order, your body will be bringing you the real thing on a regular basis.

You may think you lost your dreams in the morning, but while you're reading the newspaper, or waiting at a traffic light, a fragment of one of last night's dreams pops back into your mind. Grab the nearest scrap of paper and write it down. Tuck it somewhere safe and bring it back to enter into your dream diary. You may want to carry a notebook just for this purpose.

Don't forget to take your dream diary with you whenever you travel. Most people report that their dreams are more active than usual when they sleep in new places, with their bed oriented to a different direction, and with the light coming through different windows in the morning.

Using Your Diary after You Dream

After you wake with a dream, even a made-up dream, you want to be as complete as you can in describing it so you don't lose the important elements that will help you interpret it later. Following are some tips for recording your dreams:

- ✔ **Write the date with each dream:** Keeping track of the dates of your dreams, and the day of the week if you're so inclined, can help you track themes and relate your dreams to real life events.

- ✔ **Write in the present tense:** A dream is a living thing and continues to exist in your awareness even after you've dreamed it. By saying "I jump off the water tower and a huge crow swoops down and catches me in its beak," instead of "I jumped off and was caught," you stay immersed in the experience and can more easily access related emotions, associations, and meanings.

- ✔ **Record as many details as you can:** List the main actions, the way you feel as you act or are acted upon, your choices and decisions, the location, directionality, the characters and objects, important adjectives, any symbols or numbers, colors, sounds, names or unusual words,- messages dictated by a faceless voice or a talking head, the way the light appears in the dream, the dream's general atmosphere, and how "real" it feels. Sometimes details you consider of no consequence will reveal telling insights, so jot down everything your mind is highlighting.

✔ **Put a star next to dreams that seem especially important:** As you practice interpreting your dreams, detecting the real stand-out ones will get easier, but as you begin, try to sense which ones have the strongest "psychic weight." You'll know. Some will wake you exactly at 3 a.m. Some will seem like they're lit by a spotlight. Some will seem especially tangible, or convey a sense of warning, or feel predictive in nature.

✔ **Dream fragments can be as valuable as epic dreams:** You don't need to remember long involved theatrical productions to get profound benefit from dreams. More often than not, a simple fragment will provide the insight that is most useful to you. Fragments are highly potent symbolized messages, often containing layer upon layer of meaning.

✔ **Pay attention to dream images that have carried over from the previous day:** These seeds or trigger images from real life are called *day residue* and are as important as any other dream image. Remember that images from daily life come into your awareness the same way dream images do, so to your subconscious mind there's not much difference. The fact that you noticed a map of Arizona at a friend's house, and then dreamed you were hiking in the desert, signifies a theme that is trying to surface.

✔ **Make little drawings to illustrate important parts of the dream:** Sketches help strengthen recall and are important in interpretation. The Mayan priest in your dream wears elaborate carved earrings hanging to his shoulders. Draw them in as much detail as possible. You see a strange, star-shaped crystal set into a clay tablet with odd writing on it. Sketch it, quick, before you forget!

✔ **Notice what happens in the next few days:** Do you notice images in real life that parallel your dream symbols? Does someone you dreamed about suddenly call you? Do you dream about your car, and then have three friends tell you about their car trouble? Watch for repeating themes and a continuation of dream messages.

✔ **Apply dream material in real life:** Write about how you use your dream insights. Did you call the friend who you dreamed was standing in the rain under an umbrella by your front door? Did you start exercising after you dreamed you couldn't get enough oxygen? Could you write a poem inspired by an image from a dream? How about painting a dream? Or trying to capture the music you dreamed?

Using the Back of Your Diary

In each dream diary you start, consider creating a section in the back where you can keep several ongoing lists. Here you can excerpt and collect particularly interesting dream images, themes, and characters, along with the dates you dreamed them. As you review your dream diary periodically, you find repeating patterns and symbols. Here are some suggested lists:

- ✔ **Your many faces:** List the roles you play in your dreams. Within a few months you may be an athlete, a pilot, a doctor, a prostitute, a child, and a dying person. How often are you a teacher in your dreams? What new roles have you been exploring lately? What did being a gifted musician show you about yourself?

- ✔ **Your dreamscapes:** Where have you traveled in your dreams? Foreign countries, outer space, your mother's house? Do you repeatedly set your dreams by the Atlantic Ocean? Do you revisit the schools you attended?

- ✔ **Your dream teams:** Who do you dream about? Old lovers? A boss you didn't get along with? Religious leaders of the world throughout history? Are your dreams populated by animals who talk? Who helps you in your dreams? Whom do you help? Who fights with you?

- ✔ **Your dream symbols:** Do you have lots of books in your dreams? Do you drive many different kinds of cars? Perhaps you have a rash of numbers in your dreams one month, or see triangles upon waking. Do you dream about words from other languages?

- ✔ **Your dream themes:** What overall themes do you see in retrospect as you scan back through your diary and your lists? For the first two months of the year did you seem concerned with sex? Or health? Were you practicing new methods of flying in your dreams? Did your flying dreams turn into a series of dreams where you were driving cars, trucks, and motorcycles?

Your dreams will expand or contract to fill the time you've allotted for working with them. Therefore, simply decide how much time you can dedicate in the morning and before bed to focus on dream work. That way, your dreams won't overwhelm you. Be clear with your subconscious mind. "I want to remember my important dreams and I have 20 minutes in the morning and 30 at night to work with them."

Dreaming is a nightly dip, a skinny dip into the pool of images and feelings.

—James Hillman

Your Dream Diary

1. Describe a collage of images you might assemble to decorate the cover of your dream diary. What goes next to what?

2. List ten reasons why you can't possibly do a daily writing practice. Then list ten ways you could.

3. Write a paragraph completing each of the following:

   If I were Picasso, my dream journal would be filled with dreams about, and would look like. . . .

   If I were Mother Teresa, my dream journal would be filled with dreams about, and would look like. . . .

   If I were George Burns, my dream journal would be filled with dreams about, and would look like. . . .

   If I were Amelia Earhardt, my dream journal would be filled with dreams about, and would look like. . . .

4. Write about your process of falling asleep. Describe the bodily sensations you experience. Do you have sleep disturbances during the night? What happens to your body then? Describe your experience of waking up and how you could refine the process.

5. Write a prayer to the Powers that Be, asking for help remembering and recording your dreams.

6. Pick three well-known people or characters from books, from any time in history, who you think could help you with your dreams. Write about what each would do for you and how they'd do it.

7. Make up a dream that fills two pages of your diary.

Part II
Explore Your Dreamscape

The 5th Wave   By Rich Tennant

@RICHTENNANT

"Why don't you give your Dreamcatcher another chance before backing it up with a baseball glove, flypaper and a lobster trap?"

In this part . . .

Part II shows you what's possible in your dream world so you can discern exactly what you're doing when you're dreaming. By knowing the territory, you can navigate more intentionally and go to new places. This way, you'll increase your sense of self.

In this part, I introduce you to the idea of dreaming 24 hours a day, increasing your awareness of the connection between day and night for maximum dream proficiency. Next, you'll see how your dreams are filtered through either your superconscious or subconscious mind and how your conscious mind functions as your dream viewpoint. Finally, this part describes the "dream zones," or the kinds of dream experience it's possible to encounter. If you know the characteristics of each zone, you'll be able to interpret your dreams more accurately.

Chapter 4
Dreaming Full Time

● ●

In This Chapter

▶ Waking up to your whole self: A few revelations about dreams

▶ Aiming for 24-hour consciousness: Weaving together the day and night

▶ Becoming a great intention-setter and results-getter!

▶ Helping "Morning You" and "Night You" work together

● ●

With the coming of day
I embrace my Mother,
with the coming of night
I join my Father,
and with the outgoing of the evening and morning
I will breathe their law,
and I will not interrupt these communions
until the end of time.

—The Essene Hymns of Thanksgiving

As you begin to pay attention to your sleep dreams, you open the door to a greater knowledge of your inner self. Sleep dreams are tantalizing. Like the carrot in front of the donkey, they lead you forward into the territory of the unconscious, which is really just the inexperienced part of your own soul. Dreams, because of their magical quality, seem obviously to hold deeper meaning. But seeing that what you define as normal reality is also symbolic, and can also lead you to your soul, is more difficult. But just think: What sort of self-image might you develop if you assumed you were conscious, learning, and creating all the time? Sleep isn't some black hole, separate from your "life." And your life may hold just as magical a quality, and much more depth and wisdom than you've ever thought possible.

In this chapter, I show you how to increase your dream consciousness by connecting the day and night. But first, I want to dispel some myths you may have heard about dreams and reveal the truth about this fascinating dance of your awareness.

Demystifying Some Dream Myths

As people in a society, we hold several concepts about dreams that limit our understanding of what might be possible in the realm of dream work. As you begin to outline the territory of dreams, you need to broaden your view of the way dreams fit into the spectrum of your consciousness. Are you ready to stretch into some fresh ideas?

Myth #1: Dreams are just symbols of the intangible parts of your makeup

With the rise of science, psychiatry, and neurology, people gained a new vantage point on the study of dreams, learning to separate from their dreams, objectify them, and examine them under the microscope of their intellect. Two pioneers in this dream examination movement contributed significantly to current attitudes toward dreaming:

- Sigmund Freud's psychoanalytic theory holds that dreams are created by unconscious desires, especially sexual urges and those of people's less civilized animal nature. He developed a method for dream analysis called *free association,* in which the patient describes whatever thoughts and feelings come to mind as a way of seeing behind the facade of the dream.

- Carl Jung's theory says that people evolve from an individual identity based on the limited ego to an identity that recognizes the central, spiritual Self that is capable of unifying the conscious and unconscious awareness.

Where Freud was interested in finding the causes of dreams, Jung was more interested in their purpose. Freud believed dreams disguised the unconscious; Jung believed they revealed it. Freud saw the unconscious as containing repressed personal urges; Jung felt it contained a wealth of information that was universal in nature, pertaining to humanity as a whole. Jung called this planetary source of dream material *the collective unconscious.* Both men used dreams to explore the content of the unconscious mind.

Through these scientists of the mind, we as people have made great strides in discovering how to interpret dreams as a way of understanding the psychological underpinnings of our lives. Yet in so doing, we often "mentalize" our dreams, subjecting them to endless intellectual analysis, and reducing their reality by trying to fit them into categories that are too tight and small.

In 1977 Allan Hobson and Robert McCarley proposed a dream theory they called *activation-synthesis,* which says that dreams are simply by-products of "bottom-up" brain activity — the lower parts of the brain fire random impulses during the highly active REM sleep periods, and voila! Dreams.

Revelation #1: Dreams are real!

Most ancient societies held a much more subjective, spiritual view of dreams. Egyptian, Babylonian, Greek, Hebrew, Roman, Chinese, Hindu, and Aboriginal writings about dreams all reflect the notion that dreams depict actual travels of the soul, which is free to move beyond the body in altered states like sleep, meditation, or trance. They believed that the waking world and the dream world are two different views of the same reality. Plato called dreaming "the between state," an actual place the soul went to meet with the gods, similar to "the Dreamtime" described by the Australian Aborigines. In this ancient view, we as people are not separate from our dreams, and we don't "have" them like we have a car or house. They are an integral part of our living experience. They *are* us.

Many contemporary dream workers are now returning to this view.

- ✔ Fritz Perls, a psychotherapist who helped develop humanistic psychology, originated the method of Gestalt therapy, which deals with the "whole person" to assist personal growth. He believed that instead of analyzing dreams, dreams should be relived as if they are happening in the present moment — because they truly are living parts of us.

- ✔ Others, like Arnold Mindell, Stanley Keleman, and Eugene Gendlin, have emphasized the importance of looking at dream work as a direct physical experience, emphasizing the body's consciousness in connection with dreams and their interpretation, rather than mental theories.

- ✔ Carlos Castaneda popularized the shamanistic teachings of a Yaqui Indian sorcerer, Don Juan, which feature dreaming as one of the main pathways to self mastery. In *Journey to Ixtlan,* Carlos has this brief exchange with his teacher: "Do you mean then, Don Juan, that dreaming is real?" "Of course it is real." "As real as what we're doing now?" "If you want to compare things, I can say that it is perhaps more real. In dreaming you have power; you can change things; you may find out countless concealed facts; you can control whatever you want."

- ✔ Rosemary Ellen Guiley, in *Dreamwork for the Soul* (published by Berkeley Books, 1998), shows how to use dream work for spiritual growth. She says, "Dreams move us from beyond the symbolic to experiences of Truth. Dreams are a straight connection to the divine heart of the cosmos."

In Chapters 5 and 6, I explore this ancient idea in greater depth, so you can begin to experience how dreams are not really "things," but instead, are actual movements of your higher consciousness.

Myth #2: Dreams only occur during sleep

Because science says that people dream only during the periods of REM sleep each night, people tend to associate dreaming exclusively with sleep, and with only a few specific hours of sleep at that.

However, if you assume that dreams are the main doorways through which you can reach your inner world, then defining dreams so narrowly prevents you from fully accessing your deeper experience and from considering that *everything* you perceive might be a projection originating from the same source of awareness.

Might dreaming be a broader phenomenon than people have previously allowed it to be? *Might it not be the very act of the soul perceiving?* Goethe said, "We never stop seeing, perhaps this is why we dream." I would turn it around and say, "We never stop dreaming, perhaps this is why we see."

Revelation #2: We dream constantly!

In the fourth century BC, a Chinese philosopher named Chuang-tzu pondered the deeper nature of dreaming and being awake. "While men are dreaming," he wrote, "they do not perceive that is a dream. Some will even have a dream in a dream, and only when they awake they know it was all a dream. And so, when the Great Awakening comes upon us, shall we know this life to be a great dream. Fools believe themselves to be awake now."

Traditional Eastern philosophies commonly hold that the world is impermanent and illusory. In Hindu India, all existence is considered to be the dream of God or Vishnu. Everything people know is said to be dreamed into existence from the mind of God, even the people themselves, and we as people are dreaming our own worlds into existence and eliminating them constantly.

About the Tibetan Buddhist practice called "Dream Yoga," Namkhai Norbu, one of the great Tibetan teachers, says, "All the visions we see in our lifetime are like a big dream. If we examine them well, the big dream of life and the smaller dreams of one night are not very different." Similarly, dream theorist Medard Boss says in *The Analysis of Dreams* (published by Philosophical Library, 1958), "There is no such thing as an independent dream on the one hand and a separate waking condition on the other."

To bring this point a bit more down to earth, think about how visualizing a goal you want to achieve — whether it's having a new red sports car, or winning the Boston Marathon, or losing 15 pounds — helps it materialize more easily. Sometimes an artist has a clear vision of a painting, and then creating the artwork becomes a simple matter of spending the time to replicate it physically. On so many occasions, the results you achieve seem to be dreamed into being through the conscious use of imagination. It's not too far a stretch to consider the idea that all your waking reality is being dreamed into being by a higher force of consciousness with a much broader scope than your conscious mind can grasp. If you want to understand something about this fundamental, higher consciousness, otherwise known as your soul, one of the techniques you can use is to examine the trails and tracks it leaves — the images and symbols in your life.

Myth #3: Day and night are separate worlds

Day and night certainly *seem* different. In one, your eyes are open, your body is vertical, and you can touch solid objects. In the other, your eyes are closed, your body is horizontal, and you can pass through walls or travel from one location to another instantly. You probably routinely think of waking reality as "conscious" and sleeping reality as "unconscious." You therefore tend to overemphasize the waking world and minimize your nighttime consciousness.

But what if your supposedly unconscious, nighttime reality is where you are truly awake? Sri Nisargadatta, an enlightened master from India, said in *I Am That* (published by Acorn Press, 1973), "Most of your experiences are unconscious. The conscious ones are very few. You are unaware of the fact because to you only the conscious ones count. Become aware of the unconscious."

Revelation #3: Night and day are continuous and feed into each other

Consider this: Your daily reality is like the tip of an iceberg; most of your life is actually being lived "under the surface" in various dream worlds. What you do in these dream worlds works its way up and out into a specific focus in your physical life. Your dreams actually influence, even create, what occurs in your waking world. And what shows up in your daily life sends waves back out again into the dream worlds, influencing *them*. Consider the idea that your life on earth is a constant movement back and forth between essence and form, the energetic and the solid, the imaginary and the real. Like the classic old song says: "You can't have one without the other!"

The ancient Chinese yin-yang symbol, shown in Figure 4-1, contains a teaching that relates to dream work. In this symbol, two droplet or fish-shaped forms, one white/dynamic/masculine and one black/receptive/feminine, swim around and around in a circle.

Figure 4-1:
The yin-
yang
symbol.

Each contains an "eye," or seed, or perhaps it is the "memory of," its opposite color. You can easily look at the image and think that two separate forces
are interacting with each other. In truth, there is just one force that takes two
guises, the black/yin transforming itself into the white/yang, the yang transforming itself into the yin, endlessly. This is exactly what your soul does as it
takes on the cloak of daytime consciousness (yang) and nighttime consciousness (yin).

Weaving Day and Night to Form a 24-Hour Consciousness

There are 24 hours in a day. When you realize that you are not gone or
switched off at night, you start to feel the limitless nature of your true self.
Your soul doesn't get tired and need to rest; it's alive and aware all the time.
So, to experience the full range of your soul's activity, you must be centered
and alert during your waking hours, and increasingly aware of the many
worlds you occupy during your so-called "unconscious" hours of sleep.

You can begin by smoothing the transitions between day and night, and night
and day — creating a seamless 24-hour consciousness. It's partly the jerky
shifts people make between the two realms that perpetuate memory loss in
both. Oddly, when you see what your soul does at night, you start to see it
doing similar things during the day. Notice how your dreams affect you the
next day, and then notice how your daily experience feeds into your dreams.
Just as your breath flows in and back out, and then turns and flows back in,
so your day turns to night and night turns to day (see Figure 4-2).

Figure 4-2:
Twenty-four hour consciousness: Making clear connections between day and night.

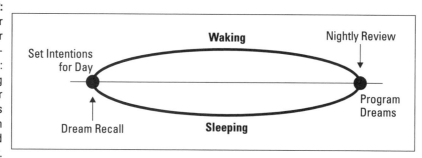

Pay special attention to dawn and dusk, when light turns to dark, and dark to light, when beta brainwaves turn to alpha and theta, and back again. Feel the curve of the turn, enter the turn, become conscious of the turn. The suggestions that follow will help you become conscious of the turns:

- ✔ **At the end of the day:** Recap what you did with the "Nightly Review".

- ✔ **At the start of the night:** Set your intentions to dream.

- ✔ **At the end of the night:** Recall your dreams.

- ✔ **At the start of the day:** Set your intentions for the day with the "Daily List".

The idea is to stop blanking out when a shift occurs. There is really no point when consciousness actually disappears. Stay alert at the end and beginning of cycles, and you maintain a sense continuity about yourself.

Ending your day: The nightly review

At the end of each day, before you fall into your dream world, make a habit of reviewing your day's activity. In this *nightly review,* take stock of what you accomplished and compare it with your original intentions that morning. In your dream diary, describe what you did, the way you interacted, the feelings you're left with at the end of the day. Before you sleep and dream, make sure you're complete and content with how you lived today. Some questions to ask:

- ✔ Did I do everything I set out to do today?

- ✔ Did I behave in a way I'm proud of?

- ✔ Did I yell at anyone, or gossip, or think negative thoughts about a friend?

- ✔ Was I kind?

- ✔ Was I wasteful?

✔ Was I disciplined?

   ✔ Was I playful?

   ✔ What am I grateful for that happened today?

What follows is a sample "Nightly Review" diary entry: *TODAY I . . .*

> *Today I felt good about visiting with Mom; we had a great conversation and I really listened to her, and she to me. I designed a flyer for my business and it looks good. I did several loads of laundry and neatened up my closets and dresser drawers.*
>
> *I feel incomplete about not changing my bedsheets, not cooking up the apples that fell off the tree, not returning the calls from Donna and Masako.*
>
> *I have a funny, nagging sense of anxiety about the trip to Santa Fe, about what to say to Robert when I see him, about whether I'll do well at my presentation next week.*
>
> *I regret I was a bit short and intolerant with a couple people on the phone today and that I forgot, once again, to tell people what's good about them. I was judgmental about the way people drive. I didn't meditate and I meant to.*
>
> *I am grateful for my new car! And for my clients, my friends, my family, and my health. I'm grateful I was offered an opportunity to speak in public, even though it scares me.*

Setting tomorrow's goals

Next, think about what you want tomorrow to be like. Would you like to do anything differently than you did today? Do you wish you had said something today that you might say tomorrow? Perhaps you'll set a strong intention to complete a project you didn't finish, or treat someone more lovingly, or take better care of yourself physically.

What follows is a sample "Tomorrow's Goals" diary entry:

> *IN THE MORNING . . .*
>
> *In the morning, I want to wake up with a positive attitude and stretch my body first thing with some yoga exercises. I want to smile at people, even in cars! I am going to return all my phone calls and write one thank-you note. I'm going to meditate for 15 minutes after I get home from work and change my clothes. I'm going to practice patience!*

Starting your night: Establish your intention to dream

As you review your day and come to a sense of completion, cast your attention ahead to what you'll do tonight during your dreams. Give yourself a pep talk. "Yes! I'm going to have fun tonight! I'm going to fly, travel, learn, meet new people, AND I'm going to remember it all when I wake up in the morning!" Try some dream incubation techniques (see Chapter 3).

What kind of experiences do you want to have? Be creative. Anything is possible! Here are some suggestions:

- ✔ I want to touch base with a relative who's died.

- ✔ I'd like to heal a psychological wound or physical illness.

- ✔ I'd like to help others tonight.

- ✔ I want to learn about plants or how to sculpt.

- ✔ I want to go to the inventor's library and learn about new technologies.

- ✔ I want to talk to of my guides.

- ✔ I'd like help solving a problem.

Here are two sample "Dream Incubation" diary entries:

TONIGHT IN MY DREAMS . . .

Tonight in my dreams, I want to go to a new place and meet people who can teach me how to be a better swimmer. I want to release any negativity I've been holding in my body. I want to wake tomorrow feeling clearer and less clogged up. I will remember my most important dreams in the morning when I wake up.

OR

Tonight in my dreams I want my soul and my helpers to give me a clear sign and some insight about this new job I've been offered. Is it good for me in the long run? What might happen? I will be able to bring this information back with me when I wake up.

When you finish setting the intentions for your dreamtime, *while you're still vertical,* turn out the light and imagine how you'll feel after you have the new knowledge or experience you want. Quiet your mind totally and release your dream intentions like a huge weather balloon until they're out of sight, out of mind. In addition, you may want to say some prayers as a way to send blessings to others — and yourself — and begin connecting with your nighttime experience, the higher dimensions of your soul, and the divine (see Chapter 17).

You can more easily to stay alert and conscious of the specific goings-on of your inner reality when your head is vertical and level. As soon as you lie down, you start to lose focus. That's why practices such as meditating and setting intentions are usually best done while sitting up.

Ending your night: Dream recall

When you wake in the morning, make sure to take those few extra moments to gently return from the depths of sleep so you can maintain a connection with your dream world. If you jerk awake, it's like throwing a boulder in a pond. The clear reflected images lying on the glassy surface will be shattered. Practice waking up consciously, without disturbance. I discuss dream recall in Chapter 2, but here are a few reminders:

✔ Say to yourself right away: "What have I just been doing?"

✔ Keep the subtle feelings and sensations from your dream state in your body before your logical mind kicks into high gear.

✔ Look internally for the most predominant images that are floating in your soft consciousness.

✔ Describe the images, subtle feelings or emotions, and actions you've taken in the dream OUT LOUD.

✔ Make your dreams real to your body. Tell someone right away, describe the dream into a tape recorder, or write it in your diary.

Starting your day: The daily list

After you summarize your nighttime activities by recording your dreams, turn your attention to the day. Collect yourself, be centered and calm. Reread your Nightly Review list from last night. What's left from yesterday that you want to complete today? Make of list of your intentions for the day by considering the following questions:

✔ What impact do you want to have on other people, and on the world, today?

✔ What kind of experience and attitude do you want to have today?

✔ What do you want to give today?

✔ What are you interested in knowing today?

Finally, tell yourself "I want to pay more attention to what I do today."

After you determine your intentions, you may want to make a more specific list of things to do. Make sure you choose goals that feed your creativity and spiritual growth, like visiting an art gallery, not just the tasks that "should" be completed like balancing your checkbook.

Getting "Night You" and "Morning You" to Cooperate

I saw comedian Jerry Seinfeld on a late night talk show, and he was telling a hilarious story about how he gets in his own way. He said that "Night Guy" likes to stay up late, party, and eat pizza. Then "Morning Guy" has to get up early to be at work and is exhausted and groggy, rushing around getting organized. Night Guy thinks Morning Guy is a wimp and Morning Guy thinks Night Guy is a jerk!

I soon started to think of myself as Morning Girl and Night Girl. Morning Girl often forgets to take the vitamins that Night Girl needs, and Night Girl sometimes forgets to exercise after work and wash her face before bed. So I started pretending that Morning Girl was doing favors for Night Girl; she'd fold the laundry or take a brisk walk. Night Girl would in turn wash the dishes and meditate. Morning Girl would make the phone calls and Night Girl would file the day's paperwork.

When developing the dream habit of becoming conscious 24 hours a day, Night You can do favors for Morning You by recapping the day and honoring what Morning You intended and accomplished. Then, Night You can intend your dream time to extend and further those goals, adding in anything new and pertinent. Morning You then picks up the flow again, bringing the dreams into waking consciousness, looking for the underlying lessons and meanings, integrating the insights into daily life, and looking for deeper meaning in the day's events. When your day and night selves work for each other's good, eventually you'll start to know the bigger Self, or soul, that underlies and fuels both.

Practicing Mindfulness All Day

While you're awake, periodically check in with yourself to make sure you're present and alert to what's happening in a 360-degree radius all around you.

Is your mind in the future, worrying or wanting some task to already be complete? Or are you in the past, wishing that you were still on that camping trip with your family?

Perhaps you've projected to another location, like the post office you need to visit this afternoon, or the bathtub you plan to get into at the end of the day. You may be in someone else's reality, thinking how it would feel to be that person — or in a fantasy reality, either positive or negative, that actually doesn't exist.

Wherever your mind goes, some of your energy goes also. The more you're absent from the here-and-now, the more stressed, drained, and unconscious you'll be. Conversely, the more present you are, the more deeply you'll be able to perceive.

Try this meditation to help trigger your mindfulness:

Remembering to be Mindful

Pick something you do a number of times each day and use it as a "mindfulness trigger." It could be every time you hang up the telephone, or whenever you sit down in a chair or pass through a doorway. Use this signal to remind yourself to come fully into the here-and-now and pay attention to what you're aware of in your body and around you. Ask yourself: "What theme am I preoccupied with right now? What message is trying to get through to me this very second? What do I already know about this situation? What's the deeper meaning of what I'm involved with right now?"

Mindfulness is a great starting point for training yourself to remember dreams. By cultivating the habit of being centered and 100 percent present, you improve your ability to focus your attention, hold your concentration, and receive insights. Amazingly, as you enter your experience fully, information will start coming to you directly, effortlessly, without you trying to obtain it.

You might normally pass by the checkout clerk, not making eye contact or really connecting. When you practice mindfulness, the experience slows and opens. You look into the person's eyes, and are present to him without an agenda. Into that pure moment, a thought may suddenly spring: "Ah, this man is sad; he feels alone." You smile, and genuinely convey that you accept him as he is. The experience becomes richer, more real, and more valuable for both of you.

Try this meditation as an exercise in mindfulness.

Becoming One with a Mundane Task

1. Pick a small, mundane task: scrubbing your teeth, washing a pot, sweeping the sidewalk, booting up your computer, writing a check.

2. Before you begin, pause, center yourself, and talk to your body and soul, experiencing cooperation inside yourself as you act: "We are going to get this pot clean now. We are going to make it beautiful." Then, "We are picking up the pot now; we are turning on the hot water; we are getting

the pot scrubber soapy ; we are holding the pot with one hand and making scrubbing motions with the other. Ah, look! The pot is shiny now right here! Now we are getting this last dark spot off the pot; now the pot is perfectly clean; now we are rinsing it; now we are putting it on the dishrack to dry; now we are finished cleaning the pot. Now the pot and I feel satisfied."

3. Feel every step, noticing how much your body, in its childlike simplicity, enjoys each part of the process. Thich Nhat Hanh, the Buddhist monk, says, "Washing the dishes is like bathing a baby Buddha."

Becoming more conscious of the known world helps you really "wake up" while you're awake. By doing this, you'll be able to gradually wake up within the heretofore-unknown worlds revealed by your dreams. By using your attention and intention to regularly penetrate below the surface of all parts of your life, you'll discover an incredibly vibrant, cohesive, loving world.

I can never decide whether my dreams are the result of my thoughts or my thoughts are the result of my dreams.

—D. H. Lawrence

Your Dream Diary

1. Write about how some of the themes from your daily life may have carried over into your dreams. Look for parallel themes, repeating symbols.

2. Write about how some of the themes from your dreams may have carried over and affected what you subsequently did in your daily life.

3. Make a list of ten images from daily life that stand out to you. What might each of them mean if they occurred in a dream?

4. If I realized I were conscious 24 hours a day, I'd feel capable of _____. (repeat ten times)

5. Write about what you observed by being mindful of a mundane task.

6. Write about why you forget to pay attention. What are your justifications? What do you lose by skimming across the surface?

7. Write about how Night You and Morning You sabotage each other and what they currently think and feel about each other (you might role-play each one). Then write about how they could do favors for each other and start championing each other.

Chapter 5

Your Two Dream Views

Only the dreamer can change the dream.

—John Logan, Scottish clergyman and poet

*H*ave you ever noticed that there are really just two basic attitudes in life? And those two attitudes can result in people having very different experiences of the same reality? One man who lives in rain-soaked Seattle is plagued with sadness and depression and is nearly suicidal from lack of sunshine, while another says enthusiastically, "This is the perfect environment for creativity — I can really focus on my writing here!"

The pessimists look at what doesn't exist and spin out fantasies into the future about what might never be, scaring themselves and feeding their fears. The optimists look at what exists, without judgment or limitation, and say, "What's right with this picture? And what's next?" They ask their body what it would have fun doing, what form of creativity seems most rewarding, and use their imagination to sense the best way to express, grow, and expand. They empower themselves and feed their feelings of trust and love.

In this chapter, I show you that, just as there are two basic attitudes in life, there are also two basic attitudes toward dreams. When you can identify your dream views, you'll be on the road to skillful dream interpretation and will be able to find the hidden gifts in what you previously thought were negative dreams.

Good Dreams, Bad Dreams

Are you a dream pessimist or optimist? Maybe you don't want to dream too much because you're afraid you'll have nightmares, or find out someone you love might die, or have to face snakes or spiders crawling out of the recesses of your mind. On the other hand, you may *love* dreaming because you feel so free and all-seeing. You can fly, breathe underwater, be young, old, male, female, a different race or nationality, a plant, or an animal.

Where do your basic attitudes, and your good and bad dreams, come from? Do you have a choice about what kinds of dreams you receive? In this section, I provide answers to these questions.

Experiencing love and fear

All people have a vast repository of past experience sorted and filed in their memory banks according to two categories, love and fear:

- The memories you hold relating to love came from past experiences in which you felt similar or connected to others, life, and the divine. You thus felt safe, whole, complete, expressive, and expansive. Love comes from the experience of unity and is life-promoting; it is always oriented toward growth and creativity.

- The memories you hold relating to fear are the result of past experiences where you felt disconnected from others, life, and the divine. You thus felt unsafe, incomplete, untrusting, isolated, and paralyzed. Fear comes from the experience of separation and is life-restricting, oriented solely toward survival.

All your dreams, and your waking experiences, too, spring either from the knowledge base of past experiences that embodied love, or from the knowledge base of past experiences that produced fear. Through these two filters, every dream and life event is perceived and given meaning.

Uncovering your attitudes about life and dreams

All too frequently what you let yourself know in the here-and-now is determined by what worked or didn't work in the past to keep you alive. Unfortunately, much of your normal mental processing is based on just surviving and avoiding pain, rather than on increasing what facilitates full soul-expression. Fear often outvotes love. Negative dramas make the news. Adrenaline often feels more real than harmony. What gets most of your attention?

Try this dream diary writing exercise to help you get a sense of how much you're motivated by love and by fear.

Is Your Dream View Based on Love or Fear?

1. Pay attention to the conversations you have with other people this week. What do you choose to talk about? What do the other people choose to talk about? Which points do you react to? Which ideas do you reinforce during the conversations?

2. Make a list of the themes and core ideas underlying these conversations. How many are love-based? How many fear-based?

3. Rate the following options from 1(least) to 10 (most). Be honest with yourself. How much energy and sense of self do you get from

- Complaining and getting sympathy?
- A crisis or emergency?
- Being spontaneous?
- Learning something totally new?
- Criticizing others?
- Creating something new from nothing?
- Being kind and of service to others?
- Refusing to participate?
- Being out in nature?

By paying attention to what attitudes are governing you're behavior, you'll be able to intentionally improve the quality of your life by not identifying yourself as a victim.

The Three Kinds of Mind

Psychology divides consciousness into three aspects: the *subconscious mind,* the *conscious mind,* and the *superconscious mind* (see Figure 5-1). These are closely related to the terms *body, mind,* and *spirit.* The superconscious and subconscious minds are actually two different realms of experience, each containing memory and information. The conscious mind, on the other hand, is simply a moving point of awareness and a point of choice. It contains no memory. When all three aspects of mind integrate and unify, the result is clarity and higher awareness.

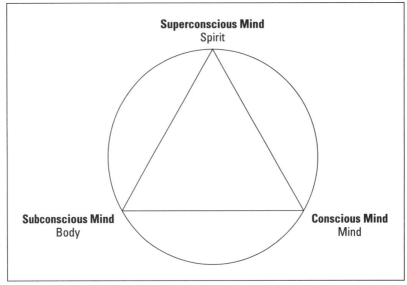

Figure 5-1:
The three
kinds of
mind.

Your superconscious mind

Have you ever had an insight about the functioning of the planet as a whole? Have you dreamed about how you could heal a serious illness in yourself, or how the next phase of your life was going to unfold? Perhaps you had a dream where a "talking head" floating in the air told you that you needed to stop eating wheat and sugar. Or an animal guided you out of a burning forest to a beautiful clear alpine lake. If so, you were perceiving from your superconscious mind — the part of your awareness that operates above your normal level of consciousness. The superconscious mind contains the Great Plan, both for the evolution of the planet and the unfolding of your life.

The superconscious mind, or realm of awareness, is known in spiritual traditions by such names as heaven, nirvana, enlightenment, the upper kingdom, the Pure Land, Father Sky, and the afterlife. Your superconscious mind is wise and compassionate and contains no fear, no ignorance. It's the part of you that contains your essence and life purpose — where you see that all your purposes and actions coexist harmoniously in perfect mutual support. The superconscious mind is really your soul's original, untainted, divine awareness. Its specific focus in the body is your heart and the neocortex of your brain (see Chapter 11).

This higher mind sees vast interconnections and knows how everything in life fits together. It understands the big picture, and sees how we constantly alternate back and forth between incarnating into physical reality then evolving back out to spiritual unity. It contains the memory of all events, throughout all time, where you acted in love, in full awareness of your true nature as a divine being. These experiences are characterized by grace, generosity, luck, and flow. My collage in Figure 5-2 gives impressions of the super-conscious mind.

Figure 5-2:
Penney's collage of super-conscious imagery.

Your superconscious dreams

When dreams emerge from your superconscious mind, they feel uplifting and light as a feather, and are often lit by a spotlight or bright sunlight. They may convey a sense of freedom and ecstatic movement, unrestricted creativity and inventiveness, confidence, and excitement. They may contain images pertaining to birth, light, height, or air — like wide-eyed babies, balloons, birds, airplanes, jets, UFOs, outer space, clouds, sunrays, stars, sky, skyscrapers, mountaintops, or angels. They may also contain symbols that represent collective consciousness or abstract patterns. To dream of large spiritual gatherings, a church, an ancient temple, a school of dolphins, a flock of birds, the inside of a large flying saucer, or pure geometric shapes like triangles or geodesic domes is a sign of superconscious awareness emerging. Your superconscious mind is speaking when you dream of having a conversation with a spiritual guide or teacher (see Chapter 17), or experience healing (see Chapter 16).

Try the following dream diary writing exercise.

Imaging your Superconscious Mind

1. Make a list of every symbol, image, scene, and action you can think of that comes from your superconscious mind. Write quickly, without rereading or questioning. Keep adding on throughout the week. Let the images come from your dreams, real life, the past, books, films, fantasies, and the lives of others.

2. Make a collage of these images, gathered from magazines, nature, and from your own artwork. Notice the subtle sensations you have as you put the images together, and how you feel afterward and whenever you look at the finished product.

Your subconscious mind

The subconscious mind contains all the physical, historical, biological, pre-verbal knowledge of the planet. In it are recorded the impressions of every insect, dinosaur, and virus, every personality, every cataclysmic event. The subconscious mind knows birth and death, healing and destruction. Because it's so primal, the subconscious mind contains information relating to survival and to the mythological human rites of passage. The subconscious records every experience where you reacted from your survival instinct and made decisions in partial awareness of your true self. These memories are characterized by contraction, confusion, panic, self-protection, cynicism, and feeling overwhelmed.

If you could see them, these memories would look like chunks of paralyzed energy, like black spots in your energy field. In the Western therapeutic tradition they're called *subconscious blocks;* in the Eastern religious tradition, they're known as *karma,* the unfinished business of the past.

Your subconscious mind contains a wealth of knowledge about humanity's physiological origins, but it also gives rise to your negative emotions and private demons. Your subconscious mind is often called hell, the lower kingdom, the underworld, the shadow, or the dark cloud — and is even associated with the Mother Earth. Its specific focus in the body is in your brainstem, reptile brain (see Chapter 11), and lower belly. My collage in Figure 5-3 gives impressions of subconscious imagery.

Figure 5-3:
Penney's collage of subconscious imagery.

Become sensitive to nuances. You can distinguish between signals that warn of real danger and signals that come from imagined danger, which are produced by memories of previous fearful experiences. If you are not in the moment and fully present in your body to assess each new experience consciously as it occurs, your subconscious will go back into the past to previous similar situations and draw parallels between then and now, even if the parallels are not appropriate. For example, if your father got angry and beat you as a child, his raised voice was a true danger signal. But today, when you hear your boss yelling at other employees, you are no longer in physical danger. Yet your adrenaline pumps because of remembered fear. If you stay present and take stock of the situation neutrally, this fresh moment offers you a new opportunity to participate in a productive, healing way. Don't let the past limit what you're capable of doing today.

Your subconscious dreams

When dreams are triggered by your subconscious mind, they usually involve the body and the five senses.

- ✔ There is often an edge of tension, frustration, confusion, or a tangible feeling of desire, anxiety, panic — even terror.

- ✔ They often have a heavy, constrictive, or sinking quality, and may be poorly lit, foggy, or seem like they're in black and white.

- ✔ Subconscious dreams may contain images pertaining to earth, water, and fire, as well as sex, illness, death, imprisonment, monsters, dangerous animals, or people who chase you.

If you dream about caves, the ocean or floods, snakes, your house burning down, paralysis, or being stuck in tunnels, your subconscious mind is trying to tell you something. Your subconscious is talking to you if you dream of having a conversation with a shady character or are injured. Because not all information in the subconscious mind is about fearful emotion, you may also dream about a food your physical body needs, or the symbolic meanings of animals or plants, or the ancient history of Egypt.

Even when your dreams *seem* negative, they always contain hidden, positive gifts. For example, dreams about death usually indicate profound psychospiritual growth and change.

Try the following dream diary writing exercise.

Imaging Your Subconscious Mind

1. Make a list of every symbol, image, scene, and action you can think of that comes from your subconscious mind. Write quickly, without rereading or questioning. Keep adding on throughout the week. Let the images come from your dreams, real life, the past, books, films, fantasies, and the lives of others.

2. Make a collage of these images, gathered from magazines, nature, and from your own artwork. Notice the subtle sensations you have as you put the images together, and how you feel afterward and whenever you look at the finished product.

Remember that you have both an individual version of the subconscious and superconscious mind that pertains to your personality and personal history (I am ME), and a collective version of each that pertains to humanity as a whole and the history of the planet (I am US). Dreams often give you information drawn from both levels of your soul's experience.

Your conscious mind: The dream viewpoint

The conscious mind contains no memory, knows nothing. It is a point of awareness, your sense of "I am," the eye of the soul. The conscious mind is also the agent of your free will; it is your conscious mind that chooses what you notice, think, intend, and do. It gives you your sense of individuality and identity, or ego, because whatever it looks at, it identifies with. In the body, the conscious mind is focused in the center of the brain. By choosing different views, your conscious mind influences your experience. Whether during the day, in the content of a fantasy or the way you interpret a life experience, or at night, in the kinds of dreams you receive, you have two filters, two attitudes, two choices about how to make it all meaningful to yourself (see Figure 5-4).

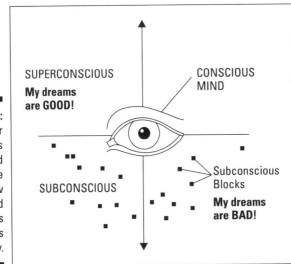

Figure 5-4: Your conscious mind chooses the dream view and interprets your dreams accordingly.

Your conscious mind can focus on the superconscious mind, or love, or on the subconscious mind, or fear — and your dreams will flow from whichever source your conscious mind has identified with. So, as your conscious mind looks out into the waking world and dream world, if it looks to the superconscious realm it will see qualities of wholeness, wisdom, compassion, truth, purposefulness, beauty, harmony, ease, and peace. You'll feel confident, free, and self-empowered. If, instead, your conscious mind looks toward the subconscious realm, it will perceive partiality, lack of self worth, doubt, anxiety, distrust, ugliness, struggle, and chaos. Eventually, you'll discover how to shift from identifying yourself solely with the subconscious reality, to an understanding that your true identity is superconscious. The game will then be about finding the superconscious insight within the subconscious blocks, and transforming fear to love.

Your Soul's Journey to Clarity

As you grow wiser and become more aware of your spiritual nature, at some point you begin to actively work on improving the quality of your character. You'll look inside, open your intuition, and try to develop greater purity and integrity. This is the process of psychological growth or the spiritual path; it is your soul trying to become fully recognized by your conscious mind. I talk more about this spiritual path in Chapter 17.

Dreams play a key role in helping you along the way toward greater clarity. What marks the beginning of an authentic spiritual journey is a yearning for a deeper experience of connectedness and all the spiritual qualities — like harmony, peace, joy, unhindered creativity, kindness, and generosity — followed by a conscious choice to change. The journey might also be triggered by a yearning to know what the mysterious "Night You" is doing during your dreamtime.

A great life guided by dreams

The great spiritual leader Muhammad believed that dreams were conversations between humanity and God. He saw no difference between the guidance that came to him at night in dreams and that which came during the day in visions. He is reputed to have assembled his followers each morning after prayers to ask them what they had dreamed, share his own dreams, and interpret the most important of the lot. Muhammad received his first revelation and the call to his life work in a dream. Later, the archangel Gabriel, believed to be the bringer of true dreams, appeared to him while he was sleeping in a mountaintop cave in the hills near Mecca, and initiated Muhammad into the mysteries of the cosmos. This profound dream is called the *Night Journey,* and in it Muhammad rides a half-human silver mare into Jerusalem, the center of the world. There he talks and prays with Abraham, Moses, and Jesus. Next, Muhammad travels through the seven celestial spheres or dimensions, each colored like layers of the rainbow, and then he spans across an ocean of white light to connect with God. Muhammad experienced many other revelations in dreams, in which light and sound affected him directly — he called these visions "the breaking of the light of dawn." The famous "Call to Prayer" was first heard in the dream of one of Muhammad's followers. Muhammad instituted it as a regular spiritual practice.

The spiritual path often begins after a crisis or an experience that shows you there is more to life than merely surviving, or working for material gain, or attracting a mate so you can feel loved. Once you've started on the path to wholeness and asked for clarity, your body (which stores your subconscious blocks) takes the request seriously. Anything that's in the way of your knowing your own true higher nature will be dredged up from the storage vaults in your subconscious and popped into your conscious mind for review.

By understanding that your fears were originally created by incomplete perception, and that all you need to do is re-perceive the experiences from a superconscious, loving point of view, you will be able to clear them once and for all (see Figure 5-5). In mythology, which has had a profound influence on the study of dreams, this process of clearing suppressed fear from the subconscious is called *the hero's journey*.

Each subconscious block contains data that is unavailable to you because you've suppressed or denied it. If you can become curious about what information your subconscious blocks contain, and even welcome the cloaked insights that are lurking down below, you can transform your attitude and behavior from avoiding "negativity" to embracing it as a new kind of fodder for self-growth. Working to understand your psychological process is a large part of your spiritual path.

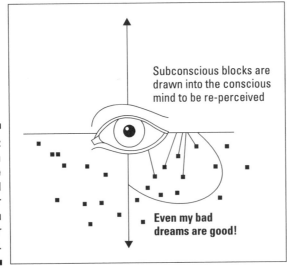

Figure 5-5:
With a positive attitude and a desire for clarity, you can clear your fears.

Subconscious blocks are drawn into the conscious mind to be re-perceived

Even my bad dreams are good!

There's no such thing as a bad dream!

The next time you have that dream of being chased by a python, or falling from a hundred-story skyscraper, or giving a speech naked, try not to cringe and contract in distaste and panic. See if you can catch yourself before your conscious mind leaps to the subconscious view and takes the subconscious attitude.

Remember: *Every dream occurs in service to your soul's greater, fuller, more authentic presence in your life.* Your soul is saying to you, "Here! I want you to look at this image of a tidal wave about to crash down upon you! I have a message encoded in it. Come find the hidden gift!"

Every dream is an opportunity to learn something new about yourself. What's so wonderful about dreams is that you are much less inhibited at night and exert much less control over your dream content than on your behavior during waking reality. So dreams can bring you information you'd never let yourself have while awake. Table 5-1 shows sample dream images that arise from your subconscious and superconscious awareness.

Table 5-1	Sample Dream Images
From the Subconscious Mind	*From the Superconscious Mind*
Falling	Flying
Being chased	Traveling
Being invaded	Exploring
Being controlled	Learning
Being killed or dying	Giving birth
Losing control	Teaching
Being naked	Creating, performing
Being lost or stuck	Healing
Shady characters	Guides and angels
Snake	Luck Dragon
Old car	Jetliner, UFO
Drowning	Swimming under water like a fish
Caves, tunnels	Clouds, sky

Your dreams may emerge from either your superconscious mind or your subconscious mind. Superconscious dreams show you about your true soul characteristics and reveal higher aspects of the soul's life in other dimensions. Subconscious dreams shed light on beliefs and emotions that block the expression of your soul. Similarly, you can interpret your dreams from either a superconscious or subconscious point of view. So just because you have a nightmare doesn't mean you have to create more fear in yourself when you contemplate it. You can reframe your nightmares and examine them. Letting them give you helpful insights.

Reframing nightmares

For several weeks, Pete had been dreaming that he was mountain climbing, and as he painstakingly made his way up a frozen waterfall, one of the pegs that anchored him to the ice pulled out and he fell fifty feet until the previous anchor caught him. As he hung suspended over a gaping chasm, he knew the support that now held him was also about to give way and he would soon fall to his death. He'd wake up shaking each time the dream occurred, but would quickly brush the upset away.

In his daily life, Pete was working on a startup Internet business in the Silicon Valley. It was hard, fast-paced work, and he had a lot riding on the new company's success. Recently he had experienced several setbacks that slowed the company's rapid progress. When Pete examined his series of nightmares open-mindedly instead of suppressing the rising terror he felt, he discovered some helpful insights.

Pete was as motivated to make his company a success as he was to reach the summit of the mountain in his dream. When he looked for parallels between the dream and real life, he saw that he was trying to do too much of the work on his business by himself. He didn't feel supported by the team of people working for him. He had an underlying feeling of anxiety that something would fail at the last minute and he would "lose ground" in his competitive market by "falling" behind schedule, then he would "fall" out of favor with his venture capital investors, and that would be it. Goodbye, Pete!

When he looked for his soul's message, he saw that he'd always tried to prove himself to his father as a young boy; maybe if he could create a company that was more successful than his father's had been, he'd feel acknowledged, loved, and successful. He was subconsciously afraid of being rejected. He realized that his sense of self really had nothing to do with succeeding as an entrepreneur — he was already quite happy with himself and he didn't have to try so hard. He could relax a bit, have more fun, and encourage his team to enjoy their work as well. When he actually did that, he found his team was much more responsive and talented than he had previously given them credit for. And, they supported him brilliantly!

Transforming negativity into insight

Suppose that you dream you're being hunted by a mafia hit man who seems to anticipate your every move to avoid him. He's getting closer and closer! What will you do next? Run? Fight? Hide? You wake up in a cold sweat. What can you do to turn an anxiety-ridden nightmare to positive use?

✔ **Get out of victim mode.** Your mind is probably caught in a swirl of adrenaline-based fight or flight urges, protestations, complaints, accusations, and a desire for vengeance, punishment, or rescue. Catch yourself obsessing in the middle of these kinds of thoughts. Suspend your thought process for a moment: "Oh, I don't have to continue to think this way right now."

✔ **Let the dream be the way it is.** Remember: Your dream is a message to you from your soul — it's not "bad." Tell yourself: "It's okay, even perfect, the way it is — even if I don't like it, even if I can't see why it's appropriate yet." There's something valuable represented in the dream; what might it be?

✔ **Make a factual description.** "Something is trying to kill me. I feel terrified, confused, confounded, alone, helpless, and exhausted."

✔ **Get centered and remember who you really are.** Bring your attention fully into the now, into your body. Tell yourself, "I am my soul!" If you need to, ask for help, either from another person or from spiritual sources. Remember you've chosen to grow, face fear, and integrate your soul's knowledge. Say to yourself, "I'm bigger than my emotions," or "Some part of me knows how to understand this dream." You are the one who dreamed the dream, so you must also be the one who knows why!

✔ **Bring your attention into your body.** Notice the simple animal-like sensations in your body. Let your body do whatever it's doing — and be with your body fully. Breathe. Don't try to escape. Feel the nuances of energy jiggling and moving. Describe the sensations to yourself: "I feel a contraction in my solar plexus, a shaking in my heart; my throat is tight, I want to cry; I want to run." Follow the energy; where does each sensation want to go next? Let go of tension and feel the flow. Extend each sensation to its next natural expression.

✔ **Notice images, ideas, and associations that spring to mind.** As energy starts to move, it may free up information about previous similar experiences that have been stored in your subconscious. Try to catch the connections. You may suddenly remember that your mother lost you at a shopping center when you were four, or a friend recently betrayed you.

✔ **Ask for understanding.** Soften and open your heart and ask for its wisdom. How does the dream show you how to retrieve a lost part of yourself? Were you depending on something or someone, or trying to get something you had thought was outside yourself — and now you can see it is within you? Instead of attacking, how might you facilitate healing between yourself and the dream characters? How can you improve yourself in the dream? Perhaps you realize you need to stop running and talk to the hitman, or call for help from the police, or turn yourself into the hitman's favorite grandmother! By doing this you suddenly understand what you were doing to cause yourself to feel like you had no right to be alive.

✔ **Validate yourself for reframing the dream.** Notice how it feels to be coming from a place of curiosity, desire for understanding, and positive intent versus a place of contraction, guilt, panic, or attack. Pat yourself on the back. Each time you change fear to love it gets easier the next time.

Try the following meditation to help you when addressing your subconscious mind.

Dialoguing with Your Shadow Self

1. Sit down, close your eyes, and be centered. Inside your body, imagine a dark, shadowy field of energy. Let it gradually step out of you through your back, until it is totally separate from you. Let this shadow self stand behind you and whisper something in your ear. What does it say? What does it want?

2. Turn around and face your shadow self. What does it look like? Say to it, "Show me something about myself that I haven't wanted to know." Let it change shape, become various personas, hold out tantalizing objects or scenes. Describe what happens.

3. Now ask your shadow self to show you the images it holds about the worst possible scenarios for your life. Write them down. Then ask it for the hidden lesson you might learn if you followed each scenario to its final outcome. (If you learn the lesson, you won't need to live out the scenario!)

4. Have a conversation with your shadow self. Ask it to tell you what kinds of information it has access to. Then ask what it needs from you. Ask: "How will I know when you want to talk to me?" Describe the signals your subconscious will give you when it needs you to stop and listen to something important. Come back and open your eyes.

Try this meditation when addressing your superconscious mind.

Dialoguing with Your Diamond-Light Self

1. Sit down, close your eyes, and be centered. Inside your body imagine a bright, clear body of light. Let it gradually step out of you through your back, until it is totally separate from you. Let this clear, diamond light self stand behind you and whisper something in your ear. What does it say? What does it want?

2. Turn around and face your diamond light self. What does it look like? Say to it, "Show me something about myself that I haven't been able to see." Let it change shape, become various personas, offer gifts or scenes. Describe what happens.

3. Now ask your diamond light self to show you the images it holds about the best possible scenarios for your life. Write them down. Then ask it for the hidden lesson you might learn if you followed each scenario to its final outcome.

4. Have a conversation with your diamond light self. Ask it to tell you what kinds of information it has access to. Then ask what it needs from you. Ask: "How will I know when you want to talk to me?" Describe the signals your superconscious will give you when it needs you to stop and listen to something important. Come back and open your eyes.

In dreams we catch glimpses of a life larger than our own.

—Helen Keller

Your Dream Diary

1. Make notes next to all the dreams you've remembered this week. How many are primarily love-based? How many primarily fear-based?

2. Using stream of consciousness — writing whatever comes into your mind — make up three superconscious dreams, writing nonstop without rereading, taking five minutes on each.

3. Using stream of consciousness, make up three subconscious dreams, writing nonstop without rereading, taking five minutes on each.

4. Make a list of the subconscious and superconscious symbols and actions in your dreams fro the past week. What might each signify? Write about how each might relate to your daily life.

5. Write about what you label this week as "good," desirable, or pleasing; write about what you label this week as "bad," undesirable, or upsetting. Why do you hold these judgments?

6. Pick a "bad" dream, then think back through your life to "earlier similar" episodes. Write out as many as you can. Then pick a "good" dream and think back through your life to "earlier similar" episodes. Write out as many as you can.

7. Transform a nightmare into a useful dream. Write about what you needed to do to shift the outcome and the insights that came as a result.

Chapter 6

Navigating Your Dreamscape

That which extends throughout the universe I regard as my body,
and that which directs the universe I regard as my own nature.

—Chang-Tsai

*Y*our mind is like a zoom lens on a camera, moving continually and in no discernable logical sequence, pliable as a jellyfish, contracting to microscopic size or expanding to encompass galaxies. Your conscious mind opens or closes down your view, zooming in and out, taking various "snapshots" along the way, at whatever focus fascinates you. Taken together, these snapshots become your life story. If you extend your consciousness away from your body, inch-by-inch, you may notice your consciousness moving out equally in all directions, always forming a ball of awareness. You can expand and contract this bubble of perception and include more, or less, inside it.

Focus on pouring a glass of juice, and your bubble is quite small. Focus on your flight from Chicago to Baltimore, and your bubble is much broader. Zoom out and be aware of your house, yard, the street. Zoom in and be aware of your body sitting in your desk chair. Zoom further in and be aware of your heart beating. Zoom out again and include your whole town. Zoom in and notice your hands preparing dinner.

Your mind has been on the move constantly since you opened your eyes! You've been expanding and contracting in and out through space and time, without even realizing it. The same thing happens in your dream life, as I explain in this chapter. But first, I explain how your conscious mind works in waking reality.

Consciously Zooming In and Out

When you notice something, that something has actually taken shape inside your bubble; therefore, it is no longer separate from you, but is coming from your own mind. Becoming aware of something that's outside your sphere of awareness is impossible. As soon as you notice something, it's inside your conscious mind. And what's inside your bubble is emerging from a field of consciousness — which, lo and behold, is actually your soul. When I speak of soul in this book, I mean your individual experience of the divine, or the function of consciousness that translates the divine into the personal experience and vice versa.

What draws you outward and inspires you to expand your consciousness? Your soul's purpose. What makes you narrow your focus to concentrate on a specific task and to create? Your soul's purpose. What gives you revelations? Your soul. Your soul regulates the seemingly haphazard flow of your conscious mind's sequence of perceptions, and this includes your dream perceptions as well as your waking ones. If you want to embody your soul's full wisdom, trusting the flow of your perceptions and the movement of your conscious mind, during the day *and* the night, is important.

Use the power of the present moment

Bring your conscious mind, your point of attention, into the present moment and focus your awareness inside your body. Now you're centered, in the crosshairs of the here-and-now. Pay attention to your body. Can you feel your pulse moving blood through your capillaries? Can you feel your lungs filling and emptying? Can you feel the temperature of the air on your skin? Now notice what's around you in a 3-foot radius: your clothes, the sofa, the pillow behind your back, the magazine you're reading, the cocktail table, the floor lamp, the carpet and floor, your cup of coffee. Now notice what's included inside a 10-foot radius: the front door, the ceiling, the television, a tall houseplant, your CD collection.

As your awareness extends, you grow more complex, and your present moment includes more. As your perceptual bubble expands, your "here" includes more space, and your "now" includes more time. Turning off the nearby light switch, which occurs in a bubble of awareness 6 feet in radius, might take 10 seconds, while walking to the car in your driveway, a bubble 30 feet in radius, takes 2 minutes.

Try this meditation to change the size of your perceptual bubble by zooming in and out through space and time.

Changing the Size of Your Perceptual Bubble

1. Hold your thumb 6 inches in front of your face and stare at it. Then focus on a spot on the wall across the room. Bring your gaze back to your thumb, and then back to the wall. Keep shifting back and forth and feel the size of your perceptual bubble change. Notice that your sphere of awareness expands and contracts behind, above, and below you as well.

2. Think of a vivid experience from your recent past. Imagine it in detail. Then shift to present time and notice what's happening in the environment around you. Then, shift to a future fantasy, and embroider it with vivid detail. Come back to the present again. Think about a current problematic situation. Now think back to what caused it. Then cast ahead to sense how it will be resolved.

3. Center yourself, close your eyes, and notice your breath moving in and out; stay with it for several full cycles. Then direct your attention to your heartbeat and feel it pulsing all through your body. Next, notice the finer vibrations of your nerves. Trace the tingling all over your body. Then imagine your cells, teeming with life. Feel their tiny jiggling. Continue down into the layers of your body, paying attention to the molecules, and then the atoms floating in space. Continuing down into an atom, visualize a subatomic particle like an electron and merge into it. At some point you will encounter open space. Hang suspended for a moment, and then come back up through the different levels of your body.

Your conscious mind expands through time and space, including the near and far distant past and future, as well as the inner space of matter and the outer space of the universe. But your mind widens and narrows in another way as well, as I explain in the next section — and here's where your dream world enters the picture. . . .

Recognize that you are multidimensional

You are much more complex than you appear on the surface. If you could see yourself from a clairvoyant's point of view, you'd look something like an egg-shaped onion, with layers of energy-and-consciousness progressing from a relatively slow, dense inner core, outward or upward.

Each successive spherical layer, or *dimension*, or *body*, or *plane*, or *zone* (as I call them later on for various purposes), includes more time and space and vibrates at a higher frequency. If you could see the layers as colors, you'd look like a rainbow; if you could listen to yourself by ear, you'd sound like a musical scale being sung. The whole thing is your soul's great body of knowledge; it's your higher identity, and the territory of your dreams. The tight focus of the physical world is just one of many worlds to which you have access. You inhabit this physical world and habitually call it "reality," but when you dream, meditate, or daydream, you open your lens and take in a wider view that includes other worlds at higher dimensions.

Dreams are snapshots of those other-dimensional views. When your lens zooms out, either during the day or at night in dreams, you may become aware of hidden emotions, or constellations of beliefs, or of the deep-seated intentions of your soul's purpose for your life. The further your conscious mind zooms out, the less you'll feel like a finite personality, restricted to linear time and space, or cause and effect. Your energy will be freer, you'll move faster, and knowledge will be more instantaneous and direct. The higher the frequency of consciousness and the broader your view, the more connected you'll feel with others, and the more you'll share knowledge and an overlapping sense of purpose with everyone.

Try the following meditation to enhance the frequency of your perceptual bubble by zooming in and out through the dimensions.

Changing the Frequency of Your Perceptual Bubble

1. Stare at the palms of your hands until you feel them tingling. Now shift from that physical focus and recall a feeling of anger or frustration; notice that you may feel you're "stretching" a bit, using a different part of your brain. Now concentrate on remembering a pleasant emotion like kindness. Can you feel the subtle shift? Next, move into an awareness of the sounds you hear in the near and distant environment. Move out to a longer focus now, and think about what you believe is necessary for success in life. From those fixed ideas, open yourself to the flow of your imagination and watch an inner movie unfold spontaneously. Shift further out and see if you can sense what your life may hold for the next year or two. Come back and be aware of what odors you're smelling right now.

2. Focus on your goals for the day. What do you need to accomplish? What feeling will you have when you complete the tasks? Now zoom out and sense how all the people who live in your city are working to accomplish goals today, and how they will all feel by the end of the day. Can you sense the group experience? Now come back and notice what you personally believe about the current political situation. Zoom back out and feel all the people in the country who hold the same views you do. Come back and imagine yourself working alone to landscape your yard. Then zoom out and imagine a big group of friends who have pitched in to do the work with you. Can you sense the co-creation and cooperation involved? Zoom out and feel the planetary identity of "Earth." Come back to yourself. Say your name.

When your conscious mind zooms out to encompass a larger view, not only do you contain more of the past and future, more space, and more dimensions of your soul, your knowledge increases as well. Your conscious mind determines how much of your total self you know at any one time. The larger the bubble, the higher the frequency, and the greater the knowledge. New insights become available — knowledge you usually cut yourself off from because you define the past, future, and other dimensions as separate from you. You may suddenly see how all the events of your life are coordinated, how other people are acting just the way they need to act in order for you to receive the insights you need, or how a specific episode is likely to unfold.

To reduce it to a formula: *your perceptual bubble = your conscious mind = the present moment = your identity = the scope of your knowledge.*

Leave your body and lose your mind

You are active in every dimension of yourself, all the time! But during waking hours, it's the physical world that counts as real and therefore, it's the only one we pay attention to and remember. Because we assume waking reality is all there is, people simply forget to pay attention to the extended views, or to look for what's happening below the surface. Similarly, because normal waking consciousness stops when we fall asleep, we tend to think of our nighttime activity as nonexistent, unreal, or unimportant.

Dreams aren't logical, measurable, or solid; they function by entirely different rules than your three-dimensional life here on earth. So, although you're asleep for approximately a third of your life, you have difficulty retaining the memory of what occurs during those hours. I believe that this is in large part because of people's unfortunate habit of defining the world of waking reality as "conscious," and the other worlds as "unconscious." By definition, then, every time you stretch out to higher realms, either in dreams or during the day, you go blank. As you focus into any one dimension of your soul, it's as though you're remembering yourself as one kind of being and forgetting your-self as another. For example, when you dream, you temporarily forget your-self as a physical being and remember yourself as an emotional, mental, or spiritual one. In dreams, you can fly, fall, swoop, and swim. When you awake, your zoom lens closes down rapidly to its shortest focal length, and you forget your dream world and recreate the physical one, where your body must walk step by step to the kitchen for food.

Being awake in your daily reality while simultaneously being active in other dimensions of yourself is quite common. When this happens, you may call it "going unconscious," "spacing out," or "leaving your body." The term "nobody's home" was invented for people who are simultaneously exploring other dimensions while awake in this one! For example, as you work at the computer, you may lose your concentration without realizing it. Minutes later, you zoom back and remember your train of thought. Where were you? Perhaps you were exploring an emotional reality triggered by something you wrote, or visiting a person you were reminded of by something you just read. Maybe you were dipping into the memory banks of the planet to find inspiration.

When you lose memory, you have gone into higher dimensions without taking your perceptual bubble, or conscious mind, with you. You have become uncentered and have entered the unconscious, which is simply the part of yourself you have not yet consciously realized. Therefore, you have no memory of what you do there. People travel in and out through their soul's great body of knowledge constantly, yet they discount these other-dimensional experiences as daydreams, lulls, or "absent-mindedness."

Occasionally, your activity in other dimensions bleeds through uninvited into this one and interrupts your concentration. For example, sometimes as I'm going about my normal routine, I get an overwhelming spacey feeling and have to make myself focus on each task three times to accomplish it. I drag on through the day until *finally* I realize something's happening at another level of myself. It feels like I'm at the end of a piece of stretched elastic and can barely hold myself here. So I surrender, lie down, and take a brief but intense nap. I'm aware that something important is happening while I sleep, but often I can't tell what I was doing until an event later "rings my bell."

This feeling of *bi-location,* having two parts of the consciousness simultaneously operating in different dimensions, has often happened just before a public figure or someone I know has died, before a cataclysmic event like a plane crash or earthquake, or when a friend is in trouble. Others describe this kind of "forced dream state" before a creative breakthrough, a scientific discovery, or a healing dream. Have you ever experienced this?

When "Nobody's Home," Where Did You Go?

The next time you catch yourself being preoccupied, or "spacey," stop. Ask yourself the following questions and write about them in your diary:

- ✔ Is there something I feel incomplete with or preoccupied by?
- ✔ If someone were trying to get my attention, who might it be? What is the message?
- ✔ If I were also in another location right now, where would I be?
- ✔ If I were also in another time period right now, when would it be?
- ✔ If I were also performing another task right now, what would it be?
- ✔ If I were also visiting another dimension right now to access information, which level would it be? What would I be trying to discover or understand?
- ✔ If I were also visiting other people right now, who would they be? What would the purpose of our exchange be?

From either/or to both/and

In your dream world, you step directly into other dimensions, unencumbered by the beliefs that determine the way reality has to function. In the higher dimensions, or "dream zones," movement is fluid, even instantaneous; communication is telepathic and undistorted; and the results you achieve are simply a matter of clear intent. Wouldn't it be fun, and useful, to move your dreams out of the unconscious into your conscious mind? Wouldn't it help you know more about yourself if you could be aware of more than one part of yourself at once?

To improve memory of your other-dimensional and dream activities, first get used to the idea that the higher realms are a normal part of who you are and that you *can* broaden your view to know two or more kinds of experience at once. For example, you can be aware of your physical body and your emotions at the same time — why not be aware of your physical world and your soul's purpose simultaneously? Or your emotions and the beliefs that cause those emotions?

Many ancient cultures believed the soul or part of the soul actually left the body at night to fly around and visit the ancestors or the gods, returning in the morning with information for the personality. The famous French thinker, Michel Foucault, in his 1954 essay "Dream, Imagination, and Existence," takes that view a bit further. Foucault believed the dream is actually the cause of human imagination, not the other way around, and that dreams begin with the origin of individual existence, namely the human soul. He believed that while consciousness (the personality) sleeps, existence (the soul) awakens. I'd like to extend the idea further still, beyond the limitations of either/or thinking into the more inclusive experience of both/and:

- First, the soul doesn't leave the body during sleep; the conscious mind is simply hypnotized into going unconscious. I believe it is now possible to take the conscious mind with you into your sleep realms.

- Second, I believe people's waking consciousness and their soul's consciousness are no longer as separate as they appeared to be. Today, people are beginning to experience the presence of the waking consciousness and the soul's consciousness within each other, and their inexorable merging.

You can now experience your soul within your waking personality and your conscious mind in your hitherto unknown soul realms. You can use dreams to really wake up that conscious mind of yours so you can recognize the totality of who you are, where you are, and what you're capable of doing. To bring the dream world more fully into your perceptual bubble, let me help you find out just where you go at night!

Exploring the Four Dream Zones

Your soul's big body of knowledge has many zones, and all are real. In your dreams, you can actually enter these zones, live in their particular realities, and bring back memory of what you did. By understanding what happens in each dream zone, you can interpret your dreams more accurately and increase your superconscious awareness. For simplicity's sake, I've divided the territory of your soul into four zones (metaphysical teachings tell of literally hundreds!). Each zone is a world unto itself, functioning according to its own principles, containing a particular kind of information and a different kind of experience. Figure 6-1 presents a model of these zones. As you expand through the zones, consciousness speeds up like a car accelerating from first through fourth gears.

The first dream zone, which you know so well, is the *physical world* in which objects appear solid and are separated by space, and where events are separated in time. Here time seems incremental, linear, and sluggish. Life is experienced as moving in alternating cycles of on and off, and the duality between here and there, good and bad, and male and female is what causes action.

The second dream zone, the *emotional,* is the realm of electromagnetic energy, desire, attraction, repulsion, and motivation. In this world of feeling and emotion, life is less dense, more interconnected; actions happen faster and are more fluid. Figure 6-2 models how your conscious mind identifies itself with Zones 1 and 2.

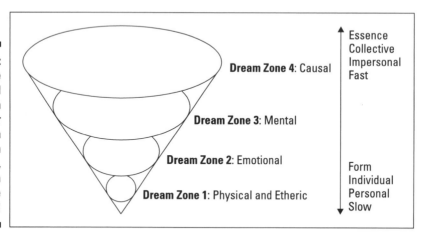

Figure 6-1: You move back and forth through four dream zones when you sleep, and even while you're awake!

Dream Zone 4: Causal

Dream Zone 3: Mental

Dream Zone 2: Emotional

Dream Zone 1: Physical and Etheric

Essence
Collective
Impersonal
Fast

Form
Individual
Personal
Slow

The third dream zone, the *mental,* is the world of logic, beliefs, conceptual thought, intuition, and inspiration. Here, time and space seem almost nonexistent. Boundaries hardly exist, and consciousness moves like lightning.

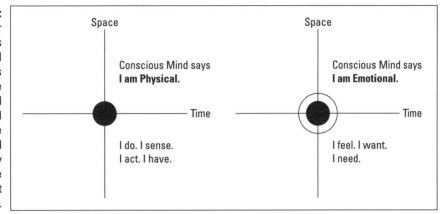

Figure 6-2:
Your conscious mind identifies with the physical zone and then the emotional zone. They produce different perceptions.

The third dream zone, the *mental,* is the world of logic, beliefs, conceptual thought, intuition, and inspiration. Here, time and space seem almost nonexistent. Boundaries hardly exist, and consciousness moves like lightning.

In *the fourth dream zone,* the *causal,* or spiritual, thought gives way to pure intent. In this zone, the soul synthesizes the lessons it has learned and determines its life purpose, based on a perfect coordination with the lessons and needs of all other beings. At this level, you have little sense of separation from other souls — indeed, you have an overwhelming sense of belonging to, and of *being,* the "Us." Figure 6-3 models how your consciousness identifies itself with Zones 3 and 4.

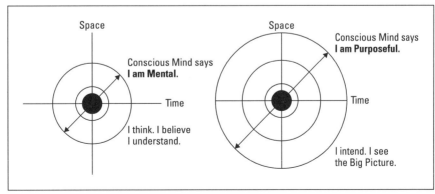

Figure 6-3:
Your conscious mind expands more and identifies with the mental zone, and then even more to enter the causal zone.

Beyond the fourth zone, dreams are virtually impossible to remember. Out here, all sense of separation ends; the soul blends into the universal bliss-consciousness of the divine and loses its individual identity as it realizes it *is* the whole. Perhaps this is Foucault's "origin of existence" — noted in the previous section — the beginning of the Great Dream of human perception.

What you focus on is what your life becomes. If you expand your awareness outward to include the causal zone, for example, you will actually *become* that amount of yourself and have instant access to all the knowledge contained in that layer, like the history or future of the planet. If you expand to include only the physical zone in your bubble, you'll be aware of the limits of time and space and your basic survival needs. If you focus your zoom lens on the emotional zone, you may feel besieged by an upset or attracted to someone. If you zoom out further and encompass the mental zone, you may become righteous about your ideas, or understand a complex mathematical problem.

Identifying Subconscious and Super-conscious Ideas in the Zones

To give you a more precise view of your soul's territory, I break things down just a bit further. You can subdivide the first three zones into two layers each — one denser and more fixed, one clearer and more fluid. The denser layer contains more subconscious information, the clear layer contains more superconscious information. Table 6-1 summarizes the contents of your dream zones, which I explain further in the sections that follow.

Table 6-1	The Content of the Dream Zones
Zone 1: Physical	
Physical	Waking world, results, form
Etheric	Energy patterns, "chi," "event waves"
Zone 2: Emotional	
Lower Emotional	Fear, desire, conflict, anger; victim/dominator patterns; instinct, survival
Higher Emotional	Motivation, creative urges, passion
Zone 3: Mental	
Lower Mental	Fixed beliefs, logic, ego
Higher Mental	Intuition, inspiration; conceptual ideas, mathematics, abstract patterns

Zone 4: Causal	
Causal	Personal "karma" and life purpose
	Collective history and future of the planet; the Big Picture, the Grand Plan of Evolution

Zone 1: The physical and etheric body

The denser level of Zone 1 is the solid physical world — the world of results and materialization. Its less dense counterpart, which many people can see in altered states of awareness, is called the *etheric body, energy body,* or *aura*. This level is made of a finer, more pliable energy that acupuncturists and martial artists call *chi,* and spiritual mediums call *ether* or *plasma*. It underlies the physical body like an energetic blueprint, and contains everything that eventually materializes in the physical. Clairvoyants often see illnesses, even signs of impending death, in the etheric body before they occur in the physical. Many methods of healing the etheric body have been developed, like homeopathic remedies, acupuncture, and chi kung, and "energetic bodywork" techniques like Reiki, laying on of hands, and acupressure. The etheric body is where you may be sensitive to upcoming dramatic events or sense danger before you encounter it.

Zone 2: The astral body and electro-magnetic energy

Zone 2 contains two layers of activity — the lower emotional zone and the higher emotional zone. The lower layer of the emotional zone contains fear-based feelings, the survival instinct, automatic reactions, obsessive desires, and even violent emotions. It is a disturbing world filled with upset, conflict, and polarization. This layer is sometimes called *the astral body,* and it may be what some religions identify as the hell realm.

The higher layer of the emotional zone contains no blocks, but transfers the superconscious intent of the soul into physical manifestation via pure electromagnetic energy. It creates and dissolves motivation by making you feel attraction, nonattraction, and repulsion, so action can occur. In this realm, the creative passion for life and ecstatic feelings exist. Note that you can be motivated by lower emotions like lust and greed, or by higher ones like joy and curiosity to learn. Sometimes you'll be motivated by both layers of the emotional zone simultaneously.

Zone 3: Beliefs and logic, inspiration and intuition

Like Zones 1 and 2, Zone 3 contains two layers of activity as well. The lower layer of the mental zone contains fear-based fixed beliefs, attachments to ideas that provide identity, opinions, and rules. This part of your awareness contains survival-oriented worldviews and slower mental processes like logic and analysis. The higher layer of the mental zone, on the other hand, is fluid and free, full of superconscious inspiration, intuition, revelation, and creative ideas. The higher mental layer is the realm of meaning, abstract-conceptual thought, geometric patterns, mathematics, music, and the superconscious worldview.

Zone 4: Your life purpose and the planetary consciousness

Zone 4, the causal or spiritual realm, contains a record of all the events you have experienced in all your lifetimes. Zone 4 is the realm where your individual life purpose originates, where your soul keeps track of your *karma* or unfinished business, and coordinates lessons for you so you can remove things that interfere with your ability to complete your evolutionary process and attain enlightenment. It's also the collective consciousness of humanity, containing the ongoing and ever-evolving purpose for all life forms and the entire planet. In Zone 4, all events are imprinted, and all souls coordinate their actions harmoniously with each other. Sometimes called *the Akashic Records,* or the *noosphere* (pronounced *NO us feer*), this realm contains blueprints for whole species and vast evolutionary trends.

Traveling through Your Dream Zones

To help you understand the zones better, let me take you on some sample sojourns through your dream territory. Table 6-2 gives some guidance on determining which zones you're visiting in your dreams.

Table 6-2	Determining Your Dream Zone
If You Dream About This	*You're in This Dream Zone*
A series of numbers	Higher Mental
A voice tells you, "Don't work with Charles!"	Higher Mental
Climbing up a tower	Rising to a higher zone

If You Dream About This	*You're in This Dream Zone*
Driving a car with no brakes	Lower Emotional
Drowning in a flood	Lower Emotional
Falling in an elevator	Dropping to a lower zone
Flying through high tension wires	Lower Mental
Gorging yourself on chocolate and sweets	Lower Emotional
Hail is dropping from the sky	Lower Mental
Skiing down a mountain	Dropping to a lower zone
Someone has called your name out loud	Etheric
Swimming under water without needing to breathe	Higher Emotional
Taking off in a jumbo jet	Rising to a higher zone
You compose some incredible music	Higher Mental
You have a baby with huge eyes glowing with light	Higher Emotional
You see a vision of the planet in the future	Causal
Your teeth fall out	Etheric/Lower Mental
You're a dolphin a school of dolphins	Causal
You're flying over an island looking at the terrain	Higher Mental or Causal
You're having reconstructive surgery	Etheric

Scenario #1: The barking dog and your own reality

During your dinner hour and for most of the evening, your neighbor's dogs bark continuously. You respond to the disturbing physical stimulus by getting emotionally upset. Your privacy and peace of mind are being invaded, and you feel like shooting the dogs and your irresponsible neighbor. That night you dream about being chased by a hunter in a bright orange vest. The next morning, as you work with the feeling of terror in your dream, you have a sudden insight that the dogs next door might have been barking out of fear. As you watch television that evening, you see a documentary about grizzly bear attacks. That night you dream about an experience similar to one you had as a child, where you were punished by being forced to sit in a chair facing the wall. In processing your dream the next morning, you realize that, because you were punished for expressing yourself as a child, you assumed you had no right to do things your own way. Suddenly, the pieces fit together, and you understand that the barking dogs made you feel that you had no right to have your reality be the way you wanted it — that you would always have to fight to be yourself, but would probably always be subjected to "attacks" from the outside world. That night you have a dream about taking a risk in your career. The dream is filled with golden light, and you feel great when you wake up!

What have you been doing? Your perceptual bubble has been moving in and out, creating links between your physical, emotional, and mental zones, until at last, the revelation your soul wants you to have can pop into your conscious mind. A subconscious block is cleared. Immediately, you receive a vision of guidance from your causal zone about what step to take next to fulfill your life purpose.

Scenario #2: Vague proddings

For weeks you've hardly remembered your dreams. All you can sense are strange feelings, moods, or colors that you wake up immersed in. Sometimes you sense geometric patterns or flat shapes like grape clusters that seem to be inside your body somehow. During the day you're preoccupied with the thought that you've outgrown your job and need to move on, but you don't know what else you can do. Emotionally, you're feeling depressed. You decide to see a nutritionist, who says you are low on several important vitamins and trace minerals. You buy some and take them. After a month of this odd vagueness, you suddenly get laid off from your job, start jogging (which helps sort out your thoughts), and go to a career counselor who helps you reinvent yourself. You finally remember a symbolic dream! You're paddling down a fast-moving but calm river in a kayak. It feels exhilarating!

What have you been doing? Your perceptual bubble has been expanded way out to your causal zone for quite some time because you are due to make a major life change. Your soul is trying to disengage you from a limited way of expressing yourself, free your mind from fixed ideas, renew your enthusiasm in life, and "rewire" your brain and body so new kinds of knowledge can come through you. You've been getting parts of the message subliminally, and helping yourself by changing your diet and exercise habits, and getting the professional advice you need. As the work at your higher dimensions completes, your physical world immediately changes to match the new blueprint, and you begin to feel the excitement of the new chapter of your life.

Scenario #3: The fork in the road

You dream a woman stands at a fork in the road. You think you should take the right-hand road but she says, "Go left. It's rocky but it will get you across the river more easily." You go left. In the next few weeks, your life begins to get rocky. You get the flu just as you're supposed to give an important presentation in another city. On the way, your plane is delayed, and the flight cancelled. You have to fly to an out-of-the-way city, stay overnight, catch a flight the next day, and you miss the meeting. Your car needs major work. Your teeth need major work. Your roof needs major work. Just when you think things can't get worse, you lose your job are forced to rethink your career. After months of this, life finally eases up and you dream you are giving a speech at a huge conference and are totally comfortable, even energized by all the attention. Shortly after this, you get a new job in a new field.

What have you been doing? Your perceptual bubble has been focused in your lower mental, lower emotional, and physical zones, because you are working intensely, day and night, on clearing emotional and mental blocks to a new level of your self-expression. You shouldn't have been surprised, however, because you saw the difficulty ahead of time and chose the path anyway when you were focused at your causal zone.

Dreaming in Cycles

Dreaming in cycles is a natural experience. You may remember many symbolic dreams in technicolor detail each morning for months on end. Then, inexplicably, your dreams seem to dry up. As hard as you try, you may only wake with a mood, a vague "quality" of something just on the edge of consciousness, a feeling that your body is being "worked on" somehow. Or you may dream about numbers and geometric patterns.

During these times, your activity has shifted into the higher mental and causal zones, and you may not remember dreams in symbolic terms. At these levels, you have no emotions or pictures from real life — only abstract "patterns of being." So don't worry that your not dreaming — you are; you're just dreaming at very high frequencies of consciousness. You will soon drop back down so you can see your life's new blueprint.

You will tend to rotate around through the dream zones, activating and loosening subconscious blocks from the lower emotional and mental zones, and then bringing them into your physical reality so you can recognize and clear them. Afterward, you may check in with the causal zone to see what your soul wants to create next, and you'll have experiences in the higher mental and emotional zones that inspire you and help you understand how to proceed with your authentic self-expression.

Remember: Dreams always serve the growth and full expression of your soul. Though your dreams may seem haphazard, the experiences you have at the different dimensions of yourself are always coordinated and purposeful.

We sometimes congratulate ourselves at the moment
of waking from a troubled dream:
it may be so the moment after death.

—Nathaniel Hawthorne

Your Dream Diary

1. Write an imaginary account of your journey into dreamland, pretending that you can remember every detail of what you're doing from the moment you close your eyes until you open them again. Don't allow any blank spots.

2. Practice taking different focal lengths with your conscious mind zoom lens, and describe what is "inside" you at each different view, and what you know about what you notice.

3. Write about a time when activity in another dimension interrupted your ability to concentrate while you were awake.

4. Notice the times today or recently that you left your body and blanked out. Write about what triggered you to leave.

5. Write, using stream of consciousness, in the present tense, and make up a dream occurring at:

   • The etheric level of your physical dream zone

   • The lower emotional dream zone

   • The higher emotional dream zone

6. Write, using stream of consciousness, in the present tense, and make up a dream occurring at:

   • The lower mental dream zone

   • The higher mental dream zone

   • The causal dream zone

7. Looking back at your dreams and waking experiences for the past couple weeks, write about what your soul is trying to do to help you.

Part III
See What Dreams May Come

In this part . . .

As preparation for knowing the meaning of your
dreams, Part III helps you see what specific kinds of
dreams are possible. Here you'll find many examples to
help you begin to sort your dreamlife into a more recognizable order. Chapter 7 describes the categories of sleep
dreams that occur in Dream Zones 1 and 2, pertaining
more to life in the world, while Chapter 8 delineates the
categories of sleep dreams that occur in Dream Zones 3
and 4, pertaining more to life beyond the ordinary world.
Chapter 9 broadens out the territory, describing waking
dreams, daydreams, synchronicity, and omens and how to
look at your waking reality as if it were a dream.

Chapter 7
Dreams of Life on Earth

. . . .

. . . .

I've dreamt in my life dreams that have stayed with me ever after,
and changed my ideas; they've gone through and through me,
like wine through water, and altered the color of my mind.

—Emily Bronte

*L*ife on earth is full of challenges, replete with drama and diversity. Here you live as an individual and can easily get caught in the experience of feeling separate from others, from your own soul, and from the divine. When you feel isolated, life can seem difficult and painful. You then develop habits of protecting yourself and using personal will to "power through" and control life's circumstances. This depresses and exhausts you.

Luckily life on earth is also full of positive actions and emotions — productivity for the sake of pure creativity, enthusiasm for learning and growth, pleasure in sensory experience, awe in the face of beauty, appreciation of other people's uniqueness, desire to help the unfortunate, laughing at the human condition, and joy in sharing, teaching, and entertaining.

Your dreams speak to you about both aspects of life on earth. They show where you've become too stuck in fear, isolation, limitation, difficulty, and willfulness — and they help you remember what's possible. They guide you to function more effectively and positively, bringing answers to daily problems and helping you stay healthy. They are useful, even if they bring uncomfortable and frightening ideas into your conscious mind. Remember that every dream, whether about the mechanics of the physical world or the hidden dynamics of your subconscious mind, aims you toward heaven.

In this chapter, I give you a sense of the kinds of dreams, both subconscious and superconscious, that originate in the first and second dream zones (see Chapter 6) that pertain to your physical and emotional experience. You'll discover that you can increase your repertoire of dreams when you know what's possible.

Zone 1: Dreams of the Physical World

Many sleep dreams, as well as experiences in your waking reality, deal with the functioning of the physical world. These dreams take place in Zone 1.

Take dinner, work, or TV shows to bed

Did you ever have chicken mole with chips and jalapeno chili salsa, a glass of orange juice, some red wine, a chocolate sundae, and a double espresso right before bed, and then notice that your dream state resembled a tornado's path through West Texas? Whether it's a crazy combination of foods, or drugs, or nervous exhaustion, the physiological processes of your body are often directly reflected in your dreams. A chaotic dream may not entirely be a sign of a disturbed emotional life, then — you may just have had too much physical stimulation.

Perhaps you're like Frank, who has been on a tight deadline at work, trying to get a new software package ready to ship. Just as he thinks it's ready to go, his engineers find more bugs in the system. The pressure is mounting. He's been dreaming about work for weeks. Most nights, his dreams seem to be simply a rehashing of the day's meetings, and reviewing data and procedures again and again. On occasion, Frank wakes with an insight about how to fix some bad code in the program, or what to say to a problematic team member, and it's usually right.

Or maybe you're like Pamela, who takes movies and TV shows to bed with her. If she watches a particularly disturbing thriller before bedtime, she often dreams she is a character in the movie, or a similar high-voltage drama of her own invention plays out in lurid detail. Sometimes it's just a little snatch of a television documentary. Pamela saw a special on women's fashion from the 1800s, and the image of a woman being laced into a corset carried over into her dreams; she saw her sister walking down a hallway with her waist cinched in to inhuman narrowness.

Both Frank and Pamela were experiencing a type of dream called *day residue*. Many dream workers discount this type of dream, but remember: There's no such thing as a bad dream! Every dream, every perception, is relevant. Part of the reason you may carry a daily activity over into your dream world is that you failed to achieve a sense of completion with it. If you make a practice of doing the nightly review and daily list processes described in Chapter 4, some of this flotsam and jetsam from your day will be eliminated.

In some cases, however, what caused you to notice something in your waking reality is the same force that causes you to dream of a parallel thing. Of all the scenes Pamela could have noticed on television that night, what caused her to focus on the corset's severe constriction of the female midsection? And then to apply that image to her sister in her dream? The other important thing about day residue dreams is that often a fascinating interplay exists between the clues you receive during the day's string of perceptions and the night's string of perceptions. A perception in your waking world triggers a response from your dream world, which triggers a new perception in the waking world, which prompts a new development in the dream world, and on and on. You notice a woman walking out of a store with a bright bouquet of party balloons. That night you dream you're riding in a helicopter with a clear bubble of glass all around you. The feeling is exhilarating, and you can see forever. The next day you have an ingenious insight about a way to improve your company's organizational structure.

Try the following dream diary writing exercise.

Tracking Your Day Residue Dreams

1. Look back through your dream records for the past few weeks and see if there are any images that might have been triggered by something that happened to you in daily life. When you find a connection, think back and notice what happened to you in daily life right after you had the dream. Was there anything that seemed like a continuation? Write about these sequences in your diary.

2. When you find a connection between a perception in waking reality and a similar dream, write about what the underlying theme is. Why were you noticing these things? What is your soul trying to tell you?

Solve sticky problems and make decisions

Just as Frank, discussed in the previous section, sometimes had insights about how to fix the problems in his software package after unwittingly taking his work to bed with him, you can solve problems from real life in your dreams by focusing on them intentionally. Here are some examples that show you how it can work.

Nora, an interior designer, needed to come up with an innovative design for an artist's studio. Every idea she thought of felt a bit too ordinary to her. She needed a design element that would stand out and be a focal point for the room. When she went to bed, she wrote out her request on a slip of paper and put it under her pillow, and then repeated her intention to receive some design help from her dream state several times out loud. In the morning she remembered a dream in which she'd been climbing a ladder, and as she descended again she stepped, not onto a rung, but into a drawer that had been pulled out from somewhere. As she recorded the dream, she suddenly saw the solution for the studio. She'd use ladders on one wall as the face for a series of storage drawers! It was an interesting and innovative idea, and the client loved it.

Perfect a new ability

When you're in the process of learning a new skill or preparing for an important track meet, public speaking engagement, or music recital, you may dream about the act, sometimes again and again. For example, as an athlete, Don attended daily workouts with his swim team. He worked conscientiously on the nuances of his stroke, breathing, and turns. As an important meet approached he tended to even dream about swimming. In his dreams he often achieved a state of perfect mind-body integration that gave him insights about improving his performance, which he was able to replicate the next day. The more he dreamed about swimming, the better he did at the meets.

Julie had just been hired as a first-time professor at a prestigious small college. She was excited that one of her life goals had come true — but now she had to show everyone that she was good at what she did. As the semester was about to begin, Julie worked on her class outlines. Though she knew she had great content, she wasn't sure about her presentation skills. Perhaps because of nerves, she had a series of dreams where she was doing public speaking in front of huge audiences. In some of the dreams she was naked. In others, she forgot what she was saying and felt acutely embarrassed. The dreams continued, and gradually the groups got smaller and more intimate; she could feel herself talking about material she loved, and the students in her dream audience started to interact with her. By the time school started, Julie felt like she'd already been teaching for years.

DREAM FACT

Solving the sewing machine problem

One of the most entertaining stories of problem-solving in dreams is how the sewing machine was invented. Elias Howe, who patented the lockstitch sewing machine in 1846, had been struggling every which way to design a machine that would streamline sewing.

Frustrated and at his wits' end, he fell asleep at his bench and had a disturbing dream. He was in the jungle, being chased by brightly painted cannibals. In spite of his attempts to evade them, he was captured, bound, and taken back to their village, where the king of the natives ordered him into a boiling kettle. His frustration continued to build, and he thought about trying to escape. He was totally surrounded by warriors, however, guarding him with sharp spears. As he looked closer, he noticed that their spears all had eye-shaped holes in the end. He commented to himself, "Holes in the points. . . ." As he came back to consciousness, he suddenly realized this was the solution to his problem of how to deliver the thread efficiently to the fabric. Put a hole at the tip of the needle!

Monitor your body's functioning

Your dreams will give you feedback about how your body is doing. Are you getting enough exercise? Are you eating the right foods? Do you need to clean up your act and detoxify your system? Do you need to raise your energy level to be successful in a new phase of your work? Do you need to calm down?

Lee dreamed she had checked into a rehab center. Or was it a health spa? During the intake meeting, one of the counselors knelt down in front of Lee and gently reached over to take a glass of wine out of her hand. She hadn't even noticed that she had it! The woman got across the idea, without talking, that Lee would need to give up drinking wine for awhile if she wanted to get healthy. Other women were being told they would need to give up an unhealthy relationship, or eating too much sugar. When she woke, Lee considered her dream advice seriously. Was she just a little too attached to the mood the wine created for her? She decided to experiment with substituting other things, like doing some Tai Chi, writing poetry, and discovering unusual herbal teas to have instead of the wine.

Use your dream diary to help you listen to your body.

Finding the Body Messages in a Dream

1. Pick any dream from the previous week and write about it as though it's a message to you from your body.

2. Consider the following questions: How might the dream relate to your energy level? Your body's circulation, assimilation, or elimination systems? How might the dream be giving you a message about your health? Is there an action implied that you sense would be good for you to take?

Nip health problems in the bud!

Not only can your dreams help you keep your body running efficiently on a daily basis, they can also alert you to potential health problems, in yourself or in others (see Chapter 15). Dr. Marcia Emery, author of *The Intuitive Healer* (published by St. Martin's Press, 1999), tells a story about how she once dreamed she was visiting a doctor's office and the doctor was telling her that she had cancer. Her dream response was to immediately yell, "You're a phony! You're a quack!" and walk out. Some time later, Marcia noticed a red spot on her nose and went to a dermatologist. Without asking her permission or telling her what he was doing, the doctor did a biopsy. Though the result was benign, the doctor insisted that she prepare herself for cancer treatment anyway. In that instant, Marcia's dream came back to her in full force and she told the doctor she wasn't interested, and walked out. She got a second opinion, which verified that she definitely did not have cancer.

You may just as easily dream about someone else's health. Henry dreamed he was talking to his sister-in-law Elaine on the phone. He heard himself say, "Who is Mary?" Elaine replied that Mary was her neighbor. "Tell Mary her test will turn out okay and not to worry," Henry said. When he woke up, he couldn't get the dream out of his mind, so he decided to call his sister-in-law and share it. Henry was surprised to hear that Mary was indeed a neighbor who lived across the street. Several days later, he was even more surprised when Elaine called him back to tell him that Mary had recently had a mammogram, which had concerned her because of several questionable spots on the x-ray. She had just found out they were fibrous, and not serious, and was greatly relieved.

Change the energy blueprint in your etheric body

Have you ever dreamed you were in the hospital having surgery? Or that you needed to find your medical records? Or that you were in a cast or bandaged, were having a shot or receiving an acupuncture treatment, or that you had a fever, were infected, or were on an IV drip? If so, you were probably focused at the *etheric* level of the physical zone, and you and other nonphysical beings may have actually been adjusting your "energy body." Spiritual healers and clairvoyants attest to the fact that when the etheric pattern of an illness can be cleared the illness has no need to materialize in the physical body. Many people have dreams of dark spots, sticky energy, or black wedges in different parts of the body. These shadowy shapes may denote the appearance of an energy blockage that if left untreated might coalesce into a tumor, infection, or disease.

I recently dreamed of a friend who pulled up her shirt and pulled down the waist of her slacks in back to reveal a very large abscess protruding from the right top of her sacrum. She seemed helpless to do anything about it. I said loudly, "This must be LANCED!" The dream felt absolutely real, like I was actually standing next to her and could have lanced the abscess myself. If I'd had the right tool, I would have. Later the next morning I called her and told her the dream. She laughed. "Guess where I just was? At the doctor's office checking on my kidney infection! I think I'm getting rid of some old toxins in my system right now because I've had several infections in the lower part of my body." My friend could have used my dream image in a meditation. By visualizing herself lancing the infection and releasing the toxins from her subtle etheric body, which responds to feeling and thought, she could help herself heal.

Understand physical zone symbolism

Scan your dreams for imagery and symbols that relate to the medical profession, healing, or to body processes like taking nourishment, assimilation, circulation, cleansing, and elimination. Also keep an eye out for anything relating to the element of earth and for vehicles or containers that might symbolize the body. The house is also a frequent metaphor for the physical body.

For example, if you dream that you're driving a car and the right front tire blows out, you might be talking to yourself about your right foot or leg, or your ability to step forward into the world. If you dream your car won't start, you may be talking to yourself about a lack of vital energy in your body, or a lack of motivation. Why don't you want to move? If you dream your car is going too fast and the brakes won't work, perhaps you need to slow down in your life and be more in the present moment. If you're driving your car from the back seat, perhaps you're afraid to come forward and "show up" or take charge. If your car crashes into a wall, you may *need* to stop! If your car drives off a bridge into a lake, you may need to deal with your emotional life. Table 7-1 presents the most common symbols and imagery of Zone 1 dreams.

Table 7-1	Symbols of the Physical and Etheric Levels (Zone 1)
Containers and Vehicles	***Body Processes***
Jars, earthenware pots, bowls	Eating, drinking, chewing, foods
Chalice, goblet	Seeing something grow
Containers and Vehicles	***Body Processes***
House, trailer, closet	Fluidity and flow, stoppage, swelling
Car, motorcycle, bicycle	Actual organs, body parts, an aura
Cave, tree	Urinating, defecating, vomiting, washing, shaving
Medical Processes	***Physical Processes***
Hospital, clinic	Building, doing carpentry
Doctors, nurses	Sculpture, 3-dimensional art
Bandages, casts, X-rays, injections	Jogging, exercising
Surgery, acupuncture	Digging in the earth
Massage, energy healing	Doing bodywork on others

When you dream about your own body and health, be sure to follow through and take your own advice. Go ahead and change your diet for a while. Or start breathing deeply to get more oxygen. When you dream about someone else's health or body, call them and share the dream. You might start by saying, "You may think this is weird, but I had this dream about you last night, and I had a strong feeling that I should call and tell you about it. It may mean nothing to you, but. . . ." You may actually help someone, and at the very least, you'll strengthen your dream recall process because you've validated the dream by speaking about it.

Zone 2: Dreams of the Emotional World

Everywhere in your life that you express or deny intensity of feeling, you can be sure there is fodder for a powerful emotional dream, the fodder of Zone 2. Whether you're overly expressive or nonexpressive, you probably have a subconscious block down below that causes emotion to gush or be dammed up. So, though dreams from the lower emotional zone can often be disturbing, they provide information about how to clear yourself of blocks to your superconscious experience.

Root out your vulnerabilities

Your dreams serve you by shamelessly pointing out all your blind spots, foibles, weaknesses, and past wounds. You may think you have the cellar door firmly latched, but when you go to bed your soul opens it up and all the gremlins, ghosts, and monsters sneak up the steps to play in your house. Why not get to know them and find out what they have to tell you?

Many dreams come from feelings of powerlessness, lack of confidence, victimization, potential failure leading to rejection, loss of security or control, loss of loved ones, fear of impending change, fear of pain, fear of death or the void. The following sections describe some dreams that indicate where you need to bring more soul presence into your life.

Your teeth are falling out or crumbling into powder

The essence of teeth is their ability to bite through, to cut and grind your food. As human animals we still retain a vestige of snarling — showing teeth as a "stay back" warning — and that is the smile we greet others with, to disarm them socially. If your teeth fall out, you lose personal power, your ability to be aggressive, and you may alienate others with a poor self-image, or feel humiliated. Where in your life are you feeling anxious about your level of competence or powerless against circumstance? With whom do you feel self-conscious or insecure? In what area should you take action to "bite through" something, or chew something thoroughly?

You're naked in public

When you realize that you are suddenly exposed and unprotected, all your "shoulds" rise to the surface. Your mind may recite a litany of conditions for popularity and success: *I should be thin, have no hair on my back but lots on my head, not wear glasses, be witty, be efficient, be smart, be seductive, be mysterious, be good in business, or be younger.*

Exposure dreams bring to light the things you haven't wanted others to see about you. What have you been hiding? Where do you feel like a phony? In what ways have you been trying to please others to be accepted? What's wrong with being seen for who you *really* are? Have you felt invisible and unnoticed and might you be preparing to become more visible? Have you felt heavily armored, and might you be ready to become more trusting? Can you tolerate — even love — your own imperfections?

You're taking an exam or performing in a play you haven't prepared for

You haven't studied! You don't know the material or your lines! And "they" will be upset if you fail the test, or flub your dialogue. Your life will be ruined! Dreams of performance anxiety often point to areas in your life where you feel judged by others. If you don't do well, you'll be rejected and ridiculed. If the setting is an academic one, and you're taking an examination, you may be showing yourself that you need to pay more attention to some part of your personal growth. If it's a play or a lecture, you may be telling yourself that you're about ready to express yourself more fully in the world. What new opportunity do you want but don't quite feel ready for? How *could* you feel ready? How could you feel more relaxed and spontaneous?

You're being chased by a wild animal, a tornado, or a serial killer and you feel paralyzed

You don't understand why, but you have drawn the attention of some dark force and it wants to annihilate you. You're running through alleyways, down corridors, through other people's houses, running so hard you may feel like you're flying. No matter what you do to outpace or outwit your pursuer, he/she/it's gaining on you. You hide, but know you will be found. Often you wake before the dreaded conclusion. What do you feel threatened by in your life? Who have you given your power away to? Where do you feel helpless and unsupported in your life? How do you deal with conflict or potential conflict? In which areas have you surrendered your right to "take up space"? Might you be fleeing from inner promptings that indicate it's time for you to let go of who you think you are, so you can grow into a bigger, healthier you?

Chase dreams can often contain elements of "I'm-paralyzed-and-can't-run" dreams. If your legs feel like lead or mush, or if you feel pinned down, your soul may be saying that you need to stand on one spot and face something. What have you been avoiding? Is there an issue you feel divided about, causing you to be unable to make a decision? You may also simply be experiencing the normal physical "paralysis" that occurs in conjunction with the REM sleep state.

You lost your wallet, money, keys, or car

You dream you come out of a restaurant and your car is gone! You make a phone call at a public phone booth and forget to put your wallet back in your purse. You go through airport security with a floppy disk in your carryon bag and all the data is erased. You can't find the money you *know* you stored in a locker when you were in college.

Dreams of loss point to areas where you may be too attached to something; your soul may be saying, "Let go and see what comes next when you don't have it all locked down." Losing your wallet may indicate it's time to reexamine your identity. Losing your car may mean you need to look at your need for movement, freedom, and independence. Perhaps others are to help you more now. Losing keys may point to a fear of losing authority. Losing money may indicate you're letting go of what's been valuable to you. How have you grown out of old ideas of who you are? Where do you need to let go and trust the unknown part of yourself to provide for you? Where do you need to experience space and emptiness instead of clutter?

A loved one has died, or you think you're going to die

Vickie dreamed on a number of occasions that her sister had died, and each time she was surprised and had to remind herself, "Oh, yes, that's right, she's supposed to die first." Nevertheless, she'd wake up sobbing. Mark dreamed he was falling in an elevator and knew he was going to die when he hit bottom. He always woke up just before he hit. Crystal dreamed she had died and an Egyptian priest was embalming her. As she watched from above, she saw that he had removed her brain and that her left hemisphere was larger than the right one. She was upset that she was so imbalanced.

Death dreams almost always signify that some aspect of you is dying, that you are making a transition into a new way of being. Is some area of your life undergoing a radical change? Are you in a process of transforming yourself? Is it time for you to totally surrender? In dreams like Mark's, where death seems imminent, you may be telling yourself to simply trust the process and pay attention to what wants to "die" in your life. Don't fight it!

Contrary to superstition, if you die in a dream, you will not die in your waking reality! Vickie's dream helped her understand that she had placed too much importance on her relationship with her sister, and she needed to let go a bit. Crystal's dream helped give her some perspective about the way she was living; she determined to balance herself out by developing her intuition and artistic abilities as well as her logic. Occasionally, death dreams are actually *precognitive,* signaling you about the impending loss of a relative or friend. Usually these dreams have a strong "psychic weight" and feel different than symbolic dreams. I talk more about precognitive dreams in Chapter 9.

Use your dream diary to look for hidden vulnerabilities.

Sleuthing for Your Subconscious Blocks

1. Look back through your dream records for the past few weeks and see if there are any images that might have been triggered by fears or blocks in your subconscious mind.

2. Make a list of the images, emotions, and actions you took in the dreams.

3. Write about what the underlying themes might be and how these emotions are connected to events in your daily life.

4. Write about how the themes might be connected with each other.

Explore taboos and suppressed desires

Considering how confused so many of us are about sex, and how unloved and unappreciated we often feel, it's no surprise that our sex life is a major dream topic — one where we explore every nuance of romance, pleasure, and societal taboos.

Gail, an accountant, was totally unashamed as she recounted her wild, sexual dream trysts with rocker Mick Jagger. She was able to get in touch with a part of her passionate nature in her dreams that she didn't seem able to tap in waking life. Sexual energy is life force energy, and freeing it in dreams can help increase your participation and creativity in waking life.

Erotic dreams can be simple escapism, yet they can also help you overcome fears and inhibitions. They may contain hints that point to your deep personal needs and desires, and to ways you can achieve greater intimacy. Being caught in the act of having sex is similar to being-naked-in-public dreams. What inhibition or self-judgment is being brought to light? Where does your dream lover touch you? You may need to give this part of your body more attention. Does a dream lover hurt you? You may be hurting yourself in a similar way. Sexual dreams can also symbolize a part of you that is longing for a greater spiritual connection.

The emotional dream zone is a malleable, rubbery world where it's possible to act out anything you want without really hurting yourself or anyone else. In your dreams, you can do things you'd never think of doing in real life. Experiencing taboos can free you to accept all of life, the bad with the good — and when you don't have to prevent yourself from being "bad," you can naturally be the best you can be, without "having to." Even the most ethical people have dreamed about stealing, or killing someone, or having sex with an unacceptable kind of partner, or indulging in a vice they'd never touch while awake. I talk more about sex dreams in Chapter 14.

Understand your psychological process

Your personality is constantly evolving, and you are discovering by trial and error how to get the best results with the least amount of struggle. Becoming psychologically mature is a matter of achieving balance among your many components and traits. Your dreams often alert you to imbalances and distortions and help you activate the underdeveloped side of the equation.

Balance your masculine and feminine energies

Everyone uses both active, dynamic masculine energy and receptive, nurturing feminine energy in their lives to be creative. If you become overly weighted in either one, your productivity and inner peace suffer. Are you too passive? Or too impulsive and impatient? Are you the actor in your dreams, or are you acted upon? Have you ever dreamed you were the opposite sex?

By letting yourself role-play the opposite gender, you can gain insight about how to integrate the dynamic or receptive aspect of yourself. Perhaps you dream you're a powerful, direct kind of man or a seductive, earthy kind of woman, or are being influenced by one. Role-playing the opposite gender helps you develop your *anima* or *animus,* the inner female and male aspects of your personality. If you dream about strong male or female role models, especially celebrities, you may be showing yourself what qualities you need to develop to achieve harmony.

Determine whether you hide and hoard or give it all away

Dreams about hiding money or hoarding treasure may indicate you're afraid you'll never have enough.

Dennis dreamed he was hiking and found a place where there were huge water-clear crystals imbedded in some boulders. He pulled on one and it came out easily, which made him greedy. He pulled out as many as he could stuff in his pockets but had to leave because tourists were arriving. He was worried they'd discover the treasure. The dream made Dennis realize that many "jewels" — talents and knowledge — had been freely given to him, so he could stop his limitation thinking and emotional hoarding, use what he has, and be generous; there were plenty of riches to go around.

On the other hand, you may dream of giving valuables, or your own energy, away. Darcy dreamed she was standing next to a group of people at a party. They were animatedly talking to each other. Whenever she tried to join in, her body faded and became more and more transparent, while their bodies got brighter, more colorful, and louder. The dream drew Darcy's attention to her habit of giving her power away, which always left her feeling drained.

Improve your relationships

Dreaming about relationships helps you work out problems with communication, understand how the other person is a reflection of you, or find hidden aspects of the core relationship that are interfering with a loving exchange. For example, Sylvia had a series of dreams about a current lover who seduced her then tried to poison her every time she opened up to him. It scared her; eventually, she realized the relationship was unhealthy, and she ended it.

Connie dreamed she had a confrontation with a woman who had betrayed her and caused damage to her career.

> *I meet up with this villainous woman and I stare into her eyes, giving her a long withering look, and she drops to the ground, unconscious. I step over her body and walk proudly into a room filled with new people who have been waiting for me for a long time. They are happy to see me, and rush over to hug me.*

The dream helped Connie get beyond the bitterness she'd been holding.

Face your monsters from the deep

Nightmares often speak to you about previous traumatic events that haven't been experienced fully. For instance, if you've suffered physical or sexual abuse early in your childhood and have repressed the memory, or if you died suddenly or shockingly in a past life and were unable to complete the experience consciously, you may have nightmares as the trauma tries to surface so you can see it, understand it, and release it.

Marina was plagued with a recurring nightmare about being with a man who was her husband (not her husband in her current reality) in a small cabin, and a terrible storm was raging. As the storm grew worse, she clung to her husband, terrified, and everything went black. After years of being haunted by this nightmare, Marina sought help through hypnotherapy. She was regressed to a memory of a previous life when she was a homesteader in Missouri and had died with her husband in a tornado. As soon as she put all the pieces together and brought the memory into consciousness, the nightmares stopped.

Jack dreamed repeatedly that he was being buried alive, and woke in a terrible panic each time he reached the point where he thought he couldn't breathe. When he was guided into the feelings of suffocation in a therapy session, he found himself back in the womb, having difficulty getting enough oxygen because his mother was a chain-smoker. Realizing his dreams had originated from cellular memory, he was able to consciously reprogram his body so it could experience having plenty of breathing room.

Jeremy Taylor, author of *Dream Work: Techniques for Discovering the Creative Power of Dreams* (published by Paulist Press, 1983), says nightmares indicate that a survival issue is being brought to your attention so you can be emotionally and spiritually authentic. In addition, he says people who are engaged in spiritual development often must clear humanity's worst case archetypal bad dreams inside themselves — because "the only place where evil can truly be faced and overcome is within."

Remember the far distant past

Because your bubble of perception expands through time and space as it expands through the dream zones, you can quite easily encompass experiences from the past in your dreams and experience them as if they were happening now. In your dream world, they are! You may dream about the forgotten years of your own childhood, or even infancy — in fact many people have dreams that seem to pertain to their time *in utero*. You might also dream about the history of the planet with no logical explanation for why you know about how it was to be traveling with Alexander the Great, for example. Is it imagination or is it literal? It's hard to tell sometimes, but many people have dreamed information about their own past and about historical facts that later proved to be true.

Similarly, it seems to be a common phenomenon to dream about having lived in other time periods. Just as memories of what can only be called past lives surface during inner work like hypnotherapy, guided visualizations, and meditation, dreams also seem to be a vehicle for opening far distant personal memory — memory that seems to go beyond your current life. Whether you choose to believe past life memory dreams are literal or symbolic, it really doesn't matter — the dreams bring you a message just the same. Past life memories seem especially convincing when they emerge in the form of nightmares. I have spoken with many people who for years had recurring nightmares about dying in a terrifying way, and in psychotherapy or meditation, realized the nightmare was a small piece of an actual past life experience they had lived through. When they understand they are fine, and alive and well again in the here-and-now, the trauma dissolves and the nightmares stop.

Other, more benign far distant "memories" can surface if something in your present life is parallel and magnetizes them. It might be that you're living through an episode that is extremely similar to one you lived in another life.

Perhaps you've just turned 53, and that was the age you died of tuberculosis in a recent past life. Now you dream you are sick and people are standing around your bedside. Perhaps you're about to visit Europe for a vacation, and you dream about a city on a river; you are young soldier in an old-fashioned uniform who always goes to a certain chalet-style building on a corner, climbs some steep steps, and gets fed by an old woman at a wooden table. Later, during your trip you find a street in a city by the Danube that feels like the exact spot!

You don't need to believe in reincarnation to work with dreams. All dreams have multiple layers of meaning and you can derive value from any interpretation that feels right to you.

Be prepared for sudden change

Just as you can experience the distant past, you can have *precognitive dreams* that bring you knowledge from the future; this can happen when there is a need in your present life that magnetizes it. If you are afraid to face a sudden change, you may give yourself a dream about losing your job six months before your company lays off a third of its workforce. Rachel dreamed about the deaths of both her grandmothers approximately two weeks before each one died, with no signs that they were ailing. In both dreams she was reassured that the women were ready, happy, and would depart easily and quickly. And their deaths happened just that way.

Sometimes you may have precognitive dreams about world events and not understand why. Perhaps it's just that these things carry a psychic weight and send off ripples or "event waves" through society. Before President Ronald Reagan was shot, I dreamed I was riding in the back of a stretch limousine looking at the back of then Vice-President George Bush's head as we drove across the tarmac to Air Force One. Bush was being called to Washington, but I didn't know why.

Remember that precognitive dreams are not meant to scare you! You bring the messages about the future to yourself for a good reason. And in the world of dreams, it's normal to know the future.

Travel out of your body

Colleen dreamed her mother had come to visit her, and though she was in bed, she could see her mother standing in the living room looking out a window. In the dream it was so real and matter-of-fact that she could hardly believe it hadn't happened when she woke the next morning.

Josh had experienced a series of auditory dreams. In one, he received a phone call early in the morning, thought he actually heard the ringing, and got up to answer it. A friend of his who was traveling in a foreign country was on the line, clear as a bell, telling Josh about a recent happening on his journey. When Josh actually awoke later, he thought the call had been real. Another time, in the dark of early morning, he heard a man's voice call his name from the other side of the room. It jolted him awake. The voice seemed physical, but no one was there.

Josh had experienced a phenomenon called *direct voice,* where a disembodied voice seems to speak to you from outside your body. Metaphysicians seem to agree this is a kind of telepathic connection to higher realms. *Telepathy,* or the direct transmission of communication, mind to mind, without speaking, is a common occurrence in emotional zone dreams.

When you experience the kind of dream where the other person actually seems to be there with you, where they're so real you could hug them, like Colleen did, you're experiencing a *visitation dream* or are *astral traveling.* It's quite common to interact in dreams with others who live far away, even with people who have died.

Out-of-body experiences, or *OBEs,* also known as *astral projection dreams,* are similar to visitation dreams, but they are more lucid and conscious. Dreamers often report that they separate from their physical body and "travel" in a dream body, or *subtle body,* to explore other worlds, parallel realities, and loved ones in this world. While engaged in the dream, it feels like it is literally happening. I once experienced this. In the dream:

> *I feel myself floating an inch or two above my physical body in bed as I lie on my back. Suddenly I perform a complex somersault-and-twist maneuver and the next thing I know, I'm facing my sleeping body on the bed, floating in the air about eighteen inches above it. Instantly my dream body zooms sideways and passes right through the wall of my bedroom! I find myself out in my front yard, about three feet above the ground, facing the grass. I realize then that I'm having an OBE, and I know I have to be careful not to jerk back to my physical body in bed. I calm my thoughts and decide to visit my mother. I immediately zoom to her bedroom on the East Coast. She's sitting up in bed looking at me. We don't talk. Then something at home disturbs me and I snap back clumsily into my sleeping body and wake up, disoriented. The next day I have a headache, and I think it's because "I came in crooked."*

Robert Monroe, author of *Journeys Out of the Body* (published by Anchor Books, 1973), studied the OBE phenomenon extensively and developed methodologies for prompting the experience. It may well be that this type of dream is one where you take your conscious mind with you while you're dreaming, and thus perception is heightened and it seems totally real to you.

Keep your heart open

Not all emotional zone dreams are fear-based. Dreams from the higher emotional zone give you messages about new forms of your creativity, how and where to express your passion, or which fork in the road will lead to the greatest fulfillment. Dreams that originate from the higher level of the emotional zone help you feel motivated, loving, and enthusiastic in your waking life.

Martha dreamed she was giving her obnoxious neighbor a cake. When she woke, she couldn't believe she would do such a thing because the man had been so negative toward her. But she realized if she could try on the feelings she'd had in the dream, she could probably find a way to open her heart and make a peace offering. Then she thought maybe this sort of kindness was a key to improving *every* area of her life.

Rekindle your passion for life

After periods of illness or depression, or as you break free of restrictive cycles of dutiful action and prepare for what's to come, you may have hopeful, uplifting dreams that encourage you to move forward. Ellen had just come out of a difficult marriage and was reinventing herself. She had an interest in the environment and animals and decided she'd like to work to protect endangered species. For months she dreamed repeatedly of certain symbols, especially of turtles and a vertical spiral. Then, on a dive trip to learn more about ocean ecosystems, she saw an inordinate number of sea turtles and a beautiful waterspout skittering across the ocean. She knew she was on the right path. Then she met a new man, and she dreamed that in the air around his head she saw neon arrows blinking on and off, pointing insistently toward him. In her waking life, as she continued to associate with the men, she soon discovered they had many things in common, and their work for the environment seemed to dovetail uncannily. Ellen's dreams seemed to literally be pointing the way for her.

Motivate yourself to create

George dreamed he was visiting a man who was an artist. The man showed George through his house, pointing out the fantastic paintings and sculptures he had made, and in his bedroom he pointed to an incredible, massive bed carved intricately with mythological scenes interwoven with scenes from his own life. The detail was awesome and the concept mind-boggling. He could hardly take it all in. When George woke, he realized that *he* was the artist — after all, he had dreamed all those creations instantaneously and effortlessly! Perhaps he could do the same thing in real life!

Understand emotional zone symbolism

Scan your dreams for imagery and symbols that relate to the elements of water or fire, or to chaotic forces of nature like storms, floods, forest fires, volcanoes, or mudslides. Keep an eye out for vehicles that might symbolize the emotional body, like trains or boats. Lower emotional level symbols are chaotic, fearful, dark, threatening, restrictive, and out of control. Higher emotional level symbols convey positive, healthy emotion, smoothness and fluidity, purification and transmutation, motivation, creative enthusiasm, and passion for life.

Here are some common symbols and imagery from the lower emotional level in Zone 2:

- ✔ **Vehicles:** Speeding train; boats, especially sinking or wrecked

- ✔ **Elements:** Water— tidal waves, lakes, ocean, rivers, floods, drowning, whirlpools, swamps; fire — houses burning, forest or brush fires, explosions; Storms — tornadoes, hurricanes, earthquakes, volcanoes, mud slides

- ✔ **Miscellaneous symbols:** Sex, relationships; conflict, betrayal; hiding, hoarding, being drained; being chased; exposure, nudity; losing important items or money; paralysis, being tied up, poison, suffocation, danger; snakes, lions, tigers, bears, sharks; weapons, traps

The following are from the higher emotional level of Zone 2:

- ✔ **Symbols:** Babies, children, birth; campfire, fire in a fireplace, smoke rising; dolphins, puppies, hummingbirds, otters, horses, elephants; fish, fishing; gifts, giving; the heart; purification; redemption, rescue' swimming, pools, carwash

- ✔ **Feelings:** Being motivated or motivating others; expressing creative passion; feeling compassion, kindness; feeling joy and ecstasy; finding important items or money

Because dreams from the first two zones are so tied to real life experience, they come to you cloaked in imagery, symbols, and sensations that feel very much like life. If you explore the higher dream zones in Chapter 8, you'll see that the dreams from those levels are not always symbolic.

I wake up in the morning with a dream in my eyes.

—Allen Ginsberg

Your Dream Diary

1. Make a list of five problems you'd like to solve, or questions you'd like insight about. Pick the most important one and program a dream to help you with it. Write about the response you get. If you don't get a dream, make one up with stream of consciousness writing. Continue to work on the other issues the same way.

2. Let the following phrases stimulate your imagination and write about what comes to you.

   • If I were my body, giving me a dream about how to heal my (ulcer, backache, carpal tunnel syndrome, and so forth), I'd project the following scenarios. . . .

   • If I were my body, giving me a dream about what I want to eat and don't want to eat, I'd project the following images. . . .

   • If I were my body, giving me a dream about how to improve my energy level and regulate the flow of my energy, I'd project the following scenarios. . . .

3. Write out a detailed description of how you see yourself optimally expressing a new skill. Program a dream to practice the skill.

4. Make a list of the symbols in your dreams from the past week. Write about how each might relate to your physical and emotional life right now.

5. Write out three of your wildest fantasies about sex, taboos, the dark side, or death. It's okay to be macabre and politically incorrect! Write about what you learn from each.

6. Write about a relationship dream, a nightmare, and a creativity dream, asking yourself about each: "If I accept what's happening in the dream and extend the action further, what happens? If I let the dream take an odd turn, what might happen that I never expected?"

7. Look through your dreams for the past week and write about the different types of Zone 1 and 2 dreams you've had. How much are you focusing on your subconscious mind? How much on the superconscious? How much physical, etheric, emotional?

Chapter 8

Dreams of the Life Beyond

· ·

In This Chapter

▶ Sleep as soul contact

▶ Types of dreams in the mental dream zones

▶ Types of dreams in the causal dream zone

▶ Symbolism associated with each type of dream

▶ Dreams of shifting between zones

· ·

> *I now believe that everyone 'dissolves' into the collective every night
> and simply does not remember it. This, I believe, is one of the main reasons
> for the great restorative and recuperative powers of sleep.*
>
> —Jeremy Taylor

*W*hat if you were made to live entirely in the physical world, with no break from its fight-or-flight survival mentality, or from the slowness of its creative cycle, its often snagged and zigzagging pathways forward, or its tendency toward attachment, pain, and suffering? Without the joy, ecstasy, and beauty of the inner worlds, you might forget to notice the gifts of this outer one. If you didn't have sleep and dreams, if you were conscious in only the three-dimensional reality, you'd no doubt be one of the dullest, most mournful, most alienated souls in the universe.

Sleep lets you remember the rest of yourself. It lets you dive into the pool of everlasting life and refuel with new spiritual enthusiasm, new breath, new plans, new knowing. As an individual in a world of individuals, you can only do so much with the power of your personal will and logical mind without having the renewing influx of help, inspiration, surprise, revelation, grace, and good luck that comes from beyond the scope of your personality.

In this chapter, I show you how to recognize dream messages from the the higher zones, and how to use those messages to improve your life.

Remembering the Rest of Yourself

Your sleep dreams are openings, ways for you to see into your Big Self and the Big Life that lies beyond daily life. The important point is to realize that your sleep self is not separate from you, but is like the top of the sliding board, the place from which you rolled down into your current existence, the state where you are still in total communion with the divine plan. You must go back to the top of the sliding board every night to check the broader view from up there, so you can roll down a fresh personality for your next new day's life on earth.

I find it curious that a newly forming fetus spends 100 percent of its time in REM sleep, then 80 percent at several months in utero, and 50 percent as a newborn. The percentage decreases gradually, until in early childhood, we spend 20 to 30 percent of our time in REM sleep, which continues for the rest of our adult life. Could it be that REM sleep is an indication of interaction between the higher levels of the soul and the lower levels of the personality? That during these times, an important exchange of information, energy, and intent is taking place? And might it also be that when we pass beyond REM sleep into the deeper levels of delta brainwave sleep, that we are actually communing with the divine, and being one with our superconsciousness?

Perhaps *being the soul* is the ultimate rest. Maybe each kind of brainwave indicates a different zone of dream activity. I postulate that beta is the soul dreaming of the waking world, alpha is the soul dreaming of creativity and imagination, theta is the soul dreaming of weaving back and forth through the dimensions between the essential self and the physical self, and delta is the soul dreaming of immersion into the divine. I believe every kind of perception can be called a dream, and that dreaming is *the* act consciousness.

Zone 3: Dreams of the Mental World

As you expand up and away from your daily consciousness during the deeper periods of sleep, your bubble of perception begins to encompass the worlds where thought, belief, ideas, and inspiration live. As you reach the lower levels of this higher "atmosphere," your dreams will talk to you about your mental structures, the places where your ideas have become fixed because you've attached too much importance to certain concepts.

Clear your fixed subconscious beliefs

Just as your dreams help you see and clear subconscious emotional blocks, they also help you discern the fear-based mental patterns that often lie hidden behind your reactionary behaviors. As you evolve spiritually, you'll find that any part of you that isn't fluid and able to be impressed by divine urges, anywhere you can't be creative and spontaneously responsive, holds you back from your goal, which ultimately is enlightenment. As you expand through the higher dream zones, you'll notice places where your thoughts have frozen, or ways you organize your basic perception that are inefficient and create an inaccurate translation of the divine. The further out you travel, the more you will value trust, and the less you'll need beliefs.

Free yourself from mental clutter

Dreams filled with symbols of old ways of doing things, old ways of thinking, or old images of yourself can help you weed through limiting ideas you may not have been able to see. Donna dreamed she was up in the attic of a house she lived in when she was a girl. It was filled with boxes of mementos and she was sorting through the keepsakes. She realized the possessions belonged to all the women in her mother's lineage and went way back into ancient history. She was to inherit them now! Expecting great treasures, instead she found tiny restrictive shoes that would not fit her, primitive sewing and cooking implements she would never use, and clothes that were virtually rags. She suddenly knew her ancestors had lived hard lives grounded in poverty. She became very sad and woke herself up, actually crying. Donna's soul was talking to her about a belief system based on limitation and difficulty that she had inherited from her mother, as her mother had from her mother, and hers before her.

Let go of too much definition

Dreams containing images of measurement, definition, sequencing, and logic can show you where your mind is stuck or functioning too narrowly. Scott had a series of dreams in which he was measuring wood for a deck he was building, but the boards kept coming out different lengths, so he'd go back and check the blueprints and remeasure the boards over and over. He also dreamed he was trying to dial a telephone number from memory, one that had prefixes, operator codes, and PIN numbers, making it about thirty digits long. He kept getting the sequence wrong. Scott needed to trust his intuition rather than cling to his logic alone.

Break out of your shackles

Joe dreamed he was flying. He took off from a street corner, steadily gaining momentum, but as he cleared the treetops he saw a wide band of high-tension lines stretching across the open fields ahead. He wasn't high enough to clear them and he couldn't muster the energy to climb any further. He knew he was going to have to fly through them! He woke in the morning exhausted, feeling all "tangled up." Similarly, Julie had a dream fragment of walking into a large spiderweb that was in front of her face. She felt it break apart with a distinct "snap." Constructs that are in your way, like Julie's spider web and Joe's high tension lines, may indicate outdated or fixed ideas that your soul wishes you to examine and break through.

Pay attention to words and numbers

Your dreams will often deliver a concise message to you in written or verbal form, with no symbolic images at all. It's common for dreams from the mental zone to be unaccompanied by real-life images, since perception through the five senses relates more to the physical and emotional realms and to the issues found in the lower dream zones. The higher you go, the more abstract and pattern-oriented your dreams tend to become.

Listen to the message — literally

Allen called to tell me that he'd had the same dream several nights in a row. In it he was repeating out loud the phrase: "I accept it, but I don't accept it as REAL!" As an aside, he said, "How's that for faith in a nutshell?"

Sheryl couldn't remember the words in this dream when she woke, but felt like she'd been hard at work for hours. She reported: "All night I'm repeating a sentence or mantra. It's clumsy or negative in some way and was given to me by a man who is out of synch with me, but I have to try to live it out, or fill it out, and dream from it, anyway. I don't like the words; they disturb my body."

Kay dreamed about an old boyfriend who had moved and his new house was on "Weird Street." In the dream she commented aloud to herself, "I should have known he'd move there."

Notice playful puns and metaphors

Your dreaming self can be very playful, and in the mental dream zones you'll often notice your own wit and cleverness. Because dreams make such use of metaphor and symbolism, it's not much of a stretch to see that your mind will dredge up puns and make connections between the various meanings of the same word to get a point across. Your dreams will also exaggerate ideas you may have under-emphasized, make important things seem absurd, or convey an idea by couching it in its opposite meaning.

Craig dreamed that a herd of deer led him through some woods and in a clearing he came upon his older brother, as he had looked when they were teenagers. Craig realized his brother was very "dear" to him, and that he needed to get "clear" about why he worshipped his brother so much. Patrick was in a process of reinventing himself — becoming a new man — and was developing confidence in his ability as an investment counselor. He dreamed that Paul "Newman" gave him some valuable advice on picking winning stocks, which proved to be accurate.

See if your dreams are numbered

I talk more about the specific meanings of numbers in Chapter 11, but if you dream of a specific number in a dream, there's usually a good reason. Numbers are symbols for various patterns of awareness, periods of time, and types of personalities.

Sheila dreamed that she looked at her digital clock and the numbers said it was 68:76 and she had the thought that it was *really* early in the morning. Later while daydreaming, her mind wandered back to a house where she had spent a couple years while growing up. Its address was "6876 Morning Glory Drive"; suddenly, she knew her night dream was reminding her that she needed to remember something important about her self-concept that had developed during that time period.

Jenny dreamed she was playing the slot machines in Las Vegas and struck a jackpot, winning $2,222,200. She was overjoyed. When contemplating the meaning of all the two's in her dream, she discovered two is the number of relationship, and she was telling herself that she was finally ready to have a relationship, having spent several years alone.

Receive instruction about life

Have you ever dreamed you were attending a class at a university? Or a seminar at a retreat setting in the mountains? Have you dreamed you were in a library, actually reading books? Maybe you were having a conversation with a professor, a historical figure, a wise grandparent, a shaman, a religious leader, or an animal. If so, you were tapping into the wisdom of the collective mind to help you learn more about your life process. Often, when you reach a turning point in your life, you'll give yourself a guidance dream to help ease the transition process.

Ross was at a point in his career where he felt he was marking time. He was asked to bid on a contract but to get it he had to reduce his fees to rock bottom. He was ambivalent about giving away his services just to survive at something he wasn't that interested in anyway. He had the following dream:

> *A man and a woman are on an icy trail on a cliff and the man slips and falls thirty feet to a ledge below. The woman instinctively goes after him, as if to help, but she loses her footing and falls to her death. The man desperately reaches up for something to hang onto and his fingers catch the sleeve of a homeless person above. The homeless person then begins to slip off the cliff, and he in turn grips the next person beyond him, and that person the next and so on, until the cliff is stripped of people all falling into the gorge below. The man alone remains.*

Ross took his dream to be a teaching; he realized that his creative, dynamic self was stuck, and his intuitive, feminine side was showing him that he should let go and surrender — and fall into the void. He saw that destitute (cheap, small thinking) people could not help him out of his dead-end situation because they weren't strong enough. He realized he didn't have to hit rock bottom if he'd let go and trust his intuition.

Susan had an odd snippet of a dream, which at first seemed totally meaningless. In it she is putting on her mascara, but she has the mascara with the wand she doesn't like. There is another kind she just bought that has a perfect wand. Where is it? This fragment expanded in meaning over several days — and Susan realized she really wanted her new business to be the way *she* wanted it to be, not the way everyone else thought it *should* be, or the way that had worked for her in her previous career. She made a special effort after that to pay attention to being authentic in every little choice that needed to be made.

Jumpstart your creative genius

In the higher level of the mental dream zone, your dreams take on a freer, more inspirational quality. Here you don't need to solve creative problems, you begin to grasp your own creative genius and the effortless quality of great creations.

Sarah recounts this dream:

> *I am with a woman who is playing the piano, spontaneously composing incredible, fluid music. I can hear every detail of it and am in awe. I have a book on how to compose music; it's divided into three sections like those books where you can mix and match human heads, midsections, and legs to make funny and different kinds of people. This book has sections of music so you can combine stanzas in interesting ways. I notice I have to read a book to do this and the woman is just IN the process totally.*

Sarah's dream gave her the insight that immersing herself in a creative process directly and trusting the flow of what came through her was better than trying to study the principles of creativity.

Carl dreamed:

> *I'm painting the air and a scene from reality reveals itself with each brushstroke as I paint. It's really fun! I can't wait to see what my magic paintbrush will create. I don't want to stop.*

Upon reflection, Carl understood that the paintbrush was really his own perception, and that he created his daily reality as effortlessly as he painted the air in his dream.

Invent new technological wonders

Just as many of the great breakthroughs in mathematics, science, and chemistry came in dreams, you too may dream of futuristic technologies, gadgets, or inventions. Here is a sampling:

- *I am given a tool that looks like a trumpet with a bell on both ends and a voice tells me it is my "rod of power." It receives information from one dimension and translates it to another. It also balances me when I become "uneven." I have to hold it with two hands.*

- *I look in a box and take out a pair of special goggles that can take instant-developing photographs of whatever you look at, even if it's in the future. There is a little button on the sidepiece.*

- *I am in a foreign country spying on a "work camp." They are making a top secret product and I sneak in and discover it's a small reddish disk made of highly fire clay that has some special mineral in it. Then I see another scene where the disks are used on some sort of "telephone poles" as part of an information transmitting system. The disks never wear out.*

- *I have a pocket "calculator" that measures the frequencies of words when I say them out loud.*

Counsel, teach, lead, and heal others

As you begin to identify your higher mental level dreams you'll make an interesting and pleasant discovery: You are much wiser, more loving, and talented than you could ever imagine! In many mental zone dreams, you'll find yourself in the role of leader, teacher, counselor, or healer to people you know and don't know. In daily life you might think you don't know enough or have enough expertise to take on so much responsibility, but in your dreams you can be excellent in many areas.

Steven, an automobile mechanic, dreamed often that he was teaching a class to a large group sitting in a theater-style lecture hall, gesturing with a piece of chalk in his right hand. There was a blackboard behind him and on it were scrawled dozens of complex mathematical formulas. He realized he must know about mathematics somewhere in his deeper recesses.

Communicate with the other side

Have you dreamed of a loved one who has died? Did your favorite grandfather give you a piece of advice or caution you about continuing down a path of action that would lead to misfortune? Perhaps you dreamed your aunt who died suddenly in an accident came back to tell you she didn't suffer, is happy where she is, and you needn't worry about her. These dreams are common in all cultures, and it seems that it is in our dreams where we can match vibrations with our dearly departed friends and relatives, and visit briefly with them.

Mental zone dreams of the dead differ from emotional zone dreams of the dead because they are often instructional, more neutral, and much less scary. Sometimes the spirits of the dead come back to ask for help in being released — as in straightening out burial or cremation plans, or to make sure their last wishes are reinforced — so they can move on to higher realms.

DJ dreamed of a friend who had died the previous year. She was worried about the man's widow, who was also a friend. In her dream she wanted to find the man and bring a message back for his wife.

> *I am hunting through the rooms of a large house for K, following clues. I go upstairs and have to pass through a series of guardian-type people who try to prevent me from continuing. Finally, I enter a room and K comes out from behind a curtain. I'm proud of myself that I've found him. He seems tired and doesn't want to talk. I have the distinct impression he wants to be left alone.*

Later, DJ realized that the man's mourning friends and relatives were holding him back and that he probably needed a period of rest to regroup before he'd be ready to move on to a higher level. This helped DJ advise his wife.

When Bill's grandmother died suddenly, he dreamed she flew out of the house she'd been living in — so fast that she blew out one entire wall. He could see the trail of golden light she left as she exited over some bright green hills. Months later, he dreamed she was jauntily driving a jeep through a green park, and though no words were exchanged, he knew she felt strong and good.

It's common to see the image of a large, serene grassy park just after people have died; perhaps it's an archetypal image of the first level of the afterworld where souls are adjusting and finding a new harmony. This in-between place is often called *summerland*.

Explore parallel realities and personas

Some metaphysicians theorize that in addition to having past and future lives, we all live other lives simultaneously with this one. These are called *parallel lives* or *alternate realities*. Some people visit these other realities during out-of-the-body experiences. In some cases, you may dream about them. These dreams are distinguished by a strong feeling of reality and a certainty that you actually are the other persona.

Parallel life dreams are also often *continuing dreams;* you may become the same persona, with the same group of people, doing similar activities that pick up where a previous dream left off — even if the previous dream was several years prior.

Daryl had a continuing parallel reality dream in which he was married to a different woman, lived in a different house, and had a different kind of job. After ten years of living this other life in his dream world, Daryl and his dream wife divorced. At that point that particular dream stream stopped. His real life marriage shifted too, as his wife took a job that required frequent travel.

I have a strange parallel reality myself, one which provides me with interesting episodes every two or three years. Here's one dream caper:

> *I'm with a special "mission impossible" team and we're sent to a small artificial moon or asteroid. We go inside it to the control room and must drill a core sample through to the outer surface, and then insert a telescopic device, camouflage it, and get out fast. Then we must get out fast. One man has many sharp flat tools like scalpels, made of a special metal, that he reinserts into a sheath after using them. I'm on lookout and see we are being invaded from the back of the little planet — something is crawling toward us through space — and we have to prepare for an attack.*

Each of the dreams of my other-worldly mission impossible team is clandestine, sometimes in foreign countries that are actually at war, sometimes in outer space. My role as a courageous undercover operative brings me a sense of skill and adventure that is strangely fulfilling.

Join the group mind

The higher level of the mental dream zone is a world of nearly instantaneous telepathic communication. All knowledge is available and it might be safe to say that here, our minds merge into one unified group mind, or huge pool of knowing, to which we all have equal access. When your zoom lens expands to encompass the group mind, you may dream of large groups.

Patty often dreamed of a council sitting around a large oval table, with a crystal ball floating in the air in the middle. She had a permanent seat at that table, and in her dreams she'd walk into the room and sit in her chair. Then streams of light would come out of the crystal ball into the mind of each person. After that they shared their visions, though she never remembered the topic of discussion.

Jerry tells this dream:

> *I am on a large saucer-shaped UFO, standing in a circle with other people, and we are all dressed in silver jumpsuits. We are a team and are preparing to take the ship from one dimension to another by aligning the vibration of our minds. We must each achieve the exact same focus then all together we must raise the frequency of our awareness seamlessly to a very high pitch. If we succeed the spacecraft will disappear and travel the distance upward. If one person falters or doubts, the ship will explode and we will all be destroyed. I feel us doing it successfully.*

Dreams of large audiences, crowds, conferences, gatherings, conventions, or colonies of organisms can be about the group mind. Are you attending summer camp? Or a large family reunion? Are you an ant in an ant farm? You may be attuning to the group mind.

Understand broad concepts and energy dynamics

The higher level of the mental dream zone contains great knowledge, and much of it is abstract and conceptual, based on mathematical patterns and sacred geometry. You may visit this zone when you're seeding new ideas to yourself, activating the general principles, blueprint, and philosophy first at the rarified level, so over time it will trickle down and become an integrated and conscious part of your waking life. Perhaps this is how revelations and "aha's" occur to us — they began their process of unfolding in a dream.

Larry has studied with a Peruvian shaman for several years, and throughout that time, has dreamed repeatedly of an infinitely tall tree penetrating into the heavens, the branches spiraling around the trunk and progressing in what looks like a *Fibonacci ratio* (numbers beginning with 1 and 1 which are the sum of the preceding two numbers) from earth to sky. Each branch holds a platform, and on each platform lies a resting puma, sacred in Peru. Larry has contemplated this dream image deeply; to him the tree is the tree of life, or the *axis mundi,* the involutionary/evolutionary process of life. The pumas represent the power of the Great Mother, the sun, and passion — the creative, motivational life force, which must be activated at each level.

Kristin, who lives above the Arctic Circle in Norway, dreamed:

> *I am in a wide-open barren landscape with an eternal horizon and little or no vegetation. I see seven stones. They are big and very round, yet progress evenly in size from larger to smaller. They are lifting up and floating maybe one meter over the ground. In the movement there is a sound like a deep flute.*

A mental zone dream that changed the way the world perceives

Rene Descartes (1596-1650), the father of rationalist philosophy and creator of the modern idea of self, ironically, was inspired by three mystical dreams on St. Martin's Eve, 1619. The first two dreams were nightmares, in which he was blown by a whirlwind against a church, and then frightened by loud noises and awakened by sparks all around his room. Falling alseep once more, he dreamed of a book entitled *Corpus poetarium,* which he opened to the line *"Quod vitae sectabor iter?"* (What path shall I follow?) Then someone handed him some verses that began, *"Est et non...."* (Yes and no.) This book mysteriously disappeared and was replaced by a dictionary. Descartes saw the first two dreams as punishment for the sins of his past and an indication of his need for remorse. He thought the book of poets indicated he should incorporate the wisdom of the poets in his work. "Est et non" was from Pythagoras, and might signify the distinctions between truth and error in human knowledge. The dictionary at the end, to Descartes, was a symbol pointing toward the unification of all the sciences, which became the vision for his work. The sense of a higher authority behind the functioning of human reason stayed with Descartes his entire life.

Kristin's pristine dream is one embodying many elements of sacred geometry: the universal power of seven (seven colors, seven musical notes, seven chakras) and its connection to sound and its manifesting power.

Practice new perceptual skills

In the higher level of the mental dream zone, you can try out new ways of organizing your perception and practice new patterns of knowing. By the time you remember these dreams, they may be symbolized in strange ways and may not make much sense to your logical mind. But if you can recognize them, they'll give you insight about how your soul is helping you grow spiritually. Here are some samples:

> ✔ *I see R and he has a little process in his hands. It's invisible but when he moves his hands out in front of him, something happens. It's a short, neat way to get information about what's happening under the surface of things.*

> ✔ *I'm chasing a beaker with water in it around a counter and it's moving because of energy coming out of my hands. Then I cup my hands around it about two inches out, and it levitates. After that I can make my body do the same thing — floating on my stomach, I can control my rise and fall. Next, I have a calcium tablet on my left index finger and I can spin the pill clockwise and think it into my thyroid.*

> ✔ *I have to fly through a shallow band of energy that has lots of little explosions in it. A man is floating above me, watching my progress, as though this is a test of my skill. I have to stretch out flat and hold steady as I go through so I won't hit the sparks. I pass.*

> ✔ *I am given a tool by a higher being. It's invisible but I can hold it in my hands. It is supposed to help me fly straight up. I try it but my balance is off and I circle around like a boomerang and smash into the ground. He picks me back up and sets me in a certain position so I can try again. I get it right and go up like a rocket into very rarified realms. I do this several times.*

Find inspiration and spiritual awakening

As your consciousness grows more sophisticated, you may dream about receiving guidance and spiritual teachings from ascended masters or angels. You may dream about trinities and triangles, which can indicate that you are working on integrating the three aspects of awareness: body, mind, and soul, to achieve unity. You may dream about snakes, and at this level the snake represents the spiraling kundalini life force.

Suzanne had been on a spiritual path for years but was feeling out of touch with her passion and purpose. She had a powerful dream that helped her get back in touch with her deeper self.

> *I am flying across the sky, Superman style, with an angelic-looking woman. I gradually become aware of a sublime sound, a cross between New Age music and classical, yet with an extra richness. My angelic companion says simply, "Listen to the music." As I pay attention, the music appears visually before me, like a billowing cumulus cloud etched intricately with a filigree of gold lines. It grows gracefully out ahead of me as I fly, beckoning me upward. As I follow it, like the donkey with the carrot, I have the sensation of actually becoming the sound and the image. As this merger occurs, I know I'm being taught a profound lesson. Suddenly my concentration is interrupted by the staccato sound of a heavy repeating rock 'n roll beat coming from way down below. It too has a shape; it looks like short, black, vertical dashes. I become distracted by it and plummet helplessly downward. "Listen to the music," my companion reminds me. "Choose which vibration to pursue." As I shift my attention back to the higher spiritual sound, I rise gently on an ever-increasing incline and stabilize.*

Suzanne needed to commit to her own inner voice and not be so distracted by the conflicting voices of the external world. If she could concentrate on the kind of feeling she wanted to have, and actively see it and feel it in herself, the vibration of that feeling would guide and lift her into her destiny.

Use the following dream diary exercise to uncover the spiritual messages in your dreams.

Finding the Hidden Spiritual Guidance in Your Dreams

1. Look back through your dream records for the past few weeks and see if any dreams that contain a teaching about improving the way you use your mind and energy. Could a spiritual guide or teacher have been working with you to help you become aware of a new principle of consciousness?

2. Write about what you think some of your dreams might mean if they had originated from the higher levels of the group mind.

Understand mental zone symbolism

Scan your dreams for imagery and symbols that relate to the element of air and for vehicles, objects, and creatures that fly through the air, like birds, feathers, dragonflies, airplanes, balloons, rockets, or spaceships. Look for images that stick up high into the sky, like tall buildings, ladders, and towers, or things that fall from the sky, like hailstones or satellites. Watch for geometric patterns and futuristic technologies and architecture. Symbols from the mental dream zone are mathematical, neutral, oriented toward definition, measurement, knowledge, and learning, or toward inspiration and intuition. Table 8-1 presents some symbols and imagery from the lower mental zone.

Table 8-1	Symbols of the Lower Mental Level (Zone 3)
Attic, hat, headband, scarf on head	Flying close to earth
Hang-gliders, sailplanes, small airplanes, balloons	Climbing ladders or mountains
Elevator, skyscraper, tower	Something falling from the sky
High tension lines, skeletal structures	Libraries, universities, classrooms
Tape measure, ruler, hourglass, numbers	Spiderwebs, spiders, dragonflies
Air, wind, storms, hail, feathers	Caged birds
Low-flying birds: owls, crows, jays, sparrows	Spoken words, written language

Table 8-2 takes the high road for images from your higher mental levels.

Table 8-2	Symbols of the Higher Mental Level (Zone 3)
Jets, rockets, space capsules, UFOs	Lotus flower, standing snake
Spiritual masters and guides, angels	Futuristic technologies
Geometric patterns, spirals, mathematics	Flying, high above earth
High-flying birds: eagles, hawks, hummingbirds	Cities, colonies, conferences

Zone 4: Dreams of the Causal Realm

Think of the causal dream zone as a place where your individual conscious-ness and your identity as a personality fade and merge into a new kind of awareness — one where you identify yourself as "We" or "the Us." There is no duality or opposition, no conflict. All beings identify themselves here as the same self, with a common purpose. There is an awareness in the causal zone that souls experience both an individual form of oneness and a unified form of oneness; the full spectrum of self is known. Here it is accepted that souls flow down through involution into the world of form and back up through evolution to the world of spirit, as do the particles and waves of physics. At this level you see the entire picture. Here all individual life purposes are coor-dinated with each other so that each individual life helps the other individual lives, just as in nature, bees by their very existence help flowers grow and forest fires help certain seeds germinate. Here we know all is inextricable.

Align yourself with your life purpose

It is in the causal dream zone that your entire history is recorded. And so is the history of everyone else and of the planet and the solar system, both into the past and into the future. When you are born, your soul has a broad blueprint from which it works, a loose plan for your life on earth. You intend to learn a handful of life lessons, to clear yourself of interferences or stuck places that prevent you from knowing who you really are. James Redfield, author of *The Celestine Prophecy* and *The Tenth Insight,* has called this your "birth vision." He says in *The Tenth Insight,* "When we have an intuition, a mental image of a pos-sible future, we're actually getting flashes of memory of our Birth Vision, what we wanted to be doing with our lives at that particular point on our journey. . . . When something happens that is close to our original vision, we feel inspired because we recognize we are on a path of destiny that we intended all along."

Visiting the causal zone in your dreams is often for the purpose of realigning your actions, thinking, and intentions in daily life with the higher vision or plan that exists at the clearer levels of your soul so life will unfold in a harmo-nious cocreation with everyone else's.

Daniel had been a ghostwriter and editor for many years and was comfortable working behind the scenes. He was shy and really didn't like confrontation with the outside world. Yet in his dreams, Daniel repeatedly saw himself being given a check for a large amount of money, being ushered up to a podium and introduced to a group of famous people, and speaking in public dressed in an expensive suit. He was at a loss as to what these dreams were saying. None of the dream images appealed to him in the slightest! Suddenly, within two months of the dreams, Daniel was sought out by his agent; a famous author needed someone to write a handbook using the content of her popular best seller. The book would officially be "co-authored" but Daniel would write the whole thing. It was an opportunity to get his name on the cover of a book, and to receive a handsome advance. Over the next couple years, Daniel made quite a bit of money from the book, learned a great deal about the subject material he was writing about, and became an expert in his own right. He soon found himself being invited to give talks, then seminars, something he never would have thought possible. It had simply been time for Daniel to open to the next step in his life purpose, and his dreams helped him orient his mind to new possibilities.

Discover the hidden "good reasons" for your life events

Sometimes the things that happen to you seem random and senseless. But from the point of view of your soul, each experience has a purpose and is conceived to help you learn a lesson. Causal zone dreams can help you find the underlying sense in confusing, even upsetting experiences. Phoebe had struggled to hold her own against a very strong, opinionated mother throughout her childhood. They had often argued and Phoebe tried to rebel, though her mother usually triumphed in the end. When she was in her mid-thirties and on her own, Phoebe had the following dream, which helped her put her childhood in perspective:

> *I am living in the attic of a house, and I am like a prisoner. The washer and dryer are there, and Mom keeps bringing up loads of laundry for me to do. It seems all I do is work for her. I want out! I want my freedom, but she won't let me leave. As I'm protesting about my situation I suddenly see through the roof into the sky. High above I see a tribunal of three judges sitting at a long bench. "I" am standing before them, but I look different. I'm arguing with the judges about what they're telling me I need to do, refusing their advice. Suddenly, I know that I have been remanded into my mother's custody until I learn what I am supposed to learn, until I calm down and stop being difficult and "in contempt." I hear her say, "I'll do it." And I know she was chosen because she is strong and will be patient with me. In the dream I am embarrassed; I realize it's been for my own good all along and that she's not the "bad guy." She has really been serving me the whole time.*

Glimpse world events

Because all time and space are included in the causal zone, dreams originating from here often provide you with a precognitive view of coming world events and trends, though there may not be a particularly logical reason why this information comes to you. Months before the nuclear accident at Chernobyl, Syd dreamed:

> *I am with a group of people who are being given a tour of farmland and farming methods in some place like Yugoslavia or the Ukraine. We are out in the fields and I see a huge factory several miles away, coughing billows of dark smoke into the air from its chimneys. I think this pollution is terrible but then I notice the factory is swelling in size, blowing up like a balloon. I realize it's going to explode and I yell to warn everyone. People start running in every direction. I see it blow up and a huge cloud of vile-looking gas comes out and rushes forward with high velocity and great force. I know I can't outrun it, so I get down on the ground, dig a hole for my face, and try to breathe the air that's in the dirt. The poisonous cloud blows over me and I think I breathe a little of it, but I'm okay. Everyone else dies.*

Paul dreamed he was standing in the kitchen and looked out the window to the backyard. There, mounted on a scaffolding was a huge rocket. He knew it was going to launch at any moment, and he was a bit worried, not knowing whether he'd be in any danger. The rocket ignited and began to rise with a terrible sound. Then it sank right back down again and crashed, falling over, breaking apart, and catching on fire. Several days later, he happened to hear on the news that China had tried to launch a rocket but it had crashed.

See the earth's hidden history

The Akashic Records — the memory banks of the planet — contain data from every nook and cranny of the earth's surface, throughout all time. Causal zone dreams can show you scenes from history, or from the future, that may not be recorded in written form. Gary dreamed repeatedly that he was exploring and mapping a coastline, flying along the jagged edge of a vast continent. It was beautiful country, and it felt exotic somehow. When he woke, he could never figure out where it was — until one day, looking at a globe, he noticed the north coast of Russia. Looking at it from north to south instead of from south to north, he realized this was his mysterious coastline; he'd been seeing it before it was covered in ice and snow.

Witness "the light"

Expanding your zoom lens to take in the causal world often results in dreams that involve what can only be called "the Light." Though there may be no pictures connected with the Light, most people report that they are given complex revelations and deep understanding about the nature of the universe.

Lisa and her roommate Yoshie, in Tokyo, decided not to take down their Christmas tree. Instead, they changed the decorations to soft glowing cream-white lights and added crystal balls and other see-through ornaments. They turn the lights on when they're meditating or when they have special company. Lisa had a dream:

> *I am looking at the Northern Lights. It is so vast and beautiful and exciting that I think I must find Yoshie and show her. I try to call Yoshie on her cellular phone but she doesn't answer.*

In the morning, Yoshie wakes Lisa up and drags her into the living room. The crystal clear tree lights are ON and the tree is sparkling! Neither of them has touched the light switch. Both women felt they had been affected deeply by something spiritual in a way they couldn't explain.

Symbolism of the causal zone

Scan your dreams for images of light, the unified field, grids of energy, higher beings, visions of the planet, or of your own history. Even more so, notice feeling states like bliss, profound peace, relief and letting go, and spaciousness. Table 8-3 presents some symbols from the causal zone.

Table 8-3	Imagery of the Causal Zone (Zone 4)
Beings of light, religious leaders	Crystals, diamonds
Grids of light or energy	Suns, planets, galaxies
Hidden history of the earth	Your own history and life purpose
Light, northern lights, stars	The unified field
World events	Outer space, the void

Dreams of Shifting Between Zones

Part of what you do during your dreams is travel in and out through the dreams zones, focusing your zoom lens first here, and then there. As you change the focus of your conscious mind you'll remember the movements as particular kinds of dreams.

Flying dreams

If you dream of ascending, you're increasing the frequency of your conscious mind, opening the lens to take in a higher view. Are you climbing a ladder or tower, taking an elevator up to the top of a high rise, or scaling a mountain? Perhaps you're flying around about two feet above the floor in your house. As long as the symbols relate to the earth, you're probably exploring Zone 1, heading up toward Zone 2. If you dream of taking off in a small plane, cargo plane, balloon, or helicopter that doesn't go too high above the earth, or if you're riding on the back of a bird, or flying above the treetops or around high tension lines and tall buildings, you're probably exploring Zone 2 and heading toward Zone 3. If you dream you're being launched from the earth in a rocket, are flying in a jetliner, riding on a cloud, hovering in a UFO, or are an astronaut floating on a lifeline in deep space, you're probably exploring Zone 3 and ascending to Zone 4. Flying can also be a metaphor for the expression of creative energy in waking life.

Falling dreams

If you dream of descending, you're decreasing the frequency of your conscious mind, closing down your lens to focus on a tighter, more concentrated view. Depending on the symbols, you can get a sense of which level you're leaving. Is your UFO dropping through the heavens suddenly? Does your jetliner crash? Do you drive your car off a high cliff? Are you flying high, suddenly forget how to use your arms, and plummet to earth? You may be returning to normal consciousness from the causal or mental dream zones. Are you skiing down a mountain, falling from a tree or the roof of a house, falling out of bed, or tripping over a doorstep? Falling dreams with earthy symbols indicate you're coming back into your body from Zone 2 or a higher level of Zone 1.

These "reentry" dreams often cause your body to jerk and wake you up. This is called a *myclonic jerk,* and though scientists don't know why they occur, they are similar to the shudder you experience when you've been daydreaming or absent-minded and suddenly "come to" and snap back into your body again. Metaphysicians say you're coming back into your body "crooked" and the shudder is actually a realignment of your body with your higher consciousness. Full trance mediums often display these jerks as they come in and out of trance.

Contrary to folk legends and popular belief, if you hit the ground in a falling dream, you won't die.

Dreams of missing connections and getting lost

If you are in a hurry to return to your body, or if you're disturbed by something you've encountered in one of the dream zones, you may symbolize your discombobulation in a variety of ways. Perhaps you dream you're supposed to catch a certain flight home from Europe. You're late, your luggage gets routed to the wrong airline, you have to take a shuttle from the gate to the plane and almost miss it, or you've lost your passport and realize you're going to have trouble getting through customs. Ed dreamed repeatedly that he was taking the subways of New York City (where he had once lived), trying to find his way home. He'd always get on the wrong train and end up in a tunnel — the train having disappeared — crawling through dank water and garbage, looking for the exit. As you pass through the lower emotional zone, also known as the astral plane, you may encounter emotional disturbances, like a plane encounters turbulence.

The lower emotional zone is the closest thing we have to a hell realm, and it is full of monsters, pests, leeches, and out-of-balance discarnate beings. Coming back to your body involves you learning to make a smooth transition through this realm, by staying centered, maintaining the knowledge of who you really are, and proceeding steadily instead of rushing. If you remain calm, you won't attract negative attention. This is true in waking life as well.

The soul in sleep gives proof of its divine nature.

—Cicero

Your Dream Diary

1. List five "shoulds" that affect

   • The way you act with other people

   • The way you act in private

   • What you do for a living

   Write about the negative consequences your subconscious thinks underlie each, for example, *"I should be quiet. If I'm too loud, people will think I'm selfish."*

2. Pick five recent dreams and write about: If this dream were talking to me about my mental clutter, which ideas might I eliminate? If this dream were talking to me about the fixed ideas that are holding me back, what might they be?

3. Examine your recent dreams for puns, exaggeration, and opposite meanings. Write about the hidden meanings you find.

4. Imagine you're a famous (painter, sculptor, dancer, architect, musician) with no creative blocks. Write a stream of consciousness dream sequence involving your creative genius as if you are them. What do you learn about the creative process?

5. List your three most pressing questions. Imagine that a guide, teacher, animal, or historical figure from the higher mental zone comes and gives you advice. Write out your dialogue.

6. Look through your recent dreams and write about the different types of Zone 3 and 4 dreams. How much are you focusing on the subconscious mind? On the superconscious? How many dreams are mental? Causal?

7. Make up five parallel realities and personas. Write a paragraph or two on each, describing what you look like, what you're doing, who your friends are colleagues are, and how you feel.

Chapter 9

Dreaming While Awake

• •

In This Chapter

▶ Recognizing your waking dreams and omens

▶ Working with time: Déjà vu, synchronicity, and coincidence

▶ Trusting daydreams, flashes, fantasies, and preoccupations

▶ Waking up while you're awake: Lucid dreams, mindfulness, sleep walking

• •

Our task is to listen to the news
that is always arriving out of silence.

—Rainer Maria Rilke

*Y*our soul is dreaming your waking world into existence, and no Hollywood director can rival its mastery over plot, detail, imagination, dialogue, split-second timing, special effects, and dramatic scenarios. When you need a wake-up call or a clue to a new direction, your soul can get through even the densest states of depression, boredom, distraction, and stubbornness. At night, this force directs you to have certain kinds of dreams, to cycle through the dream zones in a particular order, then to remember the dreams you need to know consciously each day. During the day, this mysterious force inside you guides your perception; it causes you to notice some things and not others. This selective attention and inattention fills your life with meaning and lets you flow from one set of meanings to another.

In this chapter, I focus on the kinds of dreamlike experiences that occur during the day and how you can recognize and interpret the hidden messages contained in ordinary experience. Your days are filled with omens, coincidences, fantasies, and daydreams — all chock full of clues about living more authentically and creatively. During the day, watch what captures your attention; your soul is directing you like an actor in a movie.

Watching the Movie of Your Waking Dreams

Though life itself is a dream, there are certain periods when your mundane experience seems especially dreamlike, as though underlined with a yellow highlighter. Normal everyday events take on extra significance and seem to be "adding up to something." You notice repeating themes, and images or numbers follow you around. Life seems to be tapping on your shoulder with coincidences. A message wants to break through. Are you watching and listening?

This kind of heightened life experience happened to me a few years ago. Here's the sequence of things I noticed and how I made sense of it: I am in Tokyo, working. The economy is not good. I hear a story about three CEO's of failed Japanese corporations who checked into a hotel together and shot themselves, leaving suicide notes, not to their families, but to their employees. Someone tells me about a new book — something like The Ten Best Places in Japan to Commit Suicide. A Japanese pop star kills himself and several million teenagers wail and weep in public. Next, there are two strong earthquakes; oddly, I am alone, quiet, and alert for both and sense a watery quality to the energy under the concrete city.

My clients are nervous and distracted, focusing on materialistic questions instead of their inner lives. Three clients fall on the same step in the hotel lobby; my interpreter is on crutches. At a seminar I give jointly with a Japanese spiritual teacher, she says that in the Chinese astrology system she studies, this is called the "time when the earth becomes watery and people fall and hit their heads." She herself has fallen just the week before. All this cultural "shuddering" makes me remember the sign, new this year, in Immigration at Narita Airport: "Welcome to Japan. Have a nice stay. Please follow the rules." Toward the end of my stay, nuclear tests are set off in the Middle East. I wonder if people have been sensing the precursor "event waves" of these explosions, and have been thrown off balance as a result.

My first week home, I see five clients in a row who are suicidal, two of my father's friends die, and a young man I know dies. On top of that, every clock and watch I own, even in my computer, stops! I dream I'm on a boat in the Atlantic and far to the west I see a nuclear blast. The ocean starts rocking with huge, steep waves and a voice says, "Hold on and ride it out!" When I wake, I receive an insight that the real nuclear explosions have affected the energy of the planet, and we are all feeling a subliminal disturbance. Many upsetting events are still to come (stock market crash, political scandal, genocidal war, school massacres, the death of heroes).

When I ask what this string of related omens means, my inner voice says it is difficult now to hold secure ideas of identity; our egos are dying. Sometimes, when the ego starts to die, we think we are dying. Then we're tempted to kill ourselves, like the Japanese CEOs who so thoroughly identified with their jobs that, when their companies failed, they saw their own lives as over. It is important now, my voice says, to be fluid in my thought processes. If I try to move forward in old, habitual, unconscious ways, I will fall. I am to examine myself now for any areas where I might be holding too tightly to outdated ideas of self. The message is: "Stop. Let go. Stay centered and in balance. Ride it out."

My real life buildup of "noticings" became a kind of elaborate dream sequence spanning nearly a month, eventually crystallizing in a sleep dream that included a specific piece of advice. After that I was left to watch the waves crest and crash across the world in the subsequent months, as my dream had accurately depicted, without getting caught up in the fear myself.

Find messages in ordinary life events

As a teacher of perception and intuition, I find knowing about underlying trends and shifts of energy both interesting and useful, since it helps me counsel people. I have to assume that because my soul can't send me an e-mail or call on the phone, it notifies me of an upcoming period of shakeups with whatever messengers are available — a conversation here, a repeating theme there, an omen here, a flashy dream there. Your soul will do the same thing. What doesn't get through to you in your sleep dreams will certainly find its way through the events of ordinary life.

A *waking dream* is usually a short series of perceptions tied together in a quirky, attention-getting way. The perceptions are characterized by a special psychic weight, as though some part of your awareness makes a point to mark the page on which they appear. Sometimes just one *omen* is involved. For example, suppose that you go to your local supermarket. Thereby the entrance you see a mountain man leading a black and white alpaca loaded high with camping and food supplies. The pair is so out of context in suburbia that they seem like a symbol in a dream. Can't you hear yourself telling your friend about your latest "dream"? *"And then I decided to go to the market and as I tried to go in, a mountain man with wild hair and a huge beard and an ALPACA in a colorful bridle and backpacks came up to me. I thought the alpaca might bite me but the man just said, 'You need more adventure in life!'"* Except that it's not a dream; it happened in your waking life.

Omens can be dramatic or subtle. They can be "ominous" and convey a sense of forboding, or they can be upbeat, making you laugh and open your heart with positive anticipation. Here are examples of some dramatic omens:

- ✔ You're not sure you should go out with your old lover again, and the day before your date, your car's clutch breaks and you can't drive.
- ✔ You look out in your backyard and a hawk is sitting on your lawn chair staring straight at you.

- You meet a prospective business partner who supposedly has a great track record but you have mixed feelings. Driving home from the meeting with him, a rock hits your windshield and cracks it in a huge sunburst, at a spot that's directly between your eyes.

- You've been criticized for being insensitive. You come out in the early morning to go for a jog and a three delicate spotted fawns cross your path. They're not afraid of you.

- Your sink, dishwasher, and toilet back up and overflow. The plumber can't make it until tomorrow.

- You find a dead raccoon in your driveway. The next day a robin flies into your plate glass window and dies.

After you can recognize the dramatic omens, you may want to turn your attention to the more ordinary scenes from life, for even these can be used to find deeper meaning. Here are some examples of more subtle omens — signs that don't whack you over the head, but which do capture your attention:

- A turquoise dragonfly lands on your arm and stays there for a minute.

- You break a tooth.

- You notice the word "Mozart" on an automobile license, a bumper sticker, and the side panel of a minivan as you drive an hour to see a friend.

- You're worried about a decision you have to make. A man steps onto an elevator you're taking, makes an offhand funny comment that answers your question, and then gets off at the next floor.

- You're driving to an appointment but have forgotten to bring the directions. You're 90 percent of the way there, but for one last right-hand turn. Is it here? The next block? You approach the intersection hesitatingly and as you're deciding whether to turn, a commercial on the radio says, "Go straight to MacDowell's!" You go straight, and sure enough, recognize the name on the next street corner.

- You catch yourself humming a song and realize the lyrics are the answer to a problem you've been chewing on.

Within the space of one day, you may notice an article in the newspaper about arbitration that helped a peace effort, then hear a snippet of conversation in the hall at work about how unfair a manager has been, then break three fingernails on your right hand, then have a misunderstanding with the waitress at lunch and leave her a tiny tip, then have a colleague take an opportunity away from you, and then see two tiny children hugging each other on the sidewalk as your car is stopped at a light. What has your soul been "dreaming" that day? Perhaps you're looking at ways to resolve conflict within yourself, ways to break your old habits of victimization, defensiveness, and being a crusader. If the day's experience had been a dream, what might the message be? Perhaps the answer is to reconnect with the innocence of the child, see with the child's purity, and express the child's easy affection.

Here are some other examples of what subtle omens may be telling you:

- ✔ You look at the digital clock just when the numbers reflect your month and day of birth. Your soul may be saying: "Be fresh, be new, be reborn right now!"

- ✔ You're gardening and notice that a type of plant you haven't had for two years has suddenly "volunteered" and come back to life amidst other newcomers. Your soul may be saying: "There are parts of you too that can spring back to life when you least expect it."

- ✔ A hummingbird unexpectedly buzzes past your ear, vibrating your whole head. Your soul may be saying: "Your thoughts need to raise up in frequency now. Think about what inspires you."

You can know how to interpret the omens you see by the way your body immediately responds to them. If your body energy contracts, gets a knot in the solar plexus, feels cold, numb, leaden, rocklike, or tends to back away from the idea, this is an *anxiety signal,* and the omen is telling you to pay attention to something that is either dangerous, or reminds you of a subconscious fear. If your body energy expands, feels warm, bubbly, tingly, enthusiastic, glowing, calm, aligned, and tends to lean toward the idea, this is a *truth signal,* and the omen is telling you to pay attention to something that will lead to greater love, creativity, freedom, and truth.

The following sections describe the steps you can take to recognize and interpret your waking dreams.

Step 1: Recognize the omens that appear for you

The first step in recognizing your waking dreams is to become aware of the signs and omens that seek you out. When you notice one, validate it by describing it out loud to yourself, sharing it with someone else, or writing it in your dream diary. You might keep a list in the back of your dream diary: "My Daily Omens."

Try the following dream diary writing exercise.

What Captures Your Attention?

1. Starting today, and for the next few days, make a list of the things you see, hear, smell, and feel that stand out to you or seem memorable or odd in some way. What are the punctuation marks in your day?

2. List the experiences that stop you in your tracks, make you reconsider, make time slow down, help you reconnect with your center, or provide a sense of relief. What symbols are associated with these experiences?

3. List the things that cause you to feel tense, agitated, frustrated, restless, impulsive, righteous, angry, or vengeful. What symbols are associated with these experiences?

4. List the things you do suddenly, ideas that come to you out of the blue, the reasons you reverse or change direction during the day, the people who unexpectedly come to mind or actually show up.

5. List the unexpected, surprising things that happen to you.

6. List scenes, symbols, words, or themes that have been repeating. What stands out to you? Does an isolated sentence from a conversation in a restaurant drift your way? Do you smell lavender for no reason while working at your computer? Do you notice a child holding a wiggly puppy? Do you see a lot of people dressed in red? The things that stop you in your tracks contain power. Perhaps you heard a radio interview with a famous older woman writer that nearly made you cry. Or something a friend said made you rethink one of your recent behaviors.

Watch for the punctuating moments that cause you to drop into your experience more deeply. These things contain messages. When you notice the presence of disturbing emotions near the surface, watch for the images and symbols connected to the experiences. Is your wife, boss, dog, child, body image, or car involved? When you take a sudden action, have a sudden thought, or when a person shows up suddenly in your reality, your soul is usually speaking, cutting through the usual linear, step-by-step process of living. For example, you get up from your desk for no reason, having decided that you *must* go copy some documents *right now.* And at the copy center, you meet a stranger who says something that helps solve a problem you've had for weeks.

When images, words, or numbers repeat, especially three times, pay attention. There is either a message in the repeating item, or the repetition is alerting you to the fact that something important is about to happen.

Step 2: Connect the omen with your issue

After you get used to noticing omens, the next step is to relate the omen to whatever is relevant in your life. The omen occurs in the outer world because there is a parallel issue in your inner world that needs dealing with.

A correlation always exists between your inner world, your outer world, and your dream world, because life is continuous. If something happens in one of the worlds, you can be sure it is simultaneously happening in a parallel way in all the others. Just like the musical note C can be expressed as high C, middle C, and low C, so can insights and lessons. Use your intuition and ask yourself: What might this omen symbolize? Of the things I'm currently mulling over in my life, which one might this omen pertain to? What might the message be? Then take the first impressions and insights you get. For example:

- ✔ Everyone seems to be dressed in red today: *I need to stimulate my vital energy and be a bit more upbeat and aggressive.*

- ✔ A crow sits on my fence a caws at me loudly for twenty minutes while I'm weeding the garden: *There is an urgent message my inner voice would like to deliver to me but I haven't been listening. I need to take time to meditate and write in my journal this afternoon.*

- ✔ My car's right front tire goes flat: *I need to look at whether I want to move forward in the way I thought I needed to. I might be afraid of something, or it might not be the correct choice. Maybe I need to wait for more information.*

- ✔ I have to have a tooth pulled: *I should examine my ideas about being powerful and helpless in the world. Am I feeling overwhelmed by circumstances beyond my control? Maybe I need to ask for help.*

- ✔ My VCR won't rewind or fast forward: *I'm supposed to pay attention to the present moment and not get too far ahead of myself or behind.*

Step 3: Connect a series of omens

After you start noticing the signs and beginning to grasp their meaning, the next step is to begin stringing them together into a bread crumb trail that will lead you to a deeper insight. A series of omens may begin with the repetition of a theme. In the story I share at the beginning of this chapter, I first noticed several reports pertaining to suicide within a short period of time. If I'd heard only one, I might not have given it as much weight. Next, several earthquakes occurred in the space of one week. Concurrently, I noticed people falling, heard stories of people breaking a leg, and someone near me was on crutches. I had an insight about the earth being watery that was reinforced only days later by the Japanese teacher. After that, the nuclear explosions led me to sense there were waves, not of water, but *like water,* that might be moving through us energetically. A picture, a larger puzzle, was being assembled. I needed to give it time to reveal the bigger view.

Sarita tells of an episode where a string of omens played out in her life. She had been feeling stuck for a while, and wondered how to pry herself out of some old habits that had become too comfortable and were holding her back. One night she dreamed:

A man is driving me somewhere. We come to a fork in the road and he wants to take the right fork, which is a new direction. I look ahead and see that farther down this road a skunk is spraying voluminously into the environment. I tell the driver about this and he says, "Do you want me to take the original road instead?" I say, "No, I don't mind the smell of skunk." And we proceed down the new road.

In the next few weeks, Sarita's life began to go haywire. Plans fell through, people betrayed her and misinterpreted her motivations, opportunities came and went in a single day, she had sudden setbacks and financial burdens, and she got sick. During this time, her dreams evaporated, replaced by sleep disturbances. Sarita's waking reality seemed to have become her dream life. It was full of highly symbolic events. Her car didn't pass its smog test and was labeled a "gross polluter." Her doctor found a problem with her thyroid. There was a miscommunication and emotional upset with a major client. It took two months of this before Sarita remembered her dream, and that she had agreed to take the new road in spite of the "skunk" fouling the air. She realized this was her soul's way of getting her out of her old habits. She needed to face some of the fears from her subconscious mind before a new level of creativity could emerge.

Step 4: Connect the omen with a sleep dream

In most waking dream sequences, where you play "connect the dots" with a series of omens, sooner or later a sleep dream will occur to help punctuate or make sense of the highlighted process. In my Japan experience, the dream came at the end and delivered a message that gave me some guidance. In Sarita's experience, described in the preceding step, the dream came at the beginning and helped her prepare for, and later make sense of, an upcoming period of difficulty and chaos.

Carol recently dreamed:

I have a new house on a cliff overlooking the ocean. I'm happy because I can have my friends over and they can just walk down to enjoy the beach. I put up a sign on the path up from the beach: "This way to my house." Then I notice that lots of strangers are finding my house, coming up from the beach and in from the main road. I go inside and there are people I don't know in my bedroom! I'm going to have to get down there and tape off the entrance and put up a NO TRESPASSING sign.

When Carol and I talked, I told her that the dream was a good reminder about having clear boundaries and not letting people you don't know into your intimate spaces. She said "Of course! I actually just finished reading a book called *How to Say No.* And I've been craving privacy lately." Then she "happened" to mention that she'd just had an automatic garage door installed and was having fun using her new automatic opener, bringing her car in off the street. She thought it was odd that in her whole life she'd never had an automatic garage door, and now she had really wanted one for some reason. I said, "It's totally parallel with your dream — you're focusing on being clear about your possessions, your private space, and your safety." Suddenly Carol saw the stream of connectedness between her sleep dream and her waking dream; it was all in pursuit of the experience of having it be okay to have her own personal space be the way *she* wanted it.

Step 5: Connect the omen to the future

After you practice recognizing omens and waking dreams, you will get a sense that some of them relate to something that is coming in your future. By continuing to pay attention even after you think the waking-dream sequence has completed, you'll understand the true depth of the way your soul is directing you.

Becky had been keeping a journal, working on opening her intuition. As she began paying attention to what was going on under the surface, her life started to change at "warp speed." Becky was in the habit of taking care of everyone in her family — to the point of obsession at times. She was beginning to think there should be more to life, more freedom, and other kinds of creativity, but she didn't know how to change her ways. About this time she dreamed she was in the hospital and couldn't even get out of bed to go to the bathroom because she was so tired.

The stage was set. Enter Becky's soul, to give her a wake-up call she couldn't ignore. The day before Christmas, Becky was frantically preparing to have the relatives over for Christmas dinner. She wanted everything to be perfect. Suddenly her appliances started to break down. The food processor jammed and broke a blade. Her vacuum burned up. The light in her stove went out, and it was the last straw when her dishwasher backed up and spewed gallons of dirty water all over the kitchen. She was inundated with emotion and felt overwhelmed with helplessness. Vaguely, she realized there was a message in all this. It was time to let *herself* be assisted. But she couldn't stop. Immediately after the holidays, Becky came down with a severe case of the flu and was incapacitated for the next nine weeks! Her doctor assigned her to strict bed rest and forbade her to do housework or to drive. In spite of the warnings, she felt guilty and tried to go back to her normal life. She ended up having to be taken to the emergency room and spent a few days recuperating in the hospital. As she lay there, exhausted, she remembered her dream. The whole scenario had played out, and Becky was finally able to let go.

Validating That You've Been Here Before: Déjà Vu

June had been looking for a job for nearly six months. At last she found a position at a small design studio, with people she liked. The atmosphere was cozy, and she was tremendously relieved to end her six strained months of unemployment. One day she was hanging up her coat in the office closet, and turned to see a blonde colleague standing bent over her drafting table, phone cradled between neck and shoulder. Instantly, June had a powerful feeling of familiarity. She had seen this entire scene before! She had lived it exactly — hanging up her coat, turning, seeing the blonde woman. And all at once she had a vague sense that she had dreamed the scene.

June was experiencing a phenomenon called *déjà vu,* which literally means "already seen." Déjà vu usually occurs during absolutely mundane moments, when you least expect it, and the feeling is that your outer reality is lining up with something you've already experienced. Many people connect that previous experience to a dream, though they never consciously remembered it in the first place.

What's really happening? I believe that part of the reason we all visit the causal zone in our sleep dreams is to check in with the collective consciousness so that our life purpose and actions remain in alignment with everyone else's. While we're focused at that broad view, understanding our interrelatedness with all other people, we test out various probabilities and action paths, seeing which one will best serve the purposes of all who need to be involved. In some ways, this is like having many parallel realities existing simultaneously.

For example, June's goal may be to find a job that lets her develop her technical skill, but there may be ten possible ways that result might manifest. In the causal dream zone, she may have experienced, or "dreamed" all of them. By the time her physical reality actually happens, only one of the options fits perfectly for all the participants. As it occurs, sometimes the memory of the causal plane "test run" bleeds through and matches up seamlessly with the actuality. So déjà vu, I believe, really is a causal zone dream being recalled — two levels of your reality are matching up.

James R. Lewis, in *The Dream Encyclopedia* (published by Visible Ink Press, 1995), reports a poll showing that 67 percent of Americans experience déjà vu. It has also been shown that more women than men experience the phenomenon. But why does déjà vu occur when it does? The next time it happens to you, see if you can pinpoint the central theme underlying the experience. This may have some significance to your life. June's experience revolved around feeling secure and welcome in an environment that would allow her to express herself. When you experience déjà vu, let it become an opportunity for you to connect with your soul. Say to yourself, "A higher part of me set this experience up for me because it's just right. I'm on purpose. All is well."

Paying Attention When Time Slips and Slides

Your sleep dreams are fun because they offer you an experience of increased freedom, and less restriction by the inexorable law of cause and effect. In your dreams you can think something into existence instantly, or be a shape-shifter who can change from a person to a gorilla to a tree to a crystalline pyramid to a baby. But occasionally, daily reality takes on just a tad of the same fluidity, and when it does, it astounds us.

Take note of time warps

Life-as-dream becomes most evident when you are able to keep your conscious mind centered inside your body on the crosshairs of the here-and-now. When you're entirely present in the moment, linear time seems to stop and the higher realms of the soul, or the dream zones, become accessible and their knowledge available for immediate use. When you're not centered in the present moment, your mind is probably projecting into the future or the past, and you've no doubt forgotten all about your body.

If your conscious mind projects into the future, time will seem to speed up and you'll "get ahead of yourself." Then you'll feel pressured, rushed, anxious, and impulsive. Life will seem slower than you. So if you're experiencing not having enough time, or being chronically late, you're probably living in the future. On the other hand, if your mind projects into the past and reminisces about the "good old days," or bemoans the way it was, time will slow down and you'll probably feel unprepared for life, and "behind the times." Life will seem faster than you. You may experience having too much time on your hands.

Either of these distortions of your experience of time indicate that you're missing the dream boat. . . . If you experience snags or feel the need to use too much will power in the flow of your life, your conscious mind is probably ahead or behind the present moment. When you aren't centered, your soul can't get through to you accurately.

Be aware when time collapses

If you're living in the moment, following your passion, and being authentic, you'll probably have the same experience you did as a child when you lost yourself in play. Concentrate on anything you love, and you lose track of time. Hours fly by. All you remember is that the experience felt "real." When you become aware that you have joined your reality so thoroughly that time seems nonexistent, your soul is able to communicate and act *as you*. By paying attention to these moments, when your conscious mind fills with superconscious knowing, more of your waking life can take on that magical quality of the waking dream.

Try the following dream diary writing exercise.

Increasing Your "Real" Experiences

1. Think back to your childhood and remember the activities you were naturally drawn into, the ways you preferred to spend your time. Remember how it felt when you partook of those involvements and how time seemed nonexistent. Make a list of those activities and describe the nuances of what you did and what fascinated you.

2. List the activities that have absorbed you similarly in subsequent years, and what you find totally fascinating today. Write about the benefits of what you receive from doing each thing.

Oracles and omens in ancient Greece

In ancient times, before people became too rational — before we all "went up into our heads" and started worshipping science and technology — people were much more unified with nature. We lived in our bodies, truly immersed in the physical world, and didn't perceive ourselves as separate from and controlling nature, so much as interacting smoothly with it. So the idea of looking to the collective, macroscopic natural world for rhythms, signs, and omens that would indicate the microscopic rhythms and actions in our individual lives was not far-fetched at all. Life was seamlessly interconnected. The natural world *was* our bigger self. What happened at the larger level would also happen at the smaller level. Thus was the art of divination and augury born.

Whether it was seeing patterns in the way bones scattered when they were tossed on the ground, or looking to the skies to interpret the activity of clouds or birds, or placing special importance on the behavior of snakes, frogs, or lions, our ancestors understood the power of omens. Zeus is said to have released two eagles, one from the east and one from the west, and where they intersected, he threw the Sacred Stone, or omphalos. The intersection occurred at a site on Mt. Parnassus, which eventually became the Oracle of Delphi, thereafter known as the navel of the earth. Parnassus, by the way, was the inventor of the art of telling the future from the flight of birds.

Get the message from coincidence and synchronicity

The dreamlike quality of life is nowhere more apparent than in the experience of *coincidence.* You think of a friend you haven't talked to in five years and call her. She says, "Oh, my gosh — I just *dreamed* about you last night!" Your thoughts of each other coincided. She occurred in your world and you in hers, simultaneously, out of the blue.

In her book, *The Purpose of Your Life* (published by Eagle Brook, 1998), Carol Adrienne defines *synchronicity,* a term first used by psychologist Carl Jung, as "an apparently chance encounter that nevertheless seems cosmically orchestrated." She says synchronicities "strike the participants as special, unexpected, or unexplainable by normal cause-and-effect rationales. The effect of a synchronicity on the psyche is to trigger an awareness that maybe a greater — or even a divine — purpose is at work."

Here are some examples of synchronicities:

- ✔ Your usual table is taken at the breakfast place you go to on Saturday morning and the hostess asks if you'd like to sit at the counter. You end up talking to a man sitting next to you who gives you information you've needed about what plants will do well along the shady side of your house.

- ✔ You can't remember what you dreamed last night. You turn on the television to a news show, and an actor is testifying at a hearing about an important social issue. Suddenly you remember you dreamed about that actor. The issue he's discussing relates symbolically a personal issue of yours.

- ✔ You are thinking about a problem as you drive to work. Should you listen to your husband or your boss? You look ahead and the vanity license plate on the car in front of you says, "C4YRSLF."

I had a powerful experience of synchronicity several years ago which convinced me of the importance of being deeply comfortable with the important decisions I needed to make. I had lost the organizer for my work in Japan and had made contact with a young man who was starting a consciousness institute in Tokyo. We corresponded and though my mind recited a list of the benefits of working with him, my body was distinctly uncomfortable. I sensed the young man was inexperienced and perhaps too mild-mannered to promote me successfully.

As we made plans, I developed more anxiety. I began to feel a contraction in my chest like a heart attack. I knew something was wrong, and decided I'd be willing to cancel my plans with him and lose the hefty plane fare I'd paid for, if I continued to have the heart contractions over the next couple days.

Literally an hour after I made my decision, I got a fax from a woman I'd done a reading for three years earlier. "When are you coming to Japan?" she queried. I faxed back and described my current situation. She responded immediately, saying, "Three years ago you told me I should start my own business and do public relations work. So I have! I'd be more than happy to set up a program for you. What do you need?"

Here was an enthusiastic, bilingual person with fantastic communication skills who knew my work! Plans shifted smoothly, and the young man ended up helping her. Later, when I told this story to the woman, she said, "I don't know why, but one afternoon I had a strong thought, "Contact Penney now! I didn't know why I was doing it but I guess we really are all connected!" I clearly saw that when I came from a place of deep inner truth, reality magically lined up to create a win-win situation for everyone.

Acting on Instinct and Intuition

Are you getting the idea of how it feels when your soul sneaks through and affects the quality of your waking reality? Appropriate action, natural timing, effortless "win-win" problem solving, and self-fulfillment are always available.

You may notice the quality of the waking dream in one other way, and that is when you find yourself acting suddenly, directly, without forethought. You "come to" in the midst of an action you don't recall beginning, and discover a wisdom in play that you can't take all the credit for. You might call this "direct action" or instinctive living. What's important about these kinds of experiences is that your inner critic, your subconscious emotional and mental blocks, is not interfering in the slightest with what you're doing. You are aligned perfectly with your body. Here are some examples:

✔ You are working around the house and suddenly decide to go to a drugstore across town — not the one three blocks away — to get a spiral notebook, which you don't really need. You jump in the car and when you get there, run into a person you haven't seen in ten years.

✔ You look down and notice your left hand is rubbing your upper right arm. As you become more aware you notice how much pain you're experiencing in that spot. You'd been oblivious while your body has been busy healing itself.

✔ You're browsing in a bookstore and see a book you know you need to buy, though you're not interested in the topic. Two days later a friend mentions he's having a problem — and you know the book is for him.

✔ You head out for dinner, having a nice little Mexican restaurant in mind. But when you arrive at the intersection where you should turn left, your car drives straight on through as though it has its own mind. That's okay — there's a Chinese place over this way, you think. But at the next juncture, traffic prevents you from changing to the appropriate lane. You continue, realizing it's probably the Italian restaurant downtown you want. As you park the car and start toward the restaurant, you notice a cozy little cafe down the block you've never seen before, and as you do, your body perks up with enthusiasm.

Try this moving meditation to wake up your body awareness.

Walking from Instinct

1. Begin anywhere — inside or outside. Stand and become alert, yet relaxed. Don't fix your attention on anything. Notice everything around you in a full circle.

2. When you feel the urge, let yourself begin to move. Let your body experience the natural shape of the surroundings, using all your senses. Do not describe your experience to yourself.

3. As you pass by the protruding corner of a hallway and change directions, notice the different impressions the old and new space make on you. Feel the impact of the sharp line of a corner or fence coming toward you.

4. As you walk, notice what your back is aware of. Can you feel an object in back of you when it's ten feet away, five feet away, one foot away? Let yourself feel simultaneous attraction toward and repulsion from objects and directions. Your body knows what to do. Where does the movement itself want to go? If you're walking down a busy street, notice how your body responds to people passing by, to mailboxes, lampposts, store fronts. Keep moving, at differing paces, going any direction you want, until you come to a stop. Notice what's there.

Part of living from instinct and intuition is achieving the state of "flow," described by Mihaly Csikszentmihalyi in his book *Flow: The Psychology of Optimal Experience* (published by HarperPerennial, 1991) as the "state of mind when consciousness is harmoniously ordered, and (people) want to pursue whatever they are doing for its own sake." He says that eventually actions and feelings come into alignment and "the separate parts of the life will fit together — and each activity will 'make sense' in the present, as well as in view of the past and of the future. In such a way it is possible to give meaning to one's entire life."

Trusting Your Daydreams

Just as you alternate between waking and sleeping awareness, you also alternate between a tight focus and a softer, looser one during the day. One moment you're adding up the tab for lunch and figuring the tip, and the next you're "spaced out," daydreaming about what you're going to do this weekend when you finally get some time to yourself.

Daydreams and fantasies are an important part of your daily process. Not only does this dip into the world of imagination fuel your creativity, it also helps you test out possible solutions to problems and experience various paths of action. Daydreaming rejuvenates your awareness in many of the same ways that sleep does, and also provides momentary relief from overly linear, goal-oriented mental activity, allowing for serendipitous, sudden insight. You probably know that feeling of trying to find your lost car keys, or develop an innovative angle for an ad campaign, or write the first few sentences for a talk you're going to give — and as long as you keep pushing, nothing comes. Yet as soon as you take the pressure off and turn your attention to more "frivolous" things, your keys and the answers you need pop up in front of you.

Find the deeper truths in your fantasies

Research shows that we normally daydream about one to two hours each day.

Just as with all other dreams, daydreams and fantasies can contain subconscious or superconscious material. You're sitting in a business meeting and people have gone off on tangents that don't interest you. Suddenly someone asks you a question and you realize you haven't heard anything for the past seven minutes — instead, you've been fantasizing about playing tennis, actually feeling yourself doing better than ever on your serve and backhand.

When your awareness jumps into a seemingly meaningless fantasy, there's always a good reason. Why is the deeper part of you concerned about practicing your tennis game? What might getting really good at tennis teach you about yourself and life? Maybe achieving a flow state in that physical activity will carry over into the new project you've taken on at work, and help you become a better manager.

You may also use your daydreams to access and process information from your subconscious mind. Perhaps your girlfriend had just told you she can't have dinner with you because she has plans with some new friends. Your mind dives into a negative scenario, envisioning her meeting a new man, being seduced by his charm, and eventually abandoning you. You're a wreck for the next two days. Maybe you need to examine your self-confidence.

People have a tendency to gloss over their daydreams and reduce their importance. Yet the content of your fantasies, the ideas you are preoccupied with, the very flow of your consciousness from one idea to the next, has a sanity and a cohesion that is important to uncover. Ask yourself continually throughout the day: "Why am I thinking about this now? What am I trying to tell myself? What triggered the thoughts I'm having now, and what's the common thread?"

Let your flashes and visions pop through

When your mind shifts from a tight to a soft focus, you may feel forgetful or absent-minded, but this movement also opens you to sudden intuitive insights, flashes of understanding, creative bursts, and full-blown visions. These kinds of waking dreams seem to insert themselves suddenly into your conscious mind. Here are some examples:

- ✔ You're talking to someone at a party and as you listen, the person's face suddenly seems overlaid with the image of a hawk's head. You think, "I wonder if this person has a hidden aggressive side. . ."

- ✔ You've been writing a poem and can't find the next phrase. A couple words pop into your head that don't relate to anything you've been writing. You hesitatingly write them down. Suddenly a beautiful phrase comes that ties the first part of the poem to a much greater point, all based on the contribution of the odd words.

- ✔ A friend has been talking about changing her life direction and your mind wanders to the same theme. Suddenly you see yourself in a small house with a view of a lake, and you know you're teaching at a local college. The details and feelings are crystal clear. The vision prompts you to explore teaching opportunities in other parts of the country.

Make use of dreams that come in meditation

Many people experience spontaneous dreamlike visions when they meditate. Quieting and centering your mind prepares you to receive clear messages from your soul, which often come in visual form. Michael was meditating one evening and saw a quick flash of himself sitting there meditating. In that fraction of a second he could see a large, orange-yellow flame burning brightly up from his lower abdomen through his torso, ending a foot above his head. The scene was peaceful, and after a few short moments the image dissolved. He finished his meditation and retired for the night. "The next morning," he says, "as I entered my office building, I passed a woman whose clothes looked dowdy and askew. I thought, 'This person needs help with her wardrobe!' Immediately, the image of me sitting in meditation from the night before came back into my mind's eye. This time, the flame was the size of a thimble. I knew right away that this had to do with my judgment of the woman's appearance. I said to myself, 'This person's clothing has nothing to do with her spiritual worth or who she really is.' With that, the flame shot back up and out the top of my head."

Waking Up While You're Awake

I believe that all people are meant to learn, grow, create, and evolve. To do this, you need to develop habits that let you be fully awake to the wonders of life. The following sections describe practices that enable you to live life as fully and richly as possible.

Develop the art of paying attention

Mindfulness practice is about being awake and alert in the moment. You can enter the present moment and place your attention consciously on, then in, your experience, without needing to *do* anything, without commenting about what's happening. Just be involved in existence. Just notice, just feel, just include, just appreciate existence as it's occurring. As you do, life will reveal layer upon layer of hidden meaning to you — meaning that is always there if we but merge with it. If you let it, the moment will educate you as you join it, and give itself to you, nurture, love, and embrace you. As you pay close attention, the thing you're paying attention to will seem to notice you. You have called it to life. You can "meditate" all day, eyes open, as you're involved in meetings, or going out to lunch, or even having an argument.

Live a life of inquiry

Our minds are meant to ask millions questions and answer them; therefore, it's helpful to make an art form of asking questions. Every dream, every person, and every event contains questions and answers. So, make a habit of inquiring about life. Ask yourself: "Why did I narrowly escape that serious accident on the highway today? " "What is the meaning of the daydream I had just now?" "What's the real reason behind my string of dominating girlfriends?" "What is the message in the barn owl's hoot?" "Why did six people break appointments with me this week?" Every experience can be seen as symbolic of a more fundamental reality, or lesson, or message. Contemplation, examination, and seeking: These are actually your active relationship with the unknown, which is your soul.

Waking Up Inside a Dream

Just as you can maintain your conscious awareness in an out-of-body experience, you can also take your conscious mind into dreams with you. When this happens, you feel awake while you're dreaming, yet you know the rules of your reality are different.

Experience lucid dreams

When you become aware that you are dreaming, you're experiencing a *lucid dream*. Lucid dreams often occur as the result of a nightmare, like when you dream you're being chased and reach a peak of fear, and then suddenly you say to yourself, "Oh, but this is only a dream! I don't need to be afraid, I can wake up or change the way this is going." Sometimes the "I'm dreaming" message is more subtle. Dorothy dreamed she was sitting at a table telling her mother about the dream she'd just had, and together they analyzed it. Often it is an anomaly like this that cues the dreamer to realize that lucidity is just a step away. When you are aware of a dream you had in a dream, you are experiencing what psychologist Patricia Garfield calls the *prelucid state.* These are dreams in which you suspect you're dreaming. You may actually ask yourself in the dream, "Am I dreaming?" You may comment about part of the dream you're having: "The last time I dreamed about this location, it was night and I couldn't see as much." You may even dream about your dream diary, thinking you've awakened, turned on the light, and are recording your dream. Garfield says on one such occasion she experienced a *false awakening,* in which she suspected something, reached out her hand, and actually rapped on the top of her nightstand. It seemed solid. She was surprised in the morning when she discovered the entire experience had been a dream. In false awakenings, you may dream you wake up and try all manner of ways to prove that what you're experiencing is really real, and then you may wake up again — still within the dream state — to yet another dream you think is real.

Sleepwalking and sleeptalking

When people walk and talk in their sleep, they have not awakened during their dreams. In fact, sleepwalking, or *somnambulism,* occurs during the deepest levels of sleep, and is actually more similar to the hypnotic state than to sleep. If awakened during an episode of sleepwalking, people will be disoriented and won't remember what they've been doing. Somnambulism involves involuntary motor acts during sleep and may extend to eating or having sex while asleep. Somnambulistic behavior typically lasts no more than 30 minutes. Some families seem genetically predisposed to somnambulism, which commonly occurs in young people ages 10 to 14.

Sleeptalking, also known as *somniloquy,* differs from somnambulism in that it can occur both during normal REM sleep and in the deeper sleep states. It is a common phenomenon. Sleeptalkers may utter just a single word, hold forth giving long monologues, or have conversations with invisible partners.

Both sleepwalking and sleeptalking may be connected to stress.

If you love it enough, anything will talk with you.

—George Washington Carver

Your Dream Diary

1. Make a list of the omens you notice for one week. Write about the underlying themes and the connecting threads. Now relate those themes to the themes you notice in your sleep dreams for the same period of time.

2. Make a list of the subtle omens you notice in one day. Write about the underlying messages.

3. Write several paragraphs describing a time your body acted directly from instinct and led you to discover something interesting.

4. Write several paragraphs about a time an omen or waking dream connected meaningfully to your future.

5. Write about how you are either ahead of yourself (in the future) or behind the times (in the past). What prompts you to go forward or backward in time? Write about what you might be avoiding, the seeming benefits of being elsewhere, and what happens when you bring your entire awareness into the present moment.

6. Write several paragraphs about your recent experiences of synchronicity. What were you talking to yourself about?

7. Try to catch as many of your daydreams, fantasies, preoccupations, and flashes of insight today as possible. Record them in your diary and write about what conversation is going on in you under the surface.

Part IV
Decode Your Dreams

The 5th Wave By Rich Tennant

"I wish you wouldn't jot a grocery list in my dream journal. I spent the morning trying to discern the meaning of artichokes and instant mashed potato buds in my life."

In this part . . .

Part IV helps you dig in and make sense of every type of dream experience. Chapter 10 leads you through the basic steps to interpreting a dream. You'll get started working with your dreams, discovering a number of useful methods for uncovering hidden meanings. Chapter 11 helps you work constructively with symbolism. You'll activate your intuition and use it to unlock the layers of insight in all manners of symbols. Chapter 12 actually interprets a variety of dreams, helps you work with scary/subconscious dreams to find the "gift in the garbage," and shows you what to do when you get stuck. You'll add many new techniques to your bag of dream tricks.

Chapter 10
Uncovering Dream Meanings

• •

In This Chapter

▶ Sorting out the dream variables

▶ Working with the dream zones

▶ Finding insights about your psychological and spiritual process

▶ Looking for themes in repeating and sequential dreams

• •

In a sudden burst of laughter,
the Dalai Lama slapped his knee and joked:
'It looks like there's an awful lot of work!
If you had to analyze all your dreams
there would be no time left to dream.'

—The Dalai Lama, from *Sleeping, Dreaming, and Dying*

Do you have a good sense of the lay of dreamland? Are you in a fairly productive dreaming rhythm, remembering more of your dreams, keeping your dream diary, watching for waking dreams in ordinary reality, and starting to weave together your daytime and nighttime experience into a coherent whole? If your answer is Yes, then you can start to dig in and discover the deeper meanings of your dreams.

I recently attended a dream workshop and one of the participants, who had succeeded in shifting her two-dreams-a-month dream life to one where she was writing in her dream diary every free minute, jokingly said, "I don't have time for all these dreams — and still live!" Another man sitting near me said, "I have books full of dreams — and I can't make heads nor tails out of any of it! I sure would like to know WHY I'm dreaming so much." This chapter will help you find the answer to that question. Although remembering your dreams is important, learning to speak their language and decode them is the most vital part — and the most fun. The thought of "analyzing" your dreams need not overwhelm you. Here are a few ideas to keep in mind as you begin:

> ✔ **Dream interpretation isn't hard work.** The techniques in this and the next few chapters help you arrive effortlessly at insights that make decoding your dreams easy.

✔ **Dream interpretation isn't intellectual and dry.** You may have heard dream experts on the radio talk shows, intellectualizing about how a dream of losing your job really means you didn't get enough attention from your father, or that you got too much of the wrong kind of attention, or that you want sex. Well, the study of dreams certainly has a scientific and intellectual basis, and good dream therapists can bring out amazingly helpful insights, but for the most part interpreting your dreams is a personal, passionate. and spritual exercise. Your dream is your own soul's message to you and you alone. In the best dream interpretation, you use your intuition and it guides you to an answer that's just perfect for you, one that increases your wisdom and understanding.

✔ **Dream interpretation needn't take over your life.** As you work with your dreams, the flow may increase and you'll remember more of the ones that used to slip away. At first, it's a good idea to document them all in your diary, but eventually you'll develop a sense of which ones are most important, and you'll pick those to do the deeper work with. You'll relax, letting yourself focus on the quality of your dream life, rather on the quantity of the dreams you remember. Interpreting your dreams will become a natural part of your life, just like reading the morning paper or talking to your friends.

Getting Started: Your Dream Interpretation Checklist

I'd like to sketch out a dream interpretation overview and some guidelines so you can develop an instinct about which dreams have priority and special weight. That way, you can quickly drop down to the core of a dream's meaning — the meaning that's useful for you at this particular time in your life.

Use the following meditation to help you use intuition to determine your most important dreams.

Using Intuition to Sense Your Important Dreams

1. Relax and center your awareness inside your body. Allow yourself to be receptive to any subtle cues that come.

2. Scan back through your dream diary for the past several weeks, lightly reconnecting with the essence of each dream you've recorded. As your attention moves from one to the next, notice which dreams stand out. Does one seem to have more "juice"? Does one seem to come forward while another recedes? As your attention touches each dream, notice which ones draw you back, as though you'd enjoy being in them again. Conversely, which ones do you resist dealing with? It doesn't matter whether your impression is positive or negative, just notice the strength of the connection or impact you experience.

3. Put a check next to the dreams that "talk to your body." Scan through the list of your checked dreams and, this time, see which one draws your attention the most. Trust your intuition to guide you to the most important dream. There may be absolutely no logical reason for the attraction. When you decide which dream has the most pull for you right now, you may want to begin with that one as you start your work of looking for hidden meanings.

Look for love and fear

The first questions to ask about your dream are:

✔ Does this dream originate from your subconscious or your superconscious mind?

✔ Are you *viewing the dream* from your subconscious or superconscious mind?

In many dreams, the fear-versus-love issue is fairly obvious. If you experience contraction, anxiety, worry, paralysis, or avoidance in the dream, it originates from the subconscious mind. If you experience even mild levels of any of these feelings while thinking about the dream, you may be reacting to the dream from the subconscious viewpoint. By looking for the fear responses in the dream and then the judgments you have about the dream content, you can more easily discover your subconscious blocks.

In the following dream, Bill experiences panic, indicating the dream has subconscious origins. When Bill viewed the dream later, he felt good about himself, signaling that he was moving out of fear into increasing clarity.

> *I've finished taking a sauna at a facility I visit frequently, and I'm naked. The door is stuck and I can't get out. After making a lot of noise and getting no response, I try to short out the wires to the heater but they're encased and I can't get to them. I'm getting hotter every minute. I realize I'll die if I can't escape. Then I use my towel to pick up one of the rocks from the heater and break the glass window in the door. I pick out the remaining fragments of glass. Finally I'm able to crawl out the window hole.*

Bill acknowledged that he was in a physical and emotional cleansing process in his waking life, and some "hot" emotional issues were beginning to surface from his subconscious, threatening to overwhelm him. He could see that part of his consciousness wanted to escape willy-nilly from the "danger." His calm problem-solving action in the dream helped him see that he had the resources within to deal productively with his emotions, without becoming a victim.

Sometimes, the emotion may not be quite so pronounced. In Lorraine's dream the fear-based feelings are present but somewhat camouflaged:

I have seven setter puppies of different colors in a wagon, and I take them to a park and watch as all but my two favorites get out. I don't try to stop them — I know I'm abandoning them but I trust they'll be okay. I park the wagon with the two dogs I mean to keep, and go do something else, but then forget about them. I only feel mildly guilty when I return to find them gone.

The dream has a subconscious origin, but it's hard to see at first. When Lorraine woke, however, she was quite disturbed that she hadn't felt more upset about her careless actions in the dream. Her agitation was a sign that directed her to look for the deeper roots of the dream. When she followed the uncomfortable emotions, Lorraine's first impression was that the puppies represented her wishes and goals, and the dream was showing her about her lackadaisical attitude toward having her wishes come true. Underneath her "mildly guilty" dream emotional response, she discovered a deeper level of feeling undeserving and self-sabotaging. What started off as a relatively mild-mannered dream eventually revealed some core psychological issues she needed to heal.

In yet other dreams, no negative emotion is present, neither in the dream nor in viewing it. When this is the case, the superconscious mind is giving you a message. This dream of Jack's may be his superconscious mind, reassuring him that there is an abundant source of supply and nourishment in his life. Superconscious dreams usually feel expansive, loving, and open, or neutral, objective, and informational.

I'm driving in a car with a friend. As we round a sharp curve, a passing vegetable truck swerves and some vegetables fall onto the road. I stop and pick them up. I'm excitedly stuffing them into my pack — carrots, celery, and heads of lettuce.

Recalling the dream, Jack had no feelings of guilt, greed, or desperation — just the happy sense of benefiting from a windfall.

 If you sense that your dream originates from your subconscious mind, and you may be viewing it subconsciously as well, don't add more fear by judging yourself negatively! Simply affirm that something important is surfacing, and that if you follow the dream interpretation guidelines discussed in Chapters 11 and 12, eventually your soul's true message will be revealed to you. Patience, not panic, is what counts. Just by remembering that there is a golden nugget inside every disturbing dream, you've already done the bulk of the work of readying yourself for a superconscious insight.

Determine the dream zone

Next, ask yourself: Is this dream coming from the physical, emotional, mental, or causal dream zone? (If you need more information on dream zones, see Chapter 6.) If you aren't sure, try asking: If this were a physical zone dream, what might it mean? If this were an emotional zone dream, what might it mean? If this were a mental zone dream, what might it mean? If this were a causal zone dream, what might it mean? By doing this, you'll notice that the dream fits most comfortably into one, perhaps two, categories.

Sandy dreamed:

> *I'm looking over a pilot's shoulder as he guides a commercial jet in for a landing. I'm frightened yet exhilarated when the pilot flies down a tight corridor between skyscrapers in a big city, and then finally lands the plane in a lake. He says to me, "I bet you've never seen that before!"*

In this case, Sandy decided that viewing her dream from all the levels had merit. She determined that

✔ As a physical zone dream, it might be showing Sandy that she needs to develop new skills for navigating successfully in her life.

✔ As an emotional zone dream, it might be telling Sandy that she is about to face a difficult period in which she will have to take risks that could cause her to crash if she doesn't pay close enough attention.

✔ As a mental zone dream, it might be telling Sandy that her soul is in the process of bringing higher knowledge carefully down through various fixed mental constructs, so it can be applied to her emotional life.

✔ As a causal zone dream, it might be reassuring Sandy that she has help from higher beings with greater experience and scope of vision than she.

In the end, Sandy decided that her dream was primarily based in the mental zone. She recognized that she had been in a period of depression and needed to raise the quality of her emotions by developing greater spiritual understanding.

Sense the dream's core purpose

After you zero in on the dream territory, the next question to ask yourself is: What am I showing, telling, or teaching myself in this dream? Every dream has a basic function — it may be to warn you so you won't get sick, or to bring you insight about how your energy is fixated on having to have a relationship, or to guide you in making a decision about whether to move to another part of the country, or perhaps the dream is reminding you of your innate joy and freedom. So before you start analyzing all the symbols and parts of the dream, see if you can sense the dream's core purpose. Ask yourself: "If this dream is really my soul trying to help me, what help is being given? If this dream serves my personal process of becoming authentic and enlightened, is it helping me learn to use energy more effectively? Is it helping me learn to use my perceptual skills more efficiently? Is it about balancing the components of my life to find greater harmony? Is it helping me understand the nuances of my creative process? Is it helping me see where fear is preventing my growth?"

Pearl dreamed:

> *I am part of a large group assembled on the lawn outside a university build-ing. Scattered among us is a flock of geese. We must scoot the geese into manila folders to make them less visible and noisy. Then we all join together in a chant or visualization to bring down the walls of the building. We do this and it feels good.*

When Pearl asked herself what the function of this dream might be, and how her soul was trying to help her, her first thought was that the geese were her interfering, unruly thoughts. She needed to "file them away" and get on with the business of aligning her mind with a group mind, without distraction. The group she was part of seemed to be in the process of deconstructing tradi-tional learning, or "opening the walls" of education. Pearl's soul was showing her that she was part of a collective consciousness, and that her knowing went far beyond the limits of her master's degree and the Ph. D. she was cur-rently working on. The function of Pearl's dream was to help her gain per-spective about the balance between academic credentials and inner wisdom.

Title the dream

Taking a moment to create a title for your dream can not only be fun, but it can also help you distill the essence of the dream's meaning. A title helps you quickly recall the details of your dream later when you want to compare it with other dreams or examine ongoing dream themes. Do you recognize the previous dreams from these titles: SAUNA JAILBREAK, COLORFUL LOST DOGS, VEGETABLE WINDFALL, CITY-LAKE LANDING, MANILA FOLDER GEESE?

Try the following dream diary writing exercise to make up titles for your dreams.

Titling Your Dreams

Try this dream diary writing exercise to practice titling your dreams: Go back through your dream diary, and from the beginning, give titles to all the dreams you've recorded. Use your intuition to allow the most colorful images and whimsical actions to connect with each other and form a poetic title that captures the spirit of the dream and makes it instantaneously recognizable. You might want to make a page at the back of your diary on which you list all your dreams' titles.

List the key aspects of the dream

Sorting the variables and temporarily excerpting them from the dream are helpful when looking for meaning. Sometimes, you just need to become

conscious of details you'd normally gloss over for meanings to become evident. Start by becoming aware of the following issues pertaining to location
and dream structure:

- ✔ **How would you describe the dream structure?** Did the dream have a
  beginning, middle, and end? Was it just a fragment? Was it a stream of
  consciousness — a string of episodes that might or might not be related
  to each other?

- ✔ **What were the main scenes and settings in the dream?** Were you inside
  or outside? Was it urban, rural, or unearthly? Was it the world you know
  or a parallel reality? How many scenes were there and were you comfortable in each one?

- ✔ **Did you have a sense of time?** Was it day or night? Were you in the past
  or the future? Or was time totally unimportant?

- ✔ **What was your viewpoint?** Were you a participant, not really seeing
  yourself? Were you an actor, playing the role of another person? Were
  you an observer? A commentator? Or perhaps you were the director?
  Were you above the action, at eye level, or below? Perhaps you had
  more than one viewpoint simultaneously.

- ✔ **How was the dream lit?** Were the scenes bright, as though lit by a spotlight or full sun? Were some scenes foggy or dark? Did you have a sense
  of it being in technicolor? Or was it more like a sepia-tone photograph?

- ✔ **Could you sense the four directions?** Could you orient yourself in the
  dream? Were you facing south, or west, for example?

Next, take a look at the dream elements:

- ✔ **What characters were present in the dream?** Were you alone or
  involved with other people, animals, or spiritual beings? Were there any
  characters on the periphery of the dream, who never actually showed
  up but had an impact on the dream anyway?

- ✔ **What were the primary images, objects, symbols, or patterns?** Was the
  dream filled with the objects and imagery of normal life? Or was it more
  otherworldly, abstract, and geometric?

- ✔ **Were you aware of specific colors?** Were you on a planet with an
  orange sky, or did your mother wear a kelly green dress, hat, and gloves?
  Watch for colors that stand out from the rest.

- ✔ **Did numbers occur in the dream in any way?** Did you dream of three
  owls, or as Lorraine did, *seven* setter puppies? Did you see an actual
  numeral on a house, a slot machine, or emblazoned across the sky? Did
  someone tell you their phone number or bank account balance?

After you're clear about the characters and symbols in the dream, examine
the motivations, actions, and movement:

✓ **What actions were taken and by whom?** As each action was taken, what goal was pursued?

✓ **Did you or any or character make a decision in the dream?** Action proceeds from choice points. No action can occur without an intention. What might have motivated each action in the dream?

✓ **Did you or any character make a definite statement, give an order, or ask a specific question?** Pay special attention to stand-out statements and questions. Also watch for specific words or phrases you see in print in the dream. These are often direct messages to you from your higher consciousness.

✓ **Were specific outcomes reached?** Did actions lead to results? Were you satisfied with the outcomes? Did you resist them? Not notice them?

✓ **Were there incompletions?** Were certain actions ineffectual or interrupted? What interrupted the flow? At what point did the action stop?

Next, note the emotions you or other characters experienced:

✓ **What feelings did you or the characters have?** Was there an underlying mood running throughout the dream? Did you experience mild or intense emotion at certain points?

✓ **Did you have any "sidebar" impressions about parts of the dream while dreaming?** It's quite common to be able to dream and comment about the dream to yourself at the same time. Often you'll have insights in the dream that you forget to bring back — your dream subtext. Pay special attention to these because they bring important messages.

✓ **What senses were you using to perceive?** Were you primarily aware through your sense of vision? Or did you feel someone touching you, or taste food, hear music, or smell flowers?

Look at the dream as literal first, then symbolic

The next questions to ask yourself are: "If this dream activity were literal, what would I — the true me, the soul — be doing?" And then ask: "How are the symbols telling me what I'm doing?" Consider the symbolism in the dreams described in a previous section of this chapter.

In Bill's dream of breaking out of the sauna, he was first showing himself that he was cleansing himself (sweating) of negative emotions. Second, he showed himself that it was important to keep himself safe during the process, by cooling off (breaking out) and becoming more neutral after periods of "hot" emotional processing.

In Pearl's dream, her literal action was encompassing a larger body of aware-ness at the higher mental zone. As she did, she became aware that this know-ing is shared by many people (the crowd on the lawn). She became aware of the group's power to dissolve barriers to higher knowing (the walls of the university), by focusing visually and auditorily (the group visualization and chanting), and when she experienced the alignment of minds, it felt wonder-ful. But before this focus could occur, the stray distracting thoughts (geese) had to be "filed" into folders to create order.

Watch for new information and insights

Your dreams primarily help you become spiritually authentic, but they also bring information that can help you in daily life. Pamela tells of having a dream where a friend insisted she drink hibiscus tea, so she bought and brewed some and found she liked it. Bette dreamed of a ray of light shining through the window onto the left side of her abdomen; within weeks, she dis-covered that she had a cyst on her left ovary.

Notice the change points

You may find some interesting insights when you examine how your dreams start, shift, and stop. Ask yourself: "At what point do I pick up the conscious recall of the dream action? What is happening in one scene that might cause it to shift to another? What is happening when the dream ends or when I sud-denly wake up?"

Perhaps you dream you're hiking in the woods and see smoke coming from the trees on a distant hill. In the next scene you see how fast the forest fire will spread and call a warning out to the other hikers in the area. In the last scene you hide behind some big rocks and hope the fire will burn around you. Why did you end it there? What are you telling yourself about your beliefs and behavior? You could have run away, or jumped in a lake, or helped the other people. The change points in dreams carry extra clues about the workings of your dream mind.

Put it all back together and see what's revealed

After you've done the dissecting and extracting, zoom back out from the detailed view and use your intuition to sense the bigger picture. Put the pieces of Humpty Dumpty together again. As you allow the components of your dream to hover in the same space together, you may have sudden insights about how your dream mind thinks and what message your soul is trying to get through to you. In the following dream, David gives himself a wealth of insight:

> *I'm with my girlfriend, who is driving an old car, though she doesn't drive in real life. I ask her why and she replies that she is able to drive in the evening and the early morning. Then I realize that she's gone on ahead, so I run alongside the car, shouting at the elderly man who is now driving, to stop. He finally does but acts like he can't see me. Two old ladies are sitting quietly in the spacious back seat and they don't see me either. Then I notice my sister standing on the running board. She is young, thin, and dressed prettily, like when she was a girl. She calmly tells me to go on and she'll meet me at the destination. I remove my groceries from the trunk and continue to a large house where I meet up with my girlfriend. When we go outside on the porch, I see my sister standing off in the distance, coming towards me slowly. It seems like she wants to say goodbye.*

A few days later David received a letter from his sister and her children, telling him she was dying. She was old and had been sick with Parkinson's disease for years. When David and I began to sketch out the overview of this dream, David listed the various elements that seemed most important to him:

- ✔ **The dream structure:** David thought this was a stream of consciousness dream. It had five sections — the conversation inside the car, David running outside the car, David's interaction with his sister, David taking his groceries and meeting his girlfriend at the house, and David seeing his sister again as she was about to say goodbye.

- ✔ **The settings:** Inside the car, outside the car, the house.

- ✔ **The characters:** David is himself, participating directly. His point of view is from eye level. The players are his girlfriend, the elderly male driver, the two old ladies, and his sister.

- ✔ **The images and symbols:** An old car, a running board, groceries, a big house with a porch.

- ✔ **The actions:** David's girlfriend driving and then going on ahead; David running outside the car trying to stop it; David not being seen; David gathering his groceries and going ahead; David reconnecting with his girlfriend at the house; David seeing his sister.

- ✔ **The decisions and statements:** David's girlfriend says she can drive at night and in the early morning, his sister tells him to go on to the destination, David decides to take his groceries and go.

- ✔ **The mood or emotions:** David experienced anxiety when trying to stop the car, frustration at not being seen, mild sadness as he realized his sister was saying goodbye.

- ✔ **The sidebar impressions:** David had the distinct impression that the stopped car seems to be taking people off to die. At the dream's end he "knew" my sister is saying goodbye because she's getting ready to die.

By bringing these most prominent parts of the dream into his conscious mind, David could more easily examine the meanings of the different sections.

What is the meaning of the first part where David's usually nondriving girlfriend drives and then goes ahead without him to their destination?

First, ask yourself: What is the essence of the experience of riding with some-one when they're driving? Do you feel taken care of? Guided? Perhaps you can relax your mental vigilance a bit as you share a new space of awareness (the car) with another. David decided he was experiencing a state of awareness where his girlfriend, normally oversensitive to the chaos of the world, was showing him that she was quite competent and knew exactly where she was going at times when the world was naturally quiet. His girlfriend also knew where the "destination" was, and got there ahead of him. Perhaps David's soul wanted him to see the equality of their different areas of competence.

What is the meaning of the part where David tries to stop the old car with the old people inside and then sees his sister on the running board?

First, notice that David has changed positions from inside to outside, from participant to observer. David felt that by stopping the car, he was trying to focus on a piece of information he wanted to understand. What WAS going on in that car? The old people in the car don't see him; they seem to be in a dif-ferent world. The inside of their car, in fact, is not the same environment he shared with his girlfriend moments before. The car now seems to be a vehicle taking people through the death experience. His sister is not inside the car yet, she's on the running board, as though she's just jumped on. David sees his sister as she looked in her youth, when she really liked the way she was, which is often the way people represent themselves to their loved ones after they've died. David was seeing his sister's secret image of herself. If his sister had already died, he'd probably have seen her inside the car with the old ladies.

Why does David take groceries from the car and go on to the big house?

First ask yourself: What is the essential experience of having groceries? Why would you take them with you? Groceries are synonymous with the idea of supply, abundance, and life-giving sustenance. David is clearly not in the dying mode — he is going to feed himself and move on to the next destina-tion in his physical life. What is the essential experience or function of a house? It is a space or a context that focuses and centers us in daily life. Perhaps David's new big house is the idea of a more expansive, more com-plex focus in life. And, he's going to share it with his girlfriend. And, she's arrived at the experience first.

Why does David see his sister again later, slowly approaching from a distance, not able to come too close, outside the new house?

What was happening literally? David may have wanted to be in the new place, or new point of view, to attain a kind of preparedness before he allows himself to know for sure that his sister really is dying.

Putting all this back together

What was David's soul trying to help him with? What was his own deep purpose behind the dream? What were his literal actions? In David's dream, he was literally shifting his awareness in and out of different foci. First he focused on the consciousness of his relationship with his girlfriend (inside the car), then on the idea of the process of dying (outside the moving car), then on his sister's connection to the process of dying (seeing her on the running board), and then on to a new state of awareness that would allow him to feel more expansive in life (the house). His purpose was, first, to remind himself of his girlfriend's wisdom and competence. He was showing himself that he could trust her and that he was going to share a future with her, that they were going to the same destination. Second, he was bringing an important upcoming life event — the death of his sister — to his conscious mind so he'd be prepared for it. Third, David was showing himself that he himself was not ready to die, that he still had more he wanted to do.

Examining the change points

Examining the change points in David's dream provides an interesting insight. Why did David's dream mind jump immediately from being with his girlfriend and getting a glimpse of a future reality, to seeing his sister's impending death? At first, the two scenes seem totally unconnected. How might the ideas be related?

David's insight was that before he could really face the loss of his last female relative, he wanted to know that he would be okay. Knowing that he would "go on," fortified with groceries, and that he'd be with his girlfriend in the future, whom he now could recognize as being competent in ways he hadn't seen before, served as a strong reassurance for him. Together with his girlfriend, he could face the news.

Watching for Clustering Dream Themes

To discover the themes your soul is working on, it's helpful to keep your inner eye peeled for repeating and parallel images, symbols, settings, and ideas that may span across a series of dreams. Some themes you work on are long-term and will continue for years. Others are short-term and may only occupy your waking thoughts and sleep dreams for a week or a month.

Do men and women's dreams differ?

Just as men and women are interested in different activities, communicate differently, and have different goals, so too do their dreams differ. It has been shown that women have more connecting fibers between the left and right sides of their brains, and thus tend to perceive the inner world and outer world as intimately connected, often being unable to distinguish causality between the two realms. Men, on the other hand, are much more able to compartmentalize and deal with one thing at a time instead of being overwhelmed with everything coming at them at once.

Women tend to be highly relationship oriented and value "face-to-face" conversation, while men need more silence and "shoulder-to-shoulder" involvement with others. It makes sense then that women's ability to bridge between different levels of awareness and maintain memory of two levels at once is high, as is their desire to share their dreams with others and uncover meaning. This doesn't mean that men can't do the same thing, just that they must be more intentional in the process.

Perhaps because women are naturally conscious of the more intangible, unseen realms, and use intuition as a normal part of awareness, their tendency to recall dreams tends to be slightly higher than men's. Women also seem to remember the colors in their dreams more than men. As men and women share more of the responsibilities of career and family, however, dream content tends to be much less divided along gender lines than it was in the past. With current trends toward intuition development and self-growth among women *and* men, perhaps dreaming skills will soon be practiced with similar ease in both genders.

Keep track of recurring dreams

You've probably had dreams that occur again and again, in the same sequence, with the same feelings and details, often ending at exactly the same point. In many cases these *recurring dreams* are nightmares, or border on being nightmarish. Kathy repeatedly dreamed:

> *Someone is calling me, and I become aware of the voice from a deep sleep, as though I'm rising up from the bottom of a well to respond. The voice is commanding and I try to wake up and answer. I think I'm sitting up, but then I realize I'm really still asleep on my back and I can't move. I can't speak and I can't even open my eyes. I get scared and finally wake myself up for real.*

Kathy has had this dream on and off over a 20-year period. The fact that it has never moved beyond the point where she becomes totally paralyzed is an indication that there is an internal issue she hasn't yet worked out. To find out why the recurring dream keeps knocking on her door, Kathy needs to complete the dream.

I do some deeper experiential work with extending dreams in Chapters 11 and 12, but one of the first things Kathy can do immediately to gain insight about her recurring dream is to ask: "Whose voice IS this calling me back from my faraway place?" Perhaps Kathy will discover it's her grandfather's voice, a man she dearly loved. When he died she was so traumatized that she unconsciously closed her heart — and was afraid to ever be that vulnerable again. Maybe her grandfather has a message for her now that will help her love fully again. On the other hand, Kathy may discover it's the voice of her own soul, and she's been resisting hearing something that would open her to greater freedom and creativity, but perhaps require her to give up a little security in exchange.

Often a clue to the dream's resolution lies in the very imagery that causes the mind to stick. The fact that Kathy can't open her eyes in the dream suggests that there is something she doesn't want to see. Because she can't speak either, there may be something she also doesn't trust herself to say. If Kathy wants to work on this dream, she might start by letting herself experience FULLY the feelings of paralysis. Without resistance, paralysis is very close to meditation. Instead of looking outside herself for the source of the voice, she might listen inside. When she hears the message, she might ask herself if she wants to share it. Because her eyes are stuck closed in the dream, her soul is probably indicating that the vision she needs is an internal one, so she might look within. Meditation is a terrific way to intuitively ferret out the hidden memory in a dream like Kathy's.

To complete recurring dreams, it's important to allow the piece of missing experience, which has been suppressed, to surface from the subconscious mind. You, the dreamer, must decide that it would be *interesting and useful* to know the full story. When you decide to face the thing that has frightened you, the missing memory will present itself. When it does, and when you listen to it open-mindedly, everything will make sense, and the dream will in all probability stop.

Follow sequential dreams

Sometimes your dreams deliver a message that's too complicated to be understood all at once in one episode. Your soul may dole out the under-standing to you over time, in a handful of related dreams. A series of sequential dreams like this may easily span 20 years or more. Sometimes one dream picks up exactly where a previous one left off; other times the connection is a bit more obscure. Repeating symbols may be common to many of the dreams, and you may also find waking dreams weaving in among the sleep dreams, as if to punctuate the main points. If you look for dream sequences, you'll find the same important personal issue at the heart of each of the dreams in the series. Sequential dreams can indicate much unused creative energy, and the ability to accomplish long-term projects.

Jon was only 12 when his older brother and sister died tragically in a motor-cycle accident. Though he didn't consciously realize it, he was a victim of survivor's guilt. He wondered why he hadn't died too. A year after their deaths, Jon had an extremely vivid, tactile dream:

> *My brother and sister and I are riding our bicycles together. I can tell they are in fine shape, and are happy. They seem so real! We are riding from the graveyard toward the monastery next to my grandfather's house.*

Though he was too naive to really understand much about dreams, this first dream served to partially reassure young Jon that his siblings were happy, and that he could feel happy too. Even so, he was sensitive and still harbored many irrational fears. The second dream in Jon's series of sequential dreams happened when he was a 20-year-old college student.

> *I'm in a dark building at night looking for my girlfriend. Everyone I meet and question tells me that "she went up those stairs." I follow, ascending higher and higher in the building, until someone says, "I saw her go up that ladder." I climb up and open a trap door that leads to the roof. When I flip the door back, I'm amazed! I'm at ground level and the roof is really a hill-top covered in grass. I see a large brick building nearby and watch an incredibly beautiful sunset. I am totally captivated by the beauty of every-thing around me. I don't climb out but realize I don't need to find my girl-friend any more when I have this much beauty.*

Jon says that at this time in his life he was preparing to go into the ministry, and he interpreted the dream to mean that his search for romantic love was actually leading him to a love of God. He says, in retrospect, that he remem-bers his local pastor telling him that his desire to go into the ministry was probably connected to his sense of "burial," his guilt about surviving his brother and sister. At the time it didn't make much sense to him. The third dream in Jon's sequence occurred when he was 33, just as he was preparing to *leave* the ministry!

> *I find myself standing on the grassy hilltop from my dream of years ago. I look down and see the trap door at my feet. I remember I hadn't come all the way out of that door before. But now I'm above ground. I comment to myself about how dumb it was of me not to come out all the way before. Now I dance around on the grass saying, "It's about time! I should stay up here!" Then I notice two white doves flying up out of the ground near where I'm dancing. They fly away.*

Jon thinks this dream is actually the beginning of his self-forgiveness process. He had spent almost 14 years as a minister, in many ways trying to under-stand what happened to him and his siblings, and he now felt stifled by the form of the church. He was about to embark on a more free-form, eclectic spiritual journey. The fourth episode in the sequence was more of a waking dream, and happened the following summer when Jon returned to Iowa and visited the graves of his siblings.

I'm standing at the graves and I look up and see an old brick hotel across the way. It immediately reminds me of the brick building from my earlier dreams, and I look around. Here I am — standing on a grassy hilltop! It's the exact scene from my dreams. Suddenly I realize the two doves flying out of the ground are the souls of my brother and sister, and I've let them go at last.

Jon felt that his period of being buried with his siblings was finally over, that he had emerged and could proceed with his own life. And yet, Jon's process of learning from his dream sequence wasn't quite finished. Two years later he had another dream.

I am in an attic of an old house and there is an elevator in the center. The elevator is actually more like a platform, with no walls or top. I step onto it and it begins to descend, dropping steadily down and down into a deep hole. I become extremely frightened and grasp at the walls going past, and shout loudly to the people who are above me. No one can help me. I grab a pipe on the wall and it just pulls off in my hand. The scene is getting darker and darker. Suddenly an idea pops into my head: "I'm too dense. If I can become lighter, more relaxed, and not so afraid, I can reverse the flow of this thing." I start to change my thoughts and the platform actually does start to rise a bit. I know there's more to do when I wake up.

Jon said this dream had a lucid quality. He realized later that he could control the flow of his consciousness, and that part of the lightening up process was to be willing to try new things, to not panic and grasp at externals when his process wasn't going in the direction he thought it should. Jon said that after emerging from his "burial period," he had thought his life was really together. Yet he saw that he still hadn't faced many of the deeply imbedded fears in his subconscious. From his dream he learned how to be open to the things that still scared him. He could see how the death of his siblings led him to the ministry (in his first dream, the children rode from the graveyard to the monastery together) as a way to cope, and that eventually he needed to dance on the graves and celebrate freedom. Coming up from the underworld was important, but so was going back down occasionally.

Try the following dream diary writing exercise.

Finding the Wisdom in a Dream Sequence

1. Think back through your dream life, as far back as you can remember. Have you had dreams that pick up where a previous dream left off? Have you revisited certain dream locales? Are there some dreams that contain similar images? Have you dreamed repeatedly of things that resemble each other — like tornadoes or columns of smoke from forest fires, or nuclear explosions with mushroom clouds?

2. Make a loose list of these symbols and then write about what the gist of each dream seemed to be about. Can you sense a progression from one dream to the next? Was your soul revealing different aspects of an issue to you? Were you showing yourself the next appropriate action in your process?

3. Make a list of the ideas that pop into your mind. How did the dreams parallel what happened in your waking reality over the time period involved? Write about the themes or life lessons you've been working on.

Tread softly because you tread on my dreams.

—W. B. Yeats

Your Dream Diary

1. Scan through your dreams this week and make a list of scenes where you experienced fear, worry, or anxiety. Then list scenes where you felt uplifted, excited, or inspired. Write in first person as your soul about each scene: "I caused myself to experience this so that. . . ."

2. Pick a dream, center yourself, and ask your body to write about what it knows about the core purpose of the dream. Let yourself write in a stream of consciousness, without editing or rereading. Begin by writing: "The core purpose of this dream is to show myself. . . ." "I chose the symbol of the ( ) because to me it represents ( ). Let yourself write, word by word, until you feel complete.

3. Examine the last week or two of dreams and notice their structure. Have you dreamed predominantly in fragments? Have they been epic movies? Were they composed of two, three, or four scenes? Write several paragraphs about why you like the style of your dreams lately. What does one powerful fragment give you that a longer dream might not? Why is your subconscious drawn to having a beginning, middle, and end?

4. Write several paragraphs about what one of your dreams means, as though you are (Sigmund Freud, Carl Jung, Buddha, Jesus, your grandmother, your inner five-year-old, whoever).

5. Pick a dream, go back through it in your imagination and while you're in it, look to the left, to the right, and behind you. Write about what you see.

6. Pick a dream where you woke before the action was complete, or where an action taken by a character was ineffectual. Write about why your subconscious caused the flow to be interrupted.

7. Go back through the past several weeks' dreams and make a list of all the statements, directives, specific questions, or literal words or phrases you saw or heard in the dreams. As you see them now, grouped together, out of context, write about the impressions you have about what you're really telling yourself.

Chapter 11

Finding the Secrets in Symbols

- -

- -

> *Everything's got a moral if only you can find it.*
>
> —Lewis Carroll, *Alice's Adventures in Wonderland*

To work effectively with your dreams at the deepest level, you need to enter the world of symbols and have "meaningful" relationships with them. Symbols contain volumes of encoded information which they convey directly and intuitively, without need for verbal explanation. They are the vehicles your dreams and imagination use to speak to you, a shortcut to the wisdom of your soul.

Although words themselves are symbols, it's easy to get lost in the labyrinth of misunderstanding they can create. You can use words superficially, not taking enough time to say exactly what you mean, or sarcastically to imply an opposite meaning, or ignorantly, causing confusion. Sometimes words truly can't describe a profound experience adequately.

They say that a picture is worth a thousand words. A picture cuts through to a deeper level. Look only at the photographs in *National Geographic* without reading the captions or commenting to yourself, and you will experience much of the world's cultural flavor.

Direct experience, however, is worth a thousand pictures. Immerse your whole body in the experience — actually go to Kenya or Siberia and live the life there for a few months, and a whole new dimension opens to you. This is what symbols do — they lead you from one level of perception to another and act literally as doorways. In this chapter, I help you to see the power of symbols and to understand their relationship to unlocking the language of the soul.

Symbols: The Language of the Soul

Symbols contain information. And everything is a symbol. Your name or nickname is a symbol for your identity. The words you choose when speaking tell us about you. Do you swear a lot, use slang and bad grammar, or do you speak with colorful adjectives in precise sentences? Take a look at the clothes you wear. What do they say about you? Casual T-shirt-and-jeans person? Image-conscious fashion plate? A walking advertisement for sex? How about your car? Is it red, silver, school bus yellow, black, dented, sporty, safe, expensive? Does it run well or break down often? What about your residence? What do your furnishings say about you? Are you cluttered or orderly? Feminine or masculine in your tastes? What do you love? What do you hate?

Everything you perceive in your world is a symbol of who you are and what you're focusing your attention on at that moment. The symbols that appear in your dream world are just as indicative of you as those that surround you in daily life. Do you dream repeatedly of swimming? Of eating delicious French pastries? In your dreams are you having great sex with celebrities? Or do you find money and jewelry on the street? Are your dreams populated with cats, babies, mobsters, angels, high school chums, trouble-making coworkers, or large insects with shiny eyes? Just as your choice of a pickup truck versus a luxury sedan reveals something about your lifestyle and personality, so does the fact that you dreamed about a hummingbird instead of a bald eagle. The hummingbird may represent a characteristic you need to recognize in yourself. Eventually, all symbols reveal aspects of spirit.

Symbols are always perceived through one or more of the five senses; a picture can be a symbol, a song can be a symbol, and a temperature, a smell, a texture, or a flavor can be symbolic too. Symbols can focus and center you. Think of the soul-stirring power of your nation's anthem, or of the power of "our song" to reignite a couple's original feelings of love. Countries represent themselves with symbols of nobility, inspiration, and power — the rising sun, the stars, lightning bolts, the cross, the spiral, the all-seeing eye, or power animals like eagles, lions, snakes, dragons, or bears. Corporations represent the essence of their identity with a logo. Good art and design are symbolic because they distill universal, divine qualities into functional and inspirational objects. You never tire of looking at a painting by Van Gogh, the Great Pyramid at Giza, a Japanese teapot, an Amish quilt, or a performance of Hamlet by great Shakespearean actors. These encapsulations remind you of your soul qualities and take you immediately into an experience of what is most real.

Travel up, down, and sideways

When seeking the meanings in symbols, you can travel in two directions —
moving from the first impression which may seem insignificant, down (or up)
through various layers into a deeper understanding of the essence of your
soul and life (the vertical path), or sideways, like stepping across stones over
a river, which brings a greater understanding of the interrelatedness of the
myriad forms that life can take (the horizontal path). For example:

- Tracked vertically, the letter "A" represents the sound "Ah," which when
  uttered is itself a representation of what many spiritual traditions consider to be the fundamental vibration of the universe. Tracked along the
  horizontal path, "A" may remind you of the time you first learned your
  A-B-C's or of your desire to do well on tests.

- The mathematical concept of "three," when followed vertically, can be
  symbolized as the numeral "3" or distilled into an equilateral triangle. If
  you bring that geometric pattern into your personality as an experience,
  it translates into the qualities of personal harmony and integration, of
  easy flow and natural self-expression. Following the concept horizontally
  through association, three might remind you of good luck, or the Holy
  Trinity, or "Ready. Get set. GO!"

- The letters "R-E-D" stand for the first color of the visible spectrum,
  which, when followed vertically, becomes an experience of a primal
  energy — the feeling of excitement, of rising physical vitality, of intensity, explosive beginnings or breakthroughs, survival, and even violence
  when that life force is blocked. To bridge between those three cryptic
  letters and the body's real subjective experience you follow a vertical
  pathway to the core meaning. The horizontal path of interpreting the
  symbol "red" gives you real world associations with the color — like
  birth, blood, the placenta, sex, danger, accidents, emergencies. Red
  lights mean STOP! Red clothes, lipstick, and cars mean a sexy, intense,
  potentially dangerous life force contained within. Red is fire, volcanoes,
  molten steel. Red also means anger, frustration, war.

Take the example of the tidal wave

Suppose that you dream of a large tidal wave. What's the essential meaning?
The vertical path of the symbol's meaning produce insights that lead you
back into the remembrance of your deepest spiritual nature.

- The first layer of the symbol is the verbal label you give it: "tidal wave."
  The words stand for the picture of a huge arching wall of water crashing
  on the shore.

✔ The image of the wave represents an underlying experience of what being that wave would feel like: "I'm rising up higher and higher and higher, feeling so full of power, bending over naturally and gracefully, falling smoothly like a car on a roller coaster, breaking across another wave, and together we crash magnificently onto the shore and dissipate, and I am drawn back into the ocean again."

✔ Underneath the experience of feeling like a tidal wave is a particular kind of knowing, an insight, or a state of awareness that reminds you of something eternal, essential, and divine: "I am moved to come into being by a great power that originates far beyond me, that directs me, and I never leave it even though I think I do as I'm 'cresting,' but I always return to my source. I can be as big as I want and still be connected to the divine."

Following the horizontal path of the symbol's meaning, you discover the associations your mind has made with the idea of "tidal wave." These ideas may give you a clue about your unresolved subconscious blocks.

✔ Perhaps for you the tidal wave carries connotations of wanting to be an excellent surfer, which is a way you've tried to prove your self worth.

✔ Maybe it conjures up the thought of death by drowning, being overwhelmed by gigantic emotional riptides and smashed to smithereens.

✔ Maybe it has a religious slant, indicating the end of the world, a "big punishment coming."

As you work with the symbols in your dreams it's important to follow both the vertical and horizontal pathways to arrive at the most complete understanding of all the meanings.

Interpreting Symbols Vertically

When you examine a symbol "vertically," you're looking for its essential meaning, and to do that you must fill in the gaps between your highest, most abstract understanding of the idea and your most earthy, concrete experience of it. Just as a musical note can express as high C, middle C, and low C, so can a concept.

If awareness originates at a high level, like the causal dream zone, where perception is very abstract, then for the fullest understanding you need to drop down the scale and see how that same awareness shows up when it expresses at the mental level. What thoughts does the spiritual pattern spawn? Next, drop it to the emotional level. What feelings are generated from the purity of the inspiration? Finally, sense the perception as it becomes physical. What actions want to begin? What forms want to take shape?

Conversely, if you encountered something in your physical body that you want to understand, like a wound or disease, for example, you need to move up the scale and see how that physical pattern shows up at the emotional level. What parallel feelings are present? Then, what ideas, concepts, or beliefs are contained within the feelings? Then, what intention or lesson are you, as the soul, trying to crystallize?

Dreams and the three levels of your brain

The basic flow of perception from the soul to the body, and from the body to the soul is vertical and must pass through three different "perceptual filters," or three different levels of your brain, to make ultimate and complete sense. Figure 11-1 illustrates these three levels: the reptile brain, midbrain, and the neocortex.

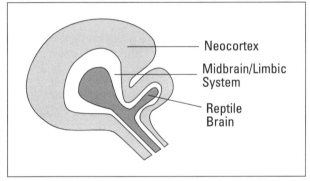

Figure 11-1:
The three levels of your brain.

The three levels of the brain function as follows:

- ✔ The first, most primal level of the brain, the *reptile brain,* concerns itself exclusively with physical survival. The reptile brain controls your body's motor responses and gives you an instinctual drive toward food, shelter, sex, and territory. Without emotion or reason, it interprets sensory stimuli in terms of either aversion or attraction, fight or flight. It relates closely to your subconscious mind and your survival behaviors.

- ✔ Nestled around the reptile brain lies the *midbrain,* or the limbic system, the seat of your conscious mind and personal self. The midbrain is involved with the creation of dreams and inner visions, symbols, relationships, emotional bonds, and the perception of similarities. Here perceptions take on sensory overlays — color, tone, texture, flavor, scent, shape.

> ✔ The highest level of the brain is the *neocortex,* your intellectual system, which is five times bigger than the two lower brains combined and is divided into left and right hemispheres. The neocortex is the home of logic, abstract creative thinking, and higher states of consciousness such as compassion and truth. It corresponds to your superconscious mind.

The following sections describe how your perception is affected as it moves through your brain.

The ascending flow of perception

As you have experiences every day and your body is motivated by attraction and aversion — love and fear — those signals travel from your cells, up your spine, and through the three parts of your brain, progressively making sense in more complex ways. Eastern disciplines like yoga refer to this rising energy as the *kundalini.*

When information from the body first enters the brain, it registers in the old reptile brain at the back of the neck. Here perception seems primitive, instinctual, reactive, and animalistic. It then progresses up into the midbrain where it becomes more civilized and takes on the nuances of the five senses. At this stage you can "have a flash," "get the picture," or "hear your 'little voice'." An idea can "smell fishy," "ring true," or "be off-color." A person can seem "yummy," "lukewarm," "real smooth," or "rough around the edges." Here you create metaphors: "She looks like a lumberjack," "The new job was a roller-coaster ride," "My dreams have been stillborn lately."

As the perception continues up into first the right, then left hemisphere of the neocortex, you begin to grasp the pattern and the overall concept, until at last it becomes fully conscious, makes sense logically, and you label it with language and create a meaning. At this point you have an "Aha!" and the proverbial light bulb goes off over your head. This is the ascending flow of perception, and it is what people do every time they try to make sense of something.

The descending flow of perception

The downward flow of perception begins as an inspirational urge or an abstract thought. As it descends from the higher zones, it first activates your neocortex, and you may receive an impression of a large, complex concept, perhaps as a geometric pattern or "energy blueprint."

The flow of perception then moves down into the midbrain where it takes on the quality of a vision, continuing downward, "fleshing out" through all the senses until the body is able to recognize it as something doable and real.

Then, as the flow enters your reptile brain, your emotional motivation and enthusiasm kick in and you move to accomplish the vision. This is the way an athlete visualizes winning a race — first she pictures her performance in every detail, then feels herself doing it, smells the dirt of the track, feels the air on her skin, hears the tape snap at the finish line — and gets her body excited. Finally she releases herself into the real act, which tends to accurately produce the outcome she pictured and felt. This descending flow is what happens every time you create or manifest something.

How to interpret a symbol vertically

Dreams are the result of both an ascending flow of information from the physical world to the spiritual, and of a descending flow of inspiration into physical realization. Dreams — and symbols — both occur as your perceptions reach the midbrain, so when trying to understand symbolism it helps to fill in the rest of the pathway, both below and above, to see both the microcosm and the macrocosm.

Try this dream diary writing exercise.

Interpreting a Symbol Vertically

Pick a dream fragment or a piece of a longer dream that stands out in your mind. Focus on the visual symbol that seems most important to you. Then, in your diary, record your responses to the following:

1. Describe the symbol in a word or two; label it. By labeling an image, you take yourself to the top of the brain's process. Say to yourself: "(Blue Pegasus) is a symbol for the image I see of (a flying blue horse)."

2. Writing in the first person, describe the experience in detail using as many sensory and emotional words as possible. Make sure to include vision, hearing, touch, taste, and smell. "If I could feel what it is like to be blue, without fear or reservation of any kind, what sensations and emotions would I be experiencing? If I could feel what it is like to be a flying horse, what sensations and emotions would I be experiencing?"

3. Ask yourself: "If I were a flying blue horse (or whatever symbol you chose), aware of all its sensations and emotions, what would I naturally know about myself, the world, and life? What insights would I have?"

4. Finally ask: "If I had all the sensations, emotions, and knowing of a flying blue horse, what lesson would I be trying to demonstrate to myself? What purpose would I be fulfilling?"

By immersing yourself directly into each of these experiences, you will fill in the vertical pathway, and the symbol will reveal itself to you.

Interpreting Symbols Horizontally

After you discover the essential meaning of a symbol, it's interesting and useful to explore the particular personal associations you have with it. Traveling the horizontal path to a symbol's meaning is a subjective journey: A snake may terrify one person because of its venomous bite, intrigue another because of its sinuous beauty, and be revered by yet another because of its connection with the earth goddess. You may have had a pet garter snake as a child and loved handling it. Jim, on the other hand, may have walked into a shed when he was six and encountered a huge rattlesnake in the shadows. Each symbol holds different meanings for different people, depending on how much love and fear are connected with the view. In addition, your mind, through selective attention, tends to perceive just what you need to perceive to learn what your soul needs you to learn.

In Freudian dream analysis, dreamers are encouraged to use *free association* to flush up a symbol's related meanings from the subconscious mind. With this associative method, you describe the thoughts, impressions, and feelings that occur to you when you think of the symbol, no matter how embarrassing or silly. Of course, it's possible to go overboard with this method, delineating a flood of associations that have no personal meaning to you and actually begin to clutter and overwhelm your mind.

When exploring the variety of associations you have with a symbol, remember to first highlight the meanings that have relevance within your own experience and then the ones that have that special "psychic weight." If the meanings become too abstruse, or if the process of association starts to make you feel sleepy, stop and go back to those few ideas that have an inner vitality.

How to interpret a symbol horizontally

Try this meditation to help you find your personal associations with a symbol.

The Flower Petal Technique

1. In your mind's eye, imagine a large, open flower with many petals. In the center of the flower, place a symbol you'd like to decode, such the snake since we started exploring it earlier. Focus on the image open-mindedly, being willing to receive any ideas that want to come into your mind.

2. Move your awareness out to the first petal, and imagine another image, an idea, a personal memory, or a word on that petal — something that is related to the snake. The first thing you get might be *poisonous*.

3. Make note of the idea, then go back to the center and touch in with the symbol again. Feel the image then go out to the second petal and see what idea or image is there. Maybe this time you get: *sexuality*.

4. Return to the center and feel the symbol. Go to the third petal. This time you get: *ancient wisdom*. Continue going back to the center, then out to a petal, until you have exhausted the meaningful associations. Don't jump from petal to petal or you might start associating the associations with each other. Soon you should have an intriguing list: *poisonous, sexuality, ancient wisdom, dangerous, slippery, sensual, "snake in the grass," lizard, dragon, cold-blooded, sacred, feminine, eel, sinuous, silent, teeth, sheds skin, constrictor, viper, rattles, cobra, Egypt, transformation, kundalini, hissing sound, forked tongue, sidewinder, Quetzalcoatl, "Don't Tread on Me."*

5. When you feel your list naturally tapering off, pull back from the associative process and review the collection of words, feelings, memories, and concepts you have. In the context of how the symbol appeared in your dream, which items on your list feel most vital and applicable?

6. Now ask yourself: "How is the snake in my dream like what's happening in my own life right now?" "How is the snake in my dream like me right now?"

Take the example of the snake

Because snakes are a common dream symbol, look at these snake dreams and see how the dreamers arrived at their personal associations with the image.

Robin dreamed:

> *I'm going down into the basement of a commercial building like a restaurant. I see all their summer umbrella tables and outdoor chairs stacked up in storage. I realize it must be wintertime. Then I look under the tables and there are huge clusters of snakes tangled together, drowsy and sleeping, looped around the wrought iron curlicues that brace the tabletops. At first I'm shocked at the teeming masses of serpents, and then I realize I don't have to be scared because they're still asleep.*

When Robin free-associated to find her personal concepts connected to the snake symbol, the most powerful ideas for her were that snakes are wise, they store up energy and use it efficiently, and they know about the underworld and the earth. As she felt further into the image of the tangle of snakes, she could tell they liked being together and were peaceful. When she asked herself how these snakes were like her own life, she realized she was in a period where she too was gestating and hibernating, soaking up knowledge from the unconscious as she prepared for a new phase in her life. She knew she was going to "wake up" and become active again soon like the snakes would in the "springtime." She realized she had the dream to reassure herself that she didn't have to worry so much just because she wasn't super busy right now. There was an important process going on in her deeper self that she knew she shouldn't disturb.

Craig dreamed:

> *I go into the bathroom and there's a cobra in the bathtub. It rises up to my eye level and spreads its hood. It's rocking slightly toward me and away. I know if I hold still it won't do anything but if I start to back off, it will shoot forward and bite me.*

Craig explored the associations he had with the symbol of the cobra and came up with "Egypt," "spiritual initiation," "truth," and "unwavering." As he asked himself, "How is the situation with the cobra like my own life right now?" he had an insight that the cobra was not evil, but more like a test of his character. He could feel how in his own spiritual growth process, he was undisciplined in a few areas. He had not committed to practice some of the things he knew were right and that at a deeper level he truly wanted to integrate into his life. To Craig, the cobra staring him in the eyes symbolized the pure, neutral, unwavering truth. If he stayed centered and could be present with the cobra — in effect, practice what he knew to be true — he would be safe. But if he indulged even the least bit in fear and started to back away, he knew he would experience immediate negative repercussions in his life from his lack of commitment.

Track a symbol back to an "earlier, similar" image

Another technique you can use for interpreting symbols horizontally is to follow the trail of an image back through your own personal history. A symbol may remind you of something you perceived in the past or an experience that happened to you before. The peach sitting on the kitchen counter may remind you of eating a hot peach you picked off a tree one summer while you visited your grandmother's farm. That might remind you of helping her bake a peach pie, watching her arthritic hands working the crust into place. That might remind you of how those hands helped you tie your shoes and how loving she was. When you finish tracking back through the past associations you have with the peach, perhaps you'll discover it has a strong connection for you with nurturing and love.

Your personal associations with common symbols

Write the first ideas that come to mind next to each word. You might write an adjective, or another noun, or a memory. Don't analyze, just write direct from your intuition.

Ant _____	Ladder _____
Apple _____	Lion _____
Artichoke _____	Luggage _____
Bear _____	Mask _____
Bed _____	Money _____
Bridge _____	Mountain _____
Camera _____	Night _____
Cave _____	Nurse _____
Clothes _____	Oak tree _____
Diamond _____	Oasis _____
Dog _____	Owl _____
Dragon _____	Party _____
Eagle _____	Pearl _____
Elephant _____	Pomegranate _____
Fence _____	Rabbit _____
Garden _____	Rose _____
Gift _____	Scissors _____
Hat _____	Skull _____
Hospital _____	Telephone _____
Infection _____	Tower _____
Jungle _____	Umbrella _____
Jury _____	Volcano _____
Key _____	Wallet _____
Kite _____	Whale _____
Kitten _____	Zebra _____

Use your dream diary to write about the roots of dream symbols.

Tracking a Symbol Back to Its Roots

1. Ask your inner self to pick an image from a recent dream that you need to understand, then let it appear in your imagination.

2. Ask: "What does this image remind me of that is present in my life now?" Let yourself receive one or more associations. Write them in your dream diary.

3. Ask: "What earlier similar experience is tied to these present ones through an association in my subconscious mind?" Write it in your dream diary.

4. Ask again: "What earlier similar experience is tied to this one through an association in my subconscious mind?" Keep asking for earlier similar experiences and images until you can't get any more or until something clicks strongly.

5. You can use the image of the core experience from your past as a dream symbol, to enter and interpret vertically. What was that experience really all about for you? Then examine the string of connected images through time to find the common themes leading into the present.

Finding Archetypal Meanings

Certain symbols and processes have meanings common to everyone because they exemplify something that pertains to the universal principles of life, or themes lived by all human beings. These universal symbols are known as *archetypes* and emerge from the collective unconscious, or the upper mental and causal dream zones. Our children's stories, folk tales, religious teachings, and world mythologies are full of archetypal characters and processes. Carl Jung used archetypes extensively in his approach to dream work, and believed that we explore the grand themes of humanity as routinely as we solve daily problems in our dreams.

Recognize common archetypes

You probably recognize these archetypes, as many people have experienced and explained them:

- ✔ **The Hero and the Hero's Journey through the Underworld:** Whether it be Buddha, King Arthur, Joan of Arc, Christopher Reeve, Han Solo, or Harry Potter, heroes undergo a similar developmental process. To be heroic we must first be cut off from our roots and misunderstood, then we must experience the call to adventure so we can discover our true self, which only comes after a difficult rite of passage where we confront temptation, challenges, demons, villains, handicaps, and our own unresolved fear. Finally, we experience an awakening and eventually reach our goal. We then must return to those who misunderstood us and enlighten them. This is the process of spiritual growth we all go through as we evolve.

- **The Divine Child:** Innocent, playful, unconditionally loving children represent the true self. If you dream of a baby or a toddler, you may be focusing on the idea of new beginnings or beginner's mind, spontaneity, fresh perspective, and trust, trying to activate more of this quality in yourself.

- **The Divine Mother:** Generous, nurturing female figures represent the principle of creativity, growth, abundance, and unconditional acceptance. They may also symbolize the idea of receptivity, sexuality, pleasure, seduction, attractiveness, and fertility. Dreaming of a mother figure can direct your attention to areas you need to nurture.

- **The Shadow:** Dark things that hide in dark corners represent the parts of your makeup that you have rejected or not owned fully, and defined as weak, evil, or ugly. These parts may scare you or trigger other disturbing emotions like jealousy, rage, or greed. Shadow imagery holds great gifts for the dreamer – you only need to ask "What part of me is like this?" Sigmund Freud believed that people often *displace* or *project* onto others the ideas they are afraid to own themselves. If you're uncomfortable with your own lustful desires, you may deal with them in a safe way by dreaming that your boyfriend acts lustfully toward another woman.

- **Death, Rebirth, and Transformation:** Mythology is full of magical creatures like the phoenix that die and are reborn in a more brilliant, spiritualized form. Jesus died and rose from the dead, Osiris was killed and cut into pieces and then was regathered, reassembled, and brought back to life by his wife Isis. The caterpillar seals itself into its cocoon and then emerges as a butterfly. Transformation is a natural result of living fully. Death imagery is almost always a profound indication of personal growth.

Although the mythology can be complex — the advantage of perusing through these meanings amassed over time is that for centuries intuitive people have contemplated archetypal images at great length. There is wisdom to be had here.

Understand the numbers in your dreams

Numbers can represent archetypal aspects of the self, the personal growth process, and stages in the creation cycle. In complex numbers, examine each of the single digits, then add them all together, and if the sum is still a double digit, add those numbers together until you have one digit left. This core number reveals a deeper meaning. Table 11-1 presents common meanings associated with numbers.

Table 11-1	The Numbers in Your Dreams
Number	**Meanings**
1	**Individuality:** authenticity, autonomy, personal will, assertiveness, self-determination, self-reliance, inner strength, leadership, dictatorship, pioneering spirit, impulsiveness, impatience, beginnings, entrepreneurial ability, originality, independence, courage, risk-taking behavior, authority, self-absorption, ego lessons, definition of personality
2	**Cooperation:** harmony, balance, receptivity, giving, mirroring, diplomacy, peacemaking, comparison, merging and dissolving boundaries, sharing, co-creation, relationships, partners, approval, agreements, linking and bridging, teaching, counseling, negotiating, indecision, conflict, sensitivity, empathy, patience, female energy, marriage/divorce
3	**Self-expression:** creativity, open-mindedness, drama, social activity, popularity, communication, release, ease, flow, outgoingness, spontaneity, imagination, verbal skill, promotion, sales, public speaking, singing, teaching, writing, performing, indecision, humor, naturalness
4	**Structure:** personal discipline, work, effort, tangible results, responsibility, tradition, builder, the body, methodical, patience, determination, practical action, endurance, loyalty, limitation, attachments, business skill, three-dimensional design and art, serious, stubborn, real estate/housing, focus, commitment, karma
5	**Freedom:** movement, change, travel, new experience and ideas, sensory stimulation, curiosity, restlessness, versatility, flexibility, cleverness, agility, mathematical and verbal ability, impatience, dancing, adventure, superficiality, temptation, communication, creativity, foreign cultures and languages, creativity, promotion, confusion, lack of security
6	**Service:** nurturing, balance, adjustment, creation of divine harmony, beauty, settling down, idealism, romance, healing, wellness, art, counseling, teaching, events and gatherings, nutrition and food, cosmic parent, home and family, intimate groups, centers, open-heartedness, sympathetic, martyrdom
7	**Truth:** universal laws and metaphysics, love of knowledge, study, academia, research, perfectionism, privacy, introspection, objectivity, abstract/conceptual thinking, analysis, refinement, precision, silence, meditation, music, investigator, behind the scenes, mathematics, science, technology and computers, alignment of personal and divine will, aloof, planning, retreats, spiritual pilgrimages, ego death, revelation of the spiritual
8	**Manifestation:** authority, power, competence, business and executive ability, organization, administration/management, systems, strategy, money, success, achievement, drive, ambition, materialism, professionalism, value system, superstructures, justice, the higher order of things

Number	Meanings
9	**Universal Awareness:** compassion, altruism, humanitarian service, collective consciousness, idealism, romance, dreams/visions, big thinking, social and political action, personal loss or disappointment, invisibility, nonphysicality, impersonality, inspiration, generosity, completion, surrender, philosophy, imagination, sympathy, broad outlook, overwhelmed, spaciousness, mysticism, death and the other side

See the meaning in your dream colors

Bright, clear color in dreams can indicate a heightened sense of reality, even a lucid, precognitive, or an important visionary dream. Colors also communicate emotion and states of energy, directly and immediately. Colors have universal, archetypal meanings, derived over thousands of years through many world cultures. If an object in your dream has an unusual color, take note! You may be providing yourself with an extra overlay of meaning. Table 11-2 presents common meanings of colors.

Table 11-2	Dreaming in Colors
Color	**Meanings**
Red	Excitement, physical vitality, intensity, explosive beginnings, birth, or breakthroughs, survival, violence, heat, blood, sex, passion, romantic love, danger, accidents, emergencies, anger, frustration, war.
Orange	Purification of impurities, expansion, creative urges, appetites, ambition, personal vitality, physical and emotional healing
Yellow	Illumination, intellect, positive attitude, creativity, open-mindedness, cheerfulness, spontaneity, imagination, communication, humor, naturalness
Green	Balance, harmony, integration of opposites, calmness, healing, nurturance, nature, renewal, growth, abundance, understanding
Blue	Mental clarity, insight, truth, neutrality, detachment from emotion (often confused with depression), overview, clear communication based on truth, faith, hope
Indigo	Intuition, spiritual insight, devotion, wisdom, compassion, communion, archetypal knowledge

(continued)

Table 11-2 *(continued)*	
Color	*Meanings*
Violet	Universal understanding, collective consciousness, spiritual knowing, awareness of unity, spiritual healing, miracles, religions/priesthoods/royalty, transformation/transmutation
Brown	The earth, stability, animalistic nature
White	The superconsciousness, purity, enlightenment, ecstasy, joy, transcendence, radiance, birth, the sacred, the yang side of God
Black	The unconscious or subconscious, the underworld, deep space, the void, gestation, absorption, receptivity, death, the yin side of God
Silver	The moon, psychic ability, magic, illusion, feminine (internalizing) force of awareness
Gold	The sun, wisdom, higher knowing, enlightened mind, generosity of heart, masculine (externalizing) force of awareness

A pale or whitish version of a color (tint) might connote an early stage of development, or perhaps gentleness, while a dark or blackish version (shade) might convey heaviness, seriousness, or over-attachment to the quality embodied by the color. Mix two colors together, like olive green (green and brown) or turquoise (green, yellow, and blue) and see how the qualities might combine to give you a special meaning.

Use dream dictionaries

You may find great insights about the symbols in your dreams by exploring the classic myths and legends of the world. Wonderful dream dictionaries exist that have done much of the work of sorting out the archetypal meanings of various symbols. You can add these meanings to your own personal associations for a broader understanding.

When you read dream dictionaries, simply throw out any meanings that don't feel right to you. Or allow all the meanings to float with you for a while until a synthesis takes place and you receive an insight of your own. Dream dictionaries are notorious for listing obscure meanings of symbols that may have made great sense in the more distant past, but don't quite compute today.

Dream dictionaries of the past

Dream interpretation dictionaries figure prominently in the literature of history. Ancient Egyptians, Mesopotamians, and Greeks used them, as well as Muhammaden scholars. After the printing press made books more widely available to the public in the mid-1600s, a dream dictionary called *Oneirocritica (The Interpretation* *of Dreams)* by Artemidorus became one of the first best-sellers, comparable only to the Bible in popularity. On the other hand, Sigmund Freud's best work, *The Interpretation of Dreams,* now read by many as a foundation for dreamwork, sold only 451 copies in two years when first published in 1900!

Trusting Your Intuition

With the myriad of possible meanings for each symbol, how are you to find the interpretation that's just right for you? Actually, you have a precise and accurate method for discerning truth — and it's built right in. Your body communicates with you constantly, giving you feedback about the truth and appropriateness of every idea you consider — it's just that you're probably not used to recognizing its cues. Using your intuition, you can quickly and directly discern these truth signals, without taking time to figure things out. The body only has two "words": *yes* and *no.* You'll recognize these signals through feelings of expansion or contraction in your body.

Feel the "yes"

When a choice is appropriate, safe, and on purpose for you, you'll experience expansion: You may sense energy rising, becoming active or bouncy, get "light-headed," or feel flushed with enthusiasm. When you light on the right meaning for a symbol, you'll feel that expanding tingle, or that mild feeling of relief, or what I often call a sense of "psychic weight," where you just know something is important. You may feel magnetically drawn to an idea or "lean toward" a certain option.

When I ask people where they experience the feeling of a truth signal in their body, many describe a warm, spreading sensation across their chest. Others feel energy bubbling up from below their diaphragm into their heart, or from their chest into their throat. Some feel it bubble up further, resulting in tears of happiness. Still others describe a variety of "clicks and clunks," as if something out of alignment suddenly snaps or drops back into its rightful place. These feelings most often occur along the vertical center line of the body and seem to be related to the sensation of something "ringing true." Another common truth signal is the sudden movement of energy up the spine or along the arms and shoulders, giving the sensation of "the chills" or gooseflesh.

Feel the "no"

But what about when something is not true for you? When the body answers *no,* you'll experience contraction: You may feel energy drop, recoil, darken, or tighten. You may feel lukewarm, even cool or perhaps you'll get a sinking feeling in the pit of your stomach. When something is not true for you, your body will try to withdraw and back away. You may feel "leaden" or "turn to stone." Instead of blushing, you may blanch. Your energy level may drop, you may feel gray, blue, even depressed. You may feel physically cold, especially in the extremities. You may actually feel pain in a specific area of your body.

Common anxiety signals are: an upset stomach or nausea, a "pain in the neck," chest pain, headaches, or a feeling like a tight fist in the solar plexus area. Yet another anxiety signal is a prickly feeling of the "hair rising" along the upper spine and neck. If a possible meaning for a symbol isn't quite right, you may simply feel thick, bored, or even sleepy. Anxiety signals can also indicate a hidden meaning in a symbol that you resist acknowledging. It's important to notice how entrenched your resistance to an idea is because the greater the resistance, the more important the buried insight.

When looking for the right meaning for a symbol, try softening your analytical mind, letting go of logic and will power for a moment or two, and dropping your awareness into your body. Next, ask for what you want and let a sensory impression pop into the center of your head. Finally, check that your whole body feels totally comfortable at a deep level with the answer.

Remember that symbol interpretation has no fixed rules. If a snake means wisdom to you in one dream, it might mean sexuality to you in the next. Stay loose and open. In addition, your system of personal symbology will evolve over time, paralleling your own character development.

Cracking Symbols Open

Have you ever designed a logo for yourself? Or a business card? What image did you pick to represent the essence of what you were offering to others? What typeface did you choose to convey the gist of your personality? What clothes would you wear to an important meeting or party where you will meet influential people for the first time? Try paying attention this week to the way you represent yourself and your ideas to others, and the way they symbolize themselves and their ideas to you.

Try the following dream diary exercise to help activate your symbol-cracking skills.

Symbolizing

1. Make a list of ten people; they can be friends, historical figures, or celebrities. Write their names in your diary. Then ask your intuition and imagination: If this person had a different name, one that accurately conveyed their essence or an important quality of their personality, what would it be? Don't be logical. Write down the impressions you get and use your truth signal to choose the best option. Then make some notes about what the name symbolizes.

2. Pick a person you know. Ask your intuition: If this person were a tree what kind would he or she be? What kind of music would represent this person? What kind of flower? What kind of car? What geometric symbol? If this person had a secret fantasy, what would it be? What would the person's dream house look like?

3. Pick just the right name for your home. Would it be "Woodside Cottage"? Or "Stonegate Farm"? Or "The Hole in the Wall"? Imagine that you're going to make a sign to put out front to welcome guests. What would it look like?

Finding juicy deeper meanings in symbols

Here are some tips for finding your symbols' deepest meanings:

✔ When looking for associations for symbols, look to your opinions and judgments. You might try to avoid these to be polite in everyday conversation, but in dreams polite interpretations are of little use. Your most forthright, candid, and judgmental ideas are often the ones that reveal the most meaning.

✔ Purely logical assumptions about what symbols stand for are often boring, and only skim the surface. Look for emotional reality and the "real response" rather than the linear, logical one.

✔ You can omit the hundred enticing details and the descriptions that wander tangentially away from the point or you may get too bogged down. Stay focused on the images that have power or that you are irrationally drawn to.

✔ Gayle Delaney, author of *All About Dreams* (published by Harper San Francisco, 1998), recommends that in addition, you might pretend to be an alien from outer space, or an "interviewer from another planet," when you ask questions of your dream self. This helps assure you get fresh, innocent answers.

✔ Sometimes the association you find for a symbol will be a story or anecdote from your current life or your past. Summarize the story and write it in your diary, or tell it to someone, then look for the key word that stands out emotionally to you. If the key word is a noun, you may need to go further to find a word that describes an experience. This final word is often tied to the meaning of the original symbol.

As you become more adept at using your intuition, you'll see that interpreting symbols is a matter of entering them with your attention, and then actually becoming them. If you stare at a symbol long enough, focusing your attention into it, trying to feel it, getting more and more involved with it, you'll begin to receive "bleedthrough" from the image, actually feeling its structure taking shape in you. Perhaps you and the symbol are exchanging energy and knowledge. You give yourself to it, and it reveals itself to you. As you merge totally into the symbol, the knowledge it represents unloads, or "downloads," directly into your body, and you can feel the living patterns and dynamics that the symbol preserves.

Enter a symbol by describing it

To enter a symbol, you need a factual description. Then you need to take it personally. Enter the symbol totally by speaking in the first person directly *as* the symbol, and finally, find nuances of meaning by extending the symbol's scope. The following sections explain how this can work.

Belinda dreamed:

> I'm in Europe and have made a huge amount of money which I now want to bring back into the United States, but I don't want to declare it at customs. I weigh many options because I don't want it to show up on the x-ray machine: Shall I divide it up and put some on my body, some scattered through books, some in shoes and boots, some tucked into dirty socks, some in my wallet? I'm paranoid and frustrated that I have so much money but don't know if I'll be able to use it.

Belinda identified three key symbols that stood out to her: a large amount of money, a foreign country that is the origin of the money, and customs and its x-ray machine. One by one, Belinda did a factual description of the symbols. She began by asking a couple key questions; then she let the answers flow directly from her intuition:

- **What is money? What is a large amount of money?** Money is a means of exchange. Money equates with value. Money is a reward. Money brings security, power, and opportunity. Money is strength and energy. If I have money I can have things. A large amount of money is the ability to have and do a lot and makes life much easier. A large amount of money means I must have done something very well or been very good. A large amount of money means I must feel deserving or I couldn't have received it in the first place.

- **What is a foreign country?** A foreign country is a place I don't normally live. It is a place where I'm not limited by what everyone else thinks about me. A foreign country is exciting. A foreign country is a place that offers unusual opportunities. A foreign country is a place where I don't feel secure, but I feel adventurous.

↙ **What is customs? What is an x-ray machine?** Customs is a guard dog. Customs is the suspicious consciousness at the outside edge of the country I live in. Customs will take things away from me if I have too much. An x-ray machine sees through the outside covering of things to reveal what's underneath.

Go deeper by taking the symbol personally

To personalize a symbol, ask yourself: "How is this symbol a part of me? How is it like what I'm doing in my life right now?" When Belinda personalized the symbols and allowed the meanings to meld intuitively together into a story that paralleled her dream, Belinda came up with these insights:

> *I shift my consciousness to a new place where I am more adventurous and not held back by habit or by the expectations of others. I take advantage of new opportunities that come from this place and I am good and excellent and am rewarded. I have more resources than ever before — a HUGE amount of abundance — and now I must go back to my regular place in the world where people remember me the old way. I have to get my new abundant nature into my old place and figure out how to use it. But first I have to get past the critic that lives at the edge of my old place. If the critic sees the new me, it will make me be small again. I will have to hide the new parts of myself but this much "wealth" will be hard to hide.*

Belinda realized the dream was about the fact that she was growing internally at a very rapid rate, and the negative part of her subconscious mind that wants her to be a victim is activated the minute she tries to express her new truth. Her dream was pointing out to her the fact that she is going to have to show up for who she really is, and let her wealth of talent and wisdom be known.

Become the symbol

To enter the symbol totally, speaking in first person directly AS the symbol, you must use your powers of imagination and childlike love of pretending. And, you must grant the symbol an intelligence of its own.

When you begin speaking as the symbol, you might start by introducing yourself and talking about what your function is. You might talk about what your particular expertise is, and what you know to be true. Then you might talk about what you really like to do, and whether you feel understood or misunderstood. Do you need to say something to the dreamer? Do you have a gripe? Do you have a secret to impart? If you could have anything you want, what would you like?

Pam dreamed:

> *I'm driving along the windy back roads in the countryside outside Baltimore and the roads are icy. My black sports car goes out of control and skids off the road.*

That morning when she got in her car to go to work, it wouldn't start, and she had to have someone jump-start her engine.

Later, when she worked with the symbol of her car in her imagination, she defined it factually as "the vehicle that takes me long distances into the world." When she "took it personally," she saw that the car was the way she wanted her body to be, sure and sleek, responsive and strong. When Pam entered and merged with the symbol, and spoke directly as the black sports car, it said in a sad voice, "I really need you to pay more attention to me. We're going too fast and not enjoying ourselves. I want you to tune in to me and our movement before you even turn me on, and I want you to stay conscious and be with me while we're moving. I feel abandoned." Pam realized that her own body was sending a message to her, reminding her that she'd been much too distracted and ahead of herself lately. The waking omen of her car not starting then seemed to fit in perfectly with the message of her dream.

Try the following dream diary writing exercise to practice merging into ordinary objects.

Pretending to Be an Object

Pick an object from the environment in your house: a vase, an overstuffed easy chair, the sheets on your bed, a shovel from the garage, the welcome mat, a candle. Enter the object, feel its life, feel what it knows and where it came from. Fall into the object and tell its story, writing directly from your intuition, allowing anything to come.

Find nuances by extending the scope

As you merge with a symbol and role-play it, use your intuition to imagine what it feels like to physically be the symbol. Then imagine that you can sense out into the environment all around you, behind, above, and below you. The environment you discover this way doesn't have to make any logical sense. As you expand your bubble of perception, anything might occur within the bubble. Is there anything interesting and pertinent that you see or hear when you extend your awareness? Douglas dreamed:

> *I row a raft out onto a lake and see two turtles swimming with their heads up out of the water. They start swimming toward my raft and I throw a half-eaten apricot to them but it sinks and they keep coming. Now I see they're really big and I think they're going to bite me in the big toe.*

When Douglas entered the symbol of the turtles, and spoke as them, they said, "We are bringing knowledge from under the water up so you can see it." When he expanded his scope he could see the apricot falling into the lake and sinking nearby, and he knew the turtles weren't interested because they weren't hungry. When he expanded a little further, he could see himself through their eyes as he sat in the raft. The turtles weren't interested in him either and they weren't angry. As he extended his scope further out, he saw a sunny little island in the middle of the lake, and on the island were thousands of other turtles, basking in the sun and drying off. The turtles wanted to be on land with their friends.

Shifting the dream from one where he felt in danger of being bitten, to one where he could feel a peaceful group consciousness, changed the whole meaning of the dream for Douglas. Now he had the sense that there were many subconscious ideas, insights, or secrets that had already surfaced in his life, but he hadn't been paying attention to the ones that were already visible. Instead of integrating the knowledge that had already been given to him, he was indulging in fear about what he didn't know.

> *Thus, learning to understand our dreams is a matter*
> *of learning to understand our heart's language.*
>
> —Ann Faraday

Your Dream Diary

1. List five symbols from your dreams this week. Write out the vertical path of their essential meaning; then the horizontal path of their associative meanings.

2. Pick five colors, other than the seven standard rainbow colors, and enter the experience of what each one represents. Write about your body's primal responses. What emotions do you feel? What impressions do you receive? What happens to your mental clarity with each? What does each color "know about"?

3. If the numbers of your home address appeared on a house in your dream, what would they mean? Write about the qualities your home is activating in you based on the archetypal meanings of the numerals.

4. List the people in your nuclear family, including grandparents, aunts and uncles, and cousins. For each one, decide: What color would symbolize them? What kind of food would symbolize them? What other odd symbol pops to mind for each?

5. Draw a symbol that represents:

- The essence of your creativity

- Your future success

- Your personal truth

- Your current health

- Something from your shadow self

6. Write a paragraph about what your full name means. What characteristics, sensations, and emotions does it elicit? What impressions might it give others?

7. Pick three to five symbols from one dream and write directly as each one, and then write directly about their interrelationships with each other.

Chapter 12

Deepening Your Dream Work

> *When an inner situation is not made conscious, it appears outside as fate.*
>
> —Carl Jung

Dreams come in so many varieties — from the merest vague impression, to a single vivid image, to literal verbal instructions, to epic technicolor sagas, to nonsensical stream-of-consciousness flows, to terrifying nightmares. In trying to decipher the diversity of inner messages, you may face innumerable brick walls and nebulous insights. Settling into that sense of intuitive "just-rightness" about your own dream meanings is an art. In this chapter, I build on the ideas about the meanings of dream symbols and give you a chance to practice interpreting a variety of dream types.

Valuing the Power of Dream Fragments

A friend who teaches seminars and does quite a bit of public speaking told me about a dream in which she insisted she wear her red Chinese house slippers as she stood addressing a large audience. In addition, she wanted her ratty old blue potholder on the podium with her. It was just a little snippet — a quick snapshot of herself — one scene out of a long series of dreams she knew she'd had that night. Why, when she knew the other, longer dreams were so juicy, had she only retrieved this single fragment?

Dream fragments are like symbols themselves. Because they're so simple and concise, you can find layers of meaning in them — they often contain everything you need to gain an important insight. When your dream fragment is like a snapshot of yourself in a particular situation, your soul may be talking to you directly about something you need to know.

The personal snapshot

Continuing her conversation with me, my friend speculated about what her dream fragment about needing red slippers and a blue potholder while speaking before a large audience might mean. "Maybe it's that I need more creature comforts now," she said. This first interpretation sounded logical to me, but didn't quite have that full ring of truth. I asked her to close her eyes and picture herself standing at the podium with her ratty potholder and slippers. Then I began a little dream interview.

I asked her to imagine what she was feeling as she addressed the audience in her dream. She closed her eyes. "I don't really want to be here," she replied, "and that's weird because I *love* public speaking. But I feel too exposed, like I really just want to be at home where I don't have to dress up and act like I'm such an expert." I asked what the potholder and slippers were doing for her. "They remind me of the way I am at home," she said, "and they make me feel more relaxed.

I asked her to go further into the feelings she was having as she stood at the podium in her Chinese house slippers and see what else was there. She was quiet for a minute and then said, "I feel uncomfortable that the audience is seeing my sloppy, casual side. I'm supposed to have it together!" I asked her what would happen next if people saw who she was when she was at home, being casual. "Maybe they wouldn't like me because it wouldn't seem like I have the answers; they'd see *my* needs instead."

I then asked what might happen next if people knew she had needs too. She was quiet for an even longer time before she said, "Well, at first I thought they'd reject me, but then I saw that they'd actually like to help me the same way I like helping them. Wow! I haven't been letting people into my private life at all. . . ." She opened her eyes and we talked more about the insight she'd just received. My friend realized she'd been keeping her public life and her private life very separate, and the effect had been isolating for her. She understood suddenly that she didn't need to reveal all the details of her intimate life to the public, nor have everybody over for lunch — she just needed to let her guard down a little, to feel more relaxed and vulnerable in her professional dealings, and to receive from the audience as much as she gave. This dream fragment put my friend on notice that she needed to shift her attitudes and adapt her behavior slightly, so she could eliminate some unconscious levels of emotional loneliness and energy drain that had been plaguing her.

Use the following dream diary writing exercise to practice interpreting dream fragments.

And Then, What Might Happen?

1. Conduct an imaginary interview with your dream self. Start by asking: "How do I feel about (image from dream fragment)?" Or, "What do I experience as I see (image from dream fragment)? Then, "What else comes to mind as I experience this?"

2. If you reach a statement based on fear, ask "What would happen if (the situation you're trying to avoid) occurred?" If you reach a positive statement, ask "What would happen if (the good situation) occurred?" When you get the answer ask, "And then what would happen?" Continue the "And then what?" questions until you feel you've arrived at the core experience. Ask yourself, "If this worst possible scenario happened, what might I learn?"

The isolated, vivid symbol

A dream fragment that reveals a highlighted single symbol is like a shortcut to an important message. By reentering a dream fragment in your imagination and asking pertinent questions, you can coax out the meaning and find the bridge to your current life situation. Marla dreamed: *I see my report card and I got straight A's.* By pretending to conduct an interview between her conscious mind (CM) and her dream self (DS), Marla zoomed right in on the dream fragment's message:

CM: What's a report card?

DS: *It's a piece of paper that tells me how I'm doing at my lessons.*

CM: What's an A?

DS: *It's the highest grade possible; it means I'm succeeding.*

CM: If you were the report card what would you want to say to me?

DS: *"I bring you a message from your teachers — you are performing at a high level in everything you're doing."*

CM: What do you experience as you see the report card?

DS: *I am surprised and excited. I've never had straight A's before and didn't realize I could possibly be doing so well.*

CM: What else comes to mind as you experience this?

DS: *Someone important must approve of what I'm doing in my life.*

CM: Who is approving of your life?

DS: *God. My parents who have both died. And my own higher self. I'm approving of myself! I've never approved of myself totally before.*

CM: So what might happen in your life from now on if you always approved of yourself totally? If you always felt like you were doing an excellent job?

DS: *I'd do an even better job! I'd give myself permission to do more of what I want to do because I'd trust myself.*

CM: Why are you dreaming about the report card now and sending me this message?

DS: *Because it's time to start a new phase in your life and expand your creativity, and I want you to be alert and ready to recognize new opportunities when they come.*

By allowing leading questions to pop into her conscious mind, and by taking her dream self's point of view and then factually describing and role-playing the vivid symbol of the report card, a dialogue was able to take shape between the various parts of herself. Marla saw how she could use the symbol of the good report card as a catalyst to help her prepare for a new, exciting period of personal growth. To accept herself as excellent and feel approved of from within was necessary so that she could embrace new, perhaps unusual, possibilities.

The geometric pattern

If you've been dreaming in one of the higher dream zones (Zone 3 or 4), you may only remember a vague impression or a geometric symbol or pattern in the morning. The meaning of this kind of fragment is likely to relate to a process within your higher consciousness, or to the way you use your energy.

Genny woke up with the feeling that four bold, black vertical lines had been drawn through the corners of her bed, from above the ceiling down through the floor into the earth below her bedroom. As she woke she thought she heard someone say that people weren't entitled to have these lines until they were 14 years old. Mystified, Genny did a meditation later in the day, visualized the lines, and pretended to be one of them. Then she wrote in stream-of-consciousness style, referring to herself in the third person:

Who are you?

I am a bold black line coming down from the heavens, connecting my power straight into the earth. I am like a lightning rod, straight and conductive. I bridge power between heaven and earth. I contain great knowledge and I am unbreakable. I am one of four lines. We function together in a square formation, serving as the corners of a new reality. We now exist around Genny. We protect her and make her strong and definite. We help her become recognizable. We are Genny's guardians. Even when she is asleep we move with her wherever she goes.

Why did the four of you come into my dream now?

We came to be around Genny now because she's earned us. She has developed inner strength and has a new level of authority. The earliest anyone is allowed to have us be with them is at age 14, when power registers in the personality for the first time. We became visible to Genny so she could know she is ready for a bigger challenge in life and so other people will recognize her more easily when they see us with their inner vision.

The words Genny wrote were a surprise to her as they flowed from her hand. She had been working with a therapist for many years, meditating, and studying spirituality. This dream fragment seemed to be telling her that she had graduated from one level of maturity and was ready for the next. Within several months, she was offered an opportunity to teach a series of classes on personal growth to a large group of businesswomen.

The cliché and pun

Sometimes a dream fragment contains words or phrases that stand out in your mind. Taylor dreamed that a man told her that in order to find a new job she had to "come from out of the blue." This made no sense to her upon awakening but later in the day she realized there were several meanings all wrapped up in that one phrase. To Taylor, *coming out of the blue* meant being intuitive. It also meant that an opportunity could come suddenly from nowhere, seemingly dropping out of the sky. She sensed she would need to follow a hunch or a gut feeling, not necessarily her logic, to find the right opportunity. Yet she also realized that she had been "feeling blue" because she felt she was wasting her life and creativity at a job she didn't like. Part of the dream fragment's message to her was that she snap out of her depression and reconnect with her enthusiasm and sense of good luck.

Use the following dream diary writing exercise to start a conversation with your own dream fragment.

Conversing with a Dream Fragment

Pick a dream fragment that intrigues you and focus on the image with your intuition. Pretend to be your own conscious mind asking questions; then switch roles and pretend to be the image in the fragment and respond. Try the following questions, in any order that appeals to you, and address them to the image directly.

- ✔ Who/what are you?
- ✔ What are you like?
- ✔ What's your special gift?
- ✔ What emotions and feelings do you trigger in me?

✔ What do you do? What's your function or role in my life now?

✔ Are you the "solidification" of something else, like a kind of energy? If so, what is the energy state trying to show me?

✔ What message do you have for me?

✔ What do you need, or want, me to do?

✔ Why are you appearing in my dream right now?

✔ How do you already exist in my life?

✔ If I internalized the quality that you represent, how might my life change? What insight might I receive that would be helpful to me?

Unraveling Complex Dreams

String together a series of dream fragments, add a few more odd characters and mysterious motivations, exotic locales, dramatic scene changes — and you've got all the makings of a sweeping technicolor epic. Some dreams can become so long and drawn out, with so many colorful details, that to delve into every one would have you glued to your dream diary 12 hours a day. How then are you to untangle your long saga dreams without wearing yourself out?

Find the structure of storylike dreams

Although some complex dreams wander and leave you with an open-ended question, a situation cut off midstream, or a scene that doesn't seem to follow the previous ones at all, many longer dreams can be divided into dramatic scenes, just like a book or play. When you separate your dreams into these basic dramatic components, use your intuition to feel the major turning points.

Listen for the places in the telling of your dream where you want to naturally insert terms like "and then," "all of a sudden, this happened," or "and it changed into. . . ."

Psychiatrist Carl Jung, as well as other dream theorists, held that a complete dream contains four basic parts, similar to dramatic structure: statement of place, exposition, culmination, and solution or summary. Table 12-1 describes how it works.

Table 12-1		The Four Basic Components of a Storylike Dream	
Scene	*Jung*	*Dramatic*	*What Happens*
SCENE 1:	*Statement of place*	Setup	Introduces the setting and initial situation, relationships
			What's the situation?
SCENE 2:	*Exposition*	Development	Introduces characters, or conflict; presents problem or dilemma; poses a question, furthers the action
			What's the problem?
SCENE 3:	*Culmination*	Climax or resolution	The situation gets critical and a turning point is reached
			How does it all work out? What has to be done?
SCENE 4:	*Solution or summary*	Denouement	Problem is solved; point is made, loose ends tied up
			What's the answer? What did you discover?

Using this dramatic structure, here's how to interpret a storylike dream:

- Divide the dream into scenes.
- Identify the main elements of each scene.
- Make associations with the elements you listed in each scene.
- Look for love and fear; identify the dream zones.
- Look at the dream as literal first; try to sense it's core purpose.
- Bridge the dream meaning to something pertinent in your life.
- Reflect on and review the meaning for a period of time.
- Decide what you're going to do and act on the dream's message.

Using Lee's dream, I discuss these steps in detail in the sections that follow.

Lee dreamed:

> *I'm on a boat at night far out in the ocean. An aggressive man comes on board and says I have to get off now. I say "No." He opens a trap door and throws me down into the dark water. I fall way down deep with great force and am trying to reverse my downward motion, swimming hard. It takes a*

lot of energy to turn and start up again, but I finally surface, gasping for air. There are ugly chunks of stuff in the water everywhere but I manage to avoid them. Then on the distant shore, I notice a community. I go there and some people invite me in to a party. It turns out to be a nudist party — like this is the latest rage. Some conservative people I know have arrived and they're taking off their clothes. I'm embarrassed and decide I will definitely not take mine off. I leave and go to another area of the community where I observe a group of people learning to do a circle dance and to become clowns and acrobats. Then they build a human pyramid and there is a grand finale like a rainbow of light. I wish I had joined in their group because it looks fun and I think I've missed out.

Divide the dream into scenes

When Lee and I broke her dream into parts, it took shape like this:

SCENE 1: (What's the situation?) *I'm on a boat at night far out in the ocean. An aggressive man comes on board and says I have to get off now. I say "No."*

SCENE 2: (What's the problem?) *He opens a trap door and throws me down into the dark water. I fall way down deep with great force and am trying to reverse my downward motion, swimming hard. It takes a lot of energy to turn and start up again, but I finally surface, gasping for air. There are ugly chunks of stuff in the water everywhere but I manage to avoid them.*

SCENE 3: (What has to be done?) *Then on the distant shore, I notice a community. I go there and some people invite me in to a party. It turns out to be a nudist party — like this is the latest rage. Some conservative people I know have arrived and they're taking off their clothes. I'm embarrassed and I decide I will definitely not take mine off. I leave and go to another area of the community where I observe a group of people learning to do a circle dance and to become clowns and acrobats. Then they build a human pyramid and there is a grand finale like a rainbow of light.*

SCENE 4: (What did you discover?) *I wish I had joined in their group because it looks fun and I think I've missed out.*

Identify the main elements in each scene

Reviewing Lee's dream scenes, we then looked for the main images, characters, objects, actions, decisions, feelings, and sidebar impressions that stood out to her.

SCENE 1: night, boat, ocean, aggressive man; wants me to get off against my wishes; I think it's dangerous to go in the water.

SCENE 2: trap door, dark water, air, ugly chunks in water; I am thrown into deep water, I swim hard to reverse direction to go up, I surface and breathe, I avoid ugly chunks; I'm afraid I'll drown, I'm afraid of hitting the chunks.

SCENE 3: distant shore, community, party, nudists, conservative people, group doing circle dance and learning to be clowns/acrobats, human pyramid, rainbow light; I go from water to land, enter community, I watch people getting undressed, I feel embarrassed, I decide not to, I watch group celebrating and making pyramid but don't participate.

SCENE 4: I feel remorseful that I didn't participate in the last group. (There are no symbols in this scene.)

Make associations with the elements you listed in each scene

The slashes represent the associations for the italicized word.

SCENE 1: *night*/unconscious, unknown; *boat*/something that keeps you safe in the water and lets you travel on water; *ocean*/huge storehouse of emotions; *aggressive man;* a part of myself that knows what's best for me and won't let me make excuses. *I have to go into the watery emotional world and I don't want to.*

SCENE 2: *trap door*/opening between dimensions or zones; *dark water*/fearful emotions; *air*/the mental zone, *ugly chunks in water*/subconscious blocks. *Even when I go down into the emotional worlds, I still try to get back to the mental as fast as I can.*

SCENE 3: *distant shore*/physical zone, daily life; *community*/a social organization or way of living in world with others; *party*/a gathering of like-minded people or a group belief; *nudists*/people who expose their vulnerabilities; *conservative people*/traditional beliefs; *group doing circle dance*/creation of unity; *and learning to be clowns*/ability to laugh at oneself; *acrobats*/ability to be flexible; *human pyramid*/aligning awareness into body-mind-spirit; *rainbow light*/experiencing the seven rays of consciousness, moving into a higher experience. *I'm intrigued but I don't feel like I belong enough to join in.*

SCENE 4: There are no symbols.

Look for love and fear; identify the dream zones

When Lee reviewed the dream scenes, it was clear to her that she had experienced fear responses when she was thrown into the ocean, tried to avoid the ugly chunks, avoided the nudist party, and didn't participate in the group that was celebrating. She realized this dream was predominantly about some process in her subconscious mind.

When she looked at the scenes to sense what dream zone she was in, she realized that boats and deep water were symbols that relate to the lower emotional zone, and that the floating ugly chunks were probably subconscious blocks. When she surfaced and breathed air, she was entering the mental zone to begin examining her beliefs.

As the scene shifted and she came ashore and entered the community, she felt she was dealing with ideas that had more to do with the way she acted socially in her physical, daily life. When Lee watched the group doing a circle dance and making a pyramid, she sensed she was looking at what it could be like in the higher mental zone and perhaps even the causal zone. Perhaps this was a key to help her deal with her fear.

Look at the dream as literal first; try to sense its core purpose

Lee said to herself, "If this dream is the record of my soul doing something real, what was I doing?" She looked at Scenes 1 and 2 and noticed that they were predominantly about resistance to leave her boat (safe emotions) in order to go underwater into the deepest, darkest part of the ocean (subconscious underworld of suppressed, scary emotions). She avoided the ugly chunks (subconscious blocks/fears) and tried to get back to the mental realm where she was comfortable. In Scene 3, she then shifted her focus toward the beliefs that limited her participation in daily life. Embarrassment at being nude (revealing herself to others), even though conservative people were doing it, caused her to leave the gathering. Hesitation again caused her to miss out on the celebratory group that formed first a circle (create unity), then learned to be clowns (laugh at oneself) and acrobats (be flexible), created the pyramid (balance the body, mind, and spirit), and then experienced the rainbow (expand via the seven rays of basic life force energy). Lee believed that the core purpose of this dream was for her soul to show her that to have the joyful experience she'd missed out on, she'd first have to face the "negative" emotions in her subconscious mind and learn to be more vulnerable and open to others.

Bridge the dream meaning to something pertinent in your life

The last scene in a dream often holds the key to bridging the dream message back into ordinary reality. In Lee's case, she felt remorse at having missed out on something that seemed fun. This helped her draw a parallel to the way she was living. She was not socializing with others much, preferring to remain at home and read books. She had an opportunity to go to France with a friend, but turned it down because it cost too much. She had stopped seeing her psychologist and bodyworker, too, because she said it was an extravagance. After her dream, Lee realized she was hiding and making excuses because she was afraid of being rejected by others.

Reflect on and review the meaning for a period of time

When you figure out your dream, the process may not be finished. Try holding your insight loosely for another week or two, or even longer, to see if other related thoughts generated by daily life begin to connect the dream to a larger constellation of issues. Perhaps the meaning you arrived at will broaden and show you more about what to do. During the week following her dream, Lee noticed a friend of hers who was acting the same way she had been. This helped her decide to change her behavior.

Decide how to act on the dream's message

The whole point of interpreting your dreams is to find the message your soul is trying to deliver. That message always points toward greater self-knowledge and self-expression, and always asks that you apply the information in an appropriate way. As a final step, ask "What are my options for action? What is the first step I can take to act on the advice or insight I've been given?" Lee decided to take a class that would get her out of the house one night a week, attend some bookstore talks, and have a few friends over for dinner and a movie.

Complete an incomplete dream structure

The final scene in a dream, like the denouement in a book or play, is often quite short. It may be a simple commentary or observation, or an action that carries a summarizing message. Sometimes the last scene may be missing, with the conclusion implied. When you can't find Scene 4, try making it up later. Here's one of my own dreams, which seemed to have three distinct parts instead of four. After working with a role-playing technique in the existing scenes, I extended the dream in a meditation to find the fourth scene and the message.

> SCENE 1: *I drive to a lake to view the full moon, and park my car (which is a Jeep) on a steep incline facing east where the moon will rise over the water. When the moon is high I see that the lake has flooded and is up to the floorboards of the Jeep. I feel helpless, stranded. I try to back out, but skid in the mud.* SCENE 2: *Then I look up into the sky and see a ghostly group of young people floating down a beam of light, lit up in a ghastly way by the moon. They are dressed in baggy clothes, huddled tightly together as they surf across the sky with empty expressions on their faces. I get a creepy feeling.* SCENE 3: *When I look back at the moon again, I notice a partially complete triangle drawn behind it in calligraphic brushstrokes.*

First, I picked the most predominant images in each scene — the ones that attracted me the most. Then I role-played each one and wrote directly in my diary, speaking as the image:

> ✔ The lake said: *"I am full of wisdom, soaked up from this spot of land for thousands of years. Now the rains have filled me with wisdom gathered from all over the world. Don't be afraid of me. Get out of your land vehicle and wade into me, swim in me! You will be safe. Swim under water, change elements, leave the safety of your four-square world. Let go of control. Feel everything!"*

✔ When I merged into the image of the group of teenagers, I found they couldn't talk. They were lost, caught between dimensions in some sort of limboland. They seemed to be looking for ordinary reality but couldn't find it. They were indeed like ghosts. My inner voice said: *"These people are part of a soul group that has not been able to incarnate all the way yet. They need help from people who understand emotion."* I realized the group of teenagers symbolized many of today's young people, as well as parts of myself that were similarly lost.

✔ The moon said: *"I reflect your own light and knowledge back to you so you can understand yourself. You came to watch me tonight so you could see something important. I am only full once in each cycle and this is when I transmit the most clearly."* The triangle said: *"I am the symbol of the unification of body, mind, and spirit. I am almost complete; it is your faith and attention that will complete the trinity so continue on your path with determination. When I am complete, the moon and I will reveal greater truth to you."*

At this point the dream made no sense. The parts seemed totally disconnected. I closed my eyes and put the three scenes back together again, but this time:

I visualize myself getting out of the Jeep instead of trying to back away. I wade into the water, then swim around and dive under water — as the lake symbol had advised. As I surface, I see the moon's reflection trailing across the water like a pathway. Then I see the ghostly teenagers somehow find their way to the moon, and they slide down the moonbeam, like kids on skateboards. They come all the way down into the lake with me. I swim over to help them learn to swim.

When I came back from my visualization, I realized that emotion truly was the missing element that would help the young people find harmony of body, mind, and spirit so that they could integrate totally into their own lives. I, or perhaps it was the societal "we," needed to surrender my earthy security and dive into the realms of intuition and feeling to open to the knowledge of what the young people needed. I realized then that this dream fell into a category that bordered on a vision; I was receiving insight about a societal issue and asking myself whether I was going to come forward to help young people. My newly invented Scene 4 seemed to indicate that, at some internal level, I had decided to help. But I also realized that a part of me needed to slide down a moonbeam into deeper emotion, too. So on another level, this dream was about my own personal process of balancing *my* emotions.

Understanding Scary Dreams

Using the information presented in this chapter, as well as in Chapters 5, 10 and 11, try to apply some dream-work techniques for yourself, so you can get a better feel for working your way through dead-end dreams blocked by fear.

Kat had been on the fast track in a marketing career in the Silicon Valley, commuting long hours, and under constant pressure to meet deadlines. She began to have a series of scary dreams where she was being chased by a tall thin man with a long, stringy ponytail. Each dream would wake her up shaking. It didn't seem to her conscious mind that the ponytail man was the most terrifying ogre who had ever lived, and she couldn't understand why he threatened her so much. Kat decided to ask her dream self to help her shift the repeating nightmare, so she could receive the information she needed from it. She did a meditation before sleep and asked for a guidance dream. Here's what she dreamed:

> *I'm running through a dense forest along a narrow path. I can't stop because the ponytail man is after me again. I run across a bridge and am far enough ahead of him that I can stop. I think, "I can't go on! What am I to do? I can't run from him forever." Just then, Buddha steps out from underneath the bridge and says, "Why don't you just listen to him?" I think "That's a good idea!" and sit down on a smooth rock to wait for the ponytail man. He catches up and I say, "I'm ready to hear you."*

Then Kat woke up. She was frustrated that the dream hadn't completed itself, but happy that it had progressed beyond its usual point.

When Kat called to tell me about her progress with this dream, I did a short dream interview with her. I asked if the ponytail man was an archetypal male figure from the business world in the Silicon Valley. She said no; she had just realized he was actually an old neighbor. The man had been heavily involved in a spiritual community, and especially in personal service to the group's guru. He was so devoted that he seemed to have no life of his own; in fact, he had donated one of his kidneys when the guru needed a kidney operation. "So what does this man represent that would be so terrifying to you?" I asked. "Well, it seemed to me he had no freedom at all, like he was tied to his work in a very sacrificial way. He even gave up one of his body parts!" she exclaimed. "And where in your life might you be sacrificing your freedom to the point of giving away a part of yourself?" I continued. "Oh, my gosh," she said, "it's so obvious! I'm just running and running for my job, and I hardly have any time for myself or my family. I haven't wanted to look at it because it means if I'm honest with myself, I'll probably have to quit and change jobs, or rethink what I'm doing with my life."

"In your dream," I asked, "what does Buddha represent to you?" She thought a minute and replied, "Buddha is a kind, neutral, detached person who can think clearly because he's not emotionally involved." I reminded her that this neutral character was probably a part of her own awareness, and that she was capable of clear thinking, too, when her emotions weren't involved. This part of her awareness had given her a specific message: *"Why don't you just listen to him?"* We decided to go back into the last dream she'd had, where she woke up before the ponytail man could tell her why he'd been chasing her. In a visualization meditation, Kat imagined the dream replaying to the point where it had been interrupted before. Then she let it continue, receiving whatever came. Here's what she saw:

> *The ponytail man sits down on a rock across from me and I notice he's out of breath from chasing me. He says, "I want to remind you that you can have your work be about what you love. You can listen for what the universe wants to tell you and you don't have to make everything work all by yourself. Your life, value, and purpose are not 'over there' but right here. Give what you want to give, but don't sacrifice yourself."*

Kat immediately realized the ponytail man was trying to help her, that he had not been sacrificing his freedom by serving his guru, but had been showing her the whole time about being totally devoted to what you love. Within four days, Kat had given notice at her job and was preparing to take a sabbatical. Within a month, she had had a new series of waking dreams — synchronous omens and elaborate deja vu experiences (discussed in Chapter 9) that seemed to be telling her, "You made the right decision. You're on the right track." Her guidance began to come to her effortlessly through coincidences in daily life, and she sensed a new path unfolding surely and amazingly.

Unsticking a Blocked Dream Message

In spite of all the techniques you can use for making sense of your dreams, on some occasions, you'll feel stymied. By playing with your dreams in a visualization meditation, you can free the flow of your imagination and find the interpretations that are meaningful. In this section, I explore some techniques that can help you create movement when you're stuck: re-dreaming your dream, backing up and extending your dream, and adding a character to gain perspective.

Re-dream and change your dream

William is a prolific dreamer, with many story-like dreams. Recently he dreamed:

> *I have taken a friend to the home of a wise old Native American man, a Don Juan type figure, with whom I have a strong connection. My friend is anxious to impress him, and interrupts him twice as we talk. I feel this is not right but let it go. It seems I have some important things to discuss with the shaman, but we never get around to talking about them. The shaman places two beautiful pottery cups on the table, though it's not clear if he is giving them to us or just displaying them. Suddenly I feel I must provide him with some fish, so I leave my friend with the shaman and walk down a hill to a*

market. I want to take one of the cups with me to hold the fish, but am again hesitant and don't do it. Once free of the house I feel energetic, and slide down the hill as if I were on skis.

When William described his feelings about this dream, he said, "The trip to the market feels like a diversion, and is symbolic of a history of my diversions in working with this man in the past. I never took full advantage of him when I was his pupil — I kept sidetracking myself, using diversions to avoid the main situation and knowledge he was inviting me into. This has also occurred several times in my career when I chose a path I knew I'd do well in rather than the more chancy one that had a bigger payoff." So overall, this dream left William feeling that he wanted to do something about his level of courage. When he re-dreamed his dream and gave himself permission to change whatever he wanted, and to allow the dream to turn out any way, here's what happened:

I am visiting the home of a wise old Native American man, a Don Juan type figure, with whom I have a strong connection. It seems I have some important things to discuss with the shaman, but I'm not sure what they are. I am a little uncomfortable but the shaman smiles and places two beautiful pottery cups on the table. He says, "One of these is empty and one is full." I look into them and they both seem empty to me. He says, "Give me something from the full one." I get scared because I can't tell what to give him, or from where. I want to go get some fish and put them in one of the cups so I can give something to him. "Just make it up," he says, like he's reading my mind. I pretend to reach in one of the cups and think I will offer him a pretend fish, but when I open my palm, there's a diamond in my hand. I give it to him.

When William thought about this strange new twist on his original dream, he liked the fact that he'd eliminated the various distractions yet he still didn't understand what the lesson was. When he did a role-playing process and spoke as the two cups, they told him that they were the same, that emptiness and fullness are flip sides of the same thing. When one filled up the other emptied. They also said that just because he couldn't see what was inside didn't mean something wasn't there. When William role-played the diamond, it told him that it was his true self and talent, and that when he reached into himself without having to know what his ability looked like, his self-expression would always be like a diamond. So William realized that his re-dreamed dream was offering him a profound teaching — showing him that he had been afraid of what he thought was emptiness inside himself. To see how full he was, he needed to trust his creative process more.

Back up and extend your dream

If your dream seems unfathomable, try re-dreaming it, but start before the point where you remember the dream actually beginning, run through it as you remember it and then extend it further beyond the point where it naturally ended. Julia dreamed:

I am being flown into a camp or outpost in the middle of a jungle in a small plane and we have to land on a dirt airstrip. There are lots of doctors and it seems like a hospital. I stay and work for a while but then I have to go back to the post I originally came from. The only way out is for me to fly myself — there are no pilots available — and I'd have to fly a huge cargo plane, not a little Cessna, and I'd have to clear a big forest and some power lines. I am scared to try but I have to leave.

This dream seemed incomplete to Julia, so she extended its scope both forward and back. First she ran through the dream once as she had originally remembered it. Then she backed up to the first scene and asked her dream self, "What was happening just before this scene took place?"

The first scene was: *I am being flown into a camp or outpost in the middle of a jungle in a small plane and we have to land on a dirt airstrip.* Backing up, she received this image: *I'm at my original post, something like a military base, which I can tell is near a coastal city, and I'm talking to a man who seems to be my "commander." The man is giving me instructions about why I am being sent into the jungle. "He tells me I'm doing it to learn to focus myself in the middle of distractions — it's a place where I can concentrate on that task."*

When Julia came to the last scene where she was scared to try to fly the huge cargo plane out of the jungle, she asked her dream self, "What happens after this scene?" Here's what she saw:

I decide I must fly the plane. I get in the cockpit and it's immense with hundreds of dials and switches! But somehow, if I go step by step, I know which buttons to push and the engines start up. They are extremely powerful. I think the runway is too short for this big of a plane, but there is so much power that there's no problem. I start down the runway and think the plane will be too heavy to lift off AND clear the power lines and forest, but the lift is incredible and steady. I go up and up and the momentum builds steadily. We clear the obstacles and continue up very high in the sky, higher than normal planes go. I have so much power that I'm just beginning to cruise when I notice I've already reached the old post where I'm supposed to land. I overshoot it because it takes time to get this plane to slow down now and come back to earth. I make a wide loop, circle back, and eventually land.

Julia went back through the whole extended dream and put the pieces together. She now had the insight that she needed to focus herself and not be distracted by outside influences. This helped explain the period of relative introversion she'd been going through recently. The last scene had a big impact on Julia. The experience of overcoming her fear and harnessing the great power of the cargo plane, and successfully flying it over obstacles, along with the great heights it was able to reach, showed Julia something about the nature of her own power — that it was possible to do much more than she previously thought she could.

Add an extra character to gain perspective

The technique of adding an extra character to gain perspective works especially well for frightening dreams where you feel helpless, or for confusing dreams where you need to clarify or learn about something. If you forgot to ask for help in the dream itself, you can always go back later in a visualization meditation and introduce a protector, a teacher, or an expert in whatever subject or activity you need help with. Carol used this technique to deal with an incomplete dream. Here's Carol's dream:

> *I am in my daughter's new apartment and it is spacious and pleasing. I see on three walls large paintings that I had done a long time ago and forgotten about. I am astonished and interested to see them again. I look at them from left to right, then right to left, and try to understand the message in each one. All I can think of is what I was doing in my life when I painted them, and I know there's more more to it.*

Carol woke before she could arrive at the insights she wanted, so she did a meditation and went back into the dream at the point where she became frustrated. She asked for someone to come help her. This is what happened:

> *Out of the dining room walks Henri Matisse! He comes over and points to the painting on the right. "This is the pictorial representation of everything you are learning about PATTERN. This one," he says, pointing to the second, "represents everything you know about how to work with SYMBOLS. And this third one embodies all the knowledge of NUMBERS." As Matisse continues to tell me what each of the paintings symbolizes, I realize how much wisdom I have gathered in the past, and how I have used these categories to make sense of the world.*

After gaining the perspective offered by her own internal Henri Matisse, Carol said, "I guess the dream is a reminder of what my real interests and essence are all about. The dream seems to be reaffirming that I should review and acknowledge the work that is ME and not forget who I am."

> *Dreams say what they mean, but they don't say it in daytime language.*
>
> —Gail Godwin

Your Dream Diary

1. Pick three dream fragments and write out an interview with your dream self about each one.

2. Pay attention to the cliches and puns you hear this week. Write them in your dream diary, then explore the underlying meaning of each.

3. Go back through your dream diary for the past few weeks and look for the four-part structure in each dream. You might make marks between the sentences where you think the scenes change. If a scene is missing, meditate and allow the gap in your dream to fill in, then write the new scene next to the original dream.

4. Go back through your dream diary and pick three dreams. Then write out your opinions and judgments about what occurs in each. See how those statements show you about your deeper self.

5. Pick three dreams from your diary and write about what has happened to you since you dreamed each one, placing special emphasis on insights, ideas, experiences, and even other dreams that tie in thematically. How has your understanding of the dream meaning deepened over time?

6. Pick three dreams from your diary and determine the message. Then decide what actions you are going to take to integrate the dream's advice. Then, act! And write about what happens.

7. Pick three dreams from your diary and go back into each one in a visualization meditation. At some point along the storyline, introduce a third character and see how that affects the outcome of the dream. Write about each one.

Part V
Make Your Dreams Come True

The 5th Wave By Rich Tennant

"Don't worry, the still life goes back as soon as I dream up a solution to _that_ particular problem."

In this part . . .

Once you can interpret dreams, Part V shows you how to use dreams intentionally to improve the quality of your life. Chapter 13 helps you apply dreams to your life work and career, while Chapter 14 helps you use dreams to improve communication and relationships. Chapter 15 gives techniques for using dreams for healing and stress reduction. Chapter 16 focuses specifically on enhancing your imagination and authentic creativity. Chapter 17 discusses ways to use dreams to expand your spiritual growth and receive superconscious guidance.

Chapter 13

Dreams and Your Life Work

- -

In This Chapter

▶ Recognizing your life work and purpose

▶ Staying in alignment with your life dream

▶ Using dreams for decision-making and problem-solving

▶ Setting and achieving goals with help from your dreams

▶ How your dreams can help you manifest what you need

- -

When you are inspired by some great purpose, some extraordinary project,
all your thoughts break their bonds: your mind transcends limitations,
your consciousness expands in every direction, and you find yourself in a new,
great, and wonderful world. Dormant forces, faculties, and talents
become alive and you discover yourself to be a greater person
than you ever dreamed yourself to be.

—Patanjali, Indian philosopher

*R*ight now, this very moment, no matter what you're doing, your soul is
prompting you from inside and out to express yourself authentically,
feeding you glimpses of your life purpose one by one, encouraging you to
make clear choices so you can do your life work. Your soul does this by
releasing visions into your higher mind that gradually filter down, become
recognizable ideas, make sense, and take on a motivating, enthusiasm-
generating quality.

You will recognize the bubbles of your life purpose when they surface
because they always attract your attention. Sometimes they'll be intriguing,
sometimes inspiring, sometimes enigmatic. The ideas may seem extra colorful, or soothing, or exciting, or even slightly frightening. You may do a double-
take with certain people, for instance, because they fit in with your life
purpose and work. You may notice the bubbles occurring outside yourself as
qualities you admire in other people's personalities, or in the things other
people like and do. Or, you may become aware of them through your own
inklings, budding desires, daydreams, and night dreams.

In this chapter, you can explore ways to improve your ability to stay attuned to your life purpose and life work through dreams.

Recognizing Your Life Lessons, Life Work, and Life Purpose

Each of us has a series of lessons to learn in life, and these lessons always pertain to achieving balanced self-expression and the integration of all the parts of ourselves into a smooth, working whole. Your *life lessons* are actually the fodder for your *life work,* and doing that work is your *life purpose.*

Life lessons capture your attention

What are life lessons? They're experiences that demonstrate a way to live that's based on the highest expression of personal character, the most harmony and compassion, the most graceful and efficient way to do things, and the true nature of the universe. Sometimes they come as revelations, sometimes as gifts, sometimes as challenges and hardships.

For example, you may need to understand how to use your masculine and feminine energies in a mutually supportive way, for example, or how to develop that fine-line balance between humility and confidence so you don't end up with the extremes of victimization and domination. Perhaps your soul wants you to heal old memories of being punished for expressing yourself so you can tap your great creative potential. Maybe you need to learn forgiveness or to be of service without being paralyzed by other people's suffering. You may need to speak more freely, or pause and think before you speak.

Whatever the focus, your life lessons will become the themes of both your waking life and your dream life. Do you always seem to attract people who cheat you? Are you chronically late for the good opportunities? Do you repeatedly find demanding jobs that deny you a personal life? These are iceberg tips that lead to life lessons. Dreaming about feeling heavy because you're wearing 15 layers of clothing? Maybe your life lesson is that you don't need so much protection from the outside world; perhaps you should shed a few skins and lighten up. Dreaming about camels crossing the desert? Maybe your life lesson is to practice conserving your energy over the long haul. Dreaming about having a baby? Maybe your life lesson is to have the confidence to release some new creation into the world. Table 13-1 presents some common life lessons.

Table 13-1	Some Common Life Lessons
Balance This	*With This*
Feel confidence in your own ideas.	Welcome other people's ideas.
Speak your truth spontaneously.	Be quiet when appropriate.
Be nurturing.	Be instigating.
Be of service.	Don't sacrifice yourself for others.
Be able to be alone.	Be able to be with others.
Be generous and unselfish.	Allow others to give to you.
Experience clarity and discrimination.	Don't criticize and judge others.
Learn your own boundaries.	Don't wall off from others and hide.
Have strong goals.	Let go of the outcome.
Be agile and flexible.	Don't spread yourself too thin.
Be strong and courageous.	Don't dominate others.
Take action at the right time.	Don't be impulsive.
Offer your ideas, help, advice.	Let each person have their own reality.
Be relaxed and centered in the moment.	Don't be vacuous and lazy.
Experience how unique you are.	Experience how similar you are to others.
Experience abundance.	Experience emptiness.
Create from nothing.	Let your creations go, and disappear.

Sometimes life lessons revolve around the development of new character traits in yourself — ones you need for well-roundedness in your personality so you can become more stable and mature. An easy way to begin to identify what these traits might be is to make a list of the things you envy or admire in your friends, colleagues, family members, and heroes. These are clues that indicate what your deeper self is starting to pay attention to. Next, take note of the personality traits in your dream characters. These, too, may point out characteristics you're trying to activate or balance in yourself. If you dream of a handsome Greek Adonis, maybe you need to see your own classic beauty. If you dream of a bum panhandling on a street corner, you may need to work on feeling more deserving and receptive.

Try this dream diary writing exercise.

What You Admire, What You Disdain

1. List your favorite actors and actresses, and why you like them.

2. List your least favorite actors and actresses, and why you disike them.

3. List other public figures, alive today, who you admire. Why do you admire them?

4. List other public figures, alive today, who you dislike. Why do you dislike them?

5. List women and men from history who inspire you, and why.

6. List women and men from history who disgust you, and why.

7. List the things you envy and detest about your friends and family members, and why.

8. List the things you are embarrassed to have others know about yourself, and why.

After you examine what attracts and repels you, see if you can determine the traits you want to develop more of in yourself, or develop a more positive expression of, or harmonize more effectively with their opposite trait. These will help you find insights about your life lessons. For example, if you wrote that you are repelled by Adolph Hitler, how might the quality of ego and need for control be present in you? Do you judge others negatively and try to get rid of them from your life? Is Hitler an extreme negative expression of something positive (like confidence in your own ideas) that you lack? Do you perhaps need to balance your aggressive energy with your receptive energy?

Life work is the soul's play

You've probably heard people speak of finding their mission in life, or having a calling. Some people are lucky enough to know from a young age what they want to do in life. Others zigzag between opportunities, moving from one that seems intolerable or okay, to another that seems a little better. You may be totally convinced about what you're doing or you may be in a process right now of zeroing in on your heart's desire. You may be an adventurer in training to climb Mt. Everest, or an entrepreneur with dreams of creating a financial empire, or a journalist who fervently believes in free speech who wants to anchor the national evening news. These focused kinds of endeavors certainly look like a mission or calling. And these people certainly seem to be doing their life work. But what if you're a waitress, or a machinist, or a landscaper? Is your day job the same thing as your life work? Is one "called" to be a housewife or a delivery man? Or is there something more lofty and glamorous that would qualify?

Life work doesn't have to be "important" and glamorous; it's really any activity that helps you learn your life lessons. If you need to learn about courage and independence, maybe mountain climbing really is for you. If you need to learn about service and patience, however, waiting tables may be just the ticket. No matter whether you feel called or just happen to fall into the work you do, it's still your soul in action, helping you at the level you're ready for.

There is no "right" life work. Your life work changes with your soul's needs. Some people maintain a primary focus their whole life, and even become famous for it. Others change careers midstream, often more than once, and sometimes to radically different careers. When your work changes dramatically, you have probably completed one series of life lessons and are off to take on a new batch. Your soul loves to play at various kinds of self-expression.

Your life work begins in childhood

Sometimes your life work is whatever you find yourself doing. Others times it's what fascinates and draws you inexorably to it, shutting out many other possibilities while you concentrate. It can be something you've always been interested in, something you even did as a child. When you were a child and became engrossed in play and other activities of your own invention, you no doubt lost track of time. There were probably activities you dreamed up that fascinated you repeatedly, that you indulged in again and again over time. In fact, you may still do these things or versions of these things. Interests and activities you naturally gravitated to early in life are often indications of your life work.

Try this dream diary writing exercise to revisit your childhood.

What You Did as a Child

1. List the activities you became fascinated with at a very early age and spent hours doing.

2. List your childhood interests. What games did you like to play?

3. What were your favorite books as a child?

4. List the activities you loved to do with your parents when you were a child.

5. What did you want to be when you grew up? What were your childhood dreams and fantasies?

6. How have your childhood interests continued through the years? Did they evolve into a career? Write about the continuity of your basic fascinations.

As you review your continuing interests, can you see how liking to draw as a child led you to become a graphic designer? Or how making hills and tunnels for your train set led you to study civil engineering? Can you remember how, when you were a child, there was very little difference between your dreams and what you allowed yourself to take action on? You had an urge to dance, and you did. You felt like coloring with the red crayon and you did. You had an idea to make ornaments for the tree in the front yard and you did. The same urges are coming to you now, it's just that there are more shoulds and cautionary ideas in the way, holding you back from expressing yourself freely. If you can remove some of the withholding thoughts, your soul can slide more of those fascinations through to you.

Your soul directives may be hidden by "shoulds"

Even now, some of these soul directives may be lurking in the back of your mind on the periphery of your awareness, hiding behind the shoulds. As you start to uncover and recognize these new inklings, and let them flow into action, you'll begin to receive even more instruction, both during the process of living each day and at night in your dreams.

Often the tiny new glimmerings of a change in your life work will show up as "floaters" in your field of awareness, ideas you may take note of and put a mental checkmark by, but which then pass from the center of your attention. In a short while, they pass back across your screen, perhaps with a slightly different nuance, or to be seen in a different light. They may pass through quite a few times, gradually registering as something of interest. Learning to recognize these inklings early can help you stay more in alignment with your soul's evolving experiential needs.

Try this dream diary writing exercise to peer into your mind's periphery.

What Lurks in the Periphery of Your Mind

1. List the things that have caught your eye or ear this week — in the news, on television or radio, in a bit of overheard conversation, in a phone call with a friend, or as you watched passersby on the street. Write about the underlying themes and why they interest you.

2. List the things you'd like to learn about.

3. List projects you'd like to start.

4. List the things you'd like to do if you had an uninterrupted month or two.

5. List the things other people have said you'd be good at.

6. Write about your recurring fantasies and preoccupations.

7. Write about the roles you play in your daydreams and night dreams.

Try this dream diary writing exercise to help you interpret your life work.

Interpreting Your Life Work Like a Dream Symbol

1. List the jobs you do: lecturer, software designer, father, magazine editor, fashion model, bodyworker, sales clerk, etc. Under each title, list the components of that job and the skills you must be good at to do it well.

2. Look at each component of the job and write about what it could be teaching you and how that quality helps balance out your personality. You might prompt yourself by asking, "If this skill/task/action were a dream symbol what would it mean?"

3. Then go back through your past and do the same thing for your previous jobs.

4. Review your work history, looking for the lessons you were learning, and how one evolved into the next. Write about your inner learning process.

Living your life purpose feels "just right"

When you become conscious of why you're doing the work you're doing, you will begin to feel you're on purpose. When you can see the life lesson you're learning from each job experience, each career change, or each new freelance project, you'll put less energy into resisting what you're doing and more into receiving the value from your chosen tasks. As you trust the flow of choices you make about what feels "just right" to do, the nature of your work will evolve. When this happens, ordinary work, even a fancy career, can transform into *right livelihood*. Right livelihood is a highly conscious version of life work; it's work that is who you are, not just about a lesson you're learning.

As you learn your life lessons and progressively do more of what you love, what feels fascinating to you, what consistently holds your curiosity, your life work will embody greater and greater amounts of your true self and talent. Life work has a natural tendency to evolve into right livelihood, especially when you pay attention to the signs that tell you if a situation or new direction is on purpose or off purpose for you. See Table 13-2 for guidelines to help you know if you're living out the purpose of your life.

Table 13-2	Know When You're Living On Purpose
When You're Not Living on Purpose:	*When You ARE Living on Purpose:*
Life is full of snags and bad timing.	Everything works; miracles happen.
No one seems to see or hear you.	It's easy to get good help.
Nothing seems interesting.	Opportunities come your way.

(continued)

Table 13-2 *(continued)*

When You're Not Living on Purpose:	When You ARE Living on Purpose:
You're pushing or pulling.	People are cooperative and agreeable.
People interpret you the wrong way.	People understand you easily.
People seem to be cheating you.	People want to help you.
Things aren't fun.	You are cooperative and agreeable.
You don't like yourself.	You like yourself and others.
You expect results too soon.	You experience "flow."
You feel a sense of urgency.	You experience synchronicity and coincidence.
You feel as though you have to do it all alone.	You feel confident but not egotistical.
You're procrastinating.	You feel lucky and generous.
You feel desperate and depressed.	You feel magnetic and radiant.
You feel like you're in two places at once.	You feel you have enough time, even if you're on a deadline.
You have no sense of direction.	You feel grateful and appreciative.
You're spending time in the past or in a fantasy world.	You lose track of time.
You have the heebie jeebies.	You see the good in everything.
You indulge in your favorite addictions.	You're doing what you love.
You lack confidence and motivation.	You're firmly in the present moment.
Your mind is fuzzy and confused.	You're focused and clear-minded.
You're trying too hard.	You're interested and continually curious.
You're being stubborn or vindictive.	You're not attached to the outcome.
You're chronically late.	You're open to surprise.
You're compulsive.	Your timing is impeccable.

Your life dream is your guide

Allowing life work to evolve into right livelihood is part of living on purpose, just as is achieving life balance, right relationship with others, and with the divine. But for most people, a vision of meaningful life work figures prominently in their *life dream,* which is the usually semi-conscious snapshot we hold about the way our life needs to look and unfold.

Having a life dream is a way of measuring how closely you're fulfilling your life purpose. A life dream is often lodged in the peripheral recesses of your consciousness, just as many of the individual components are hidden behind the shoulds of daily reality. You may think you're not clear about what your life dream is, but if an opportunity comes your way that veers from it too much, you won't find it desirable or real enough to undertake. If someone tries to force you to do something that will distract you from your life dream, you'll fight it tooth and nail.

Just as your night dreams are fluid and responsive to imagination, so is your life dream. It is capable of constant evolution, of growing to take on ever-increasing detail and depth. What you are currently doing lines up with your current life dream, but the whole thing can easily change to be an even fuller and more accurate expression of who you are spiritually. When it's time for your life to move on to the next chapter, your old interests and goals will fade and seem boring, while new ones will begin to sparkle in the dawn. Your night dreams feed your life dream and help make it recognizable. In addition, night dreams often notify you of an upcoming shift in your life direction, helping you get ready for the physical and emotional changes that will be required.

Pam, whose life work today includes working as a psychic detective and running a program called Smart Hearts, credits a dream from many years ago with helping her solve her "What am I here for?" issues. Pam dreamed:

> *I am sitting at a table facing a classroom. On the wall behind me is a projection of my natal astrological chart. I can't figure out why it's there for everyone to see like this. Then, in walk two men of great authority. They ask if that's my chart and I nod. They confer together and I hear them saying, "That's her all right, She's the one." I say, "The one WHAT?" Then they say, "You have been chosen to help people, especially children who are in danger." They show me some very scary-looking places in a ghetto and tell me I will be going there to help the children and keep them out of danger. I protest, yelling Oh, NO!" They assure me I will have nothing to fear because I will always be protected.*

Pam says it took a number of years for the dream to come to pass, but now she actually does go into poor urban areas where children are faced with danger on a daily basis. Her Smart Hearts program helps teach children how to avoid violence and protect themselves.

Your life dream needs regular updating

You may be involved with your own search, or you may be snagged temporarily on the path and confused by self-doubt. If so, you can deliberately ask for clarification of your life dream by incubating a night dream to bring you insight.

Try this meditation to focus on your life dream.

Clarifying Your Life Dream

1. Before sleep, sit up on the side of your bed, close your eyes, quiet your mind, and become centered. Imagine the spot at the back of your neck where your head and neck join.

2. Imagine a small ball of light about the size of a golfball floating in front of you.

3. Think about what you want to achieve in your dream time and formulate a concise statement describing your goal. Make it simple and specific. "Tonight I want a dream that will clarify my life work and life dream. I will wake in the morning with an insight about what I need to do."

4. Repeat the statement several times, out loud or silently, then imagine yourself waking in the morning with an answer. Put the statement inside the ball of light. Let the light activate the request.

5. Place the ball of light, with its dream seed, inside the back of your neck at that magic spot. Let the soft light gently penetrate and dissolve into your reptile brain and carry your message to the place where it can be acted upon. Relax and trust that this will occur as you sleep, and that in the morning you will have a dream.

The dream you receive may not literally make sense. If you ask about your new direction, you may not dream of a new job. You may instead dream of being at a party with a lively group of people. Perhaps this will show you that you need more work with groups or the public from now on. Similarly a clarifying dream that shows you driving a car with flat tires may indicate it's not quite time to move forward on anything. You may need to do some work on your "vehicle" first.

Decisions, Decisions!

To remain aligned with your life purpose and stay aware of the latest version of your life dream, you will have to continually check with your inner wisdom to see if the choices you've made are still relevant, or if new decisions are necessary. As your life work evolves into right livelihood, you'll be faced with a number of turning points. You may be forced to make tough decisions about whether to take a new job that would move you across country to live in a different city, or whether you should quit a job that gives you security but also makes you feel drained and depressed. Is it time to change careers? Perhaps you've been in a job search and have been offered not one, but four, jobs! Each has some particular advantage but which is best for you?

By itself, your conscious mind is capable of arguing the pros and cons of every side of every issue *ad nauseam*. You need a way to cut through the noise to make the important decisions that will further your life purpose. Your dreams can offer important, no-nonsense insight at these crucial juncture points.

Justin was part of a fast-growing, fast-paced dot-com company, working long hours under high-pressured conditions. As head of an important project team, he hardly had enough time off to do his laundry. He began to have a series of dreams that were set on boats of different kinds. In one, it was a large cabin cruiser on the ocean, and it was being rocked by gigantic waves. In another, it was a small rowboat, and Justin was alone in the middle of one of the great lakes without oars. In the final dream, which really got his attention, Justin reports:

> *I am the captain of an old paddlewheel riverboat, making its way down the Mississippi River, which seems to be flooded. I notice the boat is going faster and faster, and we are encountering rapids where there is usually calm water. The boat is tipping wildly side to side, and soon I notice I'm standing in several inches of water — on the deck. Then the water slowly starts to rise and I climb to the upper deck, but the water keeps coming after me. I know we're going down and I am preparing to give the order to abandon ship.*

When Justin woke, he realized that this was a serious message. Putting all his boat dreams together, he realized they had something to do with his job. He had been minimizing the inner disturbance his hectic work schedule was causing, and admitted he was "gutting it out" through periods of exhaustion and emotional isolation. He took the final boat-sinking-in-the-rapids dream as a strong sign that he should get out of the job. Because he wasn't sure what kind of job to replace the existing one with, and because he had a large amount in stock options, he decided to give it a little more time. Within several months, however, the stock market underwent a major correction and many of the new Internet companies, his included, lost value and went out of business. It was an extremely hard lesson for Justin, but he admitted that he'd been warning himself internally for months. Next time, he'd pay more attention!

Your dreams will often help you make decisions, whether they be about your life work or about other important components of your life purpose. Here are some types of dreams you can expect when dealing with your life work:

✔ **Early warning dreams:** As in Justin's case, your dreams may first alert you to a situation that is potentially limiting, even destructive to some degree. When you experience warnings, especially those that involve just you, pay special attention; they are often somewhat precognitive. Your dreams may also signal you about some new idea you need to pay attention to. If you dream of a new room in a house you know well, for instance, you may be showing yourself a new component of your life.

✔ **Sorting-out dreams:** If you are getting ready to make a decision, there may be considerable internal sorting of priorities, beliefs, pros and cons, and emotional fears that needs to be done before you'll be clear enough to choose what's right for you. If you dream of sorting through old boxes in your attic, basement, or garage, or throwing out items in your closet, you may be preparing for a change in life direction. Perhaps you dream of filing papers in your office, or creating binders with colorful divider tabs. You're probably just getting your mind organized and clear. Notice what you're sorting, and what you're discarding — this will give you a clue about the action to take in daily life.

✔ **Travel and on-the-road dreams:** If you've been dreaming of waiting for buses, boarding trains, catching planes, traveling to foreign countries, or taking road trips by car or motorhome, you're probably getting ready for a change. Have you dreamed of coming to a fork in the road and having to choose which direction to take? Or have you dreamed of crossing streams or rivers, trying to "get to the other side"? If you continually miss your connection, you may not be ready to make the decision. If you arrive at a destination at the end of your dream journey, see whether you like it or not, and what qualities it activates in you.

✔ **Dreams where you choose certain items:** Have you dreamed of picking certain foods from a smorgasbord, or certain objects from a tabletop? Out of all the options presented to you, why did your dream self pick the ones it did? Perhaps you dreamed of a litter of kittens, all with interesting markings and unusual colors. You picked one special one to be yours. What caught your attention? How did the choice make you feel? The choices you make in dreams indicate the way you want to feel to be most authentic.

✔ **Dreams that give you the go-ahead:** If you've been contemplating a certain course of action for a while, and the "should I?" thoughts have been floating in your awareness, if it's time for you to choose the option and move forward on it, your dreams will give you a sign. You'll dream of winning the lottery, or skiing exhilaratingly down a mountain, or driving a convertible on a country road. Maybe you'll dream of a dam breaking or an animal messenger that means something to you — like a hummingbird, or a white wolf.

Before your dreams can give you useful and accurate insight about an upcoming decision, you first need to do some preparation. Try this meditation technique.

Incubating a Decision-Making Dream

1. Fully define the problem to yourself. Describe the situation in detail and state your dilemma.

2. Examine your ideals and the feeling and experience you want the solution to provide for you. This way, when you are presented with a potential answer, you'll have something to measure it against.

3. List the solution options that occur to you. Remember to include "doing nothing at all" as one of the options. Leave a blank space for the possibility you haven't thought of yet. Your soul may have some super-solution that's much more magical and perfect than you've allowed yourself to consider.

4. Next, phrase your request clearly and succinctly and write it on a piece of paper. Before bed, read it slowly several times, and say it out loud, directing the request to your dream self. As with any dream incubation process, give your dream self the request or suggestion, and then let go in total faith that your request will be answered and your need fulfilled.

5. If, in the morning, you wake without a clearcut dream, pay attention to the mood or feelings you're experiencing, and ask for another clarifying dream the following night. Remember: Consistency pays off!

Solving Problems While You Sleep

History is full of stories about problems solved in sudden breakthroughs that came through a dream or half-sleep. Mathematical conundrums have been worked out, chemical theories postulated, books and films written, symphonies composed, and brilliant business ideas formulated — all in dreams. Chemistry's periodic table was the result of a dream, as was the entire second half of *Jonathan Livingston Seagull,* which Richard Bach wrote in a dream eight years after filing away the first parting frustration. Napoleon is said to have kept a dream journal where he recorded dreams containing military strategies which he often used in his campaigns. Warren Avis, who founded Avis Rent-a-Car, had been an Air Force combat officer in World War II, and was continually frustrated by his inability to reach destinations by ground transportation once his plane had landed. He had a dream that helped him connect strongly with the need for a solution to this problem, and eventually it led him to start a new business.

To receive insights about solving problems in your dreams, make sure to formulate and state your problem clearly and specifically first; this might include a statement like: "I'd like the solution to accomplish the following things. . . ." Then simply intend to receive a dream that will help you and proceed with you favorite dream incubation method.

Achieving Goals and Manifesting Needs

As you practice the fine art of staying on purpose, in alignment with your life dream, you find that the way you set goals may change, and that your ability to *manifest* things — to help make what you need and want into a reality — will improve. If you cultivate the habit of staying in the present moment and paying attention to the next "real" idea, the next "real" action that wants to be taken, you'll begin to understand that your goals are not really in the future, they're in a higher dream zone.

Set goals for the soul

Whenever your conscious mind, or bubble of awareness, expands up and out to the causal zone, you become conscious of your purpose and life dream, because it is in this body of collective consciousness where your destiny is lodged, coordinated with the destinies of all other people. The following sections describe how this works.

Your life dream is formulated in the causal zone

Your life lessons emerge from the areas where you have incomplete understanding and experience of yourself as a divine being. Think of it as light filtering through a sieve — the blockages produce shadows in your personality, but the open places relay the soul's wisdom and life dream accurately. Your life lessons are designed to help you remove more and more of the solid part of the sieve that prevents the fullness of your soul from shining through. The more loving you become, the more light gets through the sieve. The entire ever-changing balance between your light and dark places is held as a pattern or blueprint in the causal realm, or Zone 4. This is your life dream.

As you learn life lessons and add more light to your personality, the blueprint in the causal zone changes accordingly, and your life dream shifts. There is a magical interrelatedness between all souls in the causal zone — what you need for your personal growth always dovetails perfectly with what everyone else needs for their growth, and actions are coordinated to produce win-win situations for all involved.

Your goals emerge from your life dream

You may want to take a class on Native American drumming, or start a camp for teenagers with learning disabilities, or change careers and become a gourmet chef. Whatever ideas tickle your fancy, be assured that they wouldn't seem interesting unless they were part of your life dream. An idea that fascinates you soon becomes a desire and then a goal, if you trust the process of how your life is unfolding. You may not know yet how the goal fits in with the big picture, but you don't have to. Just trust! If the idea gives you the feeling of deep comfort, go with it. Your soul will make sure you get interested in the right things at the right time. Eventually you'll understand why it's all working the way it is.

Your goals are in the now, not the future

The reality you envision and the goals that come from it are intimately related. They are both in the present moment. Your life dream exists, contrary to popular belief, not in the future, but in the higher dimensions of your own self, which interpenetrate your waking reality right now. Thinking that you're already connected to your destiny — instead of feeling separated from it by time, distance, and difficulty — can make the fulfillment of your destiny easier and less of a struggle. You are already experiencing your life dream spiritually and mentally, but it wants to be known physically as well.

The goals that take shape in your mind are like the matches that light your passion for manifesting the vision. Your goals may come one by one, or in small batches, or as a glimpse of the whole big picture — but their function is always to point the way to an action that will help you experience what your life dream feels like as a tangible reality. Perhaps you want to become a psychologist. You can see your office and feel how it will be to work with clients and groups. That's a big picture goal. Bubbling up right along with that big goal is a thought: "I'll call around to get catalogues for all the schools, and I'll talk to my friends who are therapists." These are smaller goals that emerge from the big one.

The big goal is in the moment with you, the thoughts of which actions to take first are in the moment with you, and the enjoyment of doing each task mindfully is in the moment with you. When you finish one series of actions, more small goals will surface. For example, if you want to be a psychologist, act like one now and do what comes to you to do from that state of mind. Soon the big vision will be your physical reality.

If you project the experience of the fulfillment of your goals into the future, your body will never be able to know the reality, because it exists in the present moment. You must bring the experience of the fulfillment of your goals into the now. If you imagine that your vision already exists, your body will recognize the reality; as soon as it recognizes that reality, your vision will manifest for real. If you keep your dream in the future, it will always be there, just beyond reach, always *almost* happening.

Your life dream evolves

Every time you learn a life lesson and receive more of your life dream, everyone else's life dream shifts to accommodate your new plan. And each time they learn a lesson, you shift to adapt to their needs. And what's amazing is that everyone's life dream remains perfectly aligned for them. So today you may check your life dream and sense you'll be doing a lot of international travel over the next five years. But because millions of people are making choices minute by minute and growing and shifting continually, perhaps in a month, if you check your vision again, you'll sense that you won't need travel so much because someone else needs to do it more than you do. Instead, your life dream indicates you'll be getting interested in producing television programming for women. Where the travel sounded exciting before, now working in the media sounds exciting.

Don't lock yourself in to a life dream that may have already changed!

Because of the evolutionary nature of life dreams and their concomitant goals, you must learn to be flexible and not be too fixated about how you think the final outcome must look. Life is changing very fast these days; it's important to stay abreast of the latest version of your life dream, or you'll tend to sabotage your own progress and perhaps the growth of others as well. When your life dream gets stuck in an old version, you'll be jerked out of it to realign with what really needs to happen — and that disruptive drama is totally unnecessary. When you get stuck in an old version of your life dream, eventually you'll be jerked out of it so you can realign with what really needs to happen. That disruptive drama is unnecessary if you practice checking intuitively on your most recent, and deepest inner urges on a regular basis, and let yourself adapt easily.

Rock back and forth between worlds

Think of your consciousness as rocking out into the superconscious realms and higher dream zones to obtain the vision for your next period of life work that will manifest in the near future. Then you rock back into the physical world to take action and manifest the vision, one task at a time, enjoying each thing you're doing for its own sake. At the end of each task, you rock back out to check with the collective consciousness to see if there are any minor revisions to the "plan."

After every action, let yourself stop for a moment and regroup. What feels like it wants to happen now? You check your intuitive sense of the overall picture, while letting your body have a little rest. Then, when you feel full again, a new urge percolates into your conscious mind and you know just what you want to do next. This is the rhythm of awareness that helps you stay on purpose and fulfill your soul's goals.

Your dreams are a perfect vehicle for helping you develop this habit of bridging between the higher dream zones and the physical world. When you lose touch with your life dream, or are confused about which path to take, or even how to do a specific task, you can program a dream to bring you insight.

Manifest what you need

How many times have you decided you wanted to achieve a material goal, like buying a new house or finding your soulmate, and sat down to list all the qualities you want it or him or her to have? By focusing your mind, emotions, and body on an object of desire, you can often attract it to yourself quite rapidly. Hence the warning: "Be careful what you ask for (like your best friend's husband) because you just might get it (and all the problems that go with it)!" And then there's the saying, "If you haven't got all the things you want, be grateful for the things you don't have that you don't want." There are several subtle factors to pay attention to if you're going to try to help speed life's manifesting process along with your intentionality.

Use your will power correctly

It's easy to get a little cocky and impose your will on life, aiming to manifest things that make you feel more powerful and secure, but this will only separate you from the experience that you're connected to a divine intelligence that knows how to help you expand perfectly into your truth. And you'll end up feeling drained from "having to do it all." On the other hand, you don't need to blindly accept your "fate," relying entirely on providence to give you what you need, and assume that whatever comes *is* what you need. You don't want to think that the material world is the end-all, be-all, nor do you want to live as an ascetic, denying the importance of your physical humanity.

When you use your will power correctly, you'll know the ideas you receive naturally are part of providence, and simultaneously you should step toward the ideas with real action; no one else will do it for you. By acting in faith, the next idea you need to manifest will be drawn into your present moment and you'll realize you want it.

Remember that what you think you want may not be what you need. You may only be seeing part of the solution. Focus and stay loose at the same time.

Watch for dreams that signal a new period of manifesting

Have you dreamed you found money on the street or buried behind a wall? Did your slot machine pay off big? Or have you found stashes of jewelry, treasure, or rare old books in your dreams? Has someone presented you with a gift? Or have you given someone else a gift in a dream? Have you dreamed of possessing something valuable that multiplied or transmuted into something even more valuable? These kinds of dream themes indicate you're about to come into "an inheritance." It may be an inheritance of new wisdom, or talent, or a rash of great opportunities and contacts, or more financial abundance.

Use your dream state as a fertile field and sow your dream seeds

In addition to receiving insight about what you need next, how it might come, and what might be blocking its manifestation, you can also use your dreams as a way to amplify your intention to manifest your heart's desire. You can suggest a clearly defined goal to your dream self, with the request that it become real in the physical world in a harmonious and timely way. If the object of your desire is something that is on purpose.

This meditation works best when done before sleep. As in any incubation process, you want to plant a clear, specific suggestion in your reptile brain so your body can recognize the reality of what you want to happen.

Mocking Up Your Heart's Desire

1. Pick something you'd like to manifest. It can be something concrete, like a laptop computer, or a life situation like a new job or relationship. Do some groundwork. If it's a new laptop, get pictures of it, write down the purchase price, go to the store and see it, feel it, use it, understand it. Write about it and describe yourself using it. Let your body get familiar with the idea that the laptop is a normal part of your life. If it's a new job you want, outline the way you want to feel at work. Describe the people you're working with as if they're already present. Describe your desk and work space in detail. Describe the tasks you get to do, the challenges that stimulate you, the feeling of anticipating going to work in the morning. Create the emotional reality, and then fill it in with body-pleasing sensory details. You may not know the exact job description, but you know at a deep level the kind of self-expression and interaction with others you need to have to feel whole and happy.

2. Close your eyes and get centered. Feel your desire for the object/situation — and notice why you need it to enrich your life experience. In the clear space in front of you, visualize the energy blueprint of the object/situation you want to manifest. Feel its core vibration. Let your body get to know it, the way two friendly dogs become familiar with each other. Let your energy extend out through the blueprint and embrace it, becoming intimate and relaxed with it. Let the object/situation become a living part of your "field."

3. Get the idea now that the more transparent the energy of the object/situation is in your imagination, the further away it is in time and space. The more solid it seems, the closer it comes to present time and to your physical body. Concentrate on the energy blueprint and invest your attention and life force in it. As you do, draw in "matching funds" from the higher realms and know that the divine is also investing its attention to help this become real for you. Watch the object/situation "flesh out" with moving particles, molecules, shape, color, sound, and texture — becoming more and more real looking.

4. Say to yourself and to the divine: "I am ready to live with this *now.* I am willing to accept the growth and new experiences this will facilitate. I give permission for this to manifest immediately." Imagine capsulizing the image of you, your body, and the object/situation all living together, along with the command "I have it now" into a seed and dropping it down a chute from the center of your midbrain into your reptile brain at the base of your skull. Your reptile brain will happily launch into action.

5. Go to sleep.

By doing this exercise at least three times, you'll speed your process of manifesting your heart's desire. Keep an eye open in the following week or two for signs that what you want is becoming more real.

> *Whatever you can do, or dream you can, begin it.*
> *Boldness has genius, power, and magic in it.*
>
> —Goethe

Your Dream Diary

1. Go back through your dream diary with an eye to finding the life lessons peppered through your recent dreams. Make a list of the themes and specific issues you're working on.

2. Examine your recent dreams for the personality traits of the various dream characters. If each trait is something you might want to activate or balance within yourself, how would doing this help you learn a life lesson?

3. Make up a life work vision for yourself that has the elements of a mission or a calling. Totally blue-sky it and don't listen to your inner skeptic for once. How much does the one who's writing think you're capable of doing?

4. Write about how you're on purpose right now, and off purpose right now. What do you need to do to get back on purpose?

5. Examine the dreams in your diary to see what they may be telling you about your life dream. Have they been indicating a new direction, or new goals?

6. Scan through your diary and write about the types of decision-making dreams you've had. How have they given you direction and about what issues you've been preoccupied with recently?

7. Write about your life dream as extensively as you can. Then write about the desires and goals that occur to you as things you want to do after you've felt the reality of your life dream. List the actions you could take to bring that reality closer to you physically.

Chapter 14

Dreams and Relationships

• •

In This Chapter

▶ Discovering what dreams can tell you about relationships

▶ Easing communication problems with dream work

▶ Realizing the power of visitation dreams

▶ Understanding the hidden aspects of sex dreams

▶ Dreaming with a friend

• •

> *Only in relationship can you know yourself, not in abstraction,*
> *and certainly not in isolation. The movement of behavior is the*
> *sure guide to yourself; it's the mirror of your consciousness.*
>
> —J. Krisnamurti

Dreams, perhaps more than waking reality, are populated with a host of players, from animals to cartoon characters to old lovers to rock stars. You probably have dream relationships with a much grander assortment of personalities than you'd ever allow yourself normally. In this chapter, I show you how dreams offer countless opportunities to understand how you pick the people you relate to, how you give and receive, how you sabotage your relationships, and how you can use relationships as a path to higher awareness.

Relating More Skillfully

Dreams mirror your subconscious ideas about how you believe relationships function. They may reveal a past buildup of painful relationship experiences that has caused you to distrust others, or show the ways you protect yourself from intimacy, or how you might be jeopardizing current relationships by being too aggressive or reticent. Your dreams can alert you to the beginnings of important new relationships, or show you what's going wrong with existing ones, and can even point to the need to end a relationship. Here are some questions to ask as you prepare for sleep that will help trigger relationship dreams:

- Why don't I trust (my new boss, Cindy's daughter, women in general)?
- Why do I get (angry, sad, depressed, shy, too talkative, bored and restless) around others?
- What's blocking smooth communication between me and (my husband, secretary, son, cat, personal coach)?
- How can I feel complete and at peace with (my old girlfriend, my dead father, the person who owes me money)?
- Why are people misunderstanding me?
- Why do I repeatedly attract (losers, uptight businessmen, mother figures, expounders)?
- What was the hidden purpose of my relationship with (my last boyfriend, my yoga teacher, my grandmother)?
- How can I be of real service to (my sister, my colleagues, my neighbor)?
- How is my behavior contributing to my problems with (my boss, my tenant, my horse)?
- What will my next intimate relationship be like?
- Why am I afraid to be without a relationship?
- How can I understand what it's like to be (a man, a woman, a homosexual, an old person)?
- How can I counsel (my 5-year-old, my coworker, my editor, my lover) to help them solve the problem they're chewing on?
- How can I forgive (my greedy brother, my roommate who stole my boyfriend, the man who raped me, the coworker who claimed credit for my ideas)?
- What part of my personality do I need to develop to deal more effectively with (newspaper journalists, terminally ill patients, my narcissistic wife, artists and poets)?
- How can I increase my ability to relate to children and animals?
- Who can teach me more about my sexuality and releasing inhibitions?
- Who can teach me more about compassion and unconditional love?
- Who can teach me more about setting clear boundaries?

The following sections describe some of the ways your dreams address your relationship life and can help you improve your relationship skills.

You are alerted to new or changing relationships

Many people I've spoken with have reported at least once in their life that their dreams foretold of a coming relationship that would hold special significance. Marianne had been single for several years, when she had a dream she knew was important:

> *I see a desert like the Sahara and a caravan of camels is crossing it, coming toward me. I think it is Egypt. I sense someone I know is in that caravan. Then a voice says to me, very clearly, "In forty-three days you will meet a black man who will be very helpful to you."*

Marianne woke up, got up in a stupor, stumbled to her desk, and scribbled this message down on a piece of paper in the dark. In the morning she found the note and could hardly remember writing it. Nevertheless, she counted off 43 days on her calendar and marked the day: March 7. She forgot about it until she glanced at her daybook on March 7— she happened to be on a trip to Las Vegas for a convention, staying at a friend's house. Just before dinner, the doorbell rang and her friend answered it. Surprise! A man stood there, an old friend of her friend, who had just driven two days straight from back east to come for an unplanned visit. As he entered the room, Marianne was struck almost speechless by the chemistry between them. The fact that it was March 7 played upon her mind, as well as the fact that she was in a desert location and he had crossed a long distance to get there. The man was not black, however — in fact, he was almost a towhead blonde with light skin and blue eyes. But in dreams, she knew, it's not uncommon to represent things via their polar opposite. As they chatted over an impromptu meal, the man began to speak of a recent trip he'd taken to Egypt — a spiritual pilgrimage with a group that traveled down the Nile. After that, their relationship unfolded rapidly and lasted for many years. He was indeed helpful to her, providing guidance and the stability she had lacked.

Your dreams can also alert you to upcoming changes in existing relationships, as when a dating relationship is ready to become a marriage, or when it's time to let a friend go because you've grown apart.

You discover someone's hidden character

Many times your dreams will reveal an aspect of someone's character that you had not acknowledged consciously. Paul had just hired a new foreman for his construction business. On the surface everything seemed to be going along fine. But a couple of months into the new working relationship, Paul began to have a series of dreams about his foreman. The first was a simple dream fragment, where Paul saw the foreman hiding against a wall under the eaves of the shed they used to store tools. The next dream was a bit longer — he saw the foreman sitting at a table in a casino, playing blackjack, and losing a large pile of chips. In the third dream, Paul walks into his tool shed and catches the foreman stuffing drills and saws into a large duffel bag. When he confronts him, the foreman dives out a window and runs away.

This series of dreams seemed so odd, so opposite of the way things were running in the business, that they caused Paul to think about what the inner meaning might be. He began to watch the foreman more carefully. He noticed one Friday evening that some of the tools that should have been checked back into the shed were missing, yet on Monday they were back again. When he asked the foreman for an explanation, he received a story that sounded fishy. In time, Paul determined that his foreman had been bidding independently on small side jobs for Paul's clients, undercutting him and cheating him of business. And, he had been using Paul's tools on the weekends to do to his own work. Paul discovered the man had overwhelming personal debts that caused him to act dishonestly, and promptly fired him.

You are shown that a relationship is unhealthy and it's time to end it

Glenda had been in an on-again off-again relationship with her boyfriend Howie for three years. When she wanted to be close and develop more commitment, he backed away and became aloof. Then when she pulled back and developed more independence, he came forward with great charm and paid a lot of attention to her. She was feeling extremely drained, but couldn't seem to let go of the relationship because he did give her *some* attention, after all. One night she had the following dream:

> *I am lying on a bed and a man comes over to me who has a similar body type and coloring as Howie. He lays down with me and places a tiny black grain of some radioactive material on my left arm, just inside my elbow. It dissolves down into my tissue and starts to spread out in an ugly black line toward my hand and up toward my heart. I know it is going to poison me gradually and eventually I will die. Then he leans down and kisses me and presses his body against me and it feels fantastic. I almost forget about the black line. Suddenly I realize he is trying to distract me with sex while he kills me — that he's really just playing with me like a cat plays with a mouse.*

This dream had a strong impact on Glenda, who couldn't shake the eerie feeling. From then on, every time she saw her boyfriend, she remembered the spreading black line. It didn't take long before she decided to end the relationship.

You are warned of danger to a loved one

Veronica had a disturbing dream concerning her two young children. In it, her children were being hunted down and mangled by a mountain lion and a tiger. She saw all the gory details from a distant vantage point but was unable to move to save them. She woke in a panic and was so disturbed that she ran into her children's rooms and hugged and kissed them. Then she had to read a book and watch late night television to get back to sleep. The following week the children went on their first field trip to the local zoo. Because Veronica had to work, her husband went along on the outing. Veronica was so worried, she called her husband on his cell phone every hour. When we talked, she wanted to know, "Am I just being paranoid?"

When you have frightening warning dreams like Veronica's, should you take them as literal and precognitive, or interpret them symbolically? Was this a warning that indicated actual danger to her children, or was there some habit in Veronica's life that was harming her own childlike innocence, and she was not taking action to protect herself? Perhaps Veronica's dream self projected the danger onto the image of her children to get her attention.

When you can't tell if a dream about other people is predictive or symbolic, assume it might be both. Talk to the other person and share the information if you can — bring your concerns into the open. Or, affirm with your own actions that the situation will be as clear and safe as possible. Ask the other person to be careful and pay attention to the upcoming situation, without being fearful. Once you've communicated, let it go and remain centered and in faith.

Veronica could have talked to her children about how they felt about dangerous wild animals, or how they were to react if a stranger spoke to them. Then, she might have reassured everyone, "Dad will be with you, and just to see how you're all doing, I'll call you." After doing what you can to make the situation conscious, examine the dream as though it is also symbolic. How is it talking to you about your own fears, or a situation in your own life that has come to a head and needs immediate attention?

Try this meditation exercise to discover underlying intentions and patterns in your relationships.

Giving and Receiving Gifts

1. Pick a character with whom you're relating in some way. You can use a dream character or a person, even an animal, from your waking reality. Sit quietly, eyes closed, and be centered. Imagine you're sitting at a table facing your "partner." Make eye contact and allow yourself to feel your partner's unique energy.

2. Ask silently, "What are we doing for each other? What is the purpose of this relationship?" Then, look down on the floor next to you and you'll see a gift box — it can be any size and color.

3. Pick up the box and put it on the table in front of you. As you do, your partner will be doing the same thing. When both boxes are sitting there, let your partner give you the gift that's for you. Open the box and see what's inside. Take the gift out and look at it from all angles. What is it? What is its purpose? Why does your partner want you to have it?

4. Now you give your partner the gift you want to give. Watch as your partner opens the box, sees what's inside, takes out the gift and examines it from all angles. What is it? What is its purpose? Why do you want your partner to have it? By looking at what gifts are being exchanged, you can arrive at quick insights about the essential purpose of the relationship.

5. Thank each other.

Easing Communication Problems

How many times have you tried to say just what you mean, only to have the other person interpret it *entirely* incorrectly? And when you try to find out why they're reacting to you so strongly, they become even more agitated. When you then ask for their point of view, it makes no logical sense whatsoever, or they seem totally unfeeling. How are you to reduce these seemingly insurmountable differences in our communication styles? Your dreams may provide some relief.

You're taught to deal with difficult people

Anne had been leading meditation retreats for many years in partnership with another woman. Anne tended to be the support person, while her partner was showier and attracted more attention. After working together and building a following, Anne's partner suddenly took the mailing list, broke away, and started her own business, leaving Anne feeling betrayed and used. Anne was so shocked, she could hardly even *think* of speaking to her ex-partner. And yet, she was upset with herself for being angry and helpless. She felt paralyzed by her polarized emotions. At the height of her quandary, Anne dreamed:

> *I am standing in the lobby of a hotel watching people's comings and goings, when in troops my ex-partner in a swirl of grandeur, surrounded by an entourage of her followers. I am leaning against the registration desk, wearing a long cape with a hood that hides my face. She comes up to the counter but doesn't see me, though she's standing right next to me. I turn my head slowly and push the hood back and I stare into her eyes. She registers that it's me with an expression of great shock, but I just keep staring at her, letting her know that what she's done is despicable. I don't say a word, but she faints on the ground. I look down at her unconscious body, and I just step over her and walk into a conference room in the hotel. There I stand in the*

middle of the room and many people emerge from the shadows to greet me. They are all glad that I have become proud of myself and independent. They come up and hug me. Many say they've been waiting for me.

After her dream, Anne realized that her partner's "betrayal" was actually an opportunity for her to emerge into her own kind of work and be more visible. By not being intimidated by her partner in the dream, and simply stepping over her prone body, Anne felt she had focused herself and made an act of power. She felt more confident after that and redesigned her own workshops to reflect the new ideas she was now having.

You understand communication blocks

Denise had been experiencing an uncomfortable period where her friends and colleagues seemed to be constantly misinterpreting her. In her own mind she was being agreeable and open, but if she made a statement about what she wanted, or expressed an opinion, the people around her reacted as though she were being a prima donna. It seemed they were seeing her as aggressive and narrow-minded, which was far from her own view of herself. Stymied by the situation, Denise asked for a dream to help clarify things. Here's the dream she received:

I'm up in the attic of my parents' old house and have opened a trap door in the floor to expose a secret compartment where I keep a stash of old, very valuable jewelry I have collected for many years. No one else knows I have it and I think I am going to bring it out and let my girlfriends wear some of the special pieces for a party on Saturday. The scene changes and I'm putting diamond and ruby necklaces around the necks of my friends. I'm very proud I can do this. Then, the party is over and it's time for me to get the necklaces back to put in their storage boxes. But my friends decide they're going to keep the jewelry. I argue that it's mine but they just laugh at me and walk out together. I am frustrated and enraged.

After this dream, Denise thought about the connection to her real life problem. She finally saw that she had an attitude she'd not been conscious of: she felt she had to protect her personal "treasure" (her talents and inner self); when she did share herself with others, she believed they would not appreciate her generosity and would disrespect her, in effect "stealing" her gifts. She realized it was this unconscious belief about being misunderstood and devalued that was currently acting out in her life. To turn things around, Denise concentrated on her self-esteem and on expressing herself for her own pleasure. She let her friends react whatever way they wanted, and soon they mellowed and accepted her more at face value.

The following technique can bring some amazing results by telepathically clearing blocked communication with people in your life. You can even use this meditation to improve communication between parts of yourself.

Tossing the Ball

1. Close your eyes, be quiet and centered. In the clear space in front of you imagine an empty chair facing you. Let someone you're currently having trouble communicating with come in and sit down in the chair. Make eye contact but don't try to say anything.

2. Notice that on the floor next to you is a ball. Pick it up and set your intention to have an easy game of catch with the other person; then toss the ball to them. Notice how you throw it. How much force do you use? Notice how they catch it, and how they toss it back. Are they cooperative? If they don't cooperate, start again with a clear intention to have the game work smoothly. Continue until the exchange becomes even. Then set the ball back down.

3. Say something to your partner that you've always wanted and needed to say, and let them hear you and acknowledge you. Then let them say something to you that they've always wanted and needed to say, and hear and acknowledge them.

4. Thank each other and let the person get up and leave.

You develop empathy

Patrick had been friends with Ben for 15 years, but lately Ben had been acting stand-offish and aloof. He didn't want to socialize and would hardly even talk. He radiated an air of irritability when Patrick was with him, and Patrick wondered if he'd done something wrong or offended Ben without knowing it. When he brought up the subject, Ben would just say, "It's nothing." Finally Patrick had a dream:

> *I'm at the city zoo and I'm walking through the primate house. I get to the gorilla section and there, in a huge cage, is Ben. He's hanging onto the bars, looking scared and forlorn. Behind him is a giant silverback gorilla, who must be ten feet tall and looks quite old. The gorilla, though imposing, is sitting in the corner at the back. I can't tell if he's dangerous or sick or asleep. It just looks like Ben doesn't want to be in there with him.*

That week, Patrick decided to call Ben and tell him about the dream. Amazingly, it had a powerful impact on Ben, and he finally opened up and shared what was going on with him. It seems his father had been developing Alzheimer's disease and it had recently been progressing rapidly. It looked increasingly as though it would be Ben's responsibility to go back to his home town to care for his father, which would mean he'd probably have to give up his job and move. He was feeling just like the image in Patrick's dream — caged by the circumstances of his life. By sharing the dream, Patrick realized Ben wasn't angry at him, and opened a healthy dialogue with his friend so together they were able to discuss options and come up with viable ways for Ben to approach the upcoming change in his life.

Dreams about other people

We commonly dream about the people who are, or have been, familiar to us. Here's what it might mean if you dream about these different characters:

Mother: The archetypal mother is the one who gives love and nurturing unconditionally, but you may have your own personal symbology based on your mother's set of character traits. "Mother" speaks to your need to give new life or nurture yourself or others.

Father: The archetypal father is the provider, the authority, the protector. Your father may have differed from this, so also look at your own symbology. "Father" speaks to yourself about your need to develop these characteristics in yourself, to be stronger.

Lover/Mate: Your love partner helps you understand how to feel complete and balanced in your internal masculine-feminine energies and to know you are lovable.

Acquaintances: People you know in passing can serve as reminders to you about specific behaviors. The rude check-out clerk at the market might remind you to be kinder to others. The stuttering doorman at your apartment building might remind you to speak more clearly. The waitress at your favorite breakfast place might remind you to serve others with a cheerful attitude.

Boss/Teacher: Your boss or teacher gives you instructions and information. If you dream of them, you may be speaking to yourself about your attitudes toward authority, or your own authority.

Baby: Babies represent new life, the birth of new ideas, a new aspect of yourself, innocence, and a need to be nurtured and protected. How are you like a baby right now? What part of your life is still fragile and forming?

Pets: Your pets, past and present, represent certain "pet" emotional patterns in yourself and in your family. Your pets may show you parts of yourself that need special attention. The beloved pet often represents the state of unconditional love in your life. The type of animal can indicate traits you want to develop in yourself.

Strangers: Total strangers may introduce new aspects of your personality to you. If you dream of their name, look for puns and layers of meaning in the words.

You receive insight to counsel someone

Lynda had a young teenage daughter, Danielle, who was beginning to dress in a provocative manner. Her clothes were becoming skimpier, tighter, and shorter. For a while Lynda let it go with a few snide comments, but Danielle continued to bring home outfits from the mall that seemed increasingly questionable. Lynda threatened to cut off her allowance, and some mornings forced Danielle to go back and change into a blouse that covered her navel. But she found out from one of the other mothers that Danielle was taking little crop tops to school in her backpack and changing once she was there. One morning she came downstairs wearing an outfit in which she looked like a prostitute, and Lynda had a fit. "You look like a streetwalker!" she shouted at Danielle. "Go upstairs and change!" "No!" shouted Danielle, who promptly ran out of the house. At her wits end, Lynda had a dream — it was just a fragment but it helped Lynda to a new insight:

> *I am looking at myself in a full length mirror. I'm a little blurry around the edges and I try to focus my image by squinting. Then someone behind me throws a rock at the mirror and it turns into water and ripples spread out all across my image and I seem to disappear.*

It came to her the next day that this was possibly the way Danielle felt. Lynda had a quick intuitive understanding that Danielle was having a difficult time seeing herself, or knowing who she was. Lynda's reactionary behavior and agitation were only confusing Danielle even more. So Lynda had the idea to talk to Danielle candidly about the impression she was giving to others, especially boys, and to ask whether she understood that there could be surprising sexual responses that she might not be ready for. They had their conversation, and as Lynda stayed calm, Danielle was able to get in touch with the fact that she really wasn't clear what impressions she was giving off, and she really wasn't ready for sex and sexual attention. Together they were able to rethink Danielle's wardrobe so she felt similar to the other girls, not too much at risk emotionally, yet original.

You complete a relationship that ended badly

Cory had been very much in love with a man who rejected her suddenly for another woman, with no explanation. It had seemed incomprehensible to her that he didn't really love her because they'd seemed so close for the two years they were together. There had been no hint of trouble or incompatibility. For several years she had been plagued by recurring fantasies of wishing she were still with him. Though she knew there was no hope of him coming back, she couldn't seem to let go. Finally, she had an interesting dream that put the relationship in a new light and helped complete it for her. She dreamed:

> *I am in the lobby of a spa/resort and I'm carrying Ken around on my back. Even though he's much bigger than I am, I carry him around and around, up some stairs and back down, and as I do, he is acting out in all kinds of crazy and sexual ways on my back. I'm embarrassed because so many people in the lobby can see us and I think it's slightly crude. But finally, I just finish and I put him down and walk away. I notice there are several people leaning against the walls in various spots, who've been watching what I'm doing. They are called "emissaries." I stop next to one and she says to me, "Why did you do it?" — implying: "Why did you carry him so long?" I say, "I just wanted to say goodbye." And I knew what I meant was that I knew Ken from another time, like a past life, and I loved him but I wasn't supposed to be with him this time as a partner. But I did want to spend a little time with him for "old time's sake."*

Cory felt remarkably free after her dream, as though it hadn't occurred to her that *she* might have ended the relationship mentally and energetically before he did it physically.

Freeing Your Sexual Self

Psychologist Sigmund Freud believed there was a repressed sexual motive behind most dreams. To him, a bird represented a penis, a snake represented a penis, and a hose represented a penis. A wineglass represented a vagina, a cave represented a vagina, and a glove represented a vagina. Flying represented sex, falling represented sex, and ascending and descending stairways represented arousal and release in sex.

Today, dream therapists understand that even purely sexual dreams aren't always about sex. They can address a variety of issues, from fear of intimacy to a desire for a greater experience of the ecstasy of the soul. Sexual energies are a normal part of your body rhythms during sleep, so it's not odd at all that many categories of dreams might be remembered and symbolized in sexual terms. And, granted, our media is glutted with sexual messages.

We're profoundly influenced by our culture's unrelenting emphasis on selling consumer products via sexual imagery and innuendo. We're flooded with sexy cars, clothes, song lyrics, prime time television shows, and teenage pop stars. Is it any wonder that dreams about sex are at the top of the list of action dreams? Here's how you can penetrate through the outer layers of sexual dreams to discover what might really be going on in your subconscious mind.

The hidden meanings of sex dreams

Explicit sexual activity is a common dream theme, and though the physical experience of it is often quite literal, these dreams may not be the result of mere wishful thinking or sexual repression. The meaning of sex dreams often goes beyond the fact that you're simply horny or starved for affection — your dream self may be talking to you about merging several aspects of yourself together, or loving a part of yourself you've been judging or rejecting. Explicit sexuality in dreams often symbolizes even deeper layers of need and longing. Here are some possible meanings for a variety of sex dreams:

✔ Sex with your boss or an authority figure like a teacher, shaman, or magician, may demonstrate how it feels at a deep level to receive greater authority and knowledge so you can be clearer and more effective in the world.

- ✓ Sex with a foreigner or someone of another race might mean you are integrating the character traits of that particular culture and racial consciousness into your personality, or allowing new, more exotic parts of yourself to surface.

- ✓ Sex with someone of your own gender may simply show you how to better accept and love yourself.

- ✓ Sex with an old lover may indicate you're trying to integrate qualities from that person that you felt didn't get a chance to really take hold previously, or which you forgot. You may also be attempting to create closure concerning the relationship.

- ✓ Sex with a friend's primary partner may indicate you want to integrate a quality that you feel unentitled to, separate from, or that you feel you have to be secretive or even underhanded to obtain.

- ✓ Sex with an animal may seem outrageous to your waking mind, but in dreams anything is possible and credible. Examine the archetypal characteristics of the animal to understand what traits you're trying to activate and embrace in yourself.

- ✓ Possessing the genitalia of the opposite sex in a dream can help you understand your own opposite inner male (animus) or female self (anima).

- ✓ Sex with an extraterrestrial or energy being may indicate that you're trying to merge your awareness into a higher dimension.

- ✓ Sex with a celebrity or movie star can show that you want to elevate yourself to the level of visibility, self worth, and status represented by the other person, or that you are activating qualities in yourself represented by that person.

- ✓ Sex with cartoon characters may indicate a need to free up your imagination and become more fluid, pliable, spontaneous, and playful.

The therapeutic value of sex dreams

Many sex dreams begin as innocent explorations of romance. They often progress into territory you would be abhorrent to explore in your waking reality, since your dream self is much freer of shoulds and shouldn'ts than your waking conscious mind. In dreams you can revisit sexual trauma and abuse to start healing an old wound. Or you can move beyond your sexual comfort zone, experiencing sensations you might be too inhibited to feel while awake. Dreams even give you the opportunity to cross the boundaries of societal taboos. Taboo-breaking dreams may be quite troubling, leaving you with an experience of what rape is like, or how it feels to be unfaithful, or to sleep with someone much, much older or younger than you, or with an animal, or with many people at the same time, or with a family member.

It's important when dealing with disturbing sexual dreams to remember that the dreams are usually speaking to issues of working with energy flows and new character traits within your own makeup. You're not turning into a pervert! Remember, mistaken literalism is the single biggest stumbling block in understanding the healing messages of sex dreams.

Here are some questions to ask when analyzing a sex dream:

- ✔ Is this dream about sex or something else?
- ✔ Does the dream give me a symbolic picture of longings in me that are deeper than sex?
- ✔ Is this the result of wishful thinking or frustration?
- ✔ What am I exploring that I'm afraid to explore in waking reality?
- ✔ Is this about a psychological process inside myself?
- ✔ Does this help me learn to increase my ability to be intimate?
- ✔ Does this help me learn to set clear boundaries, or release false boundaries, between myself and others?
- ✔ Does this help me overcome my inhibitions?
- ✔ Does this help me understand a taboo?
- ✔ Does this help me heal a sexual trauma or confusion?
- ✔ Does this help me access parts of my vitality I have suppressed?
- ✔ Does this help me make a decision about sex?
- ✔ Does this give me information about how to regulate my sexual energy and desire?
- ✔ Am I trying to integrate new traits into my personality?
- ✔ What am I trying to learn to love?

The following sections give examples of how sex dreams can be helpful.

Overcome inhibitions and emotional wounding

Alyssa had had an inordinate number of short-lived relationships, never feeling confident or settled enough to commit to one person for very long. In the process of exploring so many different personality types, she ended up with many emotional wounds from being rejected and demeaned by various men. She had reached a point where every man she attracted was a repeat of the same archetypal pattern — and it was one she was now able to recognize and see as extremely dysfunctional. But Alyssa didn't know how to break out of it. How was she ever going to learn to recognize a healthy relationship? All the supposedly "good" men seemed boring to her.

Responding to her semi-conscious request, her sexual dreams began to be about making love with men she didn't know, men who were very unlike her normal "type." In some of the dreams she was surprised that someone who looked unattractive at first could be a good lover, and in other dreams her partners were especially gentle and loving, and she found she enjoyed it! After about a year of exploring new kinds of sexual and romantic partners in her dream state, Alyssa met a man who broke her old mold, and she fell in love at long last with a healthy, emotionally mature person.

Break taboos without horrendous outcomes

There is something rather fascinating about what's forbidden. We may not admit in our daily life that taboos are attractive, but at night we often step right over the "do not enter" barrier without a second thought. Certainly society has good reasons for the taboos against incest, adultery, murder, and pedophilia, to name a few. But in dreams, these things don't necessarily cause the same negative repercussions they do in physical life. By overcoming the taboo against killing his mother, for instance, David was able to access the depth of his anger and mortification, allowing him to enter a process of healing his sexual abuse.

If you've been in a marriage that's become nonsexual, dreaming of an orgy might encourage you to be more overtly sexual with your mate. Similarly, you may not be paying enough attention to your mate, preferring to look else-where for sexual fantasies or experience, thus avoiding intimacy. You might dream of having an affair with your best friend's wife, and in the dream she is so possessive that she tries to tear off your arms and legs and keep them! Maybe your wife isn't so bad after all. . . . Perhaps your conscious mind has been programmed to be prim, proper, and always cheery — to the extent that you can't even watch scary movies or hear about negativity. Your dream self may dream of making love with a famous serial killer just to put you in touch with the energy that's stored in the dark side.

Enjoying Telepathic Visitations

Have you ever dreamed you walked through other people's houses early in the morning on your way "home" from your dream excursions, and the houses seemed absolutely real, with the residents still sleeping upstairs? Have you ever visited a friend or relative, had a full conversation, or even a big hug at the end of the visit, and "knew" you'd really been there, but when you woke, realized you'd been in your bed all night? Perhaps your mother, husband, or older brother, who died several years before, visited you and gave you a reassuring message during the night.

These types of dreams are called *visitations,* sometimes also referred to as *astral travel* dreams. They are marked by communication that seems verbal but is actually telepathic — ideas are transferred directly from mind to mind, often with perfect clarity. The quality of the other person's energy also has a "real" feeling — many people say they were convinced the other person was actually there with them.

As I was in the process of writing the earlier part of this book, my father died suddenly and unexpectedly. I was unable to be with him when he died, had had no striking precognitions that he was leaving, and as a result I felt very incomplete. I hoped he would try to make contact with me in my dreams. One morning about 4 a.m., I woke quietly as though the sleep had been peeled gently away. It took a moment to realize I was awake, because I still felt the reality of the dream I'd just been in. Then, joyfully, I realized my father had been with me only moments ago! This is the dream:

> *My father has come to visit me and I suggest we walk to town to a cafe I know so we can talk. He is dressed nattily in an open-necked sport shirt and sports coat. He looks extremely rested; his face is unlined and his hair is soft and fluffy. He is obviously at peace and quite cheerful. We amble easily to the cafe and sit. I tell him telepathically about all the decisions and quandries that are weighing on my mind right now. He smiles and says, "It makes me happy to see you and your sister thinking about the same things I was thinking about at the same age." And he explains telepathically that he will be looking in on us, keeping up with our progress.*

This telepathic communication dream was satisfying at a deep level, helping reassure me that he had released the emotional pain from the last few years of his life, and that he was aware of me from whatever level he was on now. It helped me complete the experience of my father's passing and move on.

Try this meditation to help you develop your telepathy.

Sending or Receiving a Telepathic Message

1. Before bed, sit on the side of your bed, close your eyes, and be centered. Imagine your energy body or body of light is sitting restfully inside your physical body. Concentrate on being your energy body, which allows energy and thought to travel faster through the etheric zone.

2. Think of a person you want to send a message to or invite communication from. You must feel convinced about communicating with them. Visualize the person in as much detail as you can and call their name: "Sarah, I call upon you to become aware of me now." See them appear in their energy body in front of you. Make eye contact. Align yourself spirit-to-spirit with the person by feeling the quality of your soul and their soul. Align yourself mind-to-mind with them by affirming that the two of you are on the same wavelength. Align yourself body-to-body with the person by affirming that your body and their body know exactly where the other is and instinctually know how to get through to each other.

3. Form the thought you want to communicate clearly in your mind. When you're ready, speak the message into their ear, calmly and directly. Then ask the person, "Did you hear and understand what I said?" If there's any question, repeat it. If you want to receive a communication from them, imagine them beginning to whisper in your ear, and then assume the full message will be delivered during your dreamstate.

4. Thank the person and imagine both of you entering a dream state where the visitation can take place easily.

5. Make a note later of any response you receive in your waking reality or in dreams.

Dreaming with a Friend

The same way two or more people who live or work closely together often start reading each other's minds or thinking the same thoughts, two people can also dream the same dreams. Twins and siblings who are especially close to each other often dream of each other at the same time, and the content may be uncannily parallel, remembered by each person through a slightly different filter of personal symbology, but duplicating major actions and outcomes. Couples who have slept together for a long time may also align with each other so their dreams become nearly simultaneous. They often discover this by accident, sharing their dreams in the morning out loud, or later in the day or week, and the other exclaims, "Wait a minute! I had that exact same dream!"

David Lohff, author of *The Dream Dictionary* (published by Running Press, 1998), calls this phenomenon *concurrent dreaming.* Concurrent or simultaneous dreaming also occurs with dream groups that have been meeting on a regular basis. The group members begin to synchronize their energies and various processes of personal growth until they start dreaming about each other. If they develop the habit of sharing their group dreams (it can be a dream about any group, not just the specific dream group) at each meeting, they soon discover they've been pursuing similar themes in their dreams. Their dreams may contain parallel plots, similar characters, mutual dream elements, and they may even have precognition about the same event.

Another kind of shared dreaming occurs when two people set out intentionally to dream together. They may agree that, "This week let's concentrate on meeting each other in a dream, recognizing each other, and remembering what we do together." Then they may check in with each other every day to see what response they got to their incubation experiment. They may agree upon a specific dream landscape in which to meet, as a kind of focal point — like next to the big tree at the top of the hill, or in the conference room on the third floor, or in the field behind the red barn. This kind of dreaming, often

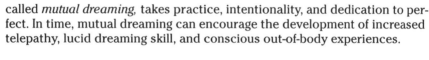

called *mutual dreaming,* takes practice, intentionality, and dedication to perfect. In time, mutual dreaming can encourage the development of increased telepathy, lucid dreaming skill, and conscious out-of-body experiences.

Try the following combination meditation and dream diary writing exercise.

Mutual Dreaming with a Friend

1. Select a dream partner whom you trust implicitly. It's important that you both feel safe. Dreams are a very private area; to allow someone that far into your dream world, that person must be mature and responsible. Choose someone you know will carry through and is serious about the experiment. It's a little easier if the person lives closer to you; long distance dream experiments can work, but are a bit more difficult.

2. Decide on your mutual goals for the experiment. Do you want to see and recognize each other in a dream first? Perhaps you'd like to try doing this simple task three times successfully before you move on to other adventures, like traveling together, healing someone together, or visiting the planetary library to obtain new information about something you're both interested in.

3. Before bed, do an incubation meditation, and repeat the mutual desire at least three times to yourself, even writing it out on paper. You might suggest that you wake up immediately after you have the dream, no matter what time of the night. Be prepared with your dream diary. In addition, do the previous exercise on "Sending or Receiving a Telepathic Message," picturing your friend and your mutual intentions, and imagining your friend doing the same meditation with you in mind.

4. Let go and wait for a dream. If you don't see your friend in your dream, record any dream in which you are with another person. The other person may be symbolic of your friend — and at least it's a start. The next night, set your intention again. Don't get discouraged, especially if your friend sees you in her dream but you don't see anyone but a giant 9-foot slug wearing a hat. Keep at it. Soon your subconscious will get the message and you'll have success.

5. Contact your friend each day and share what happened in detail. Talk about your dreams and try interpreting each other's dreams. Set your mutual intention again to continue the next night.

6. Keep up your experiment. It's important to feel you're working progressively toward a higher, more complex goal. And be specific about that goal. The longer you stay with it, the more your body and dream self will cooperate.

We cannot live only for ourselves. A thousand fibers connect us
with our fellow men; and among those fibers, as sympathetic threads,
our actions run as causes, and they come back to us as effects.

—Herman Melville

Your Dream Diary

1. Look back through your dream diary and make a list of ten dream characters you had relationships with. For each, write about what your dream self was showing you concerning how to relate more successfully.

2. List ten people or animals you have relationships with in your daily life. Then write about what character traits each represents to you and why it's important to you to develop or fully understand these traits.

3. Think of one of your friends who seems to be troubled or in need of some sort of help right now. Ask for a dream to shed light on their problem, and to show you how you might counsel them. Incubate a dream and when you receive one that seems like the answer to your request, call your friend and tell them about it. See if together, the two of you can interpret it.

4. Finish the following sentences with as many answers as you can.

   • If I could know anything about my relationship with ( ), I'd like to understand:

   • If I could help ( ), the most appropriate thing to do or say would be:

   • If I could find true forgiveness for ( ) I'd need to let go of/understand:

   • If I could begin a new relationship with someone, I'd like them to have these qualities:

5. Go back through your dream diary and list the romance or sex dreams you've had. What, besides wishful thinking, might have been the purpose of these dreams?

6. Write several paragraphs about the taboos you've broken in your dreams. How did it feel? What did you learn? Why did your dream self want to open that particular area? Did you receive increased energy as a result?

7. Write about the times you've experienced telepathy, in ordinary reality and in dreams, with someone else. How did it feel? How did the communication occur? Was it in a visitation from someone far away, or on the other side?

Chapter 15

Dreams and Healing

• •

In This Chapter

► The functions of healing dreams

► How you can use dreams to heal yourself

► How you can use dreams to help heal others

► The power of prayer and blessings

► Some symbolism of healing dreams

• •

> *(In dreams) we can heal wounds in the psyche, emotional difficulties*
> *we have not been able to overcome. We can remove energy blocks*
> *that may be inhibiting the free circulation of energy in the body.*
> *And, we can pierce obscurations in the mind by taking*
> *experience beyond conceptual boundaries and limitations.*
>
> —Tenzin Rinpoche

*U*sing dreams to facilitate healing of the body, emotions, and spirit began so far back in history that it's hard to find a culture that didn't honor and recognize healing dreams. In fact, in ancient cultures, healing was one of the three primary purposes for dreaming, the other two being to tell the future and to receive guidance. I mention the importance of the Greek dream temples of Aesculapius in Chapter 1, but the practice of seeking dreams in a sacred environment dedicated especially to that purpose can be traced to earlier Egyptian practices begun by the god of healing, Imhotep, to whom the stepped pyramid and healing temple at Sakkara are attributed, along with the complex of dream incubation temples in ancient Memphis.

Studies show that the stresses of daily life today are exacerbated by sleep deprivation. Without REM sleep, during which dreams occur, people become irritable, anxious, and disoriented. Over time, chronic sleep loss can lead to illness and accidents. Perhaps just sleeping and dreaming alone are a kind of preventive medicine, and enough to start a healing process where one is needed. But as I explain in this chapter, you can do much more to keep yourself healthy, and contribute to the health of others, when you understand the specific healing powers of dreams.

If you have a dream about your own health and feel your dreams are pointing toward something important, by all means visit your doctor. And, it won't do any harm to share your dreams — and your current work with, and belief in them — with your doctor. Your doctor may believe in dreams too. And even if he or she is a skeptic, it will help your doctor to know that you are actively working with your inner self in your healing process. In many cases, your dreams about your health will work in tandem with the real world treatments you seek from the medical profession.

The Functions of Healing Dreams

Your dream self may be one of the most effective natural healers in the world. To make the best use of your inner healing resources, you need to know what's possible. Healing dreams come in many shapes and sizes and fulfill a variety of functions: Forecasting, diagnosing, providing therapy, providing healing, and promoting wellness. I discuss each of these in detail in the sections that follow.

Forecasting dreams

Your body consciousness is extremely alert to its job of maintaining the optimal functioning of its "vehicle" and has a natural tendency to reestablish harmony and equilibrium. When imbalance reaches a critical level, the disharmony is broadcast through the body like a warning signal. That warning signal makes its way up through the three levels of the brain as you sleep, when your distraction levels are most reduced, and registers in the conscious mind as a *forecasting dream,* a dream that forecasts a potential physical problem.

Forecasting dreams can point clearly to a specific area of your body that is going out of balance. Is a pattern of emotional irritability causing such chronic contraction and stress to your stomach that you're close to developing an ulcer? You might dream that a surgeon lances your belly and smoky, foul-smelling fumes come out. Perhaps your habit of eating chocolate ice cream every night before bed is changing the acid/alkaline balance of your body, leaving you open to cold and flu germs. If so, you may dream that your throat and chest are sweating chocolate syrup.

If you dream of problems with your car, like the radiator overheating or the ignition not working, you may be warning yourself to be less emotional or to renew your motivation about life. Cars, houses, and horses often symbolize your body. Particularly when these images are stricken in some way, it's valuable to ask "Is this image bringing me a warning or suggestion about my physical health?"

Diagnosis dreams

Sometimes your dream self will give you a specific description of your health imbalances, letting you know a real problem has developed. Is your body trying to throw off toxins you picked up from environmental pollutants and does it need more water to flush the system? If so, you may dream you're thirsty and turn on the faucet to fill your glass but no water comes out. Or maybe you see a billboard that plays off the popular milk ad campaign but says: "Got water?"

You may visit a doctor's office in your dream and the doctor tells you quite clearly, "You need a pelvic exam." When you wake, you realize you haven't been to the gynecologist for over a year. You make an appointment and discover you've developed fibroid tumors in your uterine wall.

Many pregnant women dream about whether their baby will be a breech birth, or how difficult or easy their labor will be. They're usually right. In fact, studies show that many pregnant women have terrible nightmares filled with anxiety and fear of loss. Ironically, the women who had the worst nightmares had the easiest deliveries, perhaps because they'd already released their emotional tension. Some people dream they feel a cyst or tumor growing in a particular area of their body. By going for a checkup, they discover it at an early stage where it can be dealt with easily.

Therapeutic dreams

Your dreams can continue to elucidate your healing process by showing you specific things to do to reestablish the harmony in your system. *Therapeutic dreams* are about treating imbalance and promoting recovery. Sometimes they show you what to do in your waking reality, sometimes they indicate the need for adjustment in the higher dimensions of yourself — the realignment of your thoughts or clearing of energy blockages, for example.

Diet seems to be a popular topic for therapeutic dreams. You might dream you're visiting your friend John, and he makes a pot of tea and pours you some. He says, "You'll like this — it's made with ginger root and apple juice." That week you remember the dream as you do the marketing, buy some ginger and apple juice, come home, and brew it. It tastes *so good!* And, it soothes your upset stomach.

On occasion you may dream of seeing, smelling, or tasting a particular food — a head of broccoli, a ruby grapefruit, a bowl of steaming brown rice. You can rest assured your body is sending you a message: Get some of this and eat it — soon! But use your judgment; if you dream of chocolate cake, you may be looking at an addiction pattern instead.

Other therapeutic dreams help you create an energy state conducive to healing. You might regain your peace of mind by dreaming you're in natural settings of great beauty, or swimming effortlessly underwater like a dolphin. You might walk through a lush botanical garden, or rock in a hammock under a shady tree in the summer. Animals routinely heal themselves by entering long, coma-like sleep states, so it's not surprising that if you can just free your body from the grip of your buzzing daily consciousness, your internal systems will rebalance and heal much more effortlessly. Peace in sleep is a potent healing force.

Healing dreams

On occasion, people dream about being cured in their dreams, and then wake up, and, either immediately or in the very near future, have the cure come to pass. These are healing dreams. For example, you may have had chronic pain in your shoulders, feeling nearly frozen for months. In a dream, you receive a chiropractic adjustment, and when you wake up and turn over to roll out of bed, your back actually pops, freeing up greater movement and relieving much of your pain. Healing in dreams often occurs during lucid dreaming states, where the dreamer is conscious within the dream. One man reported that he reached inside himself during a lucid dream and crushed several gallstones into a fine powder with his "energy fingers." Within a few days, his real gallstones had disappeared. Other people have experiences of being permeated by a bright light in their dreams that goes exactly where it's needed. Everything inside them feels like it's in its right place and functioning the way it was intended. Emotional and physical healing often follow.

Wellness dreams

When you have undergone a process of healing, your dream self may give you a dream that signals you are well again. Just before my father died, as I was writing this book, I had the following dream, which repeated in the exact same form for three nights in a row:

> *I am given two thin leather-bound books, and a voice says, "You must use the contents of these books in the project you're already working on." The books open and hundreds of dark shadows fall out and start coming into my body. I resist, saying "But I don't WANT to!" Like, what did these awful subconscious shadows have to do with DREAMS???*

No matter my resistance, the books continued to download into me night after night. I now sense that these shadows corresponded to the upsetting experiences I would go through concerning my father's passing, and the resulting insights I would come to about "the other side," which is so strongly tied to the world of dreams. But at the time I couldn't make sense of it and wondered if something might be about to go wrong in my own body. The fourth night, however, I dreamed a short fragment:

I see my body lit up brightly by golden rays of sunshine and inside me are dozens of tiny whimsical designs — little spirals, ladybugs, springs like in a ballpoint pen, and starburst shapes. They've all been activated and are wiggling and boinging, spinning and sending off sparkles — all in a childlike, comical way.

I knew then that my "absorption" process, which had felt so disturbing, was successfully completed and I was alive in a new way — though again, I had no idea what it meant yet. Enough time has now passed that I can see the signs of a positive transformation in myself that was set into motion by my father's sudden death.

Wellness dreams have a particularly vivid look and feel, seem hyper-real, and are often lit brightly with warm light. You may see yourself looking attractive, youthful, and lively. You may even see your eyes in a mirror, or other people in the dream may comment about how beautiful you are or how shiny you look. Table 15-1 presents common dream symbols that may point to imbalances and illness.

Table 15-1	Dream Symbols That May Point to Imbalances and Illnesses
Symbol	*Possible Meanings*
Car Trouble	
Brakes don't work	Going too fast, feeling out of control
Car has flat tire/s	Problem with feet/legs, forward movement
Gas won't feed properly	Problem with assimilation of food
Headlights don't work	Eye problems, subconscious block interferes with perception
Ignition won't work	Problem with motivation, being a "self-starter"
Out of gas	Need for rest and nurturing, new ideas
Radiator is overheated	Too much volatile emotion, need more water
House Trouble	
Broken or blocked pipes	Circulatory problems
Frozen or cold temperatures	Blocked energy flow
Garbage, debris, dirt	Unhygienic conditions
House being renovated	Major healing work needs to be undertaken

(continued)

Table 15-1 *(continued)*

Symbol	Possible Meanings
House broken into	Open to infection, feeling vulnerable
House flooded	Too much/not enough water retention
House infested with pests	Possible infection brewing
House on fire	Situation leading to fever, need purification
Miscellaneous Symbols	
A past accident	Pay attention now to part that was injured
Broken bowl, spilt milk	Female problems
Drowning, suffocating	Lack of oxygen, lung problems, emotional overwhelm
Holes, punctures in body	Energy or negativity needs to be released here
Insects	Infection, cellular disturbance
Specific wounds, cuts, being hit	Energy needs to be unblocked in that area
Tied up, paralyzed	Lack of movement or exercise
Urination, defecation	Elimination problems, kidneys, bladder
Washing	Internal cleanse needed
Wolves, lions	Overeating, overindulgence
Worms, caterpillars, maggots	Illness that eats away at you

Dreaming to Heal Yourself

After you realize how informative your body is, and how your dream self tries to get a message to you when you're out of balance, you can begin to use your dreams intentionally to stay healthy and happy. First, you can familiarize yourself with the dream signals that point toward a need for healing, toward what remedy is indicated, and toward the signs that you're back in harmony again. Then you can begin to incubate healing dreams, or ask for healing guidance in dreams. The following sections describe some sample scenarios.

A diagnosis dream warns of disease

Trudy seemed to be in good health but had a sequence of dreams that added up to an intuitive knowing that something might be wrong, even though she had no overt symptoms. In the first dream:

> I'm involved sexually with a man I don't know and we've started to make love. He puts his hands on my breasts and squeezes them. A brown liquid comes out of the right one and I'm appalled. I think it's revolting and I wake up — either embarrassed or scared.

The second dream occurred several weeks later:

> A snake has somehow gotten inside my body, like it crawled up from the earth, and now it's in my chest and is laying eggs all over. I can't get it out! This dream got Trudy's attention because it tied in to the previous emotional tone of the dream about her right breast, and both dreams targeted her chest area.

The third dream convinced her to take action:

> I go to the doctor's office and get a chest x-ray, which I can see projected on the wall as it's being taken. I see a white area that is shaking and vibrating as I look at it, like it's alive. "What's THAT?" I ask the nurse. "That's your new cancer, honey," the nurse replies.

Upon waking, Trudy called for a doctor's appointment, and indeed discovered that she had a small cancerous growth in her right breast. Because she caught it early, it was successfully removed and did not spread. This dream is slightly unusual because it directly names Trudy's illness; usually dreams depict illnesses symbolically.

A healing dream removes blockage via "psychic surgery"

Brad makes his living as a seminar leader, lecturer, and personal coach. Talking is obviously important to him. For six months, he had been working for a powerful corporation that wanted him to curtail his material to suit their very particular, conservative needs. He felt like he was operating on only a few cylinders, unable to express his true self or talk about what inspired him, and the tension was slowly building. He began to feel constriction in his throat and had difficulty swallowing. He suffered increasingly from acid reflux and a burning sensation in his esophagus. Brad had a dream that changed things for him:

> *I am lying on an operating table and several surgeons are standing around talking about what needs to be done on my throat. They proceed to cut my throat open, but I don't bleed, and I don't feel any pain. They eventually take out a bright red tumor, shaped like a donut, that has been surrounding my esophagus, squeezing off the flow of nutrients to my stomach. One surgeon holds it up for me to see and says, "There it is. The ring of fire."*

When Brad woke, he thought about what "ring of fire" meant to him. He felt that because he'd been holding back on what he wanted to say, his throat area had become blocked, frustrated, and inflamed. The more he thought about it, he realized he was actually quite angry that he was being coerced into doing something he didn't want to do, just because the money was good and the corporation seemed so powerful and dominating. After his dream of being operated on energetically by what he called "psychic surgeons," Brad felt free of the mental and emotional block that had made him feel intimidated, and more in touch with his own needs. He was able to tell the managers who hired him that he wanted to beef up the program and stretch into new territory — and his newfound clarity seemed to facilitate a positive response. He was awarded a new contract for work he wanted to do.

Your dream may be literal or symbolic

When you dream of an illness or accident, it doesn't always mean the dream is literal or precognitive. Often, like in most dreams, these images are symbolic of something else going on in your system at a higher level — in your thought process, emotional habits, or energy flow. Table 15-2 presents possible meanings of dream illnesses and accidents.

Table 15-2   Possible Meanings of Dream Illnesses and Accidents

Illnesses	Possible Meaning
Allergies	You need to become more tolerant of the varieties of life and not give your authority to what you perceive to be inharmonious.
Alzheimer's disease	You need to develop trust in the unknown.
Cancer	Part of you is growing too fast, something is eating away at you; part of your true life is not being lived.
Chronic fatigue syndrome	You're focusing on what's leaving you instead of on what you're receiving and on the present moment, you're in the future too much.

Illnesses	*Possible Meaning*
Constipation	You're not letting go of what's nurtured you when it's time to move on.
Diarrhea	You're not allowing yourself to be nurtured by what's good in your life.
Epilepsy	You need to let go of control in some area.
Fever	You are burning off old limitations by raising your energy level.
Infection	You are trying to purify and get rid of harmful ideas or emotions.
Pneumonia	You are overwhelmed by sadness, grief, or heavy emotion.
Rash, skin problems	You feel self-conscious, self-critical, ashamed, uncomfortable about how you appear to others.
Rotting flesh, gangrene	You've held hatred toward self or others in the affected area.
Shortness of breath	You need to focus on what inspires you.
Tumor	Energy is accumulating and not flowing here.
Vomiting, nausea	You "can't stomach" something, something you're doing is not nurturing.
Accidents	
Being burned	Anger or censure has accumulated in that area, or purification is needed.
Being cut or punctured	The area affected needs to release pent-up energy and let go of control.
Being run over/crushed	You feel overwhelmed by an area of your life; look to area of body that is damaged and what crushes you for specific meaning.
Crashing	You're going too fast in the wrong direction and need to pay attention, regulate your energy.
Falling	You need to surrender and let go of control in some area of your life, have faith.
Losing a limb or body part	You feel disempowered concerning that function in your life.

A wellness dream models a feeling of peace that continues for months

Jeff had been in an auto accident in which he'd broken many ribs, his clavicle, his arm, and suffered a severe concussion. He'd been in the hospital and then in a private recovery clinic for weeks. His healing process seemed to be progressing slowly. As he became more and more restless, lying helplessly in bed while his bones knit back together, he had a dream during one of his afternoon naps.

> *I am wandering about in a huge park. The grass is lush and dewy, and bright emerald green, and there are fantastic gardens everywhere I look. Some are very geometric and manicured like those at Versailles, while others are like English country gardens, spilling over with all kinds of flowers. The smells are fantastic — I seem to be able to smell every tiny scent, and the distinctions in the colors are also amazing and seem extra brilliant. There are animals and birds everywhere but none are dangerous or aggressive. I come across a massive, ancient oak tree that is as broad as a house, and it has a "doorway" that leads into the inside of it, where the center has hollowed out from age. I go in and it's like being in a protective womb. I lie down on the soft mossy earth and take a nap — like I fall asleep within my sleep. I wake up to my ordinary reality, feeling profoundly rested, as though every cell in my body has been rejuvenated.*

Jeff found that this dream stayed with him, and he could recreate it easily at will. He often drifted back into it during the day, and tried intentionally to go back to the tree by meditating on the images just before sleep. Jeff found that his recovery speeded up and he was left with an ongoing mood of inner peace that continued long after he went home.

Try this meditation exercise to help elicit a wellness dream.

Visiting a Healing Spa or Clinic in Your Dreams

By creating a clear picture of a healing environment that contains everything you can imagine might help you, and then focusing on it before sleep, you will put your body into a harmonious state, or mood, and open yourself to effortless healing.

1. Imagine a place, anywhere on earth, where you might go for healing and rejuvenation. Is it an oasis in the desert? A luxurious spa in the mountains? An island paradise with sweet-smelling flowers and soothing waters?

2. Imagine the room you will stay in, the bed, the windows, the light, the natural environment, the people who are there to assist you, the food you will eat, the baths and massages you will have, the exercise and movement available, the one-on-one work with healers, therapists, nutritionists, doctors, bodyworkers, intuitives. What is a typical day like?

3. Imagine yourself checking in and going to your room, unpacking and set-tling in for your stay, which can be as long as you like. Go through the scenario of your first day, then your second, and third, and so on.

4. As you reach a point where you are being taken care of in your fantasy, let yourself dwell on that feeling and image, and fall asleep, giving your-self the suggestion that you will receive great benefit from your spa/clinic that night.

5. In the morning, write about how you feel in your dream diary, and note any dreams that seem to be about healing.

6. Continue this process every night for a set period of time — a week, two weeks, or more.

Table 15-3 presents possible meanings of body parts that show up in your dreams.

Table 15-3	Possible Meanings of Parts of the Body in Dreams
Body Part	*Possible Meanings*
Adrenals	What motivates you; your reactionary behavior, your aggressiveness or timidity
Back/spine	How you receive from your unconscious, how flexible you are, how you transmit energy from your lower self to higher self and vice versa
Bones/skeleton	How stable you are internally, how rigid, how strong, how certain
Brain	How you process information and perceive concepts; look to the three parts of brain for specific meanings
Eyes/ears	How you perceive, how you receive insight and guidance
Face	How your represent yourself to the world, your self-image
Fat	How you protect yourself, the reserves you think you might need, how you haven't used what you've already been given
Feet/toes/legs	How you take a stand, achieve grounding, make strides, move forward, find balance
Hands/fingers/arms	How you reach out to others, grasp or take hold, make things happen, embrace life
Heart/chest/breasts	How you integrate your soul's wisdom into your life, how you give unconditional love, how understanding you are, how courageous

(continued)

Table 15-3 *(continued)*

Body Part	Possible Meanings
Joints	How you bridge energy and information from one area or focus to another, how you make connections
Liver/kidney/bladder	How you filter impurities from your system and eliminate what you don't need
Lungs	How much you hold onto sadness, grief, isolation, suffering; how inspired you let yourself be
Neck/throat/esophagus	How much you communicate your truth, express yourself freely, allow trust and faith in your life, receive help
Nose	How you know through instinct
Pancreas	How you deal with sweetness in your life
Penis/vagina	How you create new life, deal with intimacy
Shoulders	How burdened you feel; how responsible you are
Skin	How you interface with the world; how sensitive you are to the environment or others
Spleen	How much you hold onto malice, bitterness, or resentment
Stomach/intestines/navel	How you nurture yourself, center yourself, assimilate your nourishing resource material
Teeth/jaw/chin	How you cut through; your determination and stubbornness
Tongue/mouth/vocal cords	How you use speech (do you gossip?); How you take in nourishment (are you greedy?)

Try this meditation exercise to intentionally dream about healing.

Incubating a Healing Dream

1. Think about what kind of healing dream you'd like to have:

   • *A forecasting dream?* Perhaps you'd like to ask your dream self to scan your physical, etheric, emotional, and mental dream zones for any imbalances or potential problems that might be brewing. You might ask, "What is the state of my overall well-being?"

   • *A diagnosis dream?* Do you already sense something might be "off" with your system? Perhaps you'd like to ask your dream self for more definitive information about what exactly is going on. Maybe you'd like to ask, "What is the cause of the chronic pain in my left shoulder?"

- *A therapeutic dream?* Once you have an idea about what's out of balance in your system, you might want to ask your dream self for guidance about the specific actions and remedies that will help heal you. You might ask, "What can I do to heal the numbness in my fingertips?"

- *A healing dream?* If you're suffering from an illness, wound, or problem that's already manifested physically, you might want to ask for a healing in your dream. You might request that you be put in touch with "The Great Physician" or "The Healing Angel."

- *A wellness dream?* If you've been in a recovery process, you might want to ask your dream self to indicate that you're once again balanced and in harmony. You might request, "Please show me a sign that I am healed."

2. Phrase your request clearly and succinctly, in positive terms, and write it on a piece of paper. Before bed, read it slowly several times, and say it out loud, directing the request to your dream self.

As with any dream incubation process, give your dream self the request or suggestion, then let go in total faith that your request will be answered and your need fulfilled.

3. If, in the morning, you wake without a clearcut dream, pay attention to the mood or feelings you're experiencing, and ask for another clarifying dream the following night.

Dreaming to Help Heal Others

Dreaming about the health of others is just as common as dreaming about your own health. People's bodies and souls are much more tuned in to each other than we acknowledge consciously. If you dream of healing someone else, it might be that you are working in a higher dream zone, like a "psychic surgeon" or "spiritual healer," helping someone clarify a pattern of thought or an emotional habit in their inner world. But receiving dreams that warn of danger to a friend, or hint that your spouse will contract a serious illness, can be very confusing. Are they literal or symbolic? Should you share the information with the other person or keep it to yourself? What is your proper and ethical role in helping others heal? This section will help you answer these questions.

Perhaps you dream about a couple you know: *You're sitting at their breakfast table with the wife and the husband is in the background. The wife has bruises all over her face, and obviously she's been beaten up. You ask her, "Why do you stay?" She says she's too tired to decide what to do.* When you wake up, you wonder why you dreamed this particular scene. You've never seen the wife actually bruised or physically injured, but some intuition inside tells you that the husband may be verbally and emotionally abusing her. What do you do?

✔ **First, always look at the dream as information about yourself.** Is the feminine/anima part of you being unappreciated or run over by the masculine/animus part of you? Is your own receptivity to fresh, original ideas and enthusiasm overwhelmed by too much structure or too many goals or shoulds? Do you in some way feel bruised by life and too exhausted internally to be clear about what needs to be done? What if this dream about other people is really your dream self giving you a forecasting dream about your own life? What debilitating situation must you take action to rectify immediately? Why would you choose the symbol of this couple to portray an insight to yourself? What do they symbolize to you? What is characteristic of their relationship? Perhaps you'd answer: *The couple bases their relationship on a rigid separation of gender roles and behavior. The man is older and dominating, the woman is seductive and dependent.* Your description of the couple may be exactly the way your own internal yin-yang balance is currently functioning. Where in your life are you feeling like a victim?

✔ **Second, assume the dream may *also* be about the other people.** Having interpreted it personally first helps remove any "messiah complex" energy that might have you rushing in to save the other person. Taking the charge off helps you determine whether and how to share the information with the person/s you dreamed about. If you do decide to share the dream, make sure you do it in a nonthreatening, nondramatic way that won't scare the other person needlessly. Let him or her decide the significance — and, remember, sometimes just having someone else dream about you out of the blue can be significant. In this case, you might telephone the wife and chat a bit, and then say, "You know, I had an odd dream about you the other night, and it had that special 'weight' that usually makes me pay extra attention. I wonder if you'd be interested in me sharing it? I'd be curious what you think it means." If she says no, let it go. If she says yes, share it, perhaps with a comment at the end like, "So I didn't know if this was really about me, or if it had any reality on ANY level in your life." Often just by sharing the dream, it will plant a seed of a new kind of thinking in the other person, or help bring an unconscious idea to the fore. That may be all you need to do. Perhap it will make your friend feel safe enough to open up about a problem she'd been keeping secret for a long time.

You may believe that you don't have one iota of doctoring or healing ability, but when you heal others in your dreams, you may prove to be quite competent. Many people use aspects of themselves and hidden talents in dreams that they do not acknowledge or access during the day. I hear numerous stories of people who visit hospitals ministering to the sick during sleep, and others who work with the terminally ill, feed the hungry, help babies be born, and visit prisons and battlegrounds. Perhaps healing is one of the most natural of human abilities, and at some level we all know how to do it. Perhaps we help each other freely as we are able to, and in whatever dimension we can.

Saying Prayers and Sending Blessings

I have to admit that I still recite "Now I lay me down to sleep" on many nights as I commend myself to my dreamtime adventures. It is a prayer I said in childhood and one that still makes me feel peaceful. Prayer has an important connection in helping facilitate healing dreams. It greases the wheels for the inflow of guidance, the body's healthy blueprint, and healing energy. Anything you can do — such as the nightly review practice — that establishes openness and a clear alignment between your personality and soul will increase the depth and spiritual content of your dreams. Prayer at its best reestablishes that connection between your earthly self and your divine self and opens the floodgates between them. We usually pray when we feel disconnected, unlucky, unloved, unprovided for, or lacking the direction we need. But remember: It's also a good idea to says prayers of thanks when you're happy and things are going well.

The natural progression of a prayer

A prayer typically begins as a request for help from a higher power — for either a general problem or a very specific one. "Please help me heal. Let me live. Please help me learn to be more tolerant and loving. Please help me find a life partner. Please help me get pregnant. Please help me get the job I want." But prayer should really be a process that reveals your oneness with your higher dimensional knowledge and with the divine. Ideally, a prayer raises your vibration and changes you so the good things you ask for can more readily manifest as natural extensions of your own goodness. The natural progression of a prayer often follows this framework:

1. Tune in to, feel, and call upon a higher source of wisdom, love, and power. As you do, you call it into being in your own reality.

2. State the truth of your current situation. How do you feel right now? What troubles you? Confuses you? Scares you?

3. Ask for help in improving your own consciousness so you can become aware of what the higher power offers you and wants for you.

4. Affirm that you have faith, that you know the perfect solution already exists, and the higher power knows exactly how to give you the revelation you need, at just the right time.

5. Express gratitude that you are a child of God, that you are alive and have all the gifts you do, and that you are watched over and provided for by divine awareness. Let go and be quietly and peacefully expectant.

Saying prayers before bed is one of the most effective ways to seed your unconscious mind with thoughts of unity, the desire for higher awareness, and an affirmation of wholeness and harmony. If, in addition to simply improving the quality of your inner peace, you are also trying to heal yourself, praying before sleep can establish a strong healing intention coupled with a profoundly calm state of mind. Used together, these things can facilitate a sleep state that allows you to sleep more deeply. Deep sleep states are quiet and allow more interpenetration between the soul and body. I believe healing is accelerated with this kind of sleep.

If you want to heal yourself in your dreams, you might take time before sleep to visualize a healing spa or clinic where you can go during your dream to find all the help you need. As you align yourself for sleep, intend to be transported to this place and pray that you receive the best help available. By creating a clear picture of a healing environment that contains everything you can imagine that might help you, and then focusing on it before sleep, you put your body into a harmonious state and open yourself to effortless healing.

The natural progression of a blessing

The second part of my childhood prayer routine, after I'd finished my out loud recitation, was "And God bless Mommy and Daddy and Grama and Grampa and my baby sister and my teacher Mrs. Hunt and the dogs and my chameleon and . . . everybody!" Blessings and prayers seem to go hand in hand, and just before sleep is a perfect time to ask for blessings for others. Because your mind quiets down and distractions fade, sending help to others is maximized in sleep, just as is facilitating your own healing process.

Blessings differ slightly from prayer. In a blessing you practice seeing the other person from the God's eye view. You might ask yourself, "How would an angel see this person? How is he already perfect? How is he not seeing himself; and can I see him in a way that is more accurate than his own view of himself?" If you practice seeing the light within others and look for their soul, for what's good about them and what's possible in their life, they will eventually feel it, and appreciate it so much that they'll try to live up to your view of them. When you bless food before you eat it, you affirm the light and life force inside and receive that life force as you eat, not just the physical form of the food. By blessing food, journeys, undertakings, and the people you know, you bring out the hidden light within to be active in the world. The natural progression of a blessing often follows this framework:

1. Tune in to, feel, and affirm your own oneness with a higher source of wisdom, love, and power.

2. Become aware that the same source of wisdom, love, and power runs through all things continuously, with no gaps anywhere.

3. Place your attention on another person. Tune in to, feel, and affirm his or her oneness with the same higher source of wisdom, love, and power. Actively look for the light within the other.

4. Say to yourself, to the other, and to the divine source, something like: "I feel the presence and the light and the perfection in this person. I know it to be their true state. I know it is real above all other realities."

5. Ask that the other person be given whatever help is needed so he or she can know this also. Let go and be quietly and peacefully expectant.

Here's an exercise to help you write your own prayer and blessing in your dream diary.

Writing Your Own Prayer and Blessing

1. Take some time with your dream diary and write a presleep prayer that aligns you with your own higher dimensions, your soul, and the divine. Keep it simple and sincere, innocent, and direct.

2. Say it out loud again and again until you are totally comfortable saying it and it feels like a comfort.

3. Say your own prayer before sleep every night, as a way to facilitate healing and inner peace.

4. Now write a blessing to say after your prayer, one that addresses your desire to help those you love, or people in need the world over. Take your time, and make it simple and heartfelt.

5. Say it out loud, after your prayer, until you feel absolutely comfortable and natural.

6. Say your own blessing every night before sleep, as a way to send healing to others.

Good thoughts are no better than good dreams if you don't follow through.

—Ralph Waldo Emerson

Your Dream Diary

1. Scan back through your dream diary, noting any dreams that might be about your health or body. Write about each: If this were a forecasting dream, what would my dream self be trying to tell me?

2. Scan back through your dream diary, noting any dreams that might be about your health or body. Write about each: If this were a therapeutic or healing dream, what would my dream self be trying to tell me?

3. Write about three possible scenarios that would put you in a state of deep peace-fulness. Write about the sensory detail, how your body responds to being there, and how you would use each setting for maximum benefit.

4. Make up three dream scenarios where you are healed of some problem you currently have — mental, emotional, energetic, or physical. How does it happen? Who helps you? Where are you when it happens? What advice do your helpers have for you?

5. Write out three dream scenarios depicting yourself in optimum health. How do you look? What are you doing? How are you interacting with others? How do you remain healthy?

6. Let yourself fantasize and write about how you would help heal a friend, relative, or even a public figure who suffers from an injury or illness. Imagine that anything is possible, and you can use any technique that comes to mind.

7. Examine your recent dreams and write about symbols and imagery pertaining to possible imbalances in your system, illnesses, accidents, parts of the body, or problems other people might be having. Are you dreaming about your own health, or the health of another? Is it literal or symbolic?

Chapter 16

Dreams and Creativity

- -

In This Chapter

▶ Activating your imagination with dreams

▶ Jumpstarting your creative process: Drawing, painting, writing, sculpting, dancing

▶ Applying your dreams creatively in art and life

▶ Living life as a lucid dream

- -

I think every creative impulse that a working writer, or artist of any sort has, comes out of that dark old country where dreams come from.

—Anne Rivers Siddons

*Y*ou have only to glance at the rich and wild imagery of artists like Salvadore Dali, Rene Magritte, William Blake, or Hieronymous Bosch to understand that much of the inspiration for their art came from an active and visionary dreamlife.

Writers and poets like Samuel Taylor Coleridge, James Joyce, Mary Shelley, Voltaire, Edgar Allen Poe, and contemporary authors like Maya Angelou and Isabel Allende credit their dreams with providing the seeds of some of their great literary contributions. Robert Louis Stevenson is said to have relied on imaginary "little people" or "brownies" to bring him stories in his dreams. He deliberately called upon them before sleep when he needed new ideas. Musician Steve Allen dreamed some of the lyrics to a song that he eventually expanded into the hit, "This Could Be the Start of Something Big."

In fact, throughout history, in every arena, dreams have been credited with helping creative ideas gel, with providing the breakthroughs to clear artists' blocks, with expanding a single creative seed into a substantial work, and with bringing new inspiration when the artist didn't know any was there. Dreams are intimately tied to creating.

Creativity, perhaps more than survival, may be *the* motivating force behind our lives. It fuels every human endeavor, from raising a family, to pushing out the boundaries of science, to finding innovative solutions to pressing social problems, to sparking new entrepreneurial business ideas, to inspiring heroic athletic achievements and great theatrical performances. The creative urge gives us the desire to make something from nothing, to begin blank and see what arises, as though by magic, from our mysterious inner, intangible, spiritual and emotional resources. For this reason, creativity is the most frightening, and most addictive, thing on earth.

Expanding Your Imagination

To find your creative genius, your inner voice and vision, you must first be willing to confront and enter the void. You must be willing to sit in the void, in faith that there is a force within it that will eventually rise to meet you, and fill you, and move you — when *it is ready,* not necessarily when you think *you* are ready. And when you least expect it, creativity does rise to meet you, often with a sense of the near-miraculous.

In so many ways, creativity is like the dream state. To dream, you must also surrender your linear, logical daily consciousness and allow the flow of awareness to take on a more random, serendipitous, streaming quality. To dream and to create, you must be slightly out of control, in a personal relationship with the unseen. You must give up your Inner Skeptic and your Inner Critic, freeing yourself from judgment and an inhibiting self-consciousness. The dreamer and the artist both must be intuitive, trusting, and innocent.

Your imagination and creativity increase to the extent that you allow surprise and happy accidents to punctuate your experience. Life is boring when you know how everything is going to turn out but it becomes alive and effervescent when you cocreate with that mysterious force of intelligence that underlies everything. That mysterious force speaks to you in the most direct way in dreams and, when you're awake, through intuition and imagination.

Dreamlike perception = creative genius

You probably know how valuable it can be to sit down by yourself or with colleagues to brainstorm an innovative solution to a marketing problem in your company, talking "off the top of your head" and verbalizing every idea, no matter how peculiar. By its very name, brainstorming implies a lack of rigid mental order, a free flow of ideas blowing around in your mind, combining in interesting, atypical ways.

Dream perception is like a brainstorm; in dreams you are not held to the logical rules of cause and effect, nor to an orderly process of growth. Anything can happen, and any two things can be linked together meaningfully, no matter how unlikely, to create surprising pathways of movement. Any new development can emerge from any previous condition. A dog show might morph into an afternoon soap opera, roots might grow from the soles of your feet, or a highschool graduation might take place on a cruise ship. The sky can be orange with green clouds, and pelicans can mate with giraffes. Why not? In dreams you can be a four-year-old again, dressing yourself in your favorite clothes. Why *not* wear a baseball cap, heart-shaped sunglasses, your father's running shoes, one red sock and one purple one, and plaid shorts with your pajama top? Think how great that would feel!

To give your creativity an infusion of vitality, you need to cultivate the child-like freedom of perception you know in dreams. You start in your waking reality by questioning your mind's penchant for coming to rapid conclusions based on how society does things, or how you did things in the past. Why do I always need to eat three meals a day? Why must I own a cellular phone? Why do I work at an office instead of at home? Why do I never wear yellow? Who says my business card can't be square? Do I really need this matching set of designer brand luggage?

Then you can ask yourself what other options or solutions are possible, especially if you look at the problem from the point of view of a 4-year-old, or a 99-year-old, or an alien from outer space. If you could do things differently, how might the process and the solution be changed? To increase your imagination, try changing your habits, developing a new vocabulary, using your opposite hand, picking things up with your toes. When you vary your routine, you use new tracks in your brain and allow new possibilities to emerge. You give yourself the message that it's okay to be innovative.

To practice changing your reality, make lists in your dream diary and write about the results of experimenting with new forms.

Questioning and Varying Your Reality

- ✔ To help you question your reality, try changing one conclusion midstream each day this week. "I can't go out shopping with you, Jean, I've got to clean my garage . . . No, wait, I can organize my time so I can fit it all in." "I hate driving on the freeway . . . No, wait, I might find it interesting if I pretend to be a chauffeur or a race car driver." "I always have my scrambled eggs and hash browns in the morning . . . No, wait, maybe I'd enjoy yogurt and fruit instead."

- ✔ List five things you think must be a certain way, or you think you must have to be happy. If each of these were not true, what might you be free to think, have, and become instead?

- ✔ List five things you do the same way every day. Then list three ways you could do each one differently. Wash your face *before* you brush your teeth, put on your right sock after your left, take a different route to work, read instead of watching TV at night. Do things differently this week.

- ✔ Watch for the times when you think you know the answer. Stop yourself and say, "Well, this is one way, but maybe there are other options that would work as well. What might they be?"

✔ Watch for the times when you repeat yourself. Stop and suspend your forward momentum. See what new idea or rhythm might want to fill the space instead. If nothing comes to you, let yourself be silent and blank, in spite of the discomfort it might cause you or others.

✔ Watch for the times when you think about how other people do things, or how you've done things in the past. Bring your attention back to the present moment and to your own unique potential to act originally. See what wants to happen when you move spontaneously from your own center.

Streaming consciousness flows anywhere

Dream awareness starts anywhere — an image or feeling pops up from the depths. Sploosh. Then it jumps off and travels in any direction, at any speed, and with any rhythm it wants. Dream awareness truly is like a river; it is pliable and fluid, but it can run through the air or be made of liquid fire or gooey molasses. Your daily reality is like this, too, but your conscious mind slows the motion by living with the illusion that you're in control, and with a sense of time that is broken into precise units instead of being continuous and uninterrupted. Creativity flourishes when your mind moves similarly in a riverlike way, one image leading surprisingly to another, and that image taking an odd turn into something else, and that something else branching off into a memory from the past or a vision of the future.

Focus on stream-of-consciousness perception this week and immerse yourself in the connections between thoughts, in the leaps of imagination, and the meandering purposefulness of your insights. Try the following dream diary writing exercise to loosen up your creative flow.

Following a Stream of Consciousness

Write fluidly, without judgment or editing, letting one idea turn surprisingly into another and another and another and another. Nothing has to make sense. Let one action suggest another action and another and another and another. Start with any of the following thoughts and let the flow continue. Write for five to ten minutes straight, without stopping or rereading, on each one.

✔ My foot began to tingle and then I stepped into a:

✔ When the wind blows from the west it brings the smell of:

✔ Right under the sidewalk, about two inches below the surface, lives a whole colony of:

✔ My mother used to dream she would be:

✔ After a sudden downpour in the desert, the flash flood came tearing down the canyon and:

✔ When I cleaned out my hall closet I found an old box that contained:

- ✔ There was a scratching at my back door and when I went to see who it was, to my surprise:

- ✔ The day after my fifth birthday, I was:

- ✔ I just won the lottery and the first thing that happened was:

- ✔ Just before I woke up all the way I heard:

All your senses are on active duty

Dreams, intuition, and creativity all make themselves known to you through the midbrain, which helps you experience the world via the senses, and through an awareness of connectedness and similarity. Both dream imagery and creative visions occur the midbrain (see Chapter 11 if you need to review the parts of the brain and their function in your dreams). To stimulate both your creative process and your dreamlife, begin to pay more attention to what you smell, how things taste, what textures and impressions you're receiving, the range of subtle sounds in the environment, and the richness of color, shape, contrast, and brightness. You may be more oriented to one of the senses, and use vision or hearing, for example, to process the bulk of incoming perceptual data. But if you pay closer attention, you might find your sense of smell tells you a great deal about other people and what's happening in the world around you. Perhaps you gloss over it because smell is a less glitzy sense than vision.

When sensory data makes itself known, try this: Let your awareness be soft, and let the stimulus enter you without defining it right away. If you hear the wind chimes tinkling, let the sounds make an impression on you. If you walk past a restaurant and smell garlic and spices cooking, let the smell do something to your body and elicit an emotion. If you enter a hot, stuffy room, simply experience what hot-and-stuffy feels like, without commenting or voting on it. See what thoughts naturally follow these pure sensory stimuli.

After you become aware of all your physical senses and can appreciate the wealth of information they bring, you can begin to pay attention to your inner senses. Each external physical sense has a subtle, internal, more rarified cousin.

- ✔ External sight deepens to inner vision or *clairvoyance.*

- ✔ External hearing deepens to *clairaudience,* the ability to hear the inner voice or celestial music with the inner ear.

- ✔ Touch corresponds to impressionability, or *clairsentience,* which is the abiliity to feel with the inner tactile sense that makes you sensitive to textures of energy.

✔ Taste and smell can also occur in subtle forms — for example, you may smell your mother's perfume before she calls on the phone, or know what certain ingredients will taste like when cooked together in various proportions.

By training yourself to be more sensorily aware, with both your outer and inner senses, you maximize your ability to dream fuller, richer dreams and increase your capacity to perceive complex creative ideas.

Everything is like something else

Seeing similarities and the possible connections between ideas catalyzes both dreams and creativity. When ideas are seen as dissimilar and disconnected, no energy or consciousness can flow between them. The fluid nature of imaginative perception is disrupted; creativity, intuition, and dreams stop dead in their tracks. The moment you see connections, similarities, and metaphors, no matter how illogical, you're back in the flow again. Where do you allow connections, and where do you split life apart, or keep things too separate and exclusive?

Try this dream diary writing exercise to practice seeing how one thing is like another.

How This Is Like That

Scan back through your dream journal and pick a handful of interesting dreams. Run through each dream, and for every character, symbol, action, feeling, and locale, say "This is similar to" and see what pops to mind. Write it down. Create a new parallel dream, replacing each original part with a new similar one.

✔ This character is similar to. . . .

✔ This action is similar to. . . .

✔ This object is just like a. . . .

✔ This symbol is similar to. . . .

✔ This location/setting is similar to. . . .

✔ This feeling is just like. . . .

See what insights about the original dream you receive by allowing the twin-like dream to appear. Write about what you discover.

Your day feeds your night, your night your next day

How did yesterday's activities, thoughts, emotions, and quandries fuel last night's dreams? And how did last night's dreams feed back into today's creative flow? Did a problem present itself in your daytime reality and was it solved in your dreams? Or did a problem make itself known in a dream, and you worked on it consciously over the next few days? Your creativity will increase as you allow the content of your waking reality to be released into the dreamworld to expand and mutate, and as you allow the content of your dreams to be released into your waking reality to help shape the events of your life.

Writers and painters, for example, often receive an inspiration for a book or painting in a dream and then begin to shape the idea in the waking world. When they get stuck, they ask for a guidance dream to help them see which direction the creative flow wants to go next. An author might take the story to bed and integrate it into a dream to see what new feeling or image surfaces in the dream flow. The surprising new twists that result can illuminate and free the next part of the work.

Susan St. Thomas is a California artist who works extensively with and teaches about the interconnection between dreams and art. Some years ago she had a dream vision that left an indelible impression on her. In the morning she wrote about the dream, titling it and sketching the vision. She called it "The Wedding Dress." She says, "I had just returned from a visit to Santa Fe with my lover and companion. I'd been with him for some time, yet we were still deepening our relationship, getting a sense about what the next steps for us might be. We were following two different spiritual paths — I was steeped in Native American practices, and he in the Sufi, and we were learning to understand each other's way. While in New Mexico we'd done a ceremony together, in which we both ad libbed with what we knew from our respective spiritual traditions. The result was magical. My dream vision came right after that:

> *I see a golden buckskin dress which just appears by itself out of thin air — as if I am being presented with this magnificent gift by an unknown benefactor. The dress has fringe and a rose-colored tint halfway up. Across the bodice of the dress, I watch as a live, movie-like scene of an Indian tribe unfolds. Instinctively I know this is MY wedding dress and that I am going to wear it in an upcoming ceremony.*

Figure 16-1 shows the sketch Susan made of the wedding dress in her dream.

"As is my practice whenever I have a visionlike dream of clarity or guidance, I honor the dream by making a painting of it. In this case, as I painted the wedding dress, I began to weave in other symbols and images from my waking reality [see Figure 16-2]. In the years since I had met my boyfriend, I had had many dreams about turtles and had seen him turn into a turtle once in a dream. Since then, I had fondly called him Turtle Man. So as I made the painting, it came to me to place the image of the turtle on the dress. For me, putting his symbol on 'my' Native American wedding dress meant that our two spiritual paths would merge into a happy union. I painted the movie scene across the top of the dress, which symbolized to me the importance of having a community to live and express ourselves within. At the time I made the painting, we had not spoken of marriage, but by the end of that year we became engaged and were married the following spring." Did Susan's honoring of her dream and careful integration of meaningful imagery into her painting of it actually help her marriage come about?

But the story continues. Susan says about six months after she and "Turtle Man" were married, she had a second dream where the wedding dress appeared again:

> *I'm walking with my husband along a road covered with clear crystals, picking up good ones as I go along. Eventually the path leads us to a cave, and the cave opens onto a bay. On the water there is a boat, piloted by a blonde woman. She indicates that I am to come aboard, but my husband is to remain on the shore. She says she's been waiting for me and it's OK because she knows all about me and even knows my dreams. To prove it to me she sketches my Wedding Dress painting.*

"When I woke I realized that once again the wedding dress had surfaced from my unconscious to remind me that an important message was being delivered. I sensed I was going to branch off slightly from my husband now, to take a new path that involved more emotional depth and feminine energy." Susan says it is this continuing interplay between her dreams, her art, and her real life that energizes her and makes life meaningful and exciting.

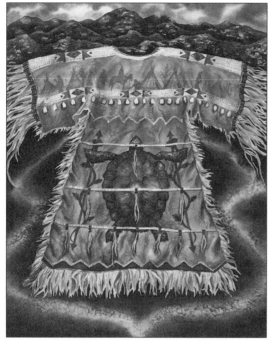

Figure 16-2:
Susan St.
Thomas's
painting of
"The
Wedding
Dress."

Finding Innovative Solutions

Creativity is not just for artists! All people use creativity every day in practical ways to "get the job done" successfully. When you embark on a new project — designing and building a custom deck for your house, rethinking the publicity campaign for a series of events you're producing, or coming up with a snappy, professional image for yourself as you start a new career — there is an early stage where dreams and creativity overlap to bring you innovative angles and fresh perspective. Without the imaginative first steps, even a utilitarian project like laying out a drip system for your garden would probably end up containing mistakes or turn out to be mediocre. You can develop your innovation muscle with the following exercises. As you loosen up your associative awareness, watch what dreams may come.

Try the following meditations to help you find innovative solutions.

Creating an Imaginary Project

Pick one or more of the suggested ideas or come up with your own, and spend a couple weeks germinating, gestating, massaging, shaping, drawing, writing, and possibly even DOING the project! As you begin, see what images, shapes, colors, smells, tastes, and sounds float in your imagination. Let the first layers of the idea come to you, and make note of them. Then let the idea evolve and shift, incorporate new elements, be extravagant or ultimately simple.

- ✔ Design your ideal bathroom
- ✔ Create an elegant flower arrangement
- ✔ Design your fantasy bedroom
- ✔ Create a place outdoors to meditate
- ✔ Design a studio for yourself
- ✔ Create an altar of your sacred objects
- ✔ Design a new kind of chair
- ✔ Create a gourmet meal for six

- ✔ Design a storage system for your closet
- ✔ Create a new hairstyle for yourself
- ✔ Redesign one of the classic old cars
- ✔ Create a clock from found objects
- ✔ Design an unusual birdbath
- ✔ Create a business card for your future self

As you formulate the vision for the end product or experience, how do you want to feel doing it? How do you want others to feel as they experience it? Watch how, as you keep your attention on the project, your dreams start to kick in with ideas, too.

Continue loosening up your creative mind by letting your imagination suggest either practical or totally silly uses for the following ordinary objects.

Making Something New from an Ordinary Object

What could you make out of each thing that wouldn't be related to its usual use? Suggest three to five possibilities for each.

- ✔ A ladder
- ✔ A red bandana
- ✔ A head of iceberg lettuce
- ✔ A pair of sunglasses
- ✔ A cake of soap
- ✔ An empty picture frame
- ✔ Tattered blue jeans

- ✔ A dead tree branch
- ✔ A bale of hay
- ✔ A bunch of bananas
- ✔ A can of worms
- ✔ A bottle of water
- ✔ Rusty nails
- ✔ A roll of toilet tissue

Feel free to add other components to complete your creative vision. You might pretend you're an alien from outer space, trying to figure out what each object is.

Jumpstarting Your Creative Process

I took a creativity seminar years ago with artist Michell Cassou, coauthor of *Life, Paint, and Passion* (published by J.P. Tarcher, 1996). She had us paint on big stretches of butcherblock paper with tempera paint, and encouraged us to not be too "precious," stiff, or formal. She helped us pay attention to what "wanted" to be painted, to what color "wanted" to go onto the paper next — not what our minds said made the most sense. At first, my paintings were tight — I actually got headaches and tense shoulders from trying to make sure my images were properly triangulated and balanced, according to the graphic design principles I had learned in art school. They were interesting, abstract, and colorful — but lacked a sense of life.

Michell let me go on for several classes that way. Then she stopped at what I thought was my finished painting and said simply, "Could you put one more thing on that painting?" I looked at her, dumbfounded. "But I'm finished," I protested. "Well, just put a black dot on the painting somewhere," she insisted. And she dipped my paintbrush into a big glob of black paint, handed it to me and waited. I sheepishly took it, hesitatingly aimed it at my perfectly balanced creation, and blobbed a thick black dot just off-center. The shock of seeing it there, suddenly wrecking and focusing my creativity at the same time, elicited an immediate and thunderous response from my body. I broke down sobbing. "The hand is connected to the soul," Michell gently reassured me. "Now paint something real from deep within yourself, until it is complete."

I put up a fresh piece of paper and stood, staring at it. Something real? Then, all at once, I was flooded with an image from a powerful dream I'd had the week before, of a dolphin who had come from a UFO, who swam up a river to find me, and rose out of the water with glowing eyes, a big smile, and a golden crown on his head. I painted it with total absorbtion and could barely stop at the end of class. From then on, my paintings came from my core imagination and were as different from my original stilted work as water is from steel. The key was to shock my mind out of its normal patterns so that my creative impulses could flourish and flow in new directions.

Draw a dream fragment

Even if you're not an artist, even if you don't think you have a creative bone in your body, you can still draw or paint a dream because there are no rules. If you don't think you can paint a whole dream, pick one fascinating image or a dream fragment and draw that. Your style can be as childlike or primitive as you want. You can draw right in your dream diary, get a larger sketchbook, or a big newsprint pad and some colored pencils, oil crayons, pastels, soft carbon pencils, fineline and thicker nibbed markers, and have at it! Try the following ideas:

- Draw the image once, draw it again with a different feel, draw it a third time maybe in proximity to a second dream image.

- Draw on a large sheet of paper, holding drawing implements in both hands. Try capturing the general mood and feeling of your dream first. Draw a little with your nonhabitual hand, and then add onto that with your stronger hand. Then add to that with the other, going back and forth. If you feel comfortable, try drawing actual images from the dream the same way.

- Play some music that has a similar mood, pace, or tone to your dream. Relive the dream until you are filled with the feeling the dream evokes. Let the music amplify the feeling until you want to overflow onto your paper. You might even dance around the room, really bringing the dream feeling into your body. Draw abstractly from the state of being that is triggered.

- Tune in to a movement in your dream; it could be running, flying, falling, swimming underwater, or feeling paralyzed. Make a gesture on your drawing that epitomizes that motion. Is it toward yourself or away? Left to right, or right to left? Angular or swooping? Stabbing or jabbing? Repeat the motion again and again, large and small, with heavy pressure and light, with different kinds of implements and strokes, with the point of a pen and the side of a piece of chalk. What feelings or memories are triggered?

- Draw a cartoon strip of your dream, or storyboard it as though for the director of a movie. You might even draw in balloons over the characters' heads with things each might be saying.

- Make a border on the page to contain your dream drawing (you might want to do this first). It might be a simple square, rectangle, or circle, or a scalloped border around the edge, or perhaps your dream wants to fit inside a bowl, or a genie's bottle, or a window divided into four panes, or maybe it wants to fit inside an organic shape like a cloud, or your own body, or the body of an animal, like a wolf, whale, or eagle.

- Draw the same dream character repeatedly all over the paper, showing the different states of mind, phases of the dream, actions, decisions, and emotions overlapping with each other. Let the interconnections and placements surprise you.

- Draw a figure from your dream with certain parts exaggerated. You don't have to keep things in perspective and know exactly how long a horse's legs are in proportion to its neck. Maybe you just want to draw all the hairs in the horse's mane and tail and make them really, really LONG!

✔ Add one more element when you think you're finished. What would the
most unlikely thing to appear in your drawing be? Could you add a
source of light? Something from another dimension? Something with
heightened contrast to the rest?

Make a collage from your dream

If you feel uncomfortable drawing or painting, you can always cut out pictures from magazines! Scan through your dream diary for a dream, or a series
of dreams, that has colorful imagery, vibrant moods, action, and emotion.
You could just as easily select a disturbing, dark dream as a whimsical, technicolor one. Make a note of the common themes and any repeating symbols
or related characters. Get a sense of the qualities the characters represent.
Pay attention to the setting, the light, the directionality.

Now scour through all your magazines, and ask your friends for their old
magazines, ripping out images that are either literally the same as those in
your dreams, or give the impression, create the mood, or modify those
images. Pick large images and tiny ones, colorful and black-and-white ones.
Cut out a few single words here and there, or a numeral. You might even
prefer tearing the images out of the magazines, leaving rough edges. The pictures you use for your collage don't even have to be recognizable. For
instance, you might take an image of a field of golden wheat and cut it up into
triangles and odd shapes, pasting those together in a starburst shape to give
the impression of provision from a divine source, which permeated your
dream. You might find a face where only the eyes intrigue you. Cut them out
and discard the rest.

If you were chased by a hideous monster in your dream but can't find that
exact image, use something that conveys the gist of a menace — a cartoon
image of Godzilla, a black panther from a nature magazine. You might want to
incorporate an actual photograph of yourself, your mother, or an old
boyfriend into the collage. Try enlarging or reducing it on a color copier.

When you paste your images together, look for odd overlaps and interconnections, for missing pieces of the dream story, and for themes that weave in,
out, around, and through the collage. Let yourself piece the parts together
impressionistically, organically, and lay them over one another or let them
bleed off the edges of the paper. You can trim away the excess later. You may
want to paint a colored or textured background first and then paste your
images. Similarly, after you're finished with the collage, you might want to
draw over it in places with gold or silver metallic ink pens.

Let a dream inspire a series of paintings

Sometimes a dream comes at the perfect time, carries that special "psychic weight," and stays with you as though it wants to talk to you. Leslie Schwing, an artist now living in Baltimore, had a dream like this that became the genesis for a series of amazing paintings — and transformed her life. Years ago Leslie lived in the Caribbean and she says her life was in turmoil. She was married to a possessive and physically abusive man who at one point had broken her right hand. Low on energy and depressed, she continually fantasized about how she would escape. One night, still suffering from the broken hand, she had a powerful dream:

> I am walking up a mountain, being led by my little dog Hecate. She takes me to a cave. There is an old woman inside the cave, standing at a beehive oven. She is baking something and when she takes it out of the oven I see it is a marble cake with swirls of black and white. She orders me to EAT THE CAKE! Then she begins to morph into many many different women and other beings.

When Leslie woke, she had a sense that the old woman was the real Hecate, the mythological goddess figure she had innocently named her dog after — just because she liked the sound of the word. She also realized she had regained her energy and felt inspired to paint. The image of the dream cave and the characters the old woman had morphed into were filling Leslie's mind, so she tried to paint them — with her *left,* nonhabitual hand. Once she started, she couldn't stop, and made five paintings in a row, full of amazing images. As she finished one, the images for the next came to her with a great urgency. These first paintings were primitive and earthy, due to her lack of facility with her left hand — yet she is sure it was this very thing that helped her access the unfamiliar imagery from her deep unconscious. See Figure 16-3 for images of two of the paintings inspired by the dream.

At points in the process of making the Hecate paintings, Leslie "thought" she knew what wanted to be painted. Yet every time she tried to paint from any sort of mental contrivance, the painting process stopped. Eventually she had enough work for a show, which she arranged in Baltimore. She was able to "escape" at last, and freed herself to live a healthier, more loving life. After moving to Baltimore, however, the paintings did not stop. There are now 24 paintings in all.

When the process was finally complete, Leslie realized she had been painting archetypal, mythological images, yet had no direct knowledge of the myths she'd been rendering. She sensed there was a story underlying the paintings, because they seemed like a series of illustrations. As she researched the Hecate myth and the strange characters that had appeared in her paintings, she says she kept asking of the higher realms, "What's the story?" In response, her life began to seem like a waking dream. Leslie says the characters from the paintings showed up in her real life in the form of people who acted out the roles and embodied the archetypal patterns. Then one night while she was lounging in the bathtub, a story came to her and spun itself out. It was a long saga, like ancient science fiction, and she intends at some point to weave the story and images together into a book.

Figure 16-3:
Two of the "Hecate's Cave" series of dream paintings by Leslie Schwing.

As a result of living out the mythologies and interacting with the characters from the paintings, Leslie realized that she had indeed eaten the marble cake — a symbol of the integration of the dark side and the light side. She had come through a difficult, depressing period and was finally ready for a mature relationship, which soon occurred. As a final "capper," when she and her new partner were on a trip to Hawaii, they were taken to a special cave by a friend. At that cave, Leslie saw fishermen, baskets, and many of the images that were directly from her dream and the dream paintings. She told me that she felt she'd come full circle.

Try the following meditation exercise to expand your creative repertoire.

Visiting the Art House

You can help jumpstart your creative process by working with this visualization technique. Try visiting this imaginary Art House consistently for a period of time. See what kinds of artistic activities your inner self is drawn toward. Next, try programming a dream to visit the Art House at night while you sleep.

1. Close your eyes, be centered and quiet. In the clear space in front of you imagine your favorite place in nature and a fabulous getaway house: a charming cabin in the woods, a mountain chalet, a beach house, a high desert adobe with rock gardens, or even a penthouse in Paris. This is your private place for creativity and self-reflection.

2. Go in and look around. You see rooms for every kind of creativity: a music room with every fun instrument you can think of, a kitchen with state-of-the-art gadgets and mounds of fresh foodstuffs and spices, a studio with huge flat tables, easels, paints, pens and brushes of every kind, and wonderful natural light. You see a place to sculpt, work with clay, make paper, or work with metal and jewelry. You see a dance studio with mirrored walls and a stack of CD's next to a CD player. There's a woodshop, or a darkroom if you want one. There's a place to write on beautiful paper with fountain pens, or to see what you type on a full-size color monitor. Anything you can think of, you can have here in your art house.

3. Let your body and your artist brain lead you to the kind of creativity you want to indulge in first. Go into that room, touch the tools and materials, smell and feel it all. Surrender yourself to a total involvement with the medium you've selected, letting yourself experiment fully. Concentrate your energy and then release it. Enjoy the natural movements of the stream of consciousness that wants to flow through you.

4. When you're finished with your art play, come back to normal awareness and make notes in your diary about what you did and how it felt.

I talk about drawing and painting here, but the same processes can be used with other forms of creative expression, like sculpture, dance, and music. If you are inclined to any of these, see what three-dimensional forms your dreams might take, what body movements flow from dream feelings, or what songs or musical compositions might arise from your dream seeds. Pay special attention to dreams that contain creations that are unfamiliar to you in waking life. Do you sometimes dream you're playing the piano effortlessly, composing fantastic music spontaneously as you play, yet in "real" life you think you have no musical ability? Dreams of undeveloped talents might serve to give you the confidence to try new areas of self-expression.

Writing from Your Dreams

The idea for *Dr. Jekyll and Mr. Hyde* came to Robert Louis Stevenson in a dream, and Mary Shelley first saw the character that would eventually become the Frankenstein monster in a dream. I have had several ideas for children's books come to me first as dreams. When I sat down to flesh them out, they nearly wrote themselves, progressing as if by magic — as though I were still inside the dream, and the dream had become lucid.

If you are a journal-keeper and enjoy writing as a practice to keep yourself clear and open, your dreams can provide endless amounts of subject material to write about. In addition, your dreams can keep you connected to the fertile state writing teacher Natalie Goldberg calls "wild mind." In her book of the same name (published by Bantam Press), Goldberg describes drawing an imaginary dot on the sky. That dot is our conscious mind, or what Buddhists call the "monkey mind." We tend to place all our attention on that one dot, she says, forgetting that the hugeness of the sky, the wild mind, surrounds us. She says our dreams are beings that travel from the wild mind into the dot to wake us up so we'll take one step out of that small world and "sink into the big sky and write from there."

Write a children's story or a fable

Even if you don't consider yourself a writer, you can certainly construct a children's story in all its glorious simplicity and innocence. Remember how children make up endless, meandering stories that can continue as long as the audience seems appreciative? That skill probably never left you. Here are some hints to trigger your children's story and put you in the right frame of mind:

- ✔ **Pick a dream character, a dream locale, a dream theme.** They don't have to all be from the same dream. Mix and match, but pick what excites your imagination.

- ✔ **Start your story with "Once upon a time. . . ."** This puts you in the fairy tale mood, and lets your fable-writing juices begin to flow. It helps you write from the place where you know nothing and can maintain your innocence and beginner's mind.

- ✔ **Enter the tale at the point that fascinates you.** As you begin the story, imagine you are entering a dream and you're going to make it up, or it's going to make itself up, as you go along. You might try showing up inside one of the characters and begin telling the story from that point of view.

- ✔ **Examine and describe the physical landscape.** What's happening around you? Is there a problem with the situation you find yourself in? Are you going somewhere? Where? What's there? Does the scene change?

- ✔ **Ask "What does this character need?"** What are the barriers in the way of the character? Who else has needs in the story?

- ✔ **Let your character ask a question.** Let the answer be a surprise.

- ✔ **Exaggerate whenever you can.** Make things smaller, larger, louder, softer, darker, lighter, meaner, or gentler than they would normally be. Embellish and add fanciful details that describe characters, places, and actions in a fuller, more colorful way.

✔ **Describe things using lots of sense-oriented adjectives and adverbs.**
Make the story as real as possible to your body and the to bodies of
those who might read it.

✔ **Who's innocent, who's the bad guy, and who's the good guy?** Let them
interact and see what trouble they get into, then see how the problem
wants to resolve itself.

✔ **End with a moral or a lesson.** What could a 5-year-old learn from this
adventure?

✔ **Create a title that a 5-year-old would like.**

Experiment with more writing ideas

After you play with writing fables and children's stories, practice expanding
your imagination by doing a series of writing exercises or making up short
stories or anecdotes for your own amusement. Try any of the following ideas
to prompt your dreams to take shape as stories:

✔ **Tell the same story from the point of view of several different characters, even inanimate objects.** Maybe the tree, or the trap door in the
attic, or the swimming pool, has a different perspective that would make
your story — and your understanding of what's behind the story —
more complete.

✔ **Create an imaginary dialogue with a dream character.** The conversation can be between you and the character, or between two characters
you make up. Have the characters ask each other questions.

✔ **Take a character on a quest.** Have your character go on a journey,
moving through doors, gateways, down alleyways, through tunnels,
around corners, and into caves and rooms where new encounters and
episodes can unfold.

✔ **Write about meeting a character that occurs repeatedly in your
dreams.** Describe the character's habits and opinions and talents. Write
about how the two of you form a surprising friendship and how you
agree to help each other.

✔ **Write your life story as if you are your dream self.** Describe your life
history in the dream world, making no reference to the waking world.
What have you been doing all these years? What is your life purpose?
Who are your friends? What are your talents and roles?

Let poems pour from your dreams

Poetry is the form of writing that comes closest to a direct replication of the
dream state. It is nonlinear, nonlogical, springs from feeling, makes odd leaps,

implies rather than defines, and leaves impressions and a sense of space. Poems are the essential jewels buried beneath the outer layers of dust and debris; they are at once both subjective/personal and objective/universal. Good poetry makes your consciousness stretch to a higher, or different — yet always enlightening — point of view.

Every dream you record in your dream diary can also be written as a poem. For example, the narrative version of a dream I once had would go like this: *I'm at a cabin bordering some woods. It has huge plate glass windows. Someone says, "The elk are here!" And I see a herd passing by in the field outside, from left to right, and they all have different colored bandanas tied around their necks — for protection. I think, "Someone has taken really good care of them."*

When I translate the dream into a poem, here's what I get:

> the elk are here!
> the elk are here!
> precious sacred creatures
> that preserve old secrets
> from mountains, woods, and plain
> they move in a positive direction
> bringing good luck to all who see them
> each has a colorful story to tell
> each has a badge of acknowledgment
> bestowed by their happy caretaker

The process of writing the poem immediately brought related ideas to my awareness that had not been apparent in the narrative telling of the dream. Concentrating on the simple phrases and connecting them together in a collage-like way caused me to access nuances of feeling as well that I had not felt in the original dream. My more intuitive poetic voice seemed to be interpreting some of the symbols naturally as I wrote. Try writing your dreams in both narrative and poetic forms side by side in your dream diary.

Turn excerpts of powerful dreams into haiku

Haiku are simple, three-line, brief Japanese poems intended to capture the essence of a moment, an experience, or a scene and leave the reader with a feeling of timelessness, spaciousness, and wonder. They are most often about nature, but can address any subject. Try writing as many haiku as you can, suggested by the imagery from one dream. Here's the narrative version of a dream:

> *I give birth to a baby boy who grows quickly to be a toddler and he talks in full sentences with memory of who he was in previous lives. I realize he has no memory blocks. His eyes are like those blue marbles with the continents painted on in green. They are like two tiny globes, like he is seeing through the planet's eyes. They radiate a calm bluegreen glow that leads back into a grayish endless field of memory that feels wise and ancient.*

Here are some haiku generated from the dream:

my baby man self	he sees as the planet sees	his clear eyes see out
has wide open eyes	knows seas, skies, secrets	and lead me in
and wide open mind	forgets nothing, all still is	two way bluegreen
		knowing

Draw your dream and then write a poem about the drawing

You might make an impressionistic drawing or collage from a dream, and then list six to eight odd pairings of images from the drawing. Try leaving out the adjectives. Compose a poem that integrates those phrases and which will be a message to you from your inner self. Fill in around the images with other ideas that arise spontaneously. Here are six pairs of words that came from a dream painting:

star/eyes	apex/light
mountain/morning	igloo/mind
wheel/wind	beam/clouds

Here is the poem that sprang from those associations:

> In the mountain morning
> I stood on the cliff
> staring with my star eyes into the pink.
> I came from my old igloo mind, breaking loose
> and feeling the wheel of wind
> spiraling me up and out —
> I let myself be lifted,
> I let myself travel the beam to the clouds;
> there I climbed the sky pyramid
> and soon was the apex light,
> and I was free.

You can also write a poem around a list of words from your dream. Go back through one of your dreams, listing the nouns, descriptive adjectives, verbs, and descriptive adverbs. Make them up if they're implied. Compose a poem integrating these words. Fill in around the words as your intuition prompts you.

The ultimate in letting your dreams help activate your creative process is to pretend your waking reality is a lucid dream. In other words, you're awake within this dream you call daily life, and just like your agile, free-spirited, imaginative dream self, you can influence the dream any way you want. You can think about anything, interact with anyone, draw anything that interests you into your world, and achieve magical results. So what if, right now, you were in a dream? What would you think of to do next if there were no restrictions?

A dream that contributed to literature

English poet Samuel Taylor Coleridge, while idly passing the hours one afternoon, randomly turned the pages of a history book called *Purchas His Pilgrimage.* His new opium habit was causing him some pain, so he drained a glass of laudanum. As he fell asleep he read the words "Here the Khan Kubla commanded a palace to be built. . ." When he awoke three hours later, the rhythmic passages of "Kubla Khan" were firmly in his mind. He estimated the original poem to be 200 to 300 lines, and said all the images rose up effortlessly before him like "things," along with their descriptions. As he recorded the 54th line, he was interrupted by someone coming on business. When he returned an hour later the remainder of the great poem had melted away!

Dream making emerges from a fundamental desire for intimacy,
the love of creation, and the necessity to speak. The story
emerges from them, but also it is a story pointing toward them.

—Deena Metzger

Your Dream Diary

1. Carry your diary around with you this week and make notes as often as you can about what thoughts and themes are occupying your mind. What are you noticing in the world? Then add in the dream themes, and then the next day's thoughts and desires. Keep adding to your stream-of-consciousness list. After a week look back at it as a whole and write about what you see.

2. Write about your least developed sense. What's good about it that you may not have noticed? What's it good for? If it were your most developed sense, how would you know about the world and other people?

3. Write about how you used your creativity recently in an everyday project. How were you innovative? How might your innovation contribute to an upcoming project?

4. Write about how you could make your perceptual process more creative.

5. Write about how you could set yourself up to experience more surprise in your daily life.

6. Pretend you're Pablo Picasso, Frank Lloyd Wright, Georgia O'Keefe, Emily Dickinson, Beverly Sills, or another famous creative person and write about what they've been dreaming.

7. Trade a few dreams with a friend and write poems for each other based on the dreams.

Chapter 17

Dreams and Spiritual Growth

• •

In This Chapter

▶ Receiving superconscious guidance

▶ Understanding spiritual teaching dreams

▶ Recognizing spiritual visions

▶ Experiencing lucid dreaming, dream yoga, and witnessing dreams

• •

> *As I began to take an interest in my dreams, I became aware for the first time in my life that God wanted to speak to me. . . . I soon noticed that there was a wisdom greater than mine that spoke to me in my dreams and came to my aid.*
>
> —Morton Kelsey

*I*f you're working with your dreams, you have entered upon a spiritual path, whether you realize it or not. Whenever you become fascinated by the Mystery, search for an answer that lies below or beyond the superficial explanation, or yearn for experiences in life that contain greater peace, more compassion, or increased joy and spontaneity — you're on a spiritual path. Your spiritual path may revolve around a specific religion, or it may be more mystical and nature-oriented, but all spiritual paths contain certain common elements:

✔ A stated intention to better the conditions of your life by improving your character, embodying noble truths, and being responsible for what you create in the world — "first, do not harm."

✔ The acknowledgment that there is an internal, intangible, underlying reality that serves as the blueprint for the external physical one.

✔ The personal discipline and followthrough to steadily achieve better physical health, mental attitudes, and emotional equilibrium.

✔ A dedication to eliminating fear or subconscious blocks from your perception and experience.

✔ An open-mindedness toward learning new ways of thinking, acting, and being so you can live in greater alignment with the natural laws, which produces harmony.

  ✔ A commitment to being authentic — you want who you are and what you do to be the highest expression of your soul that you can attain in any given moment.

  ✔ An ongoing yearning for unity with your soul, the divine, and all life.

Recognizing Spiritual Path Dreams

Once you realize you're on a spiritual path, everything in life becomes fodder for your spiritual growth, and the special states of awareness that allow you to glimpse the inner worlds of spirit — like intuition, meditation, creativity, and dreams — become especially valuable. What's interesting is that as soon as you've committed to your spiritual growth, your dreams will begin to bring you guidance from your superconscious mind.

Remember that each dream zone has a superconscious level:

  ✔ At the physical Zone 1, the superconscious level contains the body's optimal energy blueprint

  ✔ At the emotional Zone 2, the superconscious level transmits information concerning positive motivation and ecstatic experience.

  ✔ At the mental Zone 3, the superconscious level provides insight, inspiration, intuition, and abstract conceptual understanding of higher knowledge.

  ✔ The causal Zone 4 is entirely superconscious and contains knowledge of personal and planetary evolution through all time.

When you consistently ask for information to come from these levels, you accelerate your spiritual growth by receiving guidance that brings out the best in you physically, emotionally, and mentally. Keep your eyes open for the signs of dreams about spiritual growth explained in the sections that follow.

Is your body buzzing?

Many people experience physical changes as they begin to "clean up their act," whether they clean up their act by eliminating clogging foods or addictions, or by letting go of negative thinking and depressive emotions.

As energy begins to flow through the physical system more freely, you may have dreams that reflect increased mobility, intensity, or even an increase of light in the body. You may experience more electrical energy for a while, and that buzzing in your body might even prevent you from sleeping some nights. The increased energy may show up in your dreams, literally represented by electrical symbology, such as power cords, or by spirals, wave images, zigzags, lines of light, or images that convey a sense of teeming, like tiny microbe colonies or beehives.

You may on occasion experience a release of kundalini energy, which travels up the spine (see Chapter 11). These sudden bursts of life force energy may be symbolized in your dreams as nuclear explosions, tornadoes, earthquakes, or snakes. Any sort of wavelike motion, such as swimming underwater like a fish or dolphin, or winds or movements in the atmosphere, can also represent the flow of new energy in your body.

Are you lightening up? Or going up?

As you practice becoming more loving, willing, cheerful, optimistic, participatory, and open, you may have dreams that indicate this lightening up of your thoughts and emotions. Your dreams may seem to be lit up by a bright light, or have a strong feeling of sunshine permeating them. As you begin to be motivated by higher ideals and clear thinking, your dreams may symbolize this with images of ascent. You might enter an elevator and go to the top floor, climb a tower, take off in an airplane, see a bunch of balloons being released, or fly or levitate all by yourself. You might dream you are in high places like snow-capped mountains, penthouses, skyscrapers, or treetops.

Are you in a sacred place?

Being on a spiritual path may cause you to examine your old beliefs about religion and what is sacred to you, either consciously or unconsciously. If your dreams are set in places known as pilgrimage spots or "power places," such as Stonehenge, Machu Picchu, the Pyramids at Giza, Chartres Cathedral, Tulum, Mecca, the Bermuda Triangle, Delphi, Mt. Shasta, Tibet, or Jerusalem, you may be tuning in to the higher archetypal energies these places represent and embody.

If you dream you're in church, at a convent, a monastery, a chapel, a Buddhist temple, a sacred spring or well, a Druidic oak grove, or sitting at an altar, you may be focusing your attention on spiritual bodies of information or belief systems, or creating a frame of mind where you can understand spiritual teachings.

Do you socialize with fairies and trolls?

Have your dreams started to be populated with an odd cast of characters? If you've moved on beyond the everyday dealings with family, friends, colleagues, and old lovers in your dreams, and have instead taken up with helpful wild animals, fairies, trolls, angels, spaceship captains, little silver men, and 9-foot tall slugs wearing Sherlock Holmes hats, you're no doubt visiting the higher dimensions to obtain superconscious information.

Relating with famous historical figures, especially religious and moral leaders, or with ascended masters, or elders from spiritually rich traditions like those of the Aborigines, Native Americans, Tibetans, Hindus, Buddhists, Egyptians, Peruvians, or Sumerians, indicates that you're tuning in to the ideas and energies represented by those people. Similarly, speaking with children who are wise beyond their years may indicate a connection with a higher being. If you dream of people you know who have died, you may be stretching your awareness upward to match their higher state of being on the other side.

Have you visited the library lately?

If you dream of being in a classroom, or at a conference, or that you've been surfing the Internet searching for information, you may be visiting the higher mental and causal zones to access personal or planetary information from the distant past or future. Dreaming of being in a library, poring over old books in an attic, finding ancient records hidden in a cave, or secrets thought by some to be buried under the Sphinx in the legendary Hall of Records (believed to hold the history of the earth), also indicates that you're tapping into the collective consciousness and the memory banks of the planet to expand your knowledge.

Imagine there is a place where the knowledge of everything that's ever happened on earth, and in our solar system, is recorded in perfect detail. This same "library" contains future knowledge as well. In metaphysics, this is called the *Akasha,* or the *Akashic Records,* and many clairvoyants see it as an actual library.

Try this meditation exercise to plant the library imagery in your inner mind, and ask to visit the library in your dreams as well as in meditation, especially when you need guidance.

Visiting the Akashic Record Library

1. Close your eyes, get centered and quiet. In the clear space in front of you, imagine a magnificent library on a hill. Walk up the wide pathway to the giant front doors, and the guard will let you in. Walk into the great rooms and notice the endless corridors of shelves stretching as far as you can see. On the shelves is an endless array of books, scrolls, even ancient tablets — some fat, some thin, some bound, some unbound. In another room, you find an array of ancient and future artifacts with accurate descriptions of what the item was used for, how and when it was used, and who made it.

2. Let your body decide which way it wants to walk and when it wants to turn down one of the aisles. Let yourself wander around in the Akashic Record Library for a while, looking at the grand variety of books and objects, wondering what stories each might contain. Soon one of those books is going to catch your attention in a special way. Then you notice "your" book, the book of your life history throughout time. Go over and get it off the shelf. Take it to the end of the aisle where you will find a private reading room.

3. In the reading room, open the book and see how it's organized. Is there a table of contents? Is there an index? Turn to the section pertaining to your current lifetime, right now, and look back through the previous pages. Are there illustrations? Is there an explanation for the inner purpose of the events you have experienced so far? Look back to the time of your birth, then to the time before birth, then in between lives, and then to the end of the previous life. (**Note:** If you don't believe in reincarnation, just look for the history of your current life.) Keep scanning back, letting images come to you. You might also try scanning ahead. If you get confused, ring a buzzer, and a guide will come in and help you. When you are finished, put the book back on the shelf.

4. Is there a period of history you're curious about? Try looking for the book that preserves that body of information. Is there a mystery that haunts or intrigues you? Find the book that has the record of it.

5. Come back to your normal awareness and write about what you discovered.

Obtaining Superconscious Guidance

Being on a spiritual path is challenging. When you ask to clear fear, fears will be presented to you. When you ask to understand more, more will be revealed to you. When you ask to be more of your true self, more options will be given to you from which to choose. All this increase in complexity can be confusing. You have many questions, turning points, and clear decisions to be made. Being able to obtain guidance and direction from a wise source, one that has your best interests at heart, is vitally important.

A metaphysical principle that may help you find the guidance you need is: Every time you formulate a question, that question cannot exist without its complement, the answer. They arise together. Every question naturally draws forth its perfect answer. So when you assume that "if you can think of the question, the answer isn't far away," you'll maximize the ease with which your dreams and your inner mind can guide you.

Guidance dreams often involve a conversation with a wise being, such as a spiritual teacher or guide. These beings commonly appear to be surrounded by light, or dressed in light-colored garments, and sometimes look old and experienced, or can seem to be from one of the cultures you associate with spiritual knowledge.

No one can prove that nonphysical beings are really there, so the guidance may actually be coming to you telepathically from higher dimensions of your own soul, or from collectives of beings to which you belong. Or perhaps you really do have friends, relatives, and helpers on the other side who look out for you.

My sense is that we cloak the source of the guidance in whatever garb makes the advice seem most palatable and sane. To make use of a piece of advice, you may need it to seem personal, and thus you'll accept it when it comes from your favorite grandmother, who died when you were 13. Someone else may need the guidance to have the authority of coming from a guru, or from a religious figure like Jesus, Moses, or Gautama Buddha. Another person might want the direction to seem friendly and innocent, so Tinkerbell or Yoda might need to deliver the message. Perhaps your message will come as a sentence carved into a clay tablet, or written on a note in a bottle pulled from the sea. Whatever works!

Understanding the steps to obtaining clear inner guidance

As you start to familiarize yourself with the art of eliciting guidance from dreams, let me help you understand exactly how answers emerge from the inner world. Following are the steps in the process of obtaining superconscious guidance:

1. **Relax your body.** Give full attention to the rhythmic body cycles: your breath, heartbeat, electrical vibration, the vibration of the cells deep within you. Create a feeling of safety within yourself and in the environment around you. Center yourself inside your skin. Scan your body from toes to head, relaxing and softening all the parts systematically.

2. **Become alert and aware.** Bring your attention to the simplicity of what exists in this present moment. Simply notice and take inventory, allowing both comfort and discomfort in your body, in your emotions. Let go of needing to do something about everything. Make no decisions now. Suspend the personal will and notice the presence of divine will in yourself. Remind yourself that everything you notice is part of the Big You.

3. **Bring your body, mind, and spirit into perfect balance.** Acknowledge that you are fully present in your body in this moment. Feel your connection to the heavens through the top of your head, and then move your awareness to the base of your spine and feel your connection to the earth. Visualize energy passing through you in even waves without interference.

4. **Identify yourself correctly as your soul.** Affirm your true identity by feeling the quality of diamond light within you; by contemplating qualities of the soul, such as: "I am infinite beauty, I am infinite compassion, I am infinite energy," and so on. Let the voice of the true self speak within you, saying such things as: "Be still, know I am God"; "I am one with the flow of nature and grace"; "The answers which are appropriate for me, and which serve my growth, already lie within me." Breathe with a feeling of connectedness and oneness with All-That-Is.

5. **Focus on your need.** Feel any sense of incompletion, discomfort, need or desire for help or an answer. State your question clearly. Phrase your request in specific terms.

6. **Ask for help from the higher powers.** Go straight to the Source and address the higher powers with 100-percent conviction that an appropriate answer will follow immediately and easily.

7. **Release.** Trust that the great orderliness and wisdom of the universe knows what you need. Let your request go. Have no doubts. Be in peace and wait in soft receptivity. It is at this stage that, if you're programming a guidance-seeking dream, you simply fall asleep and let the higher realms do what they do.

8. **Allow the inflow.** Have no judgments about what you receive, how you receive it, or what form the answer might take. Don't second-guess or try to refine the answer after you receive it. Particularly, if you've asked for guidance in a dream, be alert for the dreams you receive in the morning.

9. **Consciously recognize the answer.** The Source may use various means to deliver its reply. It might come in a dream, or from a friend, or as an insight while you're daydreaming. Your answer may come in words, in pictures, in symbols, or omens; either in the inner mind or in the outer reality; through any of the sensory modes; from discarnate or incarnate beings; either immediately or in the near future.

10. **Record the answer.** Do something physical with your intuitive response: Write it down in your dream diary, tape it, speak it out loud to yourself or a friend, make a piece of artwork — but make it real to your body.

11. **Feel gratitude.** Give thanks and feel appreciation for the availability of truth, and to the levels of your own consciousness for cooperating with each other. Pat your body; hug yourself. This validates the experience.

12. **Implement.** Follow through on what you receive. Use the information. This completes the experience and frees you to move into a new phase of creativity.

Working with this process consciously, you'll be able to increase the speed and efficiency with which you receive the direction you need. Recognizing appropriate insight will become second-nature.

Listening to the faceless voice

In many cases, you may simply dream you hear a voice talking in your ear. The voice may seem like a man's or a woman's voice, but there may be no image accompanying it. Sometimes the voice delivers a long message with elaborate instruction, sometimes a quick, to-the-point directive. Paul recalls that, when he was about 11, he had fallen into the habit of swearing and using bad language — partly to express the frustration of preadolescent testosterone buildup, and partly to be one of the guys. He said he was walking down the sidewalk one day, drifting along in a daydream, when a voice from out of nowhere said very clearly, *"God doesn't like it when you swear."* He decided right then that he would change his ways. He picked substitute words such as heck and darn that he would use instead of the swear words, and he soon broke himself of the habit altogether.

You too may have experienced a dream voice that utters specific or enigmatic instructions to you. Or perhaps the voice seemed to come from a "talking head" floating in space nearby. Messages like this are always of primary importance, and I suggest keeping them in mind and meditating on them. If they don't make sense right away, file them in a special compartment in your mind until you can understand what they really mean.

Interacting with remarkable beings

Your experiences with dream beings can be quite literal. You may have full interactions with your guides, teachers, or mentors. Becky, who always seems to dream about Trappist monk Thomas Merton when she needs guidance, at one point was feeling a lack of confidence about her life direction and whether she was capable of moving forward into a new area of responsibility. She dreamed:

> *I am attending a fancy wedding reception and Thomas Merton is there. Everyone else is formally dressed and they're all standing around acting skeptical and stuffy. No one seems to be celebrating and no one is dancing. Thomas Merton comes over and asks me to dance. I say to him, "Why are you wearing a sweater?" curious about why he's dressed so informally. He says, "Well, you're wearing jeans. . . ."*

Becky says she realized he was telling her that she mattered to him enough that he would match his style to hers so she'd feel comfortable — and she could have a chance to feel she was parallel with him spiritually. He was encouraging her to act real, be her true self, and celebrate, even in situations where other people were acting like phonies.

Meeting and conversing with a spiritual guide in a dream may also give you hope and faith that you should continue to value the things that make you a good human being, in spite of the negativity in the world.

Incubating guidance dreams

Would you like to set up an appointment to talk to someone who's an expert in an area of concern you have? To draw a guide, teacher, or "spiritual coach" to you, try the following:

- ✔ Determine what exactly you need help with. Phrase your need to the spiritual guide as clearly and specifically as possible. You might try writing out your opening description of what you would say to this spiritual expert if you intend to summarize your situation and ask for help.

- ✔ Identify the person who comes to mind as an expert in this area. It might be a person, living or dead, famous or not. Or maybe it's an animal, or an angel. Make a list.

- ✔ Ask yourself who else might have a unique, valuable perspective on your issue — someone who might seem like an unlikely candidate. Make a list.

Now try doing the following combination meditation and writing exercise to receive guidance from an expert.

Meeting an Expert in Your Spiritual Problem

1. Imagine yourself at a sidewalk cafe, sitting casually at a table with many people coming and going all around you. Get the feeling that you'd really like to talk to one of the "experts" about your most pressing spiritual problem. Let it be okay for the experts to choose among themselves who will come to you now to help.

2. Suddenly, someone slips from the crowd and sits down at your table. He or she says, "I got word that you wanted to talk to me. I'm _____. How can I help you?"

3. Notice all the details about the person and feel the energy of the expert's body. Make eye contact. Explain your situation and see what the expert says. Let the experience unfold spontaneously in your imagination.

4. When it's finished, thank the person, come back, and record what happened in your dream diary. Or, as the expert speaks, write the advice in your dream diary, word by word, using direct writing.

If you'd like to try a different kind of incubation meditation, one that tunes you in to information from the highest dream zones, do the following exercise.

Meeting a Being from the Superconscious Realms

1. Imagine you are out camping in the desert, or in a location in nature that seems pristine and quiet. Perhaps it's night and you're sitting under a bright full moon. Feel your desire to receive help about a pressing problem. Or maybe you're hungry for higher teachings. Ask the Source to send you an appropriate teacher or guide from the higher superconscious realms.

2. Let an entity appear. Before any words are exchanged, let your body experience the entity's energy fully. Do you feel comfortable? You can set the parameters of how the other being interacts with you. How close do you want it to come? Make sure you feel safe and are able to be receptive.

3. Allow any energy or imagery transmission to occur. Higher entities often communicate directly via energy patterns and sacred symbols. Then, let a dialogue occur. Receive the message or teachings the being has for you. When you feel complete, thank the entity. Come back and write about it.

In the early days of my intuition development process, I was never sure if the individual entities I saw in my imagination were real, so I gravitated instead toward the image of merging my mind into a pool of consciousness shared by many beings, which I contributed to and received from in equal portion to the other souls. For me, the idea of this group mind often coalesced into an image of a council or a circle, like King Arthur's Knights, sitting about a Round Table in a special conference room. You might imagine the members of your council are sitting above your head in an imaginary halo, like jewels in an invisible crown. Visualize this halo and activate it before sleep — and see what dreams result.

Henry dreamed:

> *I'm standing before a council of spiritual elders to ask a question. After the council gives me an answer, I ask how it is that I — only one of billions of people with questions — could command their attention when there are so many issues in the world to be dealt with. Immediately, the council transforms into a many-faceted, prism-like structure. Each of the millions of facets is capable of reflecting yet another council, each of which, in turn, is capable of reflecting yet another council. I see there are infinite numbers of councils. The image morphs again into a sphere from which millions of small beams of light are emanating. Each ray of light, once projected from the sphere, becomes yet another sphere, and so on, and so on.*

Henry says, "The council clearly showed me how it was that Spirit could meet the needs of all seekers."

Try this meditation when you need guidance from your spiritual council.

Tuning in to Your Spiritual Council

1. Imagine a round table, or a flying saucer above your head. Let your awareness be drawn up into that space and get an image of the circular convening of your council of spiritual peers. Take your seat at the conference table. Look around and notice who's there. Do you know any of them? Are there any historical figures?

2. Define your most pressing question right now. Then join with your council and give your soul's force to the group mind. Notice that all the others are giving their essence as well, and the knowledge of all the souls from all their lives is blending together.

3. Place your pressing question in the center of the group and let go for a moment. Let the group mind digest the question.

4. Perfect guidance will be telepathically transmitted back into your mind, and you will know it either immediately, in a dream in the morning, or in a few days. Come back down to your body and open your eyes.

Spiritual tutoring

In addition to receiving guidance about your spiritual path, you may also receive teachings in your dreams. You may be shown details about how to conduct ceremonies, what certain esoteric symbols really mean, how to perfect a technique that will help you achieve deeper meditations, or what and how the ancient cultures taught their high priests. Some of these teaching dreams may not make sense to you, and you may ask, "Why is my dreamself examining sacred symbols when I'm concentrating on planting my vegetable garden?"

My answer is: "Only your soul knows for sure!" You are a multi-dimensional being, which means you live simultaneously in every dimension and have experiences in all the dream zones. In each zone, different "life experiences" are occurring, and somehow they all weave together into one big flow of evolution. It's just that your conscious mind may have trouble holding it all in a context that makes sense to your relatively simplistic earthly personality.

Here are examples of some spiritual teaching dreams:

✔ *I'm given a tool by a being; it is invisible but I can hold it in both hands. It is to help me learn to fly straight up. I try it but my balance is off and I circle back like a boomerang and smash into the ground. The being picks me up and sets me in place and I try again. I finally get it and go up like a rocket into very rarified realms. I do this several times, practicing my focus.*

✔ *I see my left palm and there is a huge whorl pattern that has just emerged, covering the entire palm, displacing the regular lines. I know I am in a similar pattern in my life, that the spiral is like a map I have to follow.*

✔ *I am looking at a book with pictures of ancient redwood or sequoia tree slices. Next to each there is a number and a paragraph interpreting the meaning of the rings. Someone shows me the picture that governs my current life pattern, and the number is 23. The person tells me something unexpected will spring to life, that I will soon need to deal with the unusual and the new.*

✔ *I'm with a man who knows how to control a jelly-like substance, but it is alive and has intelligence. He can make it take different shapes and do different things. Some are like worms, some like little balls. I want to learn this too.*

As often as not, teaching dreams will seem quirky, like many of the examples listed above, and you may never know what exactly you were doing, or why. Whether or not you consciously understand the teaching, what's important is that you maintain an expansive sense of your multi-level identity and feel empowered to be able to explore any mystery, or any body of knowledge that interests you.

How psi dreams fit in

Psychic, precognitive, or past life recall dreams — often referred to as dreams containing *psi* (parapsychological) phenomena — can often seem like spiritual guidance or spiritual teaching dreams. They might bring information that is useful in your growth or healing process; for example:

- ✔ Dreaming that you died in the frontline on an open battlefield in the Civil War may explain your nightmares of being overwhelmed by a terror you can't escape, and help heal your debilitating agoraphobia. The healing dream would open you to spiritual growth but of itself is not about spiritual guidance.

- ✔ Dreaming that a friend had polio as a child and finding out it's true, can help you broaden your understanding of the kinds of perception that are possible and natural. In this case, the psychic dream might serve as a spiritual teaching because it shows you how extensive your perceptual capabilities are. Similarly, if you dream of a missile falling out of the sky, and the next week the Challenger explodes upon launching, the precognitive nature of the dream may convince you that you can know much more than you ever thought possible, and that you are even intimately connected with events in the future. Dreams like these can open you to your own limitless intuitive abilities.

Once you understand what's possible in the realm of perception and knowledge, psi dreams simply bring more information, not necessarily the kind of guidance that helps you grow spiritually.

Similarly, *out-of-body dream experiences,* or OBEs, may seem exotic and higher dimensional, but their value as spiritual teaching dreams lies simply in demonstrating the existence of the etheric energy body and the soul's ability to freely move consciousness from one zone of awareness to another. Many saints, mystics, and philosophers have reported these experiences; the Egyptian-born neo-Platonic philosopher Plotinus (205–270) described it well, as being "lifted out of the body into myself." OBEs show you that you are more than just your physical body, and accepting that fact can open you to the spiritual life.

Out-of-body dreams serve one other purpose spiritually — and that is to lay the groundwork for you to develop lucid dreaming skills. To grasp the concept that you can be awake during a dream and direct it intentionally is to plant the seed of a greater idea — that you can wake up during the experiences you have in ordinary reality as well and direct your life as the soul fully embodied — in other words, you can become enlightened.

Becoming Lucid in Dreams

Have you ever had a nightmare and suddenly, as you were running away from the monster, a little voice inside you said, "I don't have to be afraid — this is only a dream!" Or have you ever told someone about the dream you just had, even analyzed it, while you were still dreaming? Have you dreamed you rolled over, turned on your nightlight, and reached for your pen and dream diary — but you were still asleep? These are all signs that you may be starting to explore *lucid dreaming* — the ability to wake up within the dream state and guide the flow of your own experience in the higher dream zones. (See Chapter 9.)

Researchers on the subject have found that to develop skill in lucid dreaming, you need to develop a few simple practices:

1. Expand your dream recall ability until you can remember a number of dreams every night. Program your mind to awaken right away when you have a dream and recall it as vividly as possible.

2. Have a strong, single-minded intention to learn to recognize when you're dreaming. As you fall asleep, you might tell yourself repeatedly, "Next time I'm dreaming, I will remember I'm dreaming."

3. Visualize yourself becoming lucid. You might imagine you're back in a recent dream and this time you recognize you're dreaming.

4. Watch for a sign in your dream that tells you "this is a dream." The Yaqui shaman Don Juan always advised Carlos Castaneda to look for his hand in his dreams, as a trigger to shift him into the lucid dream state. You might use those little messages like, "This is only a dream!" or "This is the point where I usually wake up from my nightmare," or "Wait a minute! My sister doesn't have green hair!" as punctuation marks that help you become awake in the dream.

5. When you see the sign, whatever it is, or have the dreaming realization, say to yourself: "I'm dreaming." Remain calm. Expressing excitement can agitate you and might wake you up. Try to take a moment to pause and sense what you want to do next to extend the dream consciously.

You may have better luck having a lucid dream during an afternoon nap, or during nights when you're slightly restless, where waking periods are interspersed with sleep.

Dream therapist Jeremy Taylor says that, "the techniques for achieving lucidity are all comparatively easy compared with the question of what to do when lucidity is achieved." How true! Your dream self is now presented with the same choices as your waking self. What actions will you take? Fortunately, the dream self and the dream mind are still functioning largely from the effortless flow of material from the unconscious, powered by imagination. And yet, you can still choose soul-enhancing activities, or soul-blocking ones. You might use your newfound dream clarity and freedom to work on healing your own body, or you might offer yourself in service to others who need help, healing, or education. You could choose to "act like an angel." Or you could decide to go to "school" and expand your knowledge, attending classes or exploring the world of lost knowledge. You might have a confrontation with an internal demon that teaches you how to overcome fear and end nightmares. Or, perhaps you might even meditate on your oneness with the divine!

Lucid dreaming demonstrates that the way your consciousness works in the dream world is parallel to way it works in daily life. Why not make a practice of pretending you're awake in a dream right now and begin to examine the choices you make about how to extend that dream?

Seeing Visions

Have you ever been awakened mysteriously at 3 a.m. with a dream so powerful it makes you cry, or leaves you stunned by a feeling of awe? If so, you have probably experienced a vision. Perhaps because 3 a.m. is the quietest time of the night, with the least distractions from the outer world, many people report having these impactful, often life-altering dreams at that hour. Dreamers often awaken with a sense that "the sleep has been peeled away" or "the curtains of sleep have been parted" leaving them wide awake but still feeling as though they are in the dream. The full impact then floods into them as the vision registers consciously.

Visions differ from ordinary dreams in that they provide an overview about your life plan and purpose, or show how you fit in with the bigger system of the planet itself. Visions may reveal pictures of the world of the future so you can learn to live more consciously today, or so you'll be prepared to take on a new part of your life purpose, which may be about service to others.

> ✔ **Some visions inspire you to think bigger, to let yourself feel more eternal and unified with the whole of life.** Visions commonly contain transpersonal content — that which takes you beyond your personal concerns into a concern for humanity or the planet. For example, Will dreamed: *I am being shown a grid that encircles the earth and am told that this is the connective conduit through which we — everyone on the planet — can access any information or insight for our collective well-being. It is like a magnetic aura of energy that is not affected by linear time, thus, all past, present, and future knowledge is inclusive.*

✔ **Some visions help you have faith.** Beth dreamed: *I wake suddenly and see my twin brother and sister, who died when they were nine, standing at the foot of my bed. They are smiling at me and seem to be glowing. They say I can come play with them, and I know they mean I can do it with my mind through meditation. My sister raises her hand quickly up to just above her head, indicating a rising level of something, and I know I can see them now because my energy level is vibrating at a high frequency, and anytime I can duplicate this, I'll be able to see them just as I can now.* As Beth shifted out of her drowsy, or hypnagogic, state, the images dissolved, but she was left with a strong feeling about the reality of the other world and her ongoing connection with her siblings.

✔ **Some visions plant seeds that work in your subconscious for years to come, reminding you about an important truth.** Some of these seed visions occur at an early age — even in childhood. JP had what he thought was a nightmare when he was ten. In the dream: *I am way out in space watching a "room" with invisible walls and a floor made of large black and white checkerboard tiles. I know there are people in the room but I can't see them. There are also "doors" in the invisible walls and bottles of milk have been delivered and set outside the doors by a milkman. As I watch, the "room" begins to recede, taking me further and further out into space, until I get so scared, I wake up crying.* JP had this same dream again and again for a year or two and couldn't figure out what it meant. He did, however, become less and less scared of the expanding and receding feeling. When JP and I talked, I suggested he was practicing moving his awareness from the lower mental zone (mental structures and beliefs — the square room, the black and white ground representing duality) into the higher, more abstract, superconscious mental zone (the receding, expanding feeling), which may have felt scary because he was still a child. The symbol of the milk (nurturing) was a reassurance that he could always come back down to the emotional zone, where he was more comfortable. In later life, JP studied Buddhism, yoga, and other spiritual disciplines. Could it be that he started getting himself ready to stretch his mind, quite early in life?

✔ **Some visions reveal aspects of your life work.** When I was in my mid-twenties, just beginning to be serious about my spiritual path, I had my first vision: *I'm floating over the rooftop of a house, looking down into the backyard, which is surrounded on all sides by an endless forest. I see rows of little people, like swaddled babies, lying stuck in a tarpit in the yard, packed together like sardines. These little "tar babies" are moving their mouths, repeating soundlessly "Help. Help. Help." I think I must go down and get them out of the tar. Then I happen to look to the right. I see a sea of points of light moving toward the tarpit through the dark forest. As I look closer I see it is an army of "light-bearers" coming to help. Then I look straight ahead and there is another army of light-bearers coming to help. And to the left, yet another. I look behind me, and there is another sea of lights, coming with me. I say to myself, "There is so much help for so few."*

When I woke, I felt a strange stirring in my heart, perhaps the beginnings of a kind of idealism, of a desire to be of service, to be one of the many to help the few. Since the vision first occurred, many nuances have been revealed to me that showed me it was not just about my own life work, but about the process of human evolution in general, and about how the physical is like the tip of the iceberg, while the spiritual and energetic reality is overpoweringly vast.

✔ **Some visions simply take you into the Light.** Many people, regardless of religious orientation, report being surrounded and saturated by a field of "living light" that makes them feel an ecstatic love for themselves, others, and God. No one knows what precipitates these mystical, numinous dreams, but they are unmistakable. They can forever convince you of the reality of the divine, the same way near-death experiences erase the fear of death and help people commit to living a fuller, better life.

Witnessing and Dream Yoga

In the Asian traditions, dreaming is seen to be similar to the way the Judeo-Christian God creates the world. In Tibetan Buddhist philosophy in particular, the experiences you have while dreaming are thought to be almost identical to those the soul has after death.

The Tibetan Buddhists believe there are several "worlds," or states of consciousness, called Bardos. There is a Bardo of the waking world, the Bardo of dreamless sleep, and the Bardo of dreams, which is very like the Bardo of Dying and Rebirth, detailed in the *Tibetan Book of the Dead,* in which the soul moves through various stages, or kinds of dreams, from satisfying and blissful, to frightening and horrifying. And yet, all the images the soul faces after death are just illusions. If you can learn to recognize them as such and let them go, you pass through this transition phase and can merge with the divine. If, during your life, you have learned to meditate, clear your subconscious blocks and fears, and develop yourself spiritually, you have a better chance of maintaining clarity in the Bardo, and you might not be forced into another lifetime just to avoid the after-death horror. So, to prepare for the after-death experience, Tibetans developed an elaborate process of learning to become mindful during the day, and lucid and clear in their dreams — a practice called *dream yoga.* In Tibetan philosophy, the goal is to become one with the *foundation consciousness,* or what they call the *clear light.* To become familiar with the clear light of dreaming helps you become familiar with the clear light of death.

To develop these consciousness skills, Tibetans practice becoming lucid in their dreams, but take it one step further. Once lucid, they use their intention to meditate on the clear light, allowing any dream images that arise to simply fade away. The more they practice, the more they experience "clarity dreams," what I have called visions. And yet, even those are allowed to dissolve. The goal is to have a *witnessing dream,* an experience of deep, peaceful inner awareness that is completely separate from any normal dream.

Creating your own visionquest

A *visionquest* is the active seeking of a vision from spiritual sources or the higher dimensions. They are commonly used in the Native American culture in conjunction with rites of passage. Typically undertaken by men at times of war, disease, famine, death, initiation into manhood, or childbirth (to seek a spiritual name for the child). Commonly, for instance, as a young person reaches puberty and is ready to become an adult, he or she may fast and purify through a sweat lodge ceremony and then spend several days and nights alone in a sacred spot in nature, meditating, praying, and opening to the spirits in hopes of attracting a vision, especially one involving the appearance of a personal power animal, that will reveal the seeker's life direction.

You can create a visionquest experience for yourself, to elicit a clarifying vision to realign you with your life direction, help you heal, or help you rediscover your connectedness with the divine. You might write about what your goals are first, and plan where you will go in nature. Prepare by fasting and cleansing your body, by letting go of distracting behaviors like watching television and reading, and begin meditating more each day. Then go camping. Set up a sacred perimeter for yourself around the area where you will sit and pray, and dedicate yourself to connecting with the highest levels of your soul and the higher dream zones. Practice mindfulness and the deepening of your concentration. Record your dreams in your dream diary.

Ideally, to practice dream yoga, you develop lucid dreaming skills and then practice mindfulness meditation before sleep — to such a degree that you meditate right into the sleep state and carry on as if there were no change. So perhaps dream yoga is the ultimate in dream work — the skill that weaves together day and night into 24-hour consciousness and allows you to know the unity that permeates and creates the cyclical flow of life and death. What begins as a curiosity about the source and meaning of the silly, esoteric, archetypal, frightening, or highly imaginative symbols and imagery filling your nighttime reality eventually broadens into an understanding of your own multi-dimensional identity and of the skills you need in order to make use of all the levels of your self to enrich your daily life. Eventually that understanding expands even more, and you see how your dreams are truly the doorway to your spiritual growth and the key to an enlightened mind.

A man who has a vision is not able to use the power of it until after he has performed the vision on earth for the people to see.

—Black Elk

Your Dream Diary

1. Write about your spiritual path. When did it begin consciously for you? What stages has it progressed through, and what are the major lessons you've learned so far? Where are you now? What's the leading edge on your spiritual path? Write, from the point of view of your soul, about how you can learn the next lessons and what you need to do.

2. Scan through your recent dreams and see how many of them have imagery that suggests you've been dreaming in the higher dream zones. Then write about what you sense you've been doing and learning in your dreams that pertains to spiritual growth.

3. Make up a dream, or stream of imagery, in which you are interacting with a spiritual guide, mentor, or teacher. Write it in your diary using direct writing and see what happens as it's happening.

4. Write out a dialogue between a part of you — like your innocent child self, your shadow self, your opinionated expert self, and so on, — and a being from the higher dream zones. You might role-play, shifting back and forth, pretending you are one being, and then the other.

5. Pick a specific activity or task you want to learn to do better — like meditating, exercising, eating or breathing properly, or developing lucid dreaming skills. Ask for a spiritual "tutor," see who shows up (either in a meditation or in your dreams) and what advice the teacher gives you.

6. Go back into a recent dream and pretend you become lucid within it. From that moment on, write about how you'd change or redirect the dream. Imagine how you might have behaved differently in the dream if you'd known it was "only a dream"?

7. Write about the visions you've had in your life. With the help of spiritual guides, write about what they might mean and why you had the visions when you did.

Part VI
The Part of Tens

"Hey - Einstein! Wake up! Your moaning and twitching about emcee this and emcee that is driving us crazy!"

In this part . . .

You can carry your dreams beyond your personal sphere with the tips in this part of tens. Children have lots of dreams, and many of their dreams are scary. Chapter 18 helps you share dreams with your children so they too can start taking control of their dream life.

Everyone can benefit from hearing and interpreting the dreams of others. Many people across the country have formed their own dream groups to share and interpret dreams. You can, too, with the guidelines I present in Chapter 19. Happy dreaming.

Chapter 18

Ten Ways to Work with Kids and Their Dreams

In This Chapter
▶ Developing a dream-sharing practice with your children
▶ Understanding how children dream

Developing a dream-sharing practice with your children has many advantages. By showing children that their inner world is real and their imagination produces meaningful and useful information, children will not tend to discount this highly important part of themselves later in life. By learning to value their inner life and wisdom from an early age, children will grow up with their intuition and the bridge to their spiritual self intact.

In contrast, children who are routinely told, "Go back to sleep. It was ONLY a dream; it's not REAL," are inadvertently trained to distrust and deny their creativity, inner voice, and connection with their deeper self. The negation of that inner world has a shaming effect and produces a kind of ineffable sadness in adulthood.

Studies show various things about the way small children dream. Dreams seem to appear after children learn to recognize objects and distill their memory of past experience. Some studies indicate that between the ages of three and five, children have dreams that tend to be disjointed, without much of a story, and without the child appearing as a main character. This shifts between the ages of five and seven — the child then develops greater intellectual ability and can begin symbolizing experience and relating it to him- or herself.

Children between ages three and seven often report nightmares. Nightmares appear to be a natural part of growing up. After that age, their dreams are populated by a greater host of characters, including themselves. This chapter presents ten things you can do to develop a dream relationship with your child.

Talk with your kids about their dreams first thing every morning, and share one of yours, too

Dreams are an intimate subject and spending time talking with your child about her dreams, and sharing some of your own, can only bring you closer and help develop a trusting rapport. Understanding the inner life of your child can help you stay abreast of her emotional and physical needs, and find a way to meet them. By monitoring the dream content of your child, you can keep an eye out for trouble spots, sense when fear is surfacing, and help her work through the issue before it becomes locked in and turns into a subconscious block she really doesn't need.

As you wake your child in the morning, or later over a bowl of cereal, you might say, "So, what did you dream last night?" As you listen to the telling of the dream, you might say, "How did you feel when that happened?" or "You can always call for help when that happens, you know." You might ask a few probing questions like, "Do you think I'll be able to give you enough attention when I start my home business in the basement?" or "Does that orange-eyed monster remind you of anything or anybody in your life right now?" Your job is to help your child understand the strange dream images that show up, and to reestablish security and a sense of well-being, especially when the dream is scary. Share a dream or two of your own, along with your feelings about some of the symbols, and what you think various images might mean. Demonstrate for your child how you connect symbols to your own life.

Help your child incubate dreams

With small children, you might read a bedtime story to help them incubate their dreams. After reading the story, talk to your children about what they want to do in their dreams that night. Do they want to play with the characters from the bedtime story? Do they want to fly? Play with their toys? Go on an adventure with you? Have fun brainstorming with them about what's possible in their dream world.

Next, you might have them get clear about what they want, and phrase their request to their dream self. For example, you might say out loud, together, "Tonight in my dreams I want to play with my Beanie Babies!" You might say it three times and have them take a sip of water at the end to make it "official." You might also say, "Okay! Let's see what dream you get in the morning! I can't wait to hear about it." If in the morning they didn't dream about Beanie Babies, listen intently to whatever dream did occur; the next night ask them if they'd like to try dreaming about Beanie Babies again. Gentle consistency pays off.

Encourage your child to invent a dream helper or protector

Help your children to deal with scary dreams by letting them know that they can control the outcome and not feel helpless in their dream world. Talk with your child about who might come to rescue her if she were in trouble. She may say, "You!" Tell her she can call you any time she needs to in her dreams, and you will always come and help her. Then you might ask, "And who else protects you?" Perhaps she'll pick the family dog or cat. You might ask, "And what does Scooter look like in the dream world? Does she look the same, or does she change?" Try having the child draw her special dream helpers, and have her show them in the act of protecting her.

Help your child start a dream diary

As soon as your child starts drawing, you can have him start a dream diary of his own. Show him yours, and read him a few of your dreams. Then let him pick out the kind of notebook he wants to keep his dreams in. He may want to decorate it in a way that makes it his very own. At first he might just draw a picture of his dream, or of the main character in the dream, and he might dictate the story to you for you to write next to the picture. Have him make up a title for each dream. In time, he can write his own dreams in the diary, and even make up stories about the dreams. Encourage him to keep his dream diary and a pen right next to his bed.

Connect your child's dream concerns with real-life remedies

Very young children typically have anxiety about basic trust issues: Will I be fed, picked up and held, be kept warm/cool, have my diaper changed, and be put down for naps in a consistent manner? Early nightmares might result from a visit to the doctor to get a shot or have the temperature taken, or from dealing with a strange baby-sitter.

As children begin to walk and talk, their dreams may reflect themes of independence/dependence. Nightmares can result from overhearing arguments and loud noises or from encounters with imposing strangers in the world, such as the delivery man. As children begin to want more attention focused on themselves, they can have dreams based on jealousy — "I want my baby sister to disappear because Mommy isn't giving me enough attention anymore." As children grow, they begin do deal with sexual feelings and aggressive urges, and at this point their dreams may be filled with wild animals, giants, and monsters.

After age seven, when children become more social and involved with friends, they may experience anxiety about rejection and popularity. This is also the age where performance in school begins to be measured, and doing well on tests may become a dream issue. In addition, the child may experience being bullied at school, which could translate into a nightmare.

By the time a child reaches the teen years, the sleep pattern is similar to that of an adult. Dreams become quite sophisticated; yet, because of the stresses most teenagers go through, nightmares can once again become common. Teens may stay up later and sleep longer than when they were younger due to changing hormone and melatonin levels. Dream content may revolve around the definition of new identity.

If you can be sensitive to the issues children face at different ages, you can take actions to help them feel validated and secure in their waking life. For example, if your child has a nightmare that she's going to be held underwater by one of the boys at the public pool, you might want to sign her up for swimming lessons. If she dreams about horses, let her begin riding lessons as soon as she's able. Your son's aggressiveness in his dreams might be channelled effectively into karate classes.

Make a dream-based collage together

Try spending a few hours now and then with your child, cutting up old magazines, saving pictures in a clip file that you can later use to make dream collages. Save pictures of wild animals, cars, bicycles, monsters, flowers, trees, toys, dolls, dogs, cats, birds, fish, foods, kids doing different things, old people, adults in sunglasses, mountains, lakes, backyards, bedrooms, shoes, and school buses.

Start pasting images down on a big sheet of paper with your child, perhaps in conjunction with some crayon or pencil drawings of the dream. In a short time you may find the dream begins to expand as your child takes a fancy to different images and wants to put the fire hydrant next to the picture of the St. Bernard. As the "dream" grows in complexity, you might have your child tell the new story that's taking shape. When you're finished, have the child tell the complete story from beginning to end, and together you can write it down on the back of the collage, or in the dream diary.

Suggest your child perform a dream-based puppet show

Your child and some of her friends might want to create a performance — a skit or a puppet show — based on their dreams. If they want help, you could show them ways to weave their dreams together into a larger storyline, and suggest costumes or puppets to make for the different characters. Acting out the dream dramas can have a positive effect on the child's psyche, helping allay fears and integrate unconscious insights. Having a group of kids enact their dreams together helps validate their inner world and collective creative process.

In a simpler version, you and your child could interact, both using hand puppets — perhaps a different one on each hand — to talk out the various roles spontaneously. Your child could wear a puppet representing herself and her dream helper, while you might wear puppets representing the monster and a victim of the monster. After you work the story out one way, try trading puppets and playing different roles.

Transform scary dreams with your child

A child's nightmares are extremely vivid, and young children have difficulty distinguishing between fantasy and reality. In addition, approximately 40 percent of children's dreams are nightmares, or night terrors, which are a different phenomenon than nightmares. In a night terror, the child may make choking sounds, sweat, feel paralyzed, or even scream out or sit bolt upright, without remembering any dream details at all. Often the child is not frightened once awake; in fact, she may not remember anything. Helping the child feel secure and safe is always a good idea anyway. If the child hasn't awakened, let her continue sleeping. Sometimes night terrors reflect the child's sense that there are unspoken conflicts between the parents concerning religious, spiritual, and emotional matters. Strangely enough, when this is the case, the child's night terrors often simply disappear when the parents have the talk they've been avoiding

To help a child take more control over scary dreams and learn to transform nightmares, first help her create her dream protector and helper. Talk to her about how to call for help when she needs it. Second, talk about the frightening dream with her afterward. When she gets to the scary part, you might have her introduce an extra character. It could be her dream helper or one the neighbor kids, or her music teacher, or her giant stuffed gorilla in the corner. Ask her, "And then what happens?" Help her continue the dream's action, letting the fear transform into something positive and happy. You might continue on with the story, asking leading questions like, "And what did the gorilla want to eat?" "Were they going to go on a trip somewhere?" "Did your music teacher show you about any new kind of musical instrument after she blew the whistle?" By transforming the fear in the dream, and then extending the dream into a bigger story, your child will be encouraged to dream in a similar way in the future.

Write a dream-based story together

Make up a bedtime story together with your child based on a dream he had earlier in the week. He could start telling the dream and you could add in another scene. Then let him add on to what you said. Then you add more. Keep on going this way until it feels like a natural end. The next night you might take the dream from that morning and add it on to the end of the previous night's story and continue. One technique you can use, if you get stuck, is to suggest that your child change the dream's ending. Ask him, "What else could have happened at this point?" Try making a little blank book by folding sheets of paper into quarters and stapling them together to make a spine. Then do a project with your child to write and illustrate the dream story you've been creating that week. Have your child think up a title for the story when it's finished and write it on the cover in big letters.

Program a creativity dream together

Going a step beyond simple dream incubation, you might help your child program a creativity dream for a specific creative purpose. Together, pick a medium, like painting, sculpture, or papier-mache, or a project like decorating a T-shirt, making ornaments for the Christmas tree, decorating a birthday cake, or creating a Halloween costume.

Before bed, talk to your child about the idea of dreaming about the shape she'll make out of her clay, or the picture her dreamself wants her to draw with colored markers. Talk about how her dreamself probably has a great idea for a costume for trick or treating. Together, say out loud, "In the morning I'm going to remember a dream about what I want to be for Halloween this year." Repeat it three times, and have her do something physical at the end, like taking a drink of water, to make it into a little ceremony that her subconscious will remember.

In the morning, help her remember any responses she received in her dreams. If nothing pertinent came, try the same procedure again the next night. When a response does come, help her make the dream into a reality any way you can. After the dream has been made real, make sure to mention to your friends and hers, in front of her, "She got the idea for this in a dream!"

Chapter 19

Ten Tips for Creating a Successful Dream Group

In This Chapter

▶ Deciding whether to form a dream group

▶ Determining the format and setting ground rules

▶ Adopting proven techniques

*B*efore you join or start a dream group, it's important to have a clear sense of what suits your needs, and what kind of people you'd like to interact with in the pursuit of higher dreaming. Part of this assessment revolves around your capacity for intimacy. Sharing dreams in a group is a highly personal experience. You may think you're just going to talk about what flying or falling might mean, but dreams have a way of dredging up your deepest secrets, and everyone else's as well. Having someone suddenly "see through you" and blurt out something like, "Are you afraid of sex?" or "Were you abused as a child?" might be disorienting and upsetting if you're not prepared to see certain things about yourself. On the other hand, if the environment is set up to be safe, you can make short work of many of your subconscious blocks.

Decide if a dream group is right for you

Ask yourself: "Am I comfortable with intense one-on-one situations? Am I willing to participate fully, even if it means I might show some vulnerability in front of others on occasion? Can I be honest? Am I willing to listen patiently to what others say with my full attention? Do I trust lay people, rather than a trained therapist, to give me insights about my inner self? Am I strong enough to make my own decisions about what my own dreams mean, and can I receive the ideas of others as helpful suggestions, rather than judgmental pronouncements?" Also determine whether you want a general dream discussion and interpretation group or a group, composed of artists and aspiring artists, that focuses mainly on the creative process. Would you be comfortable if the group had both men and women members?

Determine the best format

Think about the dream group atmosphere you want to establish, which should be one of trust and openness. When you look for group members, interview people briefly about their motivations for exploring their dreams, their comfort levels with group work, and their willingness to be vulnerable. Group members should agree about how best to cooperate and derive value from their dreams.

In my experience, ongoing groups with no end date in sight can become psychologically draining. Having the group meet once a month for six months, or once a week for eight weeks, tends to focus the energy and the work within the context of the allotted time and keeps group members more enthusiastic. Groups that meet weekly or biweekly tend to intensify your focus on your dreams and may give you faster, deeper results. A group that meets monthly, often mandated by today's frighteningly busy work schedules, will keep dream work an important part of all your lives but give you time to focus on other interests as well. Group members need to decide what kind of focus they want — intense or more casual.

Because each person in the group shares a dream, and you want to devote enough time to have each member give feedback on each dream, make sure the meeting is the right length and that you don't strain the limits with too many group members. An evening meeting from about 7:00 p.m. to 9:30 p.m. is doable for most people who work and gets them home at a decent hour. If you limit the group to four to six members, you should have plenty of time for each person's needs to be met.

Evaluate what works best attitudinally

I encourage you to be clear about your dedication to the dream work process, to the process you're undertaking by joining a group, and to the other group members. Ask yourself a few questions about logistics: "Do I want to devote the time to this sort of endeavor — if I commit to it, will I go to every meeting? Do I have any 'yes, buts' that might interfere with my involvement in the process? Will I maintain confidentiality about what happens within the group and not reveal material about group members' inner lives to others, no matter how innocuous the material seems?"

Make it a top priority to attend all the meetings and be on time. A process of trust and respect must be established among group members. If people don't think it's important enough to attend each time, after they've given their word, a subtle sort of internal sabotage begins to occur. If you must miss a meeting, notice how the themes of your dreams that week might be a key to your growth that you might not be allowing yourself to face fully. Make a point to discuss this later with the group.

Understand group facilitation

Dream groups are most effective when a leader, practicing "beginner's mind," both facilitates and participates in the process. I find that groups without a leader tend to waste time and lack focus. The facilitator should be able to perform these basic tasks:

- ✔ Keep the group on purpose and on time.

- ✔ Know how much material can be covered in each gathering and control group sharing to encourage conciseness, equal participation by all members, and content that enriches everyone.

- ✔ Deal with emotion compassionately but neutrally when and if it comes up in the sharing process.

- ✔ Help group members remember to share their dreams and give feedback in the preferred formats.

Group facilitators function best when they trust the process of the "group mind" and "group heart" to guide them. They should not function as therapists or high priests. No one in the group needs "fixing" or healing. Occasionally, group members may share the facilitating task, rotating it from meeting to meeting.

Set ground rules and basic principles

Following are some ground rules and principles that work well with dream groups:

- ✔ Group members agree to maintain confidentiality about what transpires inside the group and to actively work on developing respect and support for each other.

- ✔ Group members agree to be honest about sharing themselves. If they feel uncomfortable revealing something, it's okay to say so and be quiet instead.

- ✔ Group members accept that all dreams have multiple meanings and, therefore, agree to be open to hearing a melange of interpretations as suggestions to trigger their own deeper understanding.

- ✔ Group members accept that there are no right or wrong dreams, no good or bad ones, and therefore agree not to compare their dreams to other people's. Each dream comes in service to increasing the authentic self-expression of the dreamer, and group members commit to find the compassionate, positive interpretation that will add to the dreamer's feeling of aliveness and wholeness. Some innocent-looking dreams may contain the deepest, most heart-wrenching issues, while a highly emotional dream may be neatly worked out and fairly matter-of-fact.

✔ Group members accept that the only meaning that works is the one the dreamer decides is real. The dreamer is in charge of his or her own inner reality.

✔ Group members agree to empower the facilitator to help keep the flow of the meeting on track — even if it means that they may be asked to rephrase an insight, or wind up a lengthy narrative.

Develop an agenda for meetings

At the first meeting, discuss the ground rules, your attitudes, commitment, goals, and past experience with dreams. Why does each person want to participate in the group experience? Similarly, the start of each meeting might contain a brief period of sharing — a "touch-in" — where group members say what they've been aware of in the time between meetings, how the process of their dreaming has been going, what they've noticed in their waking life that connects to their dream themes, and any successes they've had with dream incubation experiments.

Next, take a few minutes to do a centering meditation that helps everyone gather in all their energy and raise the level of their consciousness to a lighter level. Then go around the circle and have each member share a dream, without any commentary. This allows the group to connect with each person's inner life and helps establish a mood of safety. If dreams have occurred that follow up on dreams shared the previous week, this is a good time to mention those.

After the dreams have been related, go back and work with each person's dream in more detail. First, have the person repeat the dream while everyone else pays close attention. Allow some time to ask clarifying questions, if necessary, like "What breed of dog was it?" or "Was the airplane full of people or was it just you and your wife?" Finally, let each person have a turn to share insights about what he or she thinks the dream might mean. If time is limited, try allotting 10 or 15 minutes apiece to each person's dream interpretation process.

At the end of the current cycle of dream group meetings, review your progress and share about the experience each group member had. Could the group functioning be improved? Would everyone like to continue for another eight weeks to six months? Do you need a short break? Make concrete plans for the next time.

Be respectful when sharing about dreams

How you share and receive from each other contributes immensely to the effectiveness of the process. Look at each group member as a vital component of yourself, one that you may not see or want to see. Empower the others to be messengers to you from your soul and then be surprised at what insights they trigger in you. When participants share, don't try to help or change them; let them be an influence in your own process. No one should be forced to share a dream or insights about a drean involuntarily. Remember: There's no right way to dream! If you judge yourself or others, simply use it as a lesson in what doesn't work. Stay out of long "stories" that wander from the point and don't comment unnecessarily on other people's insights.

When you share a dream, try to keep it in the present tense. This makes the dream come alive again and allows other people to "enter it" as if it were happening to them. By engaging directly and intimately with another person's dream this way, you may have insights that are more potent than you would if you viewed the dream as already over and in the past. Listen for the times when the dreamer reverts to past tense in the telling of a dream, or goes off on a tangential commentary — it may indicate a part of the dream she wishes to distance from, perhaps because there is a live issue just below the surface. Also, listen for any slips of the tongue — the dreamer may mean to say "chiropractor" but says "chirocracker" instead. There's almost always an important insight lurking around the corner when double meanings surface. If you already have some thoughts about what your dream means to you, hold those back for later. You don't want to plant ideas in anyone's mind prematurely; wait and see what insights about your dream come to the other group members spontaneously.

Respond to dream-sharing sensitively

When responding to another person's dream, remember that you are always talking about yourself. Every idea you share comes from your own associations and inner dynamics. Your interpretation of a dream tells the group about your perceptual process, not necessarily about the other person's. To minimize the possibility of unconsciously projecting your ideas onto the dreamer, which could have a tendency to feel dominating, have your group develop an etiquette for sharing insights. Try beginning your sentence with, "If this were my dream, I'd think it was about. . . ." or "If I'd been dreaming this, I'd be aware of the fact that. . . ." If the word "you" creeps into the sharing, stop and begin again with, "If this were my dream. . . ."

When the other group members share their impressions of your dream, you don't need to comment right then. Let all the ideas come in and meld around. The most accurate insights will trigger your "truth signal," and you'll immediately feel that sensation of "aha!" or tingling, chills up your arms, warmth spreading across your chest, something clicking into place, or two halves of yourself coming together. When someone's interpretation doesn't fit your dream, or when it touches on an interpretation that you don't want to hear, you may experience your "anxiety signal," which can seem like a contraction in the stomach, chest, or throat, or can make you feel cold or clammy and tight. After everyone has shared, give some feedback about how it all relates to your perceptions, inner process, and daily life.

Try other techniques and activities

If you want variety, try the following processes with your dream group:

- After everyone shares a dream, each person can spend 20 minutes drawing a picture of the dream. Then spend another 15 minutes writing a poem from the picture, and share one by one with the others.

- Have several group members volunteer to play roles in one person's dream. Act out the scenes as the dreamer originally dreamed them, then ad lib and let the drama play out spontaneously and see where it goes.

- After everyone shares a dream, do a group meditation and have each person go back into the dream and extend it. Then come back and share what happened.

- After sharing a dream, each person picks a dream symbol. The group meditates, and each person pretends to be the symbol and does a direct writing process for 10 minutes, speaking as the object, describing its purpose, what it needs from the dreamer, why it showed up in the dream, and so on.

- Have one person share a dream. The others make lists of six word pairs from the dream and write a poem. Continue on to the next person, and the next. At the end, give each person the poems relating to her dream.

Watch for the emergence of group mind, group dreaming

After your group has been meeting for a while, you may find that the group synchronizes itself uncannily and starts a special process in which participants activate and empower each other, both while attending the group and when apart. Common themes may begin to run through the group members' lives, and some people may dream parallel dreams, or even show up in each other's dreams. Watch for group dreams — members may dream about the dream group itself, or another small group that feels similar to the dream group. The likelihood is that the work begun during waking reality is continuing at night, as well as in between meetings. Let the group mind help direct the flow of the group and show participants the specific lessons to be learned. You might try an experiment where the group intentionally sets out to incubate a common dream they will have together, or have individual responses to a common dream goal. When the dream group session has completed, find your own way to personally acknowledge the other participants for their contributions to your life.

Appendix A
Dream Resources

* *

*H*ere are some resources, including organizations, publications, and Web sites, that will be useful in your dream work.

Organizations and Publications

Alfred Adler Institute
1780 Broadway, New York, NY 10019

American Sleep Disorders Association (ASDA)
1610 14th St. NW, Suite 300, Rochester, MN 55901

American Society for Psychical Research
5 W. 73rd St., New York, NY 10023

Association for Research and Enlightenment (A.R.E.)
(Also known as the Edgar Cayce Foundation)
PO Box 595, Virginia Beach, VA 23451

Association for the Study of Dreams (ASD)
PO Box 1600, Vienna, VA 22183
Publishes newsletter, sponsors conferences.

C. G. Jung Foundation for Analytical Psychology
28.E. 39th St., New York, NY 10016

Community Dreamsharing Network
PO Box 8032, Hicksville, NY 11802
Publishes *The Dream Switchboard.*

Delaney and Flowers Dream Center
Gayle Delaney and Loma Flowers, Directors
PO Box 320402, San Francisco, CA 94132

The D.R.E.A.M.S. Foundation of Montreal
Craig Webb, Director
Box 513, Snowdon, Montreal, QC H3X 3T7

Dream Network
1137 Powerhouse Lane, Suite 22, Moab, UT 84532
Publishes quarterly journal, *Dream Network.*

Lucidity Association
43 Midland Ave., Berwyn, PA 19312
Publishes *Lucidity*

Lucidity Institute
2555 Park Blvd., Suite 2, Palo Alto, CA 94306

National Sleep Foundation
122 S. Robertson Blvd., 3rd Fl., Los Angeles, CA 90048

Novato Center for Dreams and Dream Library
Jill Gregory, Director
29 Truman Dr., Novato, CA 94947

The Pacific Northwest Center for Dream Studies
219 First Avenue S, Suite 405, Seattle, WA 98104

Santa Fe Center for the Study of Dreams
Dr. Erik Craig, Director
113 Camino Escondido #3, Santa Fe, NM 87501

Saybrook Institute
Dr. Stanley Krippner, Director
1772 Vallejo Street, San Francisco, CA 94123

Sleep Research Society (SRS)
c/o Wallace Mendelson
Cleveland Clinic S-51, Dept. of Neurology
9500 Euclid Ave., Cleveland, OH 44195
Publishes a bimonthly journal, *Sleep.*

Sigmund Freud Archives (SFA)
c/o Harold P. Blum
23 The Hemlocks, Roslyn, NY 11576

Web Sites

www.asdreams.com	The Association for the Study of Dreams; extensive resources, networking, conference announcements, online journal *Dreaming,* online magazine *Dream Time*
www.dreamgate.com	Created by Richard Wilkerson; publishes online magazine *Electric Dreams,* many articles and resources for dreamers
www.dreamloverinc.com	Dream discussion, dictionary, analysis
www.dreamresearch.net	Psychological research into the nature of dreams
www.dreamtree.com	Resources, products, conferences, links
www.dreamdoctor.com	Resources, dream analysis, education
www.dreams.ca	The D.R.E.A.M.S Foundation of Montreal, Canada, created by Craig Webb, provides resources, education, networking, dreaming canoe trips
www.lucidity.com	Web site of The Lucidity Institute, directed by Dr. Stephen LaBerge, offers training, articles; publishes newsletter *NightLight*
www.sleepnet.com	Information on sleep disorders
www.saybrook.edu	Web site of The Saybrook Institute, directed by Stanley Krippner
www.sawka.com/ spiritwatch	Web site organized by Jayne Gackenbush, publishes *The Lucidity Letter,* offers courses
www.jeremytaylor.com	Web site of author and teacher Jeremy Taylor, full of articles, resources

Appendix B

Dream Dictionary

• •

A

Actor/Actress/Acting: Actors represent the side of yourself that you present to the public, your persona. The image can signify falsity or superficiality. When unpleasant, acting dreams can refer to situations where you feel forced to please others or put on an act to avoid rejection.

Airplane/Airport: Airplanes represent the vehicle of your mental or spiritual body, and the kind of plane shows how far up through the dream zones you're traveling. They may symbolize freedom, the power to rise above challenge, or the need to obtain higher perspective on a situation. Taking off in a plane may signify a new idea or venture is ready to occur. If a plane can't get off the ground, the venture may be stuck. Landing a plane signifies bringing inspiration and ideas back to earth to incorporate into your life. An airport can represent a transition in your life. A plane crash may indicate the end of your involvement with a series of beliefs, especially those you may hold in common with a group mind.

Alley: An alley may symbolize "the path," which indicates seeking and the transition from one stage of life to another. Because alleys often contain refuse, there is a connection to the subconscious mind, and passing through territory that has a slightly negative, even dangerous connotation. They are often narrow and limited, and can be a place where you might be attacked. Alleys can imply you're taking a shortcut or are headed into a dead end.

Ambush: An ambush may represent some unpleasant surprise or unanticipated challenge in your life. If you were headed for a clear destination at the time of the ambush, it may represent your progress being blocked. Ambushes may also be symbols of hidden enemies, unconscious fears surfacing suddenly, or upcoming loss and emotional upheaval.

Amputation: Amputation can refer to the radical removal of something from your life. It may no longer be necessary or it may represent the neglect or abandonment of an ability or talent symbolized by the amputated part.

Angel: Angels symbolize purity, goodness, protection, and guidance. Traditionally, they are the messengers of God to humanity and thus can symbolize a bridge between the superconscious and subconscious mind. Angels signify blessing and faith. Their messages are trustworthy.

Ants: Ants represent diligence, hard work, and foresight (because they store food). Less positively, they symbolize conformity and mass action. They may symbolize something that "bugs" you.

Apple: Apples stand for wholeness and knowledge. To dream of ripe apples on a tree signifies good fortune and the realization of the fruits of your work. Rotten apples or apple cores may mean that the dreamer's goals are not what they seem to be, have no real value, and may even be harmful.

Ascent: Dreaming of moving up in an elevator or by other means indicates a movement up through the dream zones. It can represent a desire for the big picture and attention placed on accomplishment.

Attic: Attics represent a place where old things are hidden and stored from the past, and have an association with the subconscious mind.

Avalanche: An avalanche signifies a sudden release, often accompanied by feelings of being overwhelmed, of emotions that have been piling up and denied, which are "frozen" and immobile. It may indicate you're doing too much and need to stop and let go.

Awakening: A dream of waking up while still dreaming may indicate awakening to new states of consciousness, new kinds of creativity, or a new phase in your life. It can also indicate the beginning of a lucid dream.

B

Baby: A baby represents a new idea or phase of life that's just beginning. It could relate to an actual pregnancy, or desire for a child. It can also represent dependent behavior or infantile desires. Babies symbolize innocence, unconditional love, and fresh perspective.

Balloon: Balloons symbolize celebration and the freeing and releasing of feelings or creative ideas, while the strings keep them from flying away. A deflated balloon may indicate disappointment, exhaustion, or energy drain.

Bank: A bank may signify something that needs safekeeping. It symbolizes solidity, stability, and security. Look for what is being kept in the bank.

Basement: Basements indicate activity in the subconscious mind where old ideas, beliefs, and memories from the past are stored. Since they also contain equipment, like the furnace and water pump, that powers your house (body), it may give hints about your basic physical condition.

Bear: The bear symbolizes power and the unpredictable instinctual nature. It has the capacity for introspection and patience due to its tendency to hibernate through the winter; it draws energy from the earth.

Bed: Beds (and bedrooms) can represent the way in which you allow yourself to rest and be nurtured in your inner life. They also symbolize marriage, romance, and sex and the health of an intimate relationship. Something underneath a bed may show an idea that subconsciously threatens or affects the nurturing.

Birds: Birds represent freedom and the ability to reach higher realms of knowledge. Like angels, birds often serve as messengers of the divine, symbols of the soul, and heralds of spiritual aspiration. Blackbirds and ravens are seen as messengers from the dead or from the other side.

Birth: Giving birth symbolizes the beginning of a new idea, project, aspect of the self, or stage of life, in which you feel "reborn" in some way.

Blood: Blood represents vitality and the life force. Images of bloody violence can indicate emotional upheaval. Menstrual blood may symbolize fertility or cleansing. Bleeding to death can indicate a situation where something is draining your creativity and energy.

Boat: A boat helps you traverse an emotional experience, or helps protect you from being overwhelmed by one. A boat can show how you deal with emotion — is it a power boat, a canoe, a steamer? Are you dead in the water with no wind? Sinking boats indicate an approaching and possibly overwhelming emotional encounter you may be afraid to experience.

Bones: Bones can represent death, either literal or metaphorical. They can also symbolize a state of reduction to the essence or deprivation, as in "bare bones" or looking bony and skeletal. Bones may also refer to the inner structure of something or inner strength.

Book: Books symbolize knowledge and wisdom. Old books may represent neglected or forgotten knowledge, or an earlier "chapter" of one's life. Opening or closing a book may symbolize opening or closing a stage in your life.

Boss: A boss may represent a parental figure — the father if the boss is a man, the mother if a woman. The symbol may show how you give your power away or how you deal with internal and external authority.

Bread: Bread symbolizes basic nurturing and sustenance. Bread crumbs symbolize a sense of lack of abundance. Burned toast represents nurturing that was unattended, unappreciated, and wasted.

Bridge: Bridges indicate literal travel and life transitions. Because bodies of water symbolize the subconscious and the emotions, a bridge may indicate a structure that keeps you from becoming overwhelmed by emotion. Bridges are also links between two separate shores, or life experiences, and they may also symbolize unresolved paradoxes in your life.

Building: Buildings, especially houses, may represent the self, particularly the physical body. In many-storied buildings, movement between floors can symbolize rising or falling in status or awareness. In general, buildings symbolize a life focus, an environment, definition, or context within which an experience can occur. A cityscape indicates a complex mental structure, often involving a collective consciousness.

C

Cafeteria: Cafeterias provide an abundance and variety of food, symbolizing a wealth of ideas and the availability of nurturing. You may be ready to receive nurturing in an "all you can eat" fashion.

Camera: A camera symbolizes your world view, attitudes, or credo. Taking snapshots represents your daily perceptions, observations, or decisions.

Cancer: To dream about cancer does not mean you have or will contract this disease. It may symbolize a condition in your life that is growing out of control, and has been consuming physical or emotional resources for too long. It can also symbolize the revenge of unlived life — creative energies that have been bottled up.

Captivity: Captivity represents a feeling of being out of touch with free will, being limited by a life situation, or being forced to concentrate your energy and attention on something you've been avoiding.

Car: A car is the vehicle you use to move through the physical world, so it symbolizes your body, personality, and daily life in general, as well as indicating the nature of your relationships with others. Driving a car indicates you're in control of your own decisions. Riding in the passenger seat or back seat means you may be deferring to another's influence. Mechanical problems with a car can indicate blockages in your body or forward movement.

Cat: Cats symbolize independence, mystery, magic, feminine energy or the anima, sexuality, grace, and cunning. That cats have "nine lives" makes them a symbol of good luck and longevity.

Cataclysm: Natural disasters and upheavals symbolize sudden shifts or releases of energy within your body or emotions.

Cave: Caves represent the deep inner self, the place of connection to ancient wisdom, the earth, and the feminine. A cave can symbolize the womb, childbearing, new life, contemplation, or creativity. Coming out of a cave may mean the emergence of the self.

Chased/Chasing: Being chased in a dream suggests running from a situation you find threatening, or avoiding an experience of being overwhelmed or self-destruction. If you are the pursuer, you may be chasing after a goal.

Cheating: Cheating on tests, or stealing, can indicate you feel you're innately lacking in knowledge, creativity, or natural talent.

Choking: Choking indicates an inability to "swallow" something, like a lie or an idea that is inappropriate for you. Someone else may be forcing you to behave in a certain way and you're experiencing revulsion. Someone else choking off your air may indicate you're feeling strangled by a condition in life that doesn't give you enough space to breathe.

Church: A church represents a sacred context, space, or religious beliefs. It may indicate you need to pray for yourself or others, or receive grace, spiritual nourishment, or atonement.

Circle: A circle represents wholeness, spiritual oneness or the soul, protection from evil, and the focus of attention in the present moment.

Cliff: A cliff symbolizes an edge of consciousness, a point where you either turn around and go back to what you've known before or leap off into the precipice of the unknown. It asks you whether you can let go of control, or whether you're afraid of falling.

Climbing: Climbing symbolizes a steady upward progression toward a mental or spiritual goal, requiring persistence and strength. It can also indicate an increase in social, economic, or artistic pursuits and intellectual and spiritual growth.

Clock: Clocks symbolize the idea of being on time, and can denote an anxiety about falling behind. A clock may also symbolize that time is ticking away, and procrastination about achieving life goals needs to be overcome.

Clothing: Clothing depicts the persona and the way you portray yourself to others. Changing clothes or costumes can suggest the need for change, or trying to adapt to a new way of being in the world. New, beautiful clothes suggests new things such as social or economic improvement.

Computer: A computer symbolizes your connection to knowledge and the storage of your personal body of information. It can symbolize the way your mind is working; if the computer crashes, you may need to take a break from being so mental.

Crown: A crown symbolizes spiritual authority and responsibility, often indicating an initiation. The crown acts as the transmitter of knowledge from the collective consciousness to your conscious mind.

D

Dam: A dam signifies repressed emotional energy. You may be holding back tears, or you may feel like your energy is jammed up.

Dancing: Dancing symbolizes psychological and spiritual release or communion with the rhythms of life. It may be associated with romance, freedom from constraints, participation in life, frivolity, gracefulness, or fluid cooperation with others. Dancing alone in a partner dance symbolizes a feeling of isolation.

Death/Dead People: Dreams about the dead or death are not necessarily omens of literal death but often symbolize letting go of an old part of the self or the destruction of a prior stage of life leading to personal growth and transformation. A lifeless corpse may represent a feeling of devitalization, or adherence to a lifeless routine. Talking to people who have died may bring resolution of incomplete communication or may symbolize the traits represented by the person in life.

Deer: Deer symbolize grace, gentleness, innocence, purity, and willing self-sacrifice. In folklore, deer are messengers of fairies and help you open your heart.

Descent: Descending in an elevator, or by any other means, symbolizes a contracting movement through the dream zones, or may indicate a decline in energy or status. It may symbolize descent into the subconscious in a journey of self-discovery.

Desert: Deserts symbolize barrenness, poverty, lack, or loneliness. They can also represent a space of openness and freedom from distraction in which you can attain spiritual clarity.

Diamond: Diamonds symbolize the clear light consciousness, or an absolute clear, pure state of mind. They also symbolize permanence, the enduring power of truth, and the unending love that marriage vows are based upon.

Digging: Digging symbolizes the desire to reach down into the unconscious or subconscious to unearth buried information or talent. On occasion it can represent the desire to bury or deny something.

Doctor: A doctor is someone with healing authority and may symbolize that actual healing has occurred or is about to occur or there is a desire for healing.

Dog: Dogs symbolize loyalty, friendship, protection, family values, and tenacity. They can indicate a trustworthy relationship, or conversely, a fierce adversary. Also, as animals who guard the underworld, they can be messengers of the unconscious. They are often a symbol of masculine energy or the animus.

Door: Doors are passageways between two different states of awareness. An open door indicates a new opportunity. Stepping through a door symbolizes entering a new phase of life. A choice of many doors shows a juncture at which a choice must be made. A locked door indicates something repressed or hidden. A closed door may represent an opportunity that is unavailable to you, or one you must exert effort to "open."

Drawer: Drawers contain things (ideas, issues) that are hidden away, and represent your inner state, whether it be disorderly and full of internal chaos or neatly organized with psychological order.

E

Eagle: Eagles are the most noble, high-flying bird and represent the ability of the mind to reach the spiritual realms. They are associated with the sun, authority, clear perception, pride, fierceness, and courage.

Earth: The earth represents solidity, stability, practicality, fertility, and being grounded in time and space. It symbolizes the physical body and world, and the area beneath the surface of the earth represents the unconscious. The earth seen as a globe indicates wholeness, the mother principle, and global awareness.

Eating: Eating represents a need for nurturing, or a desire for gratification based on an indulgence in physical pleasures of all kinds. To eat something is to make it part of yourself, as in accepting and integrating a previously denied part of your psyche. It can. It can also represent the partaking of more spiritual forms of nourishment.

Egg: Eggs symbolize wholeness, fertility, new birth, unhatched ideas, or new life that still needs to gestate. Broken eggs may mean you're breaking out of your shell, or spilling your ideas before they're "fully cooked."

Elephant: Elephants represent wealth, steadfast character, memory, the power to overcome a daunting task, and the intelligent gentle giant.

Elevator: An elevator is a vehicle that helps you move between levels or dimensions of yourself. It symbolizes that you're shifting upward or downward in consciousness or status. If it is stuck between floors, you may need to get clear about your intent and goals, and clear a subconscious "sticking point." A falling elevator represents a rapid descent into the unconscious or a need to let go of control.

Escape: An escape indicates you may be resisting something in your life that you need to face, or you've allowed yourself to become dominated and must take back your own authority.

Explosion: Explosions symbolize a sudden release of energy or emotion in your life. It might be a release of anger and frustration, or it might be basic kundalini energy (see Chapter 9) that helps free you to move in the higher realms. Something in your life needs to move.

F

Falling: Falling represents the basic downward momentum of consciousness from the higher realms through the dream zones, and can sometimes symbolize loss of control, the need to let go and surrender, or a fear of failure.

Father: The archetypal father represents an almost kingly power, protection, provision, love, the law, tradition, and the values of discipline and structure. Your own personal relationship with your father colors the meaning for you.

Feces: Feces represent that which is eliminated and of no use to the body, therefore it may signal that you need to be rid of something in your life. Feces can symbolize the giving up of denial and self-deception. If the feces belong to others, you may need to be free of their unessential refuse as well.

Fence: A fence symbolizes a challenge or barrier to forward movement, the need for boundaries or respect for others' boundaries, the need to pause and reconsider goals, or the feeling of being limited and contained by a situation. It can also represent being "on the fence" about an issue or decision.

Fire: Fire symbolizes passion, desire, anger, destruction, purification, illumination, transformation, and burning away what's false and unnecessary in the self or the life.

Fish: Fish inhabit the realm of the emotions (water) and the collective unconscious and represent feelings, creative ideas, or a message from the deeper part of your mind. They also symbolize Christ Consciousness and the spiritual quest.

Flower: Flowers represent beauty, peace (the lily), attraction, sexuality, harmlessness, and delicacy. They are often symbols for the essential self and the heart (especially the lotus and the rose), and can symbolize stages of spiritual unfoldment (bud to wide open).

Flying: Flying symbolizes the basic upward movement of consciousness through the dimensions or dream zones. It can represent a desire for freedom, joy, and spiritual knowledge. Flying high can signal you're looking for the big picture or a higher perspective on a situation. The way you fly may symbolize the way you express creative energy and ideas in waking life.

Forest: Forests and jungles are symbols of the subconscious, since they are full of wild animals, darkness, and tangled vines. They may symbolize an experience where you feel overwhelmed by the unknown or uncontrollable. On the other hand, they may signify a need to retreat from the world and soak up the greenness of nature, and recuperate. A forest fire might imply that the density of a period of your life is finally clearing.

Fork in the Road: Coming to a fork in the road signifies you have a choice to make, especially concerning your life direction.

Fruit: Fruits represent abundance, the ripeness of your talent, the fullness of what you have to offer, sensuality, seductiveness, sexuality, lusciousness, feminine love, and temptation.

G

Garden: Gardens represent the need for beauty, your sense of inner abundance, and the conditions of your life. A dry, weedy garden indicates you need to tend to your life to cultivate a new talent and clear away the old growth that's choking you. A lush garden indicates a rich spiritual life.

Gift: Gifts represent inner talents and rewards for doing excellent work. They also signify that you may need to focus on your lovable nature, or that you should express gratitude to others or to a higher power for what's good in your life.

Gold: Gold represents something of high value, untarnishable, pure, a bright event, person, or idea. It can represent wealth, internal and external, as well as satisfactory spiritual development.

Groups: Groups represent the collective consciousness, group mind, societal beliefs, and the need for community.

Gun: Guns symbolize power (especially exerted from a safe distance), aggressive male energy and the need for protection. Shooting yourself or others by accident or on purpose may indicate an over-active, destructive or vengeful animus, or a need to assert personal control over a situation. Firing guns often represents "shooting off your mouth."

H

Hair: Hair represents health, strength, and sexuality as well as sensitivity to the environment. It also symbolizes habitual patterns of conscious thought and opinion. Hair is known to "stand on end" in response to a strong stimulus. White hair denotes wisdom. Loss of hair signifies worry. Being covered in hair symbolizes the animal nature.

Hat: Hats symbolize the containment of knowledge, or a body of knowledge. They also can mean concealment, and can denote a role you are playing. A feather in your hat denotes achievement.

Hawk: Hawks are high-flying birds, second only to eagles, and denote clear-sightedness and keen discrimination. They can convey messages from the higher mental and spiritual realms.

Horse: Horses symbolize freedom, power, majesty, courage, and sexuality, as well as the physical body. Through history they have been associated with the powers of instinct, intuition, and prophecy.

Hospital: Hospitals indicate you may need to heal a part of yourself, or pay more attention to health. Seeing someone else in a hospital could indicate they are weakened.

Hotel: A hotel is a temporary home, and can signify you need a break from your normal mindset before a new idea or change can occur in your life. Hotel lobbies can represent an environment where ideas are coming and going, and new ideas are being considered.

House: A house is a symbol of your personal self or life situation, and gives an indication of your current state. Does the house need repair? Is it under construction and not yet complete? You may be doing inner psychological work. Is it too small for you? You may be ready to begin a new chapter in your life. Many rooms can indicate specific talents or aspects of yourself.

I

Ice: Ice is frozen water (emotion) and denotes emotional issues that have been suppressed or denied. Skating on thin ice or falling through ice may indicate an approaching emotional breakthrough.

Infestation: Infestations, whether by people, animals, insects, bacteria, or objects, represent feeling invaded, overwhelmed, overrun, and undermined. You may be neglecting important things because of an obsession with one thing. Look to the location of the infestation for the area of life it's affecting.

Initiation: An initiation ceremony means a change is taking place in your life. You have officially recognized a new level of authority and are about to take responsibility in a new way. You may be evolving to a new level of spiritual awareness or advancing in status.

Insects: Insects indicate that something or someone is "bugging" you, or making a pest of itself.

Island: Islands represent solitude, isolation, the solitary self or ego, and because they are surrounded by water, there may be a connotation of needing to acknowledge the presence and power of emotion or the unconscious in your life.

J

Jewels: Jewels symbolize inner wealth, spiritual ideas and thoughts, or high-minded values. They also represent protection and have healing powers.

Journey: A journey represents your life path, transitions between phases of life experience, and developing personality traits. Some journeys may be challenging, some may be quests, some involve traveling companions. Short journeys symbolize the need for change.

Judge/Jury: Judges and juries represent authority and morality. You may be examining an aspect of your behavior that has been out of line, or feel that others are judging you. Sitting on a jury indicates you need to make a decision about something in your life or you're judging others. You may feel guilty about something.

Jumping: Jumping over hurdles can indicate you're experiencing success and a strong forward flow in your life. Jumping off high places can indicate you need to let go and surrender to the unknown. Jumping up may be the beginning of flight, or a leap of faith.

Junk: Junk symbolizes that you need to let go of or discard something. It can also indicate parts of the self you have rejected that may need to be reclaimed.

K

Key: Keys indicate authority, the ability to enter where others cannot, to access knowledge, and conversely, the tendency to lock away or protect things, ideas, or parts of the self.

Kidnapping: Kidnapping represents a feeling of victimization or being overwhelmed and carried away by the needs, desires, and plans of others. It may indicate an area of your life that has usurped your autonomy.

Killing: Killing someone (or suicide) may symbolize the killing off of a part of the self, either for better or worse, or that incentive or motivation has been killed by some idea.

Kiss: A kiss represents the bestowing of affection, romance, approval, love, and can indicate budding intimacy and passion. It sometimes represents betrayal (kiss of death).

Kitchen: A kitchen represents physical, emotional, and spiritual nourishment. You may also be in the process of "cooking something up."

Knife: A knife is a symbol of male aggression and sexuality. It also symbolizes intellect and the ability or need to think clearly, analyze, cut through or penetrate into something in your life. A knife in the back symbolizes betrayal, or the need to penetrate into and open the unconscious.

Knot: A knot symbolizes a complex problem that needs to be solved. It may indicate anxiety and worry (being tied up in knots), something that restricts you, or something you're trying to control. It can also represent security and commitment, as in marriage (tying the knot).

L

Ladder: A ladder symbolizes climbing to a new level of awareness, status, material prosperity, and spiritual growth. In dreams relating to health, ladders symbolize the spine.

Library: Libraries symbolize a search for knowledge and ideas. It may indicate you are seeking new meaning in life or preparing for a new phase where you will need new skills.

Lightning: Lightning can symbolize the wrath of God, or having something pointed out to you by divine intelligence. It may serve as a warning to you from your higher mind, a sudden insight or revelation, or a purification or purging.

Lion: The lion symbolizes royalty, dominion, majesty, courage, strength, and ferocity. It also can represent laziness, pride, fierce protection of family, the sun, and showmanship.

Lips: Lips symbolize sensuousness, seductiveness, romance, sex, and communication.

Loss: To lose something means you may need to release an attachment to what the lost item symbolizes. Losing money means letting go of materialistic values or worry about finances, while losing a wallet may indicate a loss of identity, often a necessary step to discovering a more mature identity.

Luggage: Luggage may indicate it's time to pack up and move on, take a break, that you need to determine what's important to take with you (identity traits), or that you are weighed down by excess baggage and need to jettison a few old ideas, prejudices, fears, or possessions.

M

Magic: Magic can represent a process in your life that is working miraculously and easily. On the other hand, it may have a connotation of "black" magic, performed to manipulate others and get results through control. You may be exposed to deceit in your life.

Makeup/Mask: Either of these symbols represent a "cover up" of your true self, or a face you put forward to the public due to discomfort revealing your true feelings or nature. If others are wearing masks, some situation in your life is not truthful.

Map: A map indicates you are beginning a journey, searching for a new path, or are studying the variables inherent in a change of direction and what the ensuing experience will entail.

Metal: Since metal is cold and hard yet is malleable and can melt, it represents an attitude or personality that might be rigid but not brittle, and may in fact be capable of conducting great "heat" or passion. It can, however, represent technology and the more inhuman part of society.

Milk: Milk is symbolic of deep inner nourishment and mother love. You may be receiving love or giving love or caring.

Mirror: The mirror is a symbol of self-examination. A clear mirror shows the the self, a cloudy or cracked one reflects the distortions of character you project into the world. A broken mirror can symbolize a fragmented personality or a disturbed sense of self.

Money: Money symbolizes your sense of self-worth and your values concerning limitation and abundance, deservingness and provision. It is often a symbol for energy, both physical and emotional. Loss of money may indicate a depletion of inner resources. It can also represent power and influence. Investing money in the stock market can signify you are investing in your own talent and potential.

Moon: The moon represents feminine energy, travel, your fluctuating emotional nature, and the cycles of your self-expression. A full moon represents full self-expression, the new moon conveys a sense of gestating, waiting, and resting. A full moon may convey a sense of crazy emotional expression, or "lunacy."

Mother: The archetypal mother is a symbol of life, nurturing, comfort, and unconditional love. Being a mother in a dream indicates caretaking to a part of your own self, or to others in your life. Your relationship with your own mother colors the meaning of the symbol for you.

Mountain: Mountains represent a challenge or a major decision, and climbing to the top symbolizes achieving your goals or reaching the heights of success through steady work. Mountaintops can represent spiritual evolution and involvement with a sacred process or consciousness.

Movie: Watching a movie may symbolize a segment of your own life you're trying to understand by stepping outside to view it neutrally. Notice what kind of movie it is, who's starring in it and what happens. Starring in a movie can symbolize your need to receive more attention, to express yourself more colorfully in your life, or to take more authority and have a greater impact in what you do. Being in a movie and watching it simultaneously can provide a trigger that launches a lucid dream. In addition, movies often symbolize the process of dreaming itself.

Mud: Mud is a mixture of water (emotion) and earth (the physical) so symbolizes emotions that have become stirred up and are active in the body, creating confusion and lack of clarity.

Museum: A museum signifies you may be looking for old artifacts and treasures (memories, talents, motivations, knowledge) you have stored away from the past. They may need to be dusted off and brought into the light of day. You may be visiting the higher dimensions looking at the records of planetary history.

Music: Hearing or composing music indicates you are flowing through the upper emotional and mental dream zones, possibly reorganizing patterns in your inner awareness to incorporate increased harmony.

N

Nausea: Nausea symbolizes the need to purge or get rid of a situation you "can't stomach," or that is making you sick.

Net: A net can symbolize the need to gather in your resources, or that you feel caught in a net of confusion, intrigue, or limitation. It can also symbolize the internet or the grid of energy that encircles the planet.

Newspaper: A newspaper indicates you are receiving current information or breaking news about your life, or you're trying to catch up with what's happening in your world.

Nudity: Nudity symbolizes the feeling of vulnerability and exposure. You may need to examine part of yourself you've been hiding from others or you may be weary of maintaining a facade.

Nut: Nuts symbolize the core, kernel, or meat of an idea. There is a connotation with "squirrelling away" these valuable creative ideas or talents for a later time.

O

Oak: The oak symbolizes strength, stability, truth, wisdom, and endurance.

Ocean: The ocean symbolizes the collective unconscious, the memory banks of the planet, and deep emotion.

Octopus: The octopus symbolizes an entanglement in your life, or someone is acting possessive or clingy. It can also indicate an involvement with many different things.

Old Age: Old people represent life experience and wisdom, or feelings of letting go and allowing yourself to be taken care of. Old age can bring forgiveness, frailty, and the need to reconcile your life.

Operation: Having a surgical operation indicates that you are removing or cutting away old issues from your life and personality. Deep unconscious issues are being faced, eliminated, and you are in a healing process.

Orphan: An orphan may mean you feel unloved, unwanted, invisible, misunderstood, or needy. You may be experiencing a fear of abandonment or isolation.

Outer Space: Outer space, or deep space, represents the highest dream zones – the upper mental and causal, which pertain to the collective consciousness.

Owl: The owl symbolizes wisdom, the ability to "see at night," to know in spite of darkness. For this reason it is often considered a messenger that works with the astral or emotional dream zone by Native American people.

P

Paralysis: Being paralyzed may indicate you feel helpless about a situation in your life. On the other hand, it may indicate you need to totally stop and pay attention to something you've been avoiding, or just do nothing for a while.

Pets: A past, current, or new pet, like a dog or cat, may be symbolic of an aspect of yourself that you need to love and accept, or of a relationship that embodies a quality symbolized by the animal. The pet may teach you a lesson, like being more compassionate, because you trust it. The death of a pet may symbolize your need to let go of paying special attention to a quality of yourself, so it can integrate into you fully.

Poison: Poison may represent a condition in your life that is physically or emotionally toxic to your well-being. Either ingesting poison yourself, or poisoning another might be symbolic of something that weakens your life force. It carries a connotation of secret sabotage and vengeance.

Police: Police symbolize authority figures and the need to adhere to, or enforce, the "rules" or to live in alignment with the universal laws. You may be reminding yourself to be more conscientious, keep your word, live a more balanced life, or avoid reckless behavior. Police also symbolize conventionality and social mores.

Pool: Pools can symbolize recreation, a release of tension, and an experience of an easier flow of energy. They can indicate you're becoming more comfortable with your emotions.

Pregnancy: Pregnancy, like birth dreams, can symbolize that new creativity, wealth, or a new life episode is about to begin. You may not be able to recognize it yet, but you're receiving a sign that something new is imminent.

Public Speaking: Speaking in public represents your ability to express your creativity and truth and often reveals your feelings about being judged by others, your confidence in what you have to offer, and your comfort level with being visible.

Pyramid: A pyramid symbolizes the preservation of esoteric knowledge, secrets, and energy. It is a sacred structure designed to focus wisdom to the apex, often crystalline or gold, which symbolizes the point at which knowledge becomes conscious.

Q

Quicksand: Quicksand is symbolic of feeling that you've been tricked into getting involved with something that traps you, from which it is nearly impossible to escape. It may signify you feel you energy is being drained, that you are being dragged down into your subconscious without choice.

Quilt: A quilt is symbolic of a desire for a warm, protective "covering." A patchwork quilt represents many aspects of yourself or your life that you are seeing as interrelated, even forming a beautiful harmonious pattern, and that pattern serves as a comfort.

R

Rabbit: Rabbits are symbols of fertility, magic, and luck. A rabbit might symbolize a coming increase in abundance.

Rain: Rain symbolizes cleansing and growth. It may signify a new period of expansion is about to occur or that you're receiving the nurturing you've needed. Too much rain can indicate you are feeling overwhelmed by heavy or depressing emotions.

Ram: The ram symbolizes aggression, impulsiveness, and ambition. It might suggest you are rushing headlong into situations, or being "hot-headed."

Refrigerator: A refrigerator represents nurturing and provision. A stocked refrigerator shows that you have the resources you need to accomplish what you want to do. The refrigerator is also the place where you put your ignored feelings and ideas "on ice."

Renovation: Renovating a house or building can show that you are reorganizing and reinventing yourself, your ideas, and your life. You are changing the way you see and act in the world.

Riding: Riding in a vehicle can indicate you are seeking a new destination, in the world of thought, or emotion, or in life in general. It may indicate that you feel someone else is in control, or that you are just being carried along by a process.

Ring: A ring represents commitment, completion, and wholeness. It can be a symbol of marriage, or a pledge of fidelity in relationships or to a group or cause.

River: A river indicates an emotional process — either a gentle one or a violent one, if the river is flooded. Watching a river flow by may indicate you need to take a more direct role in actively living your life. Being on a boat or swimming in a river can indicate that you are more immediately involved in an emotional process.

Roof: A roof symbolizes protection for your personality and earthly life, yet it can also represent a barrier between your daily awareness and the higher realms. A leaky roof can mean new information is making its way into your awareness.

Roots: Roots symbolize the need to connect more deeply with the unconscious or subconscious mind. They also represent commitment to a place, or to your life or origins. In addition, they may signify that you need to go back to basics.

Running: You may need to slow down and face something, or you may be avoiding a situation in your life that feels dangerously overwhelming.

S

Saint/Spiritual Guide: You may be receiving a special spiritual message from a higher level of your own self. As with messages from angels, these are important.

School: A school may signify you are learning something in the higher realms, bringing knowledge back to your daily life from the collective consciousness. It may signal you to pay attention to new information or points of view.

Searching: You may be looking for something that is missing or needed in your life, or may be just becoming aware that you need more than you currently have.

Separation: Feeling separated or abandoned can symbolize deep-seated concerns about being alone, not being competent enough to survive, or feeling unloved.

Sex: Sex can represent repressed desire for sexual relations or emotional love, and can also symbolize a desire to activate, merge or bond with aspects of yourself and life. Explicit sexual and sensual experience often represents deeper longings, often of a spiritual nature.

Sheep: A sheep can indicate that you feel like one of the flock, without personal power or influence. It may mean you feel panic and skittishness at a deep level about some issue in your life. You may need to develop self-confidence.

Skunk: A skunk may indicate an approaching period of difficulty or discomfort, or someone who may be difficult to deal with or who could "foul the environment" for you.

Slow Motion: Moving in slow motion, like wading through deep water, snow, or mud, is akin to paralysis, and often indicates anxiety and stress in waking life.

Snake: The snake is a symbol of life force energy (kundalini) and sexuality, as well as ancient wisdom from the earth, healing, and the feminine energy. It can indicate contact with the underworld or the subconscious, as well as potential danger. Freud thought snakes were phallic symbols.

Spaceship/Flying Saucer: Spaceships are symbolic of a movement of your consciousness up into the higher realms of collective consciousness.

Spider: Spiders are the weavers of webs, so you may feel caught in some entanglement in your life caused by someone who seems to be trying to trap you. The spider is also believed to be the keeper of knowledge, the creator of mathematics, and the weaver of the world energy grid, by many tradition peoples.

Stealing: Stealing, like cheating, may indicate that you don't feel entitled to abundance in your life, or feel limited or unworthy. You may be taking energy, identity, or authority from others, or others may be taking from you.

Stranger: A stranger may symbolize a new part of your own self that is emerging, or an actual being from another dream zone.

Subway: A subway may indicate you are traveling through your subconscious mind.

T

Taking Tests: Tests and exams can symbolize your entry into a new level of expertise and authority. They can also reflect your anxiety about measuring up, being worthy, entering a new phase of self-expression, or advancing in life.

Teeth: Teeth are symbols of aggression, of your ability to cut through or bite through tough or confusing situations. Losing your teeth indicates you feel like you're losing power or your grasp on a situation.

Telephone: Talking on the telephone may indicate you are communicating telepathically with someone in a higher dream zone. It may also show your attitude toward communicating in daily life.

Tidal Wave: A tidal wave symbolizes the fear of being overwhelmed by a surge of emotion, or a chaotic emotional situation that seems unbearable in your life.

Tornado: Tornadoes symbolize situations where there is a release of anger or rage with ensuing chaos and confusion. There may be a tremendous upset in your environment.

Tower: Towers represent individuality and the need to isolate yourself to focus on who you are, or the need to obtain a higher world view or broader perspective about a situation. Coming down from a tower means you are rejoining the world and becoming accessible.

Traffic: Traffic on the highway, at airports, in hallways, or on the sidewalks symbolizes that you may feel overcrowded and need time and space to yourself to regain clarity and peace of mind.

Train: Trains are vehicles that take you through life along a track, usually with other people, so they may represent your work life, social life, or the momentum of your life's evolution in general. Missing a train may mean a missed opportunity. A derailed train means you've gotten off track and need to reassess your life purpose.

Treasure: Discovering treasure, like gold coins or jewels, can indicate you are revealing new skills and talents to yourself that you are about to develop.

Tunnel: A tunnel symbolizes a transition from one phase of life to another, often involving a period of restriction from which you cannot escape. The period of difficulty must be lived through and learned from until you naturally come out the other side.

U

Umbrella: An umbrella protects you from being deluged by too much emotion (water/rain) yet also acts as a barrier between you and higher information. An umbrella can also symbolize the unification of ideas under a common theme.

Underwear: Underwear symbolizes modesty, or a feeling of exposure. Something you normally keep hidden is being revealed or you feel like your layers are being peeled away.

Urination: Urinating can symbolize a release of energy, emotion, or ideas that have served their purpose and need to be eliminated. It can also represent an uncontrolled release of emotion that proves embarrassing.

V

Vehicles: A vehicle is a symbol of how you focus yourself and move through the zone you're inhabiting. A car, bicycle, or train symbolizes your physical body, personality, or life; a boat or other water vehicle symbolizes how you traverse through the emotional world; airplanes, hang-gliders, rockets, or UFOs symbolize how you move through the mental zones, and elevators symbolize moving between realms. Vehicles can also represent characteristics of your relationships.

Volcano: A volcano represents tension that has built up within you or someone else and a potential emotional eruption. It may warn you to relax and let off some steam or deal with someone else in a way that avoids a violent outburst.

Vomiting: Like nausea, vomiting symbolizes that you've been putting up with a situation that you "can't stomach" and are finally getting rid of it, or purging yourself to avoid making yourself sick.

Vulture: A vulture can symbolize loneliness and scavenging for your livelihood. You may feel that others are hovering around to feed off your energy and you must remain constantly vigilant to ward them off. A vulture often signals the approaching death of a part of your life, or your need to face something in your own underworld.

W

Wallet: A wallet symbolizes your financial resources and your identity. Losing your wallet may indicate that you need to let go of an aspect of your identity or develop more trust about finances.

Washing: Washing may symbolize you're in the process of cleansing and purifying an aspect of yourself. Trying to get a stain out can indicate you're focusing on a feeling of guilt or shame.

Water: Water is a symbol of the emotions and the unconscious. It also has connotations concerning sexuality and letting go.

Wedding: A wedding symbolizes the unification or balancing of two parts of yourself, like the anima and animus, the physical and spiritual, or the internal and external.

Wheel: A wheel can symbolize the completion of a phase of life or a project. It can also represent a feeling of being caught in a repetitive cycle that's going nowhere.

Window: A window represents your outlook on life or world view. It can also represent how you "let the outdoors in," how much you allow yourself to be affected by the world. If you're on the outside looking in, you may feel you've been excluded from a situation or an experience of belonging.

Wolf: A wolf can symbolize the seduction of an innocent part of yourself, or a ravenous part of yourself or a life situation that wants to devour your energy or creativity. On a positive note, the wolf symbolizes healthy family values and wisdom.

Worm: The worm can symbolize sneakiness, or the entrance of a force into your life by covert means. Worms also can indicate a feeling of being "eaten away at" by some subtle, underlying condition in your life.

X

X-rays: X-rays represent a picture of what's going on inside you, often revealing a hidden problem. They also reveal a desire for greater inner knowledge.

Y

Young Person: Youthful people can symbolize your original innocence or lost vitality. They can remind you that you need rejuvenation of your attitudes or health.

Z

Zebra: A zebra, or any black and white animal, can symbolize the need for integration of the dark and light, good and evil, ideas of right and wrong, or two distinctly different roles, in yourself and your life.

Zipper: A zipper symbolizes quick action or closure to a situation, or the need to be quiet (zip up your lips). To dream of being unzipped symbolizes loss of control or a feeling of exposure. A stuck zipper indicates a frustrating situation that must be untangled.

Zoo: A zoo symbolizes a situation that is chaotic and wild. You may need to create more order and neatness in your life. Zoos can also represent feelings of being on display or being caged in an artificially tame world.

Index

Notes

Discover Dummies Online!

The Dummies Web Site is your fun and friendly online resource for the latest information about *For Dummies®* books and your favorite topics. The Web site is the place to communicate with us, exchange ideas with other *For Dummies* readers, chat with authors, and have fun!

Ten Fun and Useful Things You Can Do at www.dummies.com

1. Win free *For Dummies* books and more!
2. Register your book and be entered in a prize drawing.
3. Meet your favorite authors through the IDG Books Worldwide Author Chat Series.
4. Exchange helpful information with other *For Dummies* readers.
5. Discover other great *For Dummies* books you must have!
6. Purchase Dummieswear® exclusively from our Web site.
7. Buy *For Dummies* books online.
8. Talk to us. Make comments, ask questions, get answers!
9. Download free software.
10. Find additional useful resources from authors.

Link directly to these ten fun and useful things at
http://www.dummies.com/10useful

For other technology titles from IDG Books Worldwide, go to
www.idgbooks.com

Not on the Web yet? It's easy to get started with *Dummies 101®: The Internet For Windows® 98* or *The Internet For Dummies®* at local retailers everywhere.

Find other *For Dummies* books on these topics:
Business • Career • Databases • Food & Beverage • Games • Gardening • Graphics • Hardware
Health & Fitness • Internet and the World Wide Web • Networking • Office Suites
Operating Systems • Personal Finance • Pets • Programming • Recreation • Sports
Spreadsheets • Teacher Resources • Test Prep • Word Processing

IDG BOOKS WORLDWIDE
BOOK REGISTRATION

We want to hear from you!

Register This Book and Win!

Visit **http://my2cents.dummies.com** to register this book and tell us how you liked it!

✔ Get entered in our monthly prize giveaway.

✔ Give us feedback about this book — tell us what you like best, what you like least, or maybe what you'd like to ask the author and us to change!

✔ Let us know any other *For Dummies*® topics that interest you.

Your feedback helps us determine what books to publish, tells us what coverage to add as we revise our books, and lets us know whether we're meeting your needs as a *For Dummies* reader. You're our most valuable resource, and what you have to say is important to us!

Not on the Web yet? It's easy to get started with *Dummies 101*®: *The Internet For Windows*® *98* or *The Internet For Dummies*® at local retailers everywhere.

Or let us know what you think by sending us a letter at the following address:

For Dummies Book Registration
Dummies Press
10475 Crosspoint Blvd.
Indianapolis, IN 46256

...FOR DUMMIES™

**BESTSELLING
BOOK SERIES**